BROOKLYN
THEN AND NOW

Pavilion
An imprint of HarperCollins*Publishers* Ltd
1 London Bridge Street
London SE1 9GF

www.harpercollins.co.uk

HarperCollinsPublishers
Macken House
39/40 Mayor Street Upper
Dublin 1
D01 C9W8
Ireland

10 9 8 7 6 5 4 3 2 1

This edition first published in Great Britain by Pavilion
An imprint of HarperCollins*Publishers* 2025

ISBN 978-0-00-871610-3

This book contains FSC™ certified paper and other controlled sources to ensure responsible forest management.

For more information visit: www.harpercollins.co.uk/green

Publishing Director: Laura Russell
Managing Editor: Shamar Gunning
Copyeditor: Kate Reeves-Brown
Editorial Assistant: Daisy Gudmunsen
Designer: Lily Wilson
Layout Designer: Cara Rogers
Production Controller: Louis Harvey
Photographer: Evan Joseph
Proofreader: Sarah Epton
Indexer: Ruth Ellis

Printed and bound by Papercraft in Malaysia

DEDICATION

Dedicated to our Brooklyn friends and clients, who helped carve out the spots in this book that highlight the best of the past and bring in the future to come.

ACKNOWLEDGEMENTS

Thank you to Shamar Gunning and the team at HarperCollins UK who believed us when we said that Brooklyn had transformed in the past decade. Thank you to Dov Elul for being our research assistant, and to Rex Uhlfelder and Ginger Uhlfelder for beta reading and photo review. Thank you to our families and our Evco team who supported us through this process.

BROOKLYN

THEN AND NOW

EVAN JOSEPH AND AMY EVANS

PAVILION

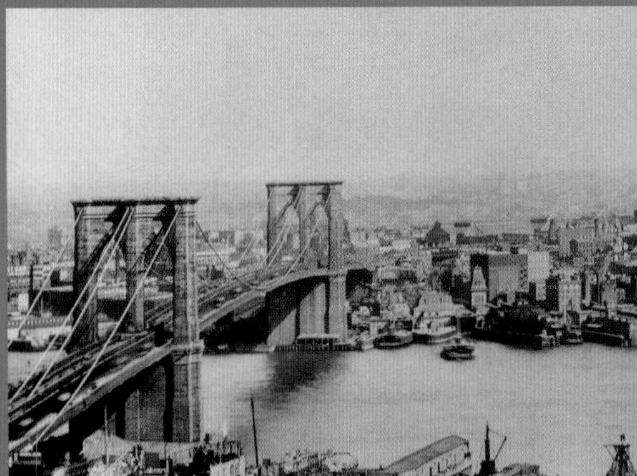
Brooklyn Bridge and Waterfront, c. 1900 p. 8

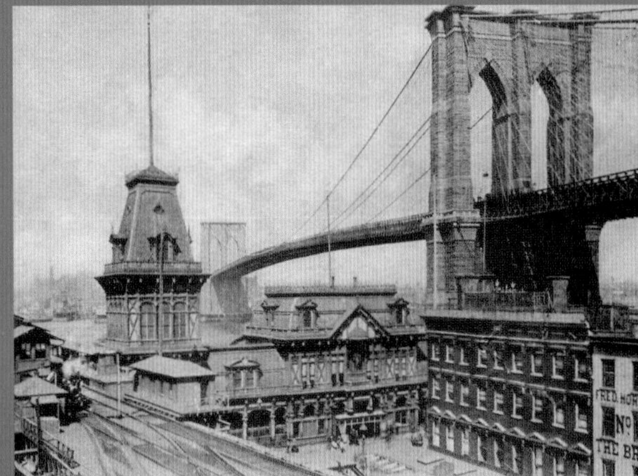
Fulton Ferry Landing, c. 1910 p. 14

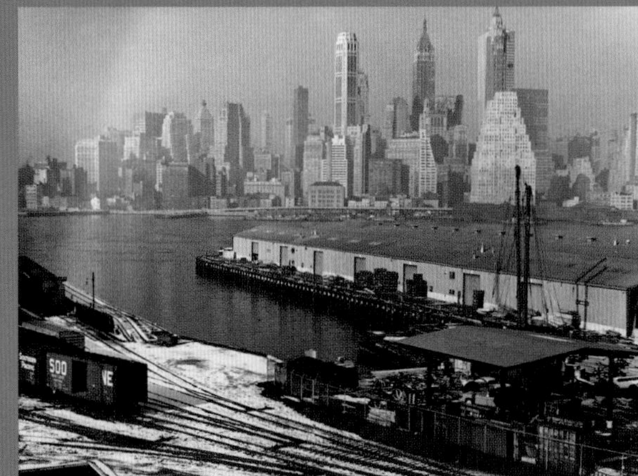
Brooklyn Heights Promenade View, 1961 p. 16

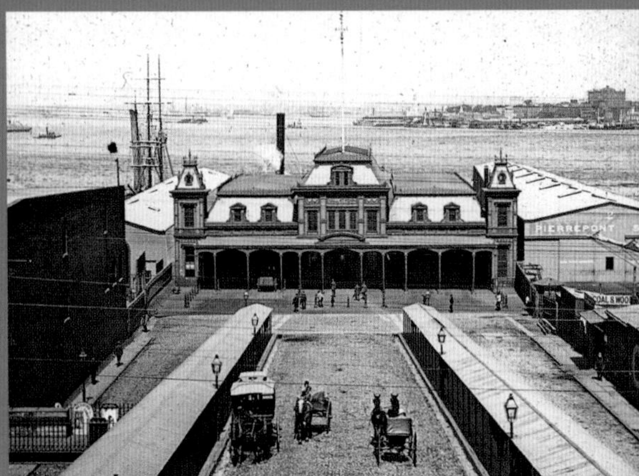
Montague Street Ferry, c. 1890 p. 22

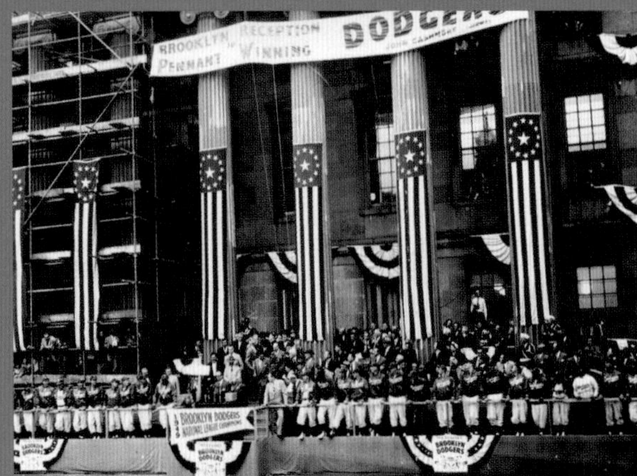
Borough Hall Steps, 1949 p. 32

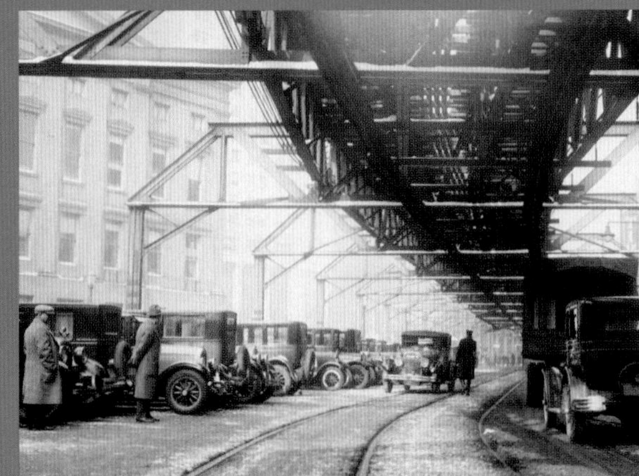
Cadman Plaza, c. 1920 p. 36

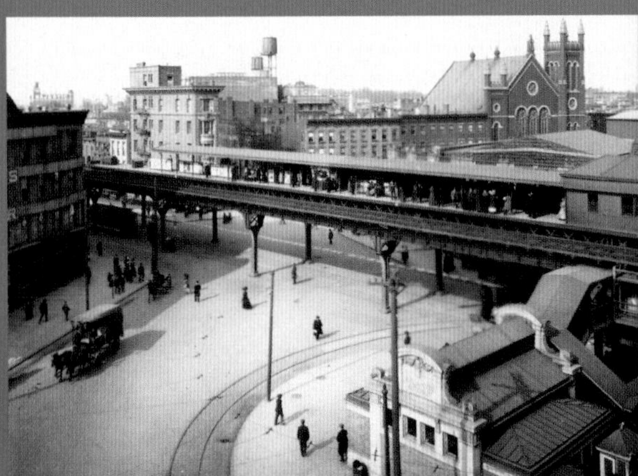
Flatbush and Atlantic Avenues, c. 1908 p. 46

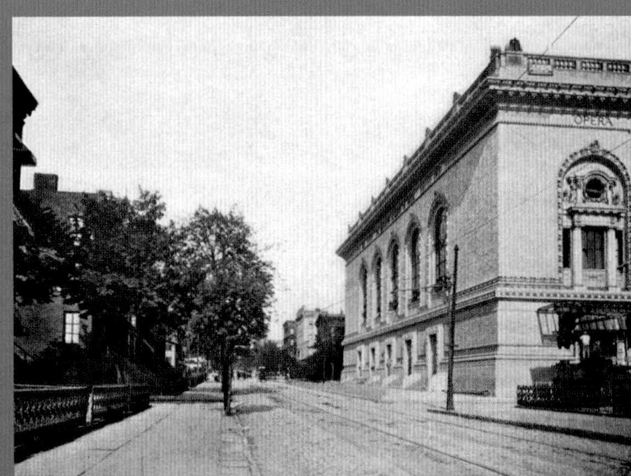
Brooklyn Academy of Music, 1908 p. 48

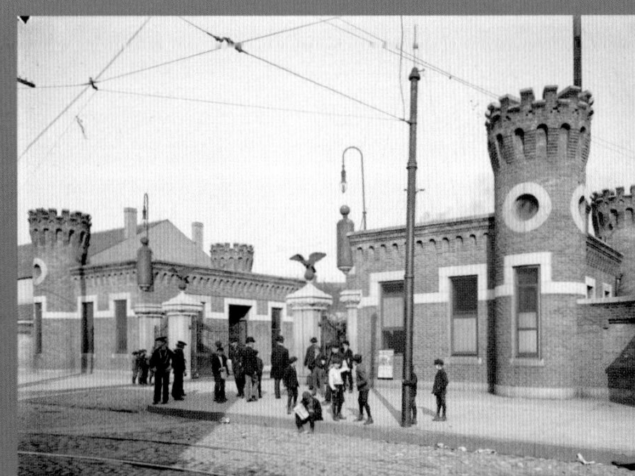
Brooklyn Navy Yard, c. 1904 p. 56

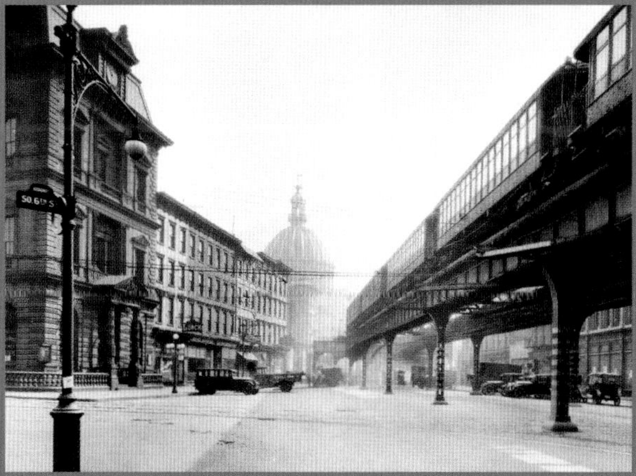

Williamsburg, c. 1924 *p. 60*

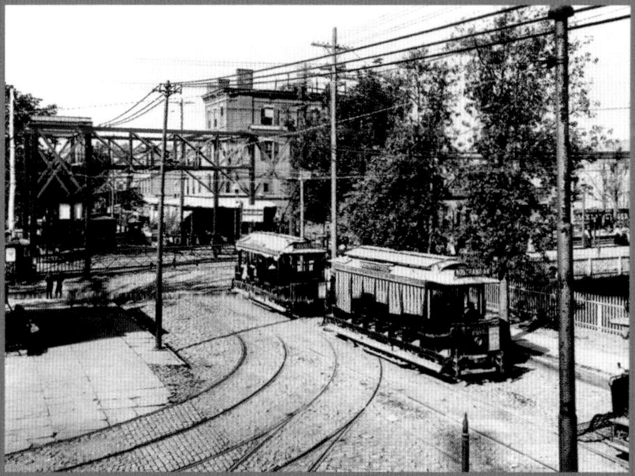

Bedford-Stuyvesant, 1896 *p. 70*

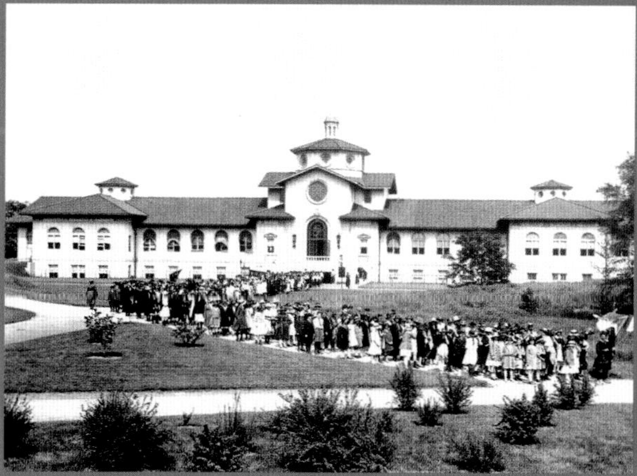

Brooklyn Botanic Garden, c. 1920 *p. 86*

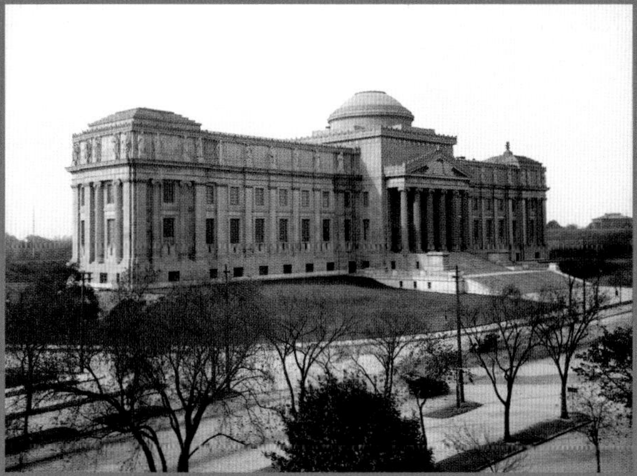

Brooklyn Museum, c. 1910 *p. 88*

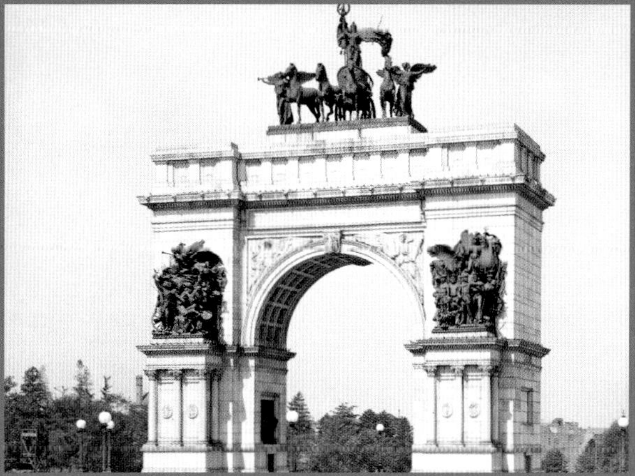

Grand Army Plaza, c. 1900 *p. 90*

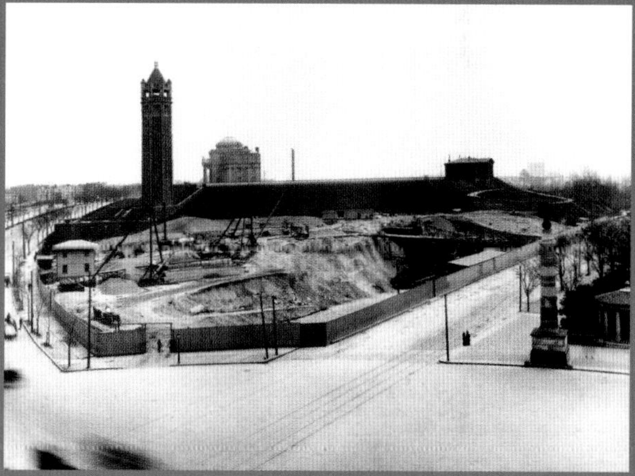

Brooklyn Public Library, 1913 *p. 92*

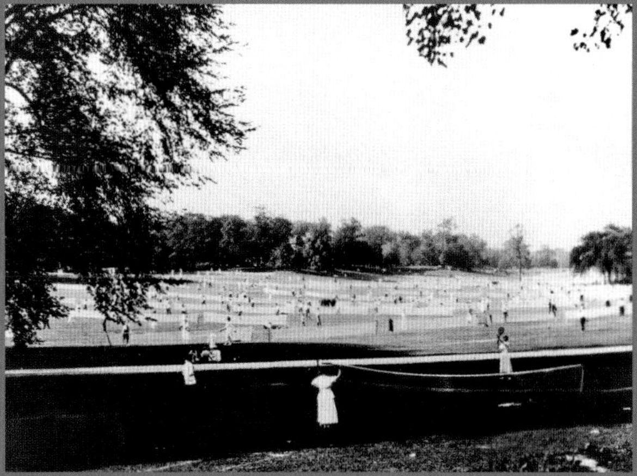

Prospect Park Long Meadow, c. 1890 *p. 98*

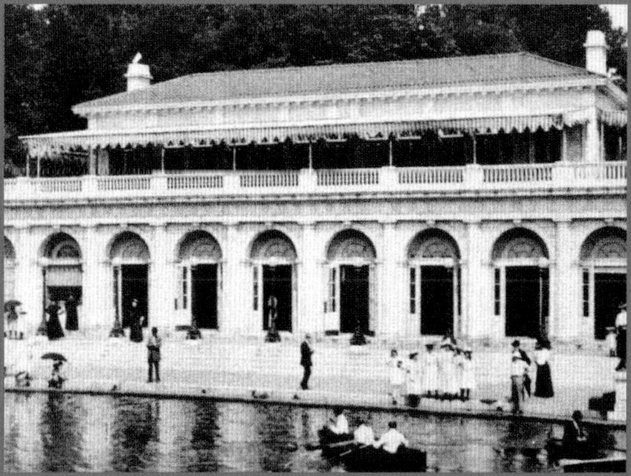

Prospect Park Boathouse, c. 1910 *p. 100*

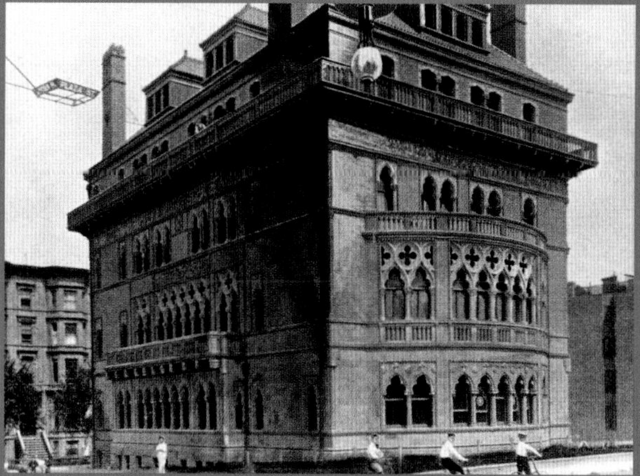

Montauk Club, c. 1907 *p. 108*

BROOKLYN
THEN AND NOW INTRODUCTION

OPPOSITE: The sun rises over the new Brooklyn cityscape, with skyscrapers and green spaces to rival Manhattan.

From the beginning of America's story, Brooklyn has played a quintessential role, though the geography was far different from the urban landscape we know today. Native American tribes, including the Canarsee and Lenape, lived along the fertile lands of the East River, fishing from the abundant waters and farming the rich soil on the shore. The first Dutch settlers in the 1630s found an unspoiled coastline and a ribboned terrain that reminded them of their homeland—the name Brooklyn was inspired by the town of Breukelen in the Netherlands, which had a similarly hilly, marshy terrain.

Brooklyn played a critical role in America's fight for independence during the Revolutionary War. The biggest fight of the conflict, the Battle of Brooklyn in 1776, played out along what is now known as Brooklyn Heights and the surrounding areas. While the Americans suffered a significant defeat, General Washington's masterful, dexterous retreat across the East River was only possible due to Brooklyn's unique topography, saving the Continental Army and, ultimately, the revolution itself.

The waterfront hummed with commerce during the first half of the nineteenth century, with sugar refineries and glass factories fueling community wealth, and new affluence all over Brooklyn. It was the Civil War that completed Brooklyn's metamorphosis into an industrial powerhouse. The Brooklyn Navy Yard, established in 1801, was instrumental to the Union's naval efforts. Thousands of workers built and repaired warships, including the USS *Monitor*, famously built in only 101 days. All efforts in the "Walled City of Warehouses" along the shore had shifted to support the war. Brooklyn's Atlantic Basin in Red Hook became an important military supply hub, with shipping vessels crowded full of munitions and soldiers. Encouraged by notable progressive voices in the area at the time, like Henry Ward Beecher, many Brooklyn boys left from the East River to join the fight, not knowing if they would make it home again.

Brooklyn's population growth tells a story of extraordinary urban expansion. There were only 16,000 residents when it became a municipality in 1834, but the borough exploded to 1.2 million individuals when it joined Greater New York in 1898. This population surge was driven by increased accessibility thanks to the opening of the Brooklyn Bridge in 1883. John, Washington, and Emily Roebling's engineering marvel, the Brooklyn Bridge forever changed the borough's relationship with Manhattan.

A number of architects and urban visionaries were responsible for transforming Brooklyn from farm land to busy suburb. James Stranahan, the "Father of Prospect Park," worked with Frederick Law Olmsted and Calvert Vaux to create Brooklyn's crown jewel of urban pastoral design in 1873. In the 1800s, Charles Pratt's wealth from his oil refineries funded Pratt Institute, while Henry Havemeyer's Domino Sugar Refinery defined the Williamsburg waterfront. These entrepreneurs built magnificent mansions along Clinton Avenue's "Gold Coast", as well as in Brooklyn Heights, and the factories employed thousands in the surrounding neighborhoods. Coney Island emerged as a seaside playground, where young and old went to enjoy the sea air, the iconic rides, and the amusements on the boardwalk.

The mid-twentieth century saw Brooklyn nurture some of America's greatest talents. Aaron Copland composed in Prospect Heights, while Leonard Bernstein conducted his first orchestra in Bed-Stuy. Jackie Gleason, Mae West, Danny Kaye, and Barbra Streisand are just some of the many celebrities who came of age and developed their talents in mid-century Brooklyn.

The Seventies and Eighties marked a challenging period in Brooklyn's history. The financial crisis that ensnared New York City hit Brooklyn brutally, compounding issues of an already declining infrastructure and leading to reduced social services. The closure of the Brooklyn Navy Yard in 1966 dealt a severe economic blow, and this manufacturing exodus continued throughout the Seventies. Pollution in the river and on its banks decimated the natural beauty and ecosystems in the immediate area, and following the 1977 blackout and subsequent urban riots, neighborhoods like Bushwick faced severe disinvestment and neglect.

Despite difficult times, Brooklyn's creativity pushed through. The Brooklyn Academy of Music, under the visionary leadership of Harvey Lichtenstein, morphed into a cutting-edge performing arts center. In spite of budget cuts, the Brooklyn Museum maintained its dedication to both historical collections and contemporary art. Community leaders, like Al Vann in Bedford-Stuyvesant and Luis Garden Acosta in Williamsburg, worked tirelessly to maintain their neighborhoods through community mobilization and cultural engagement.

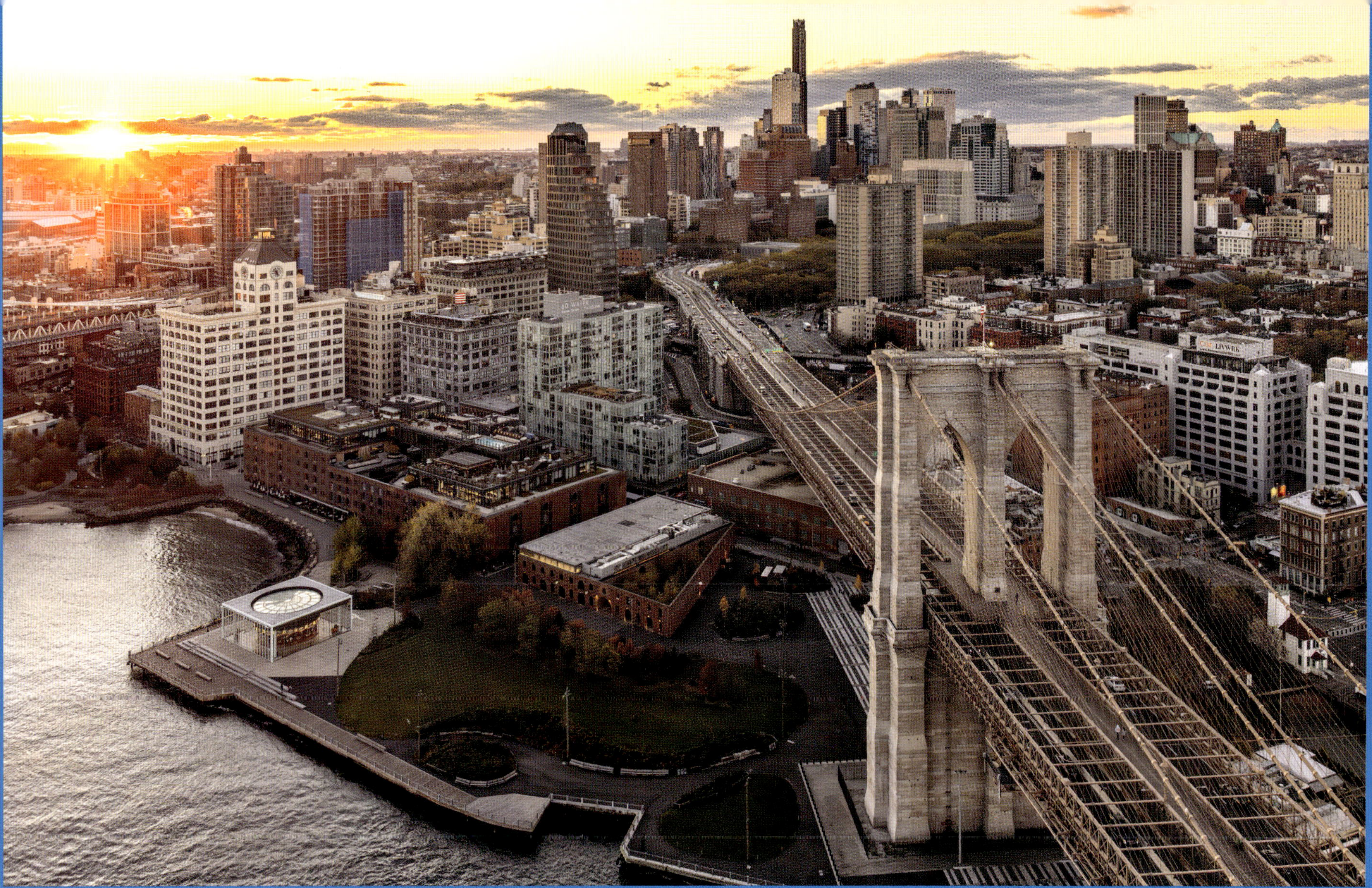

The seeds of recovery began to finally take root in the early Nineties. The DUMBO neighborhood, championed by developer David Walentas, began its transformation from a legacy industrial site to an arts district. On Atlantic Avenue, trailblazing gallery owners and small businesses helped revive the commercial center. Neighborhoods like Park Slope and Carroll Gardens, anchored by strong community organizations and historic residential architecture, began attracting new residents and investment. This grassroots revival, led by artists, entrepreneurs, and community activists, set the stage for Brooklyn's dramatic renaissance in the following decades.

Contemporary Brooklyn has experienced a remarkable transformation over the past two decades. Former industrial wastelands like DUMBO and Williamsburg have evolved into global cultural destinations. Modern architects and developers have reconceptualized the waterfront, with projects like Brooklyn Bridge Park reclaiming industrial spaces for public use. The Environmental Protection Agency is facilitating the clean-up of the Gowanus Canal and the Newtown Creek. These two superfund sites have attracted billions of dollars to complete the remediation of their waterfront communities.

Today's Brooklyn stands as a cultural nexus where artists, entrepreneurs, and innovators thrive in repurposed industrial spaces. Architecture firms like Marvel Architects and Morris Adjmi have added contemporary layers to the borough's structural evolution. A new generation of cultural icons has emerged from these streets: Lil' Kim from Bedford–Stuyvesant and Spike Lee from Fort Greene. Brooklyn's rare fusion of shared history, unique architecture, and neighborhood intimacy creates America's most compelling urban landscape, and it emerges as America's undisputed cultural crown jewel.

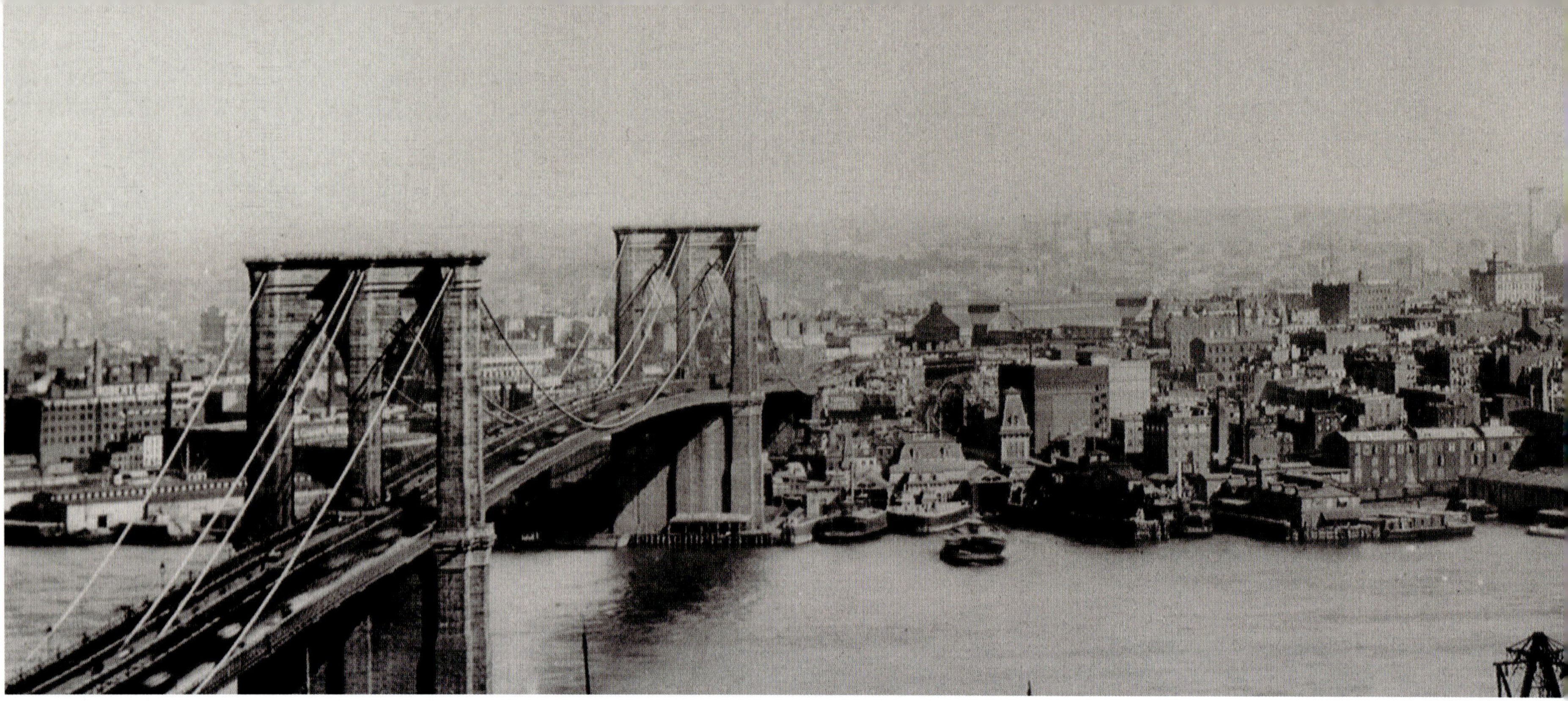

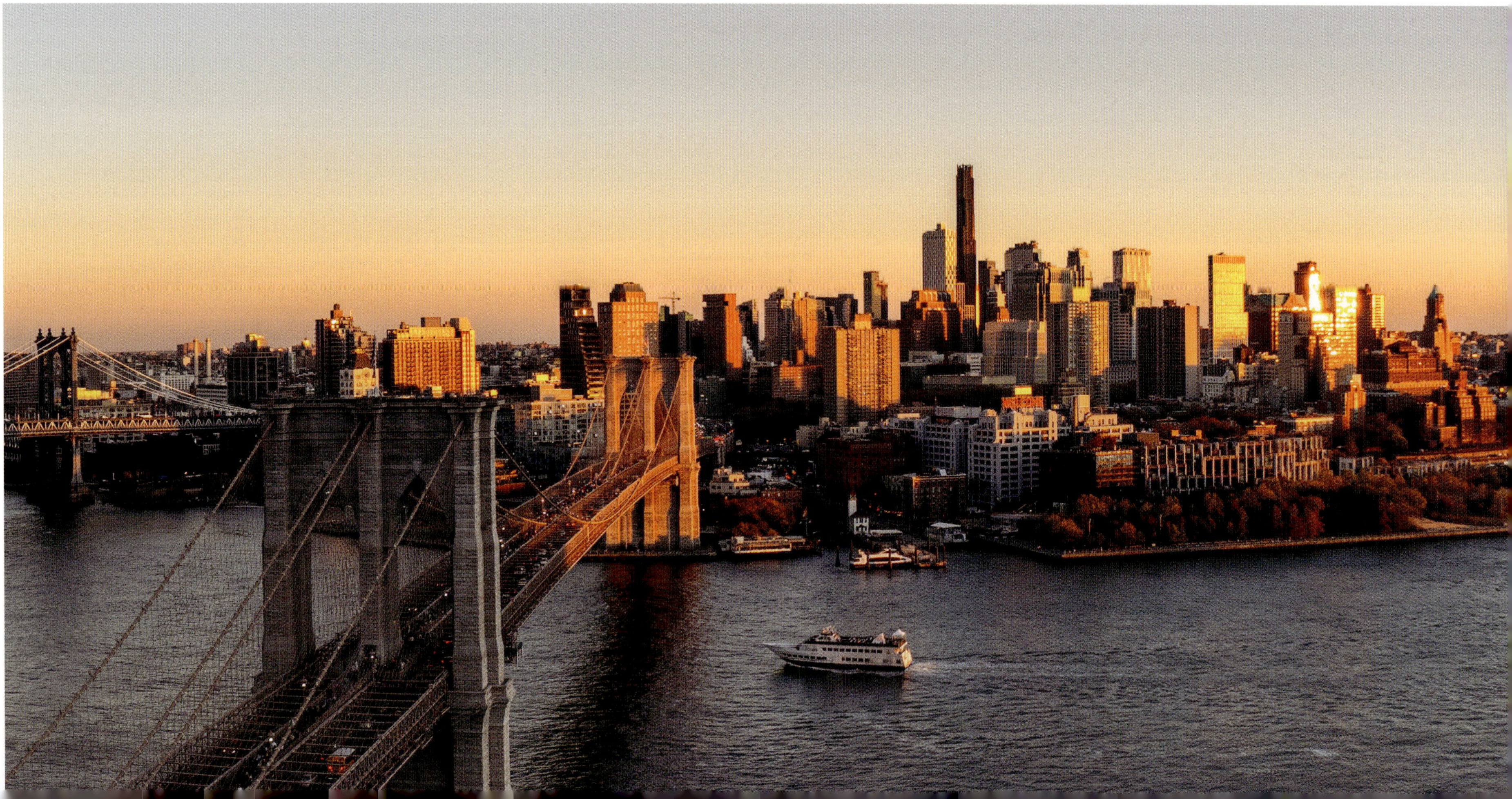

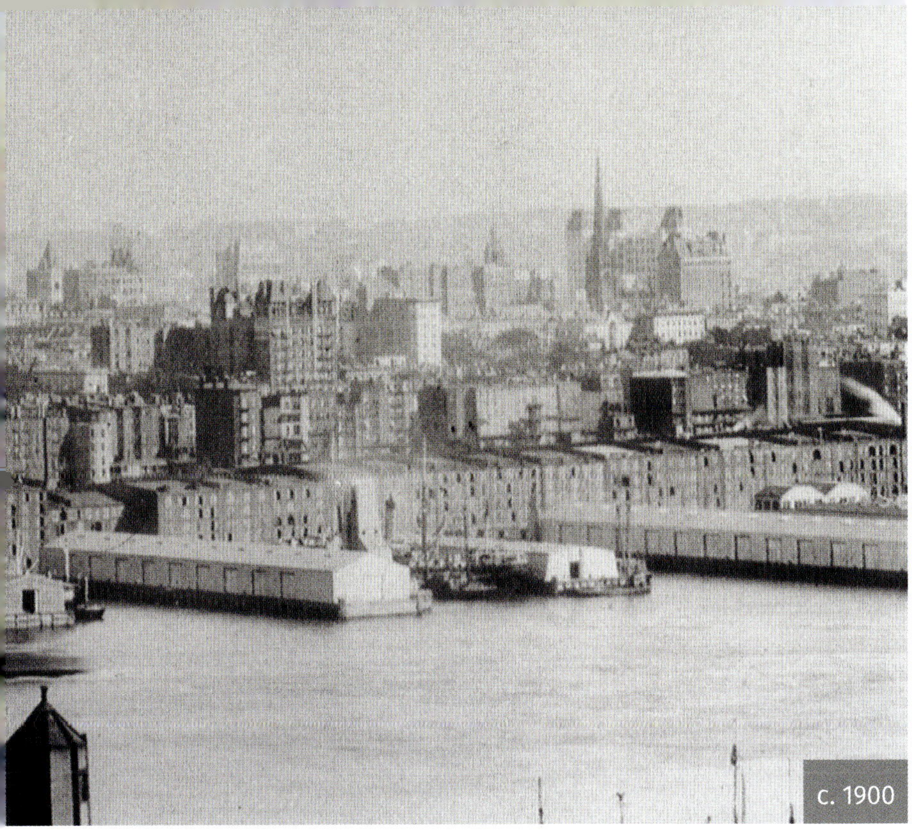

c. 1900

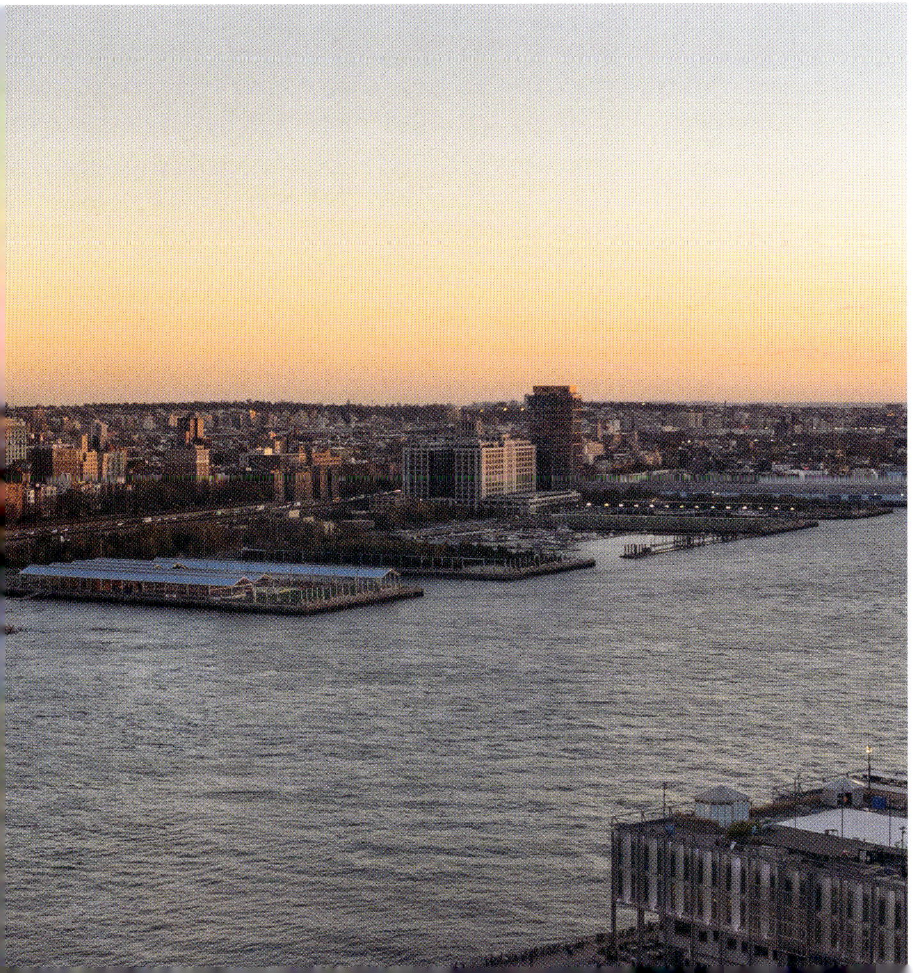

BROOKLYN BRIDGE AND WATERFRONT

A river away from Manhattan and a whole separate world

THEN: At the turn of the twentieth century, the Brooklyn waterfront was a bustling maritime hub connecting the borough of Brooklyn to the world. Warehouses stood tall along the East River, facilitating the shipping of raw materials and consumer goods in and out of New York City, and the Fulton Ferry Company was using their steam-engine-powered ferries to facilitate almost all of the trade and transport between Brooklyn and Manhattan. It was the end of the Gilded Age, when commercial fisheries, sugar refineries, boat builders, and manufacturers packed the harbor, fighting for space. Passenger ferries soon crowded in, carrying commuters back and forth from Manhattan, and ocean liners brought immigrants to the United States from all over the world. Beyond the port, a sprawl of neighborhoods reflected the changing dynamics of American life, and the challenges faced by a city trying to meet them all. From the picturesque brownstones of Brooklyn Heights and Park Slope to the factories and warehouses of Williamsburg and Bushwick, Brooklyn held family life and commerce in constant tension as it transformed to make space for the industrial boom and the gradual expansion of the residential areas required to provide the labor needed to keep it all moving.

NOW: Today, the waterfront has changed dramatically. South of the bridge, the waterfront warehouses and refineries have been reimagined as Brooklyn Bridge Park, a decades-long rehabilitation and rezoning project that, even today, is still being worked on and improved upon. The city took on the extraordinary challenge of transforming the waterfront, including: refurbishing it environmentally; repurposing the docks into green space, recreational facilities, and playgrounds; and upgrading the infrastructure with new roads, paths, and traffic patterns, without blocking the view from any of the historic neighborhoods. New neighborhoods have popped up in the spaces among the older ones, full of new developments built into the frame of Brooklyn's history, dotting the skyline with new architectural marvels from the world's leading architects.

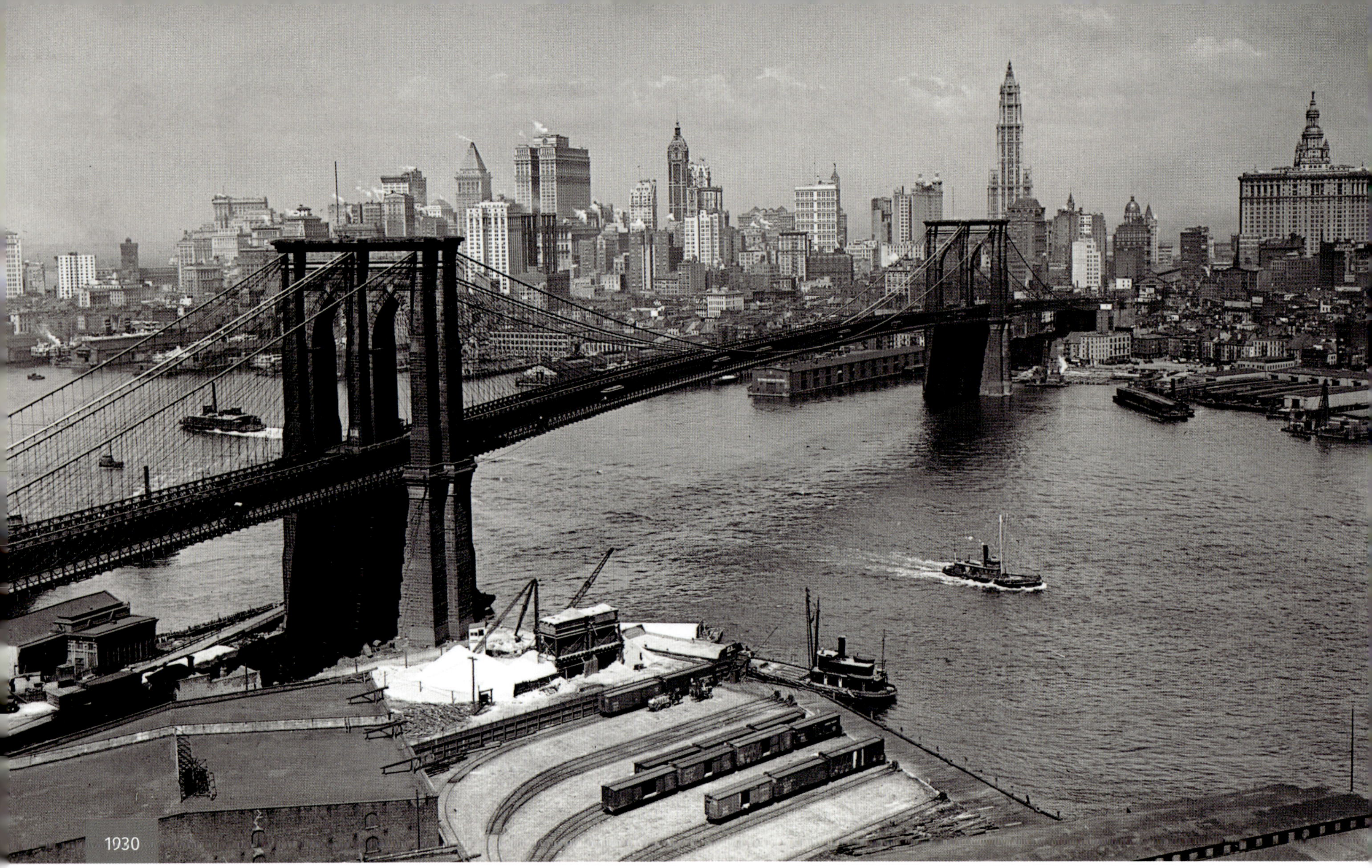

BROOKLYN BRIDGE

Cables and concrete convene to create a crucial connection

THEN: In the 1800s, Brooklyn and Manhattan were distinctly separate cities. Both were growing exponentially, Manhattan with commerce and Brooklyn with industry. The ferries that carried commuters back and forth between them were unreliable and extremely weather sensitive, so those with a vested financial interest in Brooklyn's expansion began pushing for a bridge in the 1850s. Naysayers argued that Brooklyn would lose its charm and independence, but those voices were frozen out in 1867 after a winter so cold that the ferries were grounded for months by blocks of ice, creating an economic and social bottleneck. Construction of the Brooklyn Bridge began in 1870, and when it finished fourteen years later, the bridge was open for pedestrians, cable cars, and horse-drawn carriages, with train tracks in the works. The first day 1,800 vehicles and 150,300 pedestrians crossed on the East River Bridge, as it was originally named. Cable car and carriage passengers paid five cents each, per person or per horse, but many crossed the bridge on foot to save money. In 1884, its first full year open, 8.5 million people would cross the bridge, and that number would

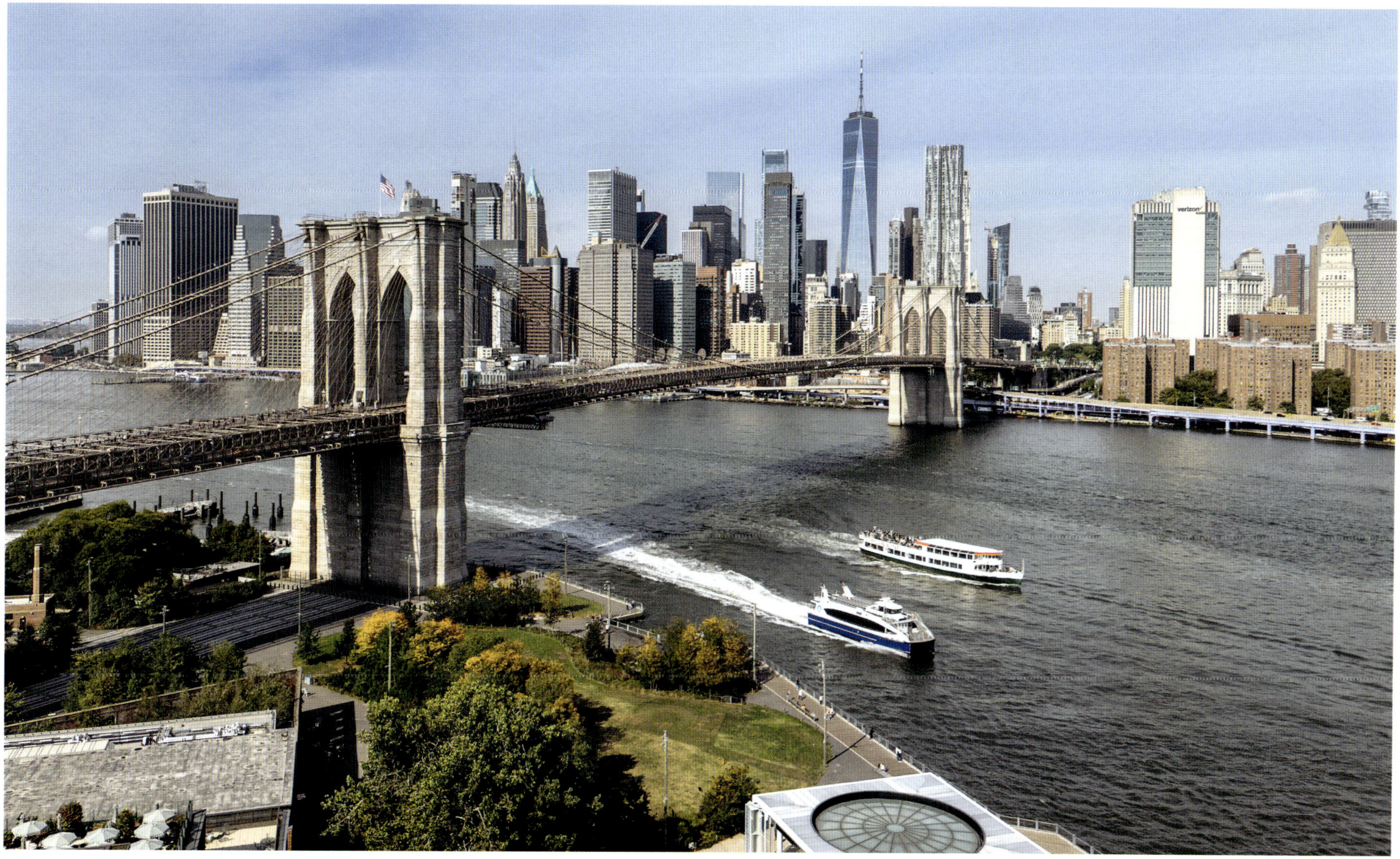

double and then double again by 1889. By 1930, the bridge had been officially renamed the Brooklyn Bridge, with thousands of pedestrians, vehicles, trains, and trolleys crossing daily, creating traffic congestion, as well as wear and tear on the structure that had become concerning to local officials. However, it was the middle of the Great Depression and repair funds were not easily available. Fortunately, federal New Deal programs like the Public Works Administration provided money for large-scale public infrastructure projects, which provided construction jobs for local workers and saved the bridge at this critical time.

NOW: Today, the Brooklyn Bridge continues to serve as both a vital transportation artery and a symbol of Brooklyn's identity. The bridge carries roughly 116,000 vehicles, 30,000 pedestrians, and 3,000 cyclists daily, while its elevated promenade offers tourists and locals alike spectacular views of both boroughs' evolving skylines. The walk between Manhattan and Brooklyn is a treat in good times, and a lifeline when needed, like during the blackouts of 1965, 1977, and 2003. When the subways stopped after the September 11th attack on the World Trade Center, over 500,000 people walked home across the bridge to Brooklyn together.

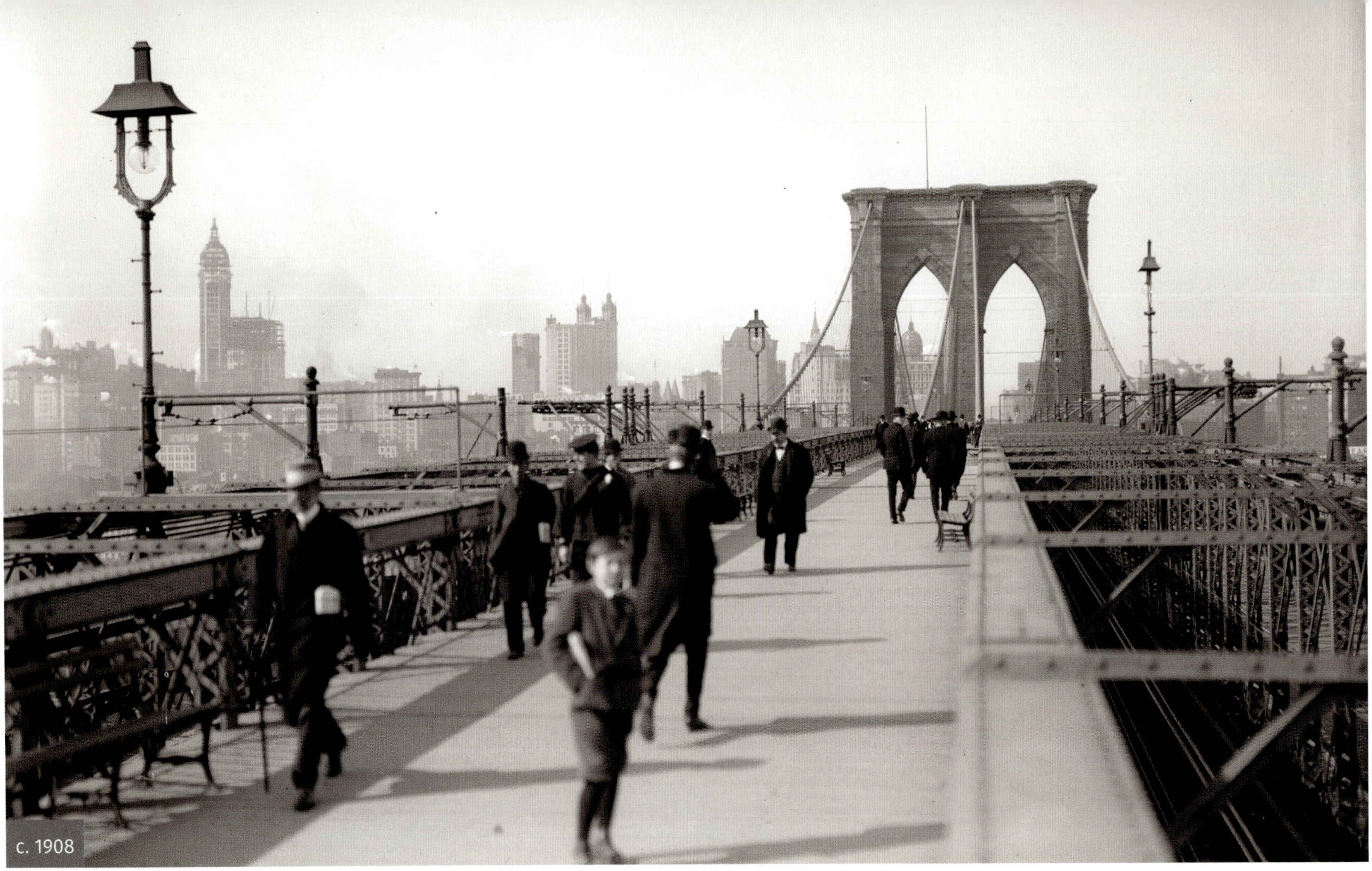

c. 1908

BROOKLYN BRIDGE WALKWAY

A pioneer of modern bridge design still standing strong

THEN: The Brooklyn Bridge was designed by German immigrant John Roebling, who died from tetanus after a ferry accident crushed his foot during the initial stages of development, long before the bridge would be completed. Work started in 1869 and finished in 1883, led by Roebling's son Washington, who took over as Chief Engineer until he developed health complications due to decompression sickness in the pressurized underwater chambers used to excavate the bridge's foundations. Washington's wife, Emily Warren Roebling, stepped in quietly as manager, learning engineering principles and facilitating communication from her sick husband, and saw the project to completion. Building the bridge was dangerous, taking at least twenty-seven lives from decompression sickness, falling from towers, and getting stuck in cables or struck by dropped tools. The impact of these deaths led to several significant changes in workers' rights and construction safety laws. It also highlighted the need for better safety measures in infrastructure projects, as some of the cables were laid with defective wire from a corrupt supplier. When it was completed in 1883 it was the world's longest suspension bridge, and it remained so until 1903 when the Williamsburg Bridge opened. The Brooklyn Bridge represented the pinnacle of masonry-tower suspension-bridge design and in 1903 when the above photo was made, it handled horse-drawn carriages, automobiles, elevated railways and pedestrians, displaying a remarkable adaptability to Brooklyn's many transportation needs.

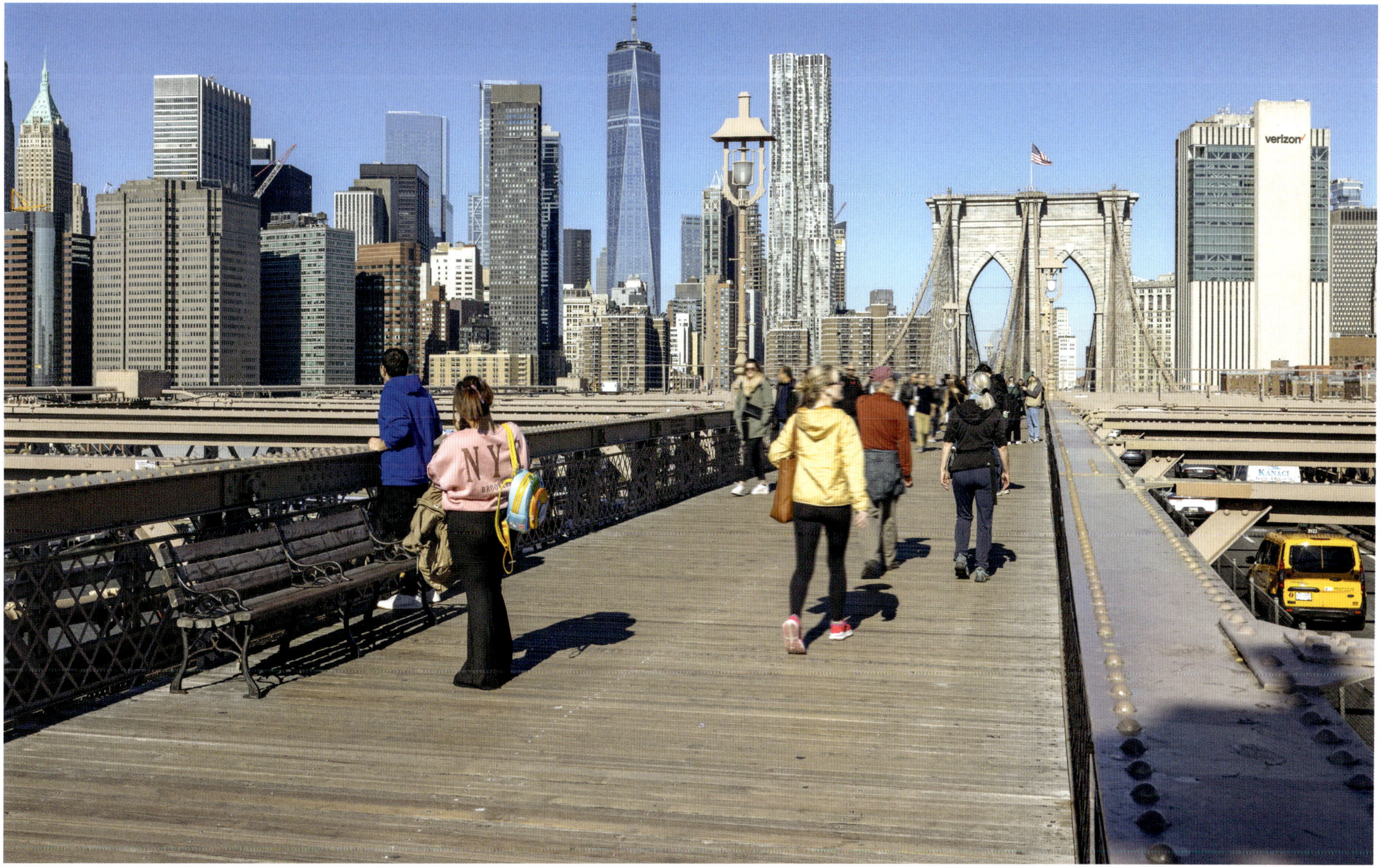

NOW: In spite of its early ingenuity, the Brooklyn Bridge has required many upgrades and adjustments over the years for solving safety and capacity issues. In 1944, the elevated train was removed from most of Brooklyn, including on the Bridge, allowing for the widening of lanes to accommodate more vehicles. In 1950, lights were added to increase night-time visibility, and the trusses were strengthened with increased bracing for modern traffic loads. Suspension cables were replaced, fencing was added, and the Manhattan-side approach was renovated in the 1980s, along with improvements to the pedestrian promenade. The bridge's 1983 Centennial Celebration brought enhanced protection for the historic structure, ensuring that the iconic design of the bridge will still be there for generations, and twenty-first-century technological improvements have brought computerized traffic and security monitoring to ensure that the bridge will stay safe to use no matter the changes in the types of transportation it conveys.

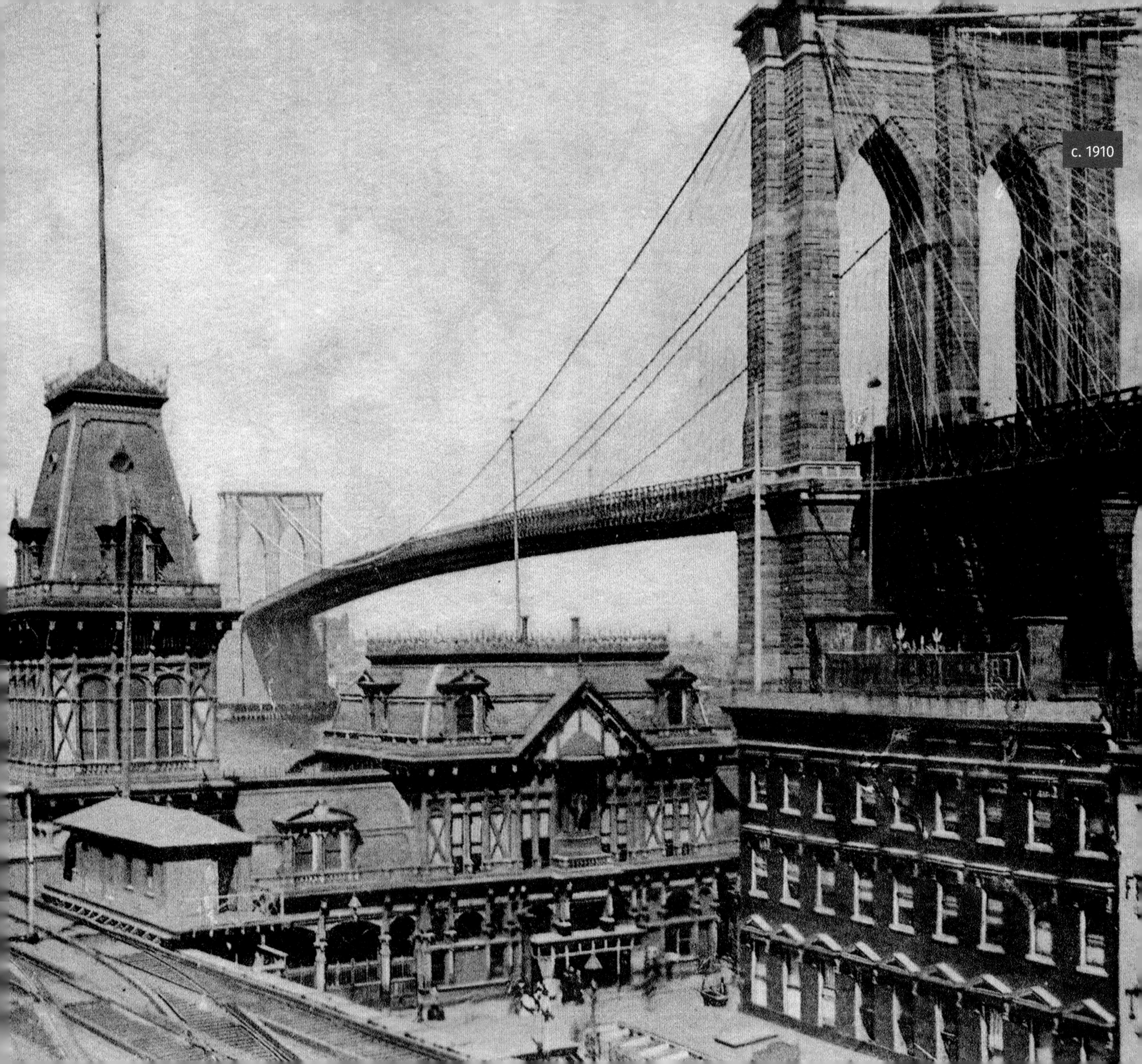
c. 1910

FULTON FERRY LANDING

Brooklyn built out from the ferry terminal

THEN: In 1910, Fulton Ferry Landing was a busy transportation hub connecting the village of Brooklyn to the city of New York through Manhattan and beyond. Ferries brought passengers and freight between the two boroughs, landing at the foot of Old Fulton Street in Brooklyn. Built by the Fulton Ferry Company and named for Robert Fulton (the engineer credited with building the first successful commercial steamboat), the Company ran its first ferry trip in 1814, almost seventy years prior to the opening of the Brooklyn Bridge in 1883. For many years, the landing was an essential part of the Brooklyn skyline and the East River infrastructure, as elevated trains continued from the east onto platforms at stations on the landing. But eventually, especially after the construction of the Brooklyn Bridge, the ferries stopped, and the landing officially closed in 1924. The trains were then rerouted to other stations deeper in Brooklyn, and by 1926, the dramatic main buildings were demolished.

NOW: Today, Fulton Ferry Landing is a busy, beautiful, and popular part of Brooklyn's waterfront and an entry to Brooklyn Bridge Park, which has six piers full of waterfront pathways, sports fields, playgrounds, and green spaces for cultural events and public gatherings. The landing also serves as the southern-most part of the thriving neighborhood of DUMBO (Down Under the Manhattan Bridge Overpass), a district of renovated waterfront warehouses between Brooklyn Bridge and Manhattan Bridge. A modern ferry service resumed in 2006, and wherever new amenities have replaced the old infrastructure, informative plaques give visitors historical information to honor the rich heritage of one of the oldest and most important pieces of Brooklyn's past.

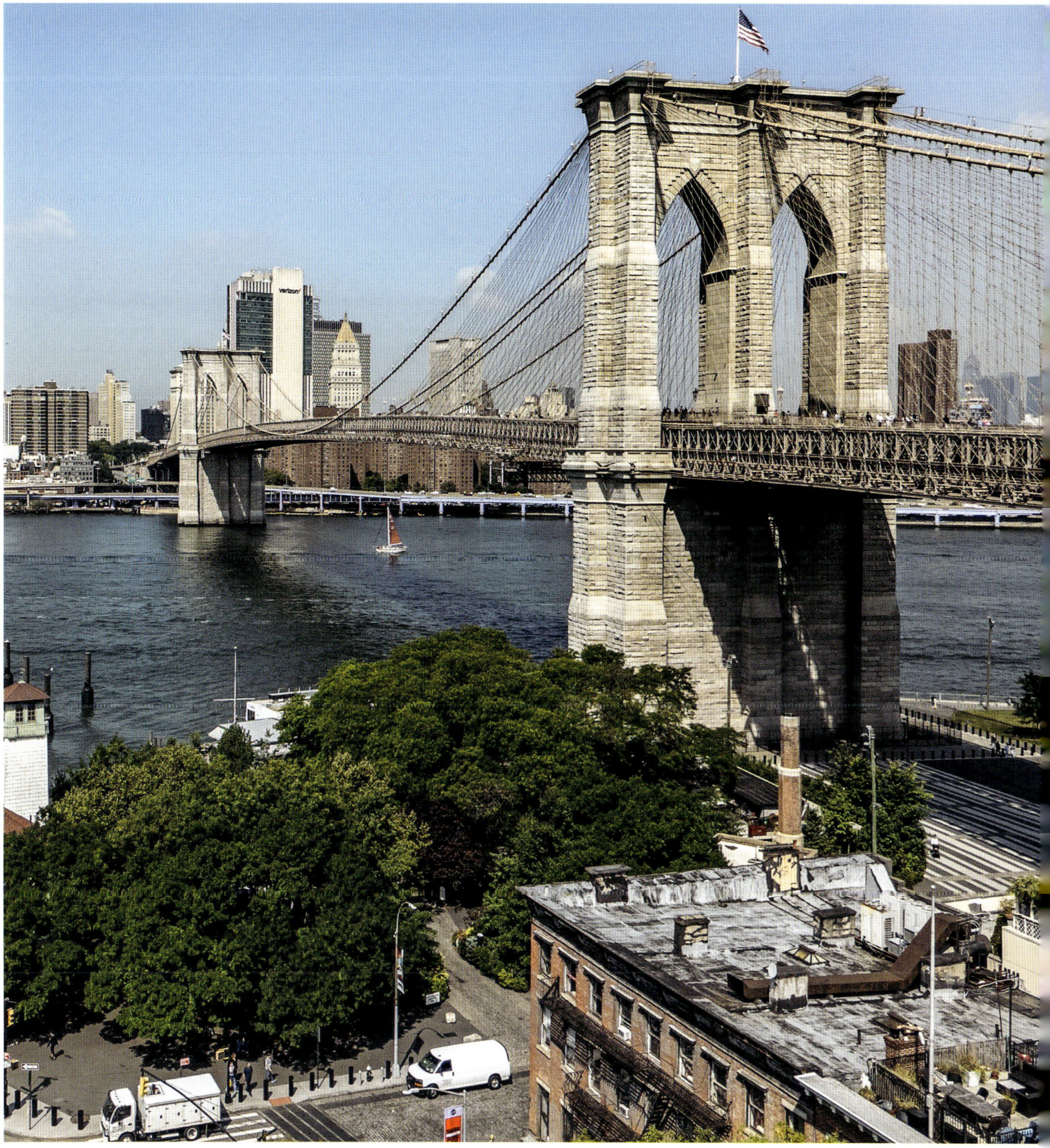

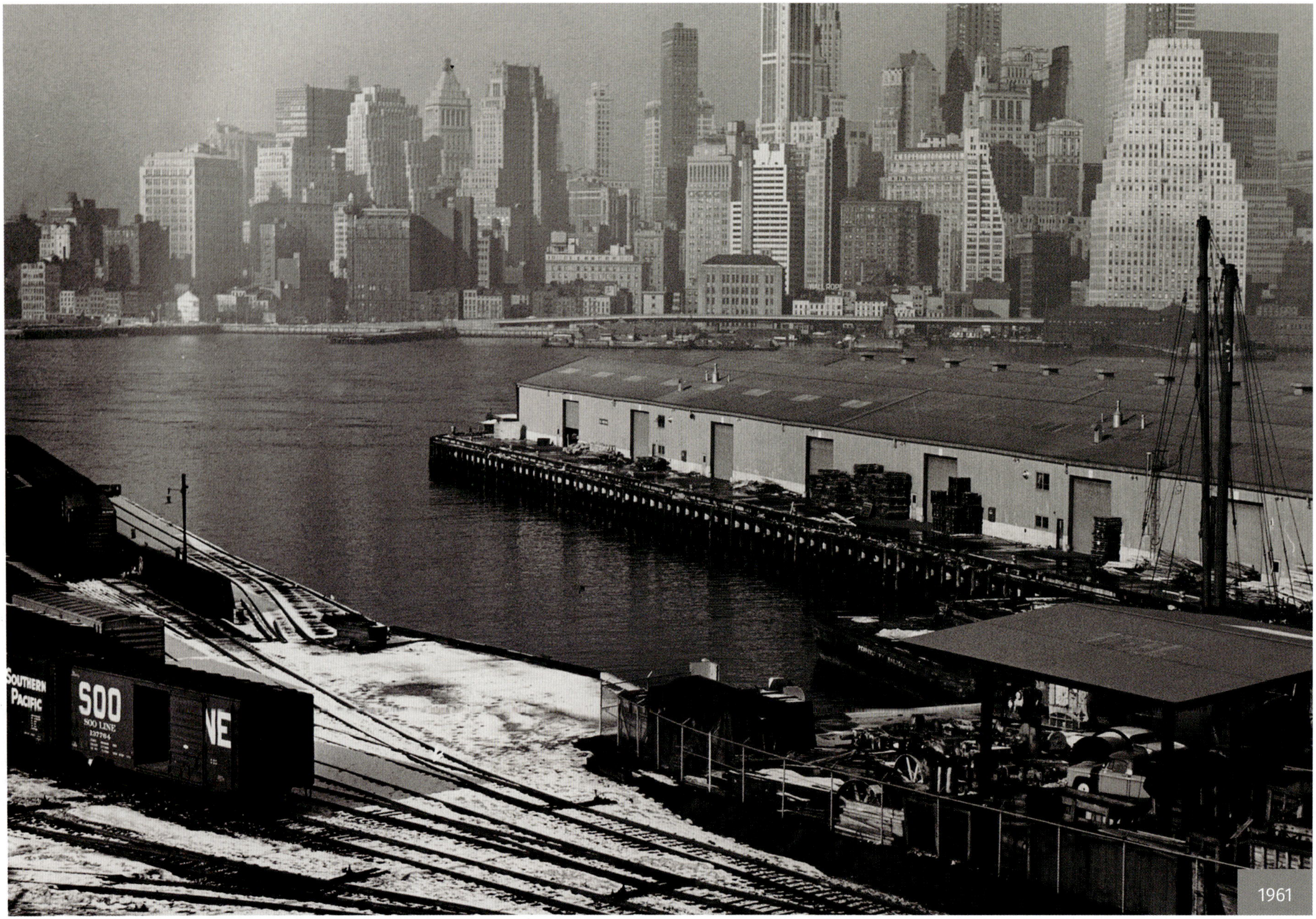

BROOKLYN HEIGHTS PROMENADE VIEW

A historic waterfront transformed a commercial center to a cherished public esplanade

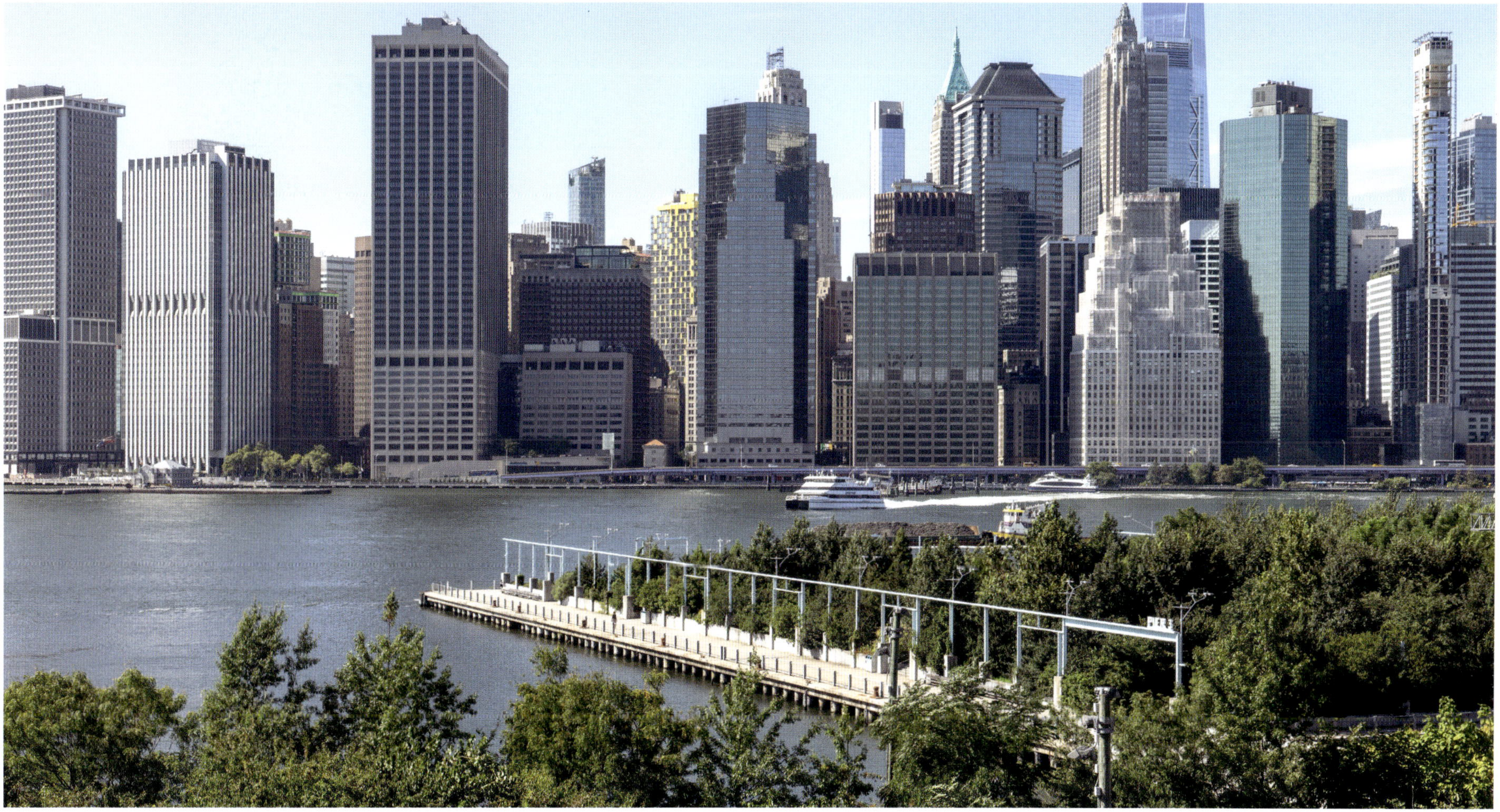

THEN: The Brooklyn Heights Promenade, initially known as the Esplanade, emerged as an important feature of Brooklyn's landscape in the mid-twentieth century. The site had long been valued for its spectacular views of the East River and Manhattan, but the area was primarily functional, reflecting Brooklyn's role as a major port and industrial center. The shoreline was dominated by commercial activities, with ships constantly loading and unloading goods and passengers. In 1961, much of the Manhattan skyline was visible, and the area was a crowded waterfront bustling with piers, warehouses, and various maritime industries. Residents of Brooklyn Heights, one of America's first suburbs, enjoyed the views of the harbor from their homes on the bluff above, but there were no formal public spaces for taking in the panorama.

NOW: Today, the Brooklyn Heights Promenade stands as an iconic public space, representing the community's successful effort to balance progress and preservation, and offering one of the most breathtaking views of Lower Manhattan, the East River, and the Statue of Liberty. Developed in the Fifties as part of the construction of the Brooklyn-Queens Expressway, the promenade preserved the character of Brooklyn Heights while accommodating modern infrastructure. The cantilevered design placed a pedestrian walkway above the expressway, creating a 1,826-foot-long elevated park maintained by the NYC Parks Department. Warehouses and piers have been replaced with benches, trees, and flower beds, and the Brooklyn Heights Promenade has become a beloved public space, attracting locals and tourists alike for strolls, jogging, or simply soaking in the views and maintaining a connection to the waterfront that has defined Brooklyn's identity for centuries.

BROOKLYN HEIGHTS PROMENADE

The Promenade protected historic charm and provided access to Manhattan views for all

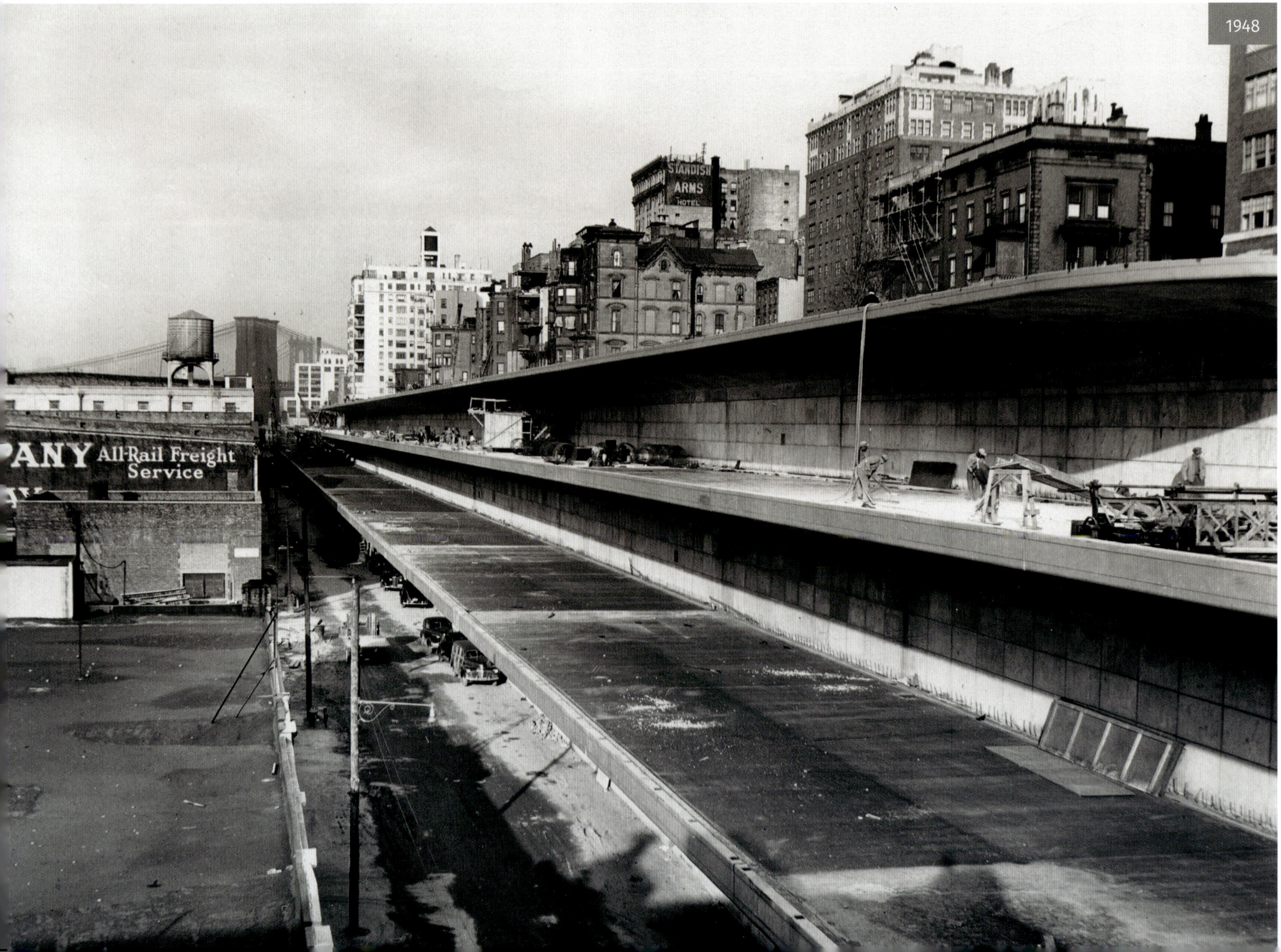

THEN: The Brooklyn Heights Promenade is a cantilevered walkway built along the top of the Brooklyn-Queens Expressway, which runs from the west end of Remsen Street to the west end of Orange Street. Urban planner Robert Moses initially proposed building the expressway right through Brooklyn Heights, which would have bisected the neighborhood and destroyed many historic buildings. Politically connected residents fought the plan in court, an alternative design was implemented, and the expressway was built along the edge of the neighborhood instead. The promenade opened in 1950, buffering the residential areas from the noise of the highway below, and protecting the view that George Washington called 'the most strategic view of Manhattan.'

NOW: Fast-forward to today, and the Brooklyn Heights Promenade is still a local treasure filled with bikers, joggers, and families with strollers looking to relax near the river and take in the views. The warehouses on the water were demolished long ago, making way for Brooklyn Bridge Park, which opened in 2010. Accessible from the promenade, the park offers a variety of recreation activities, including playgrounds and ball fields on six piers, right along the water-level of the East River. The promenade itself is also seen as one of the most romantic and beautiful places in Brooklyn, thanks to its elevation and view—making it a very popular proposal or first-date spot even to this day. The area still faces similar challenges from ongoing development proposals, which often mobilize neighborhood conservation efforts. But despite the challenges, the promenade continues to shine as a quintessential Brooklyn landmark, where history and contemporary life beautifully collide.

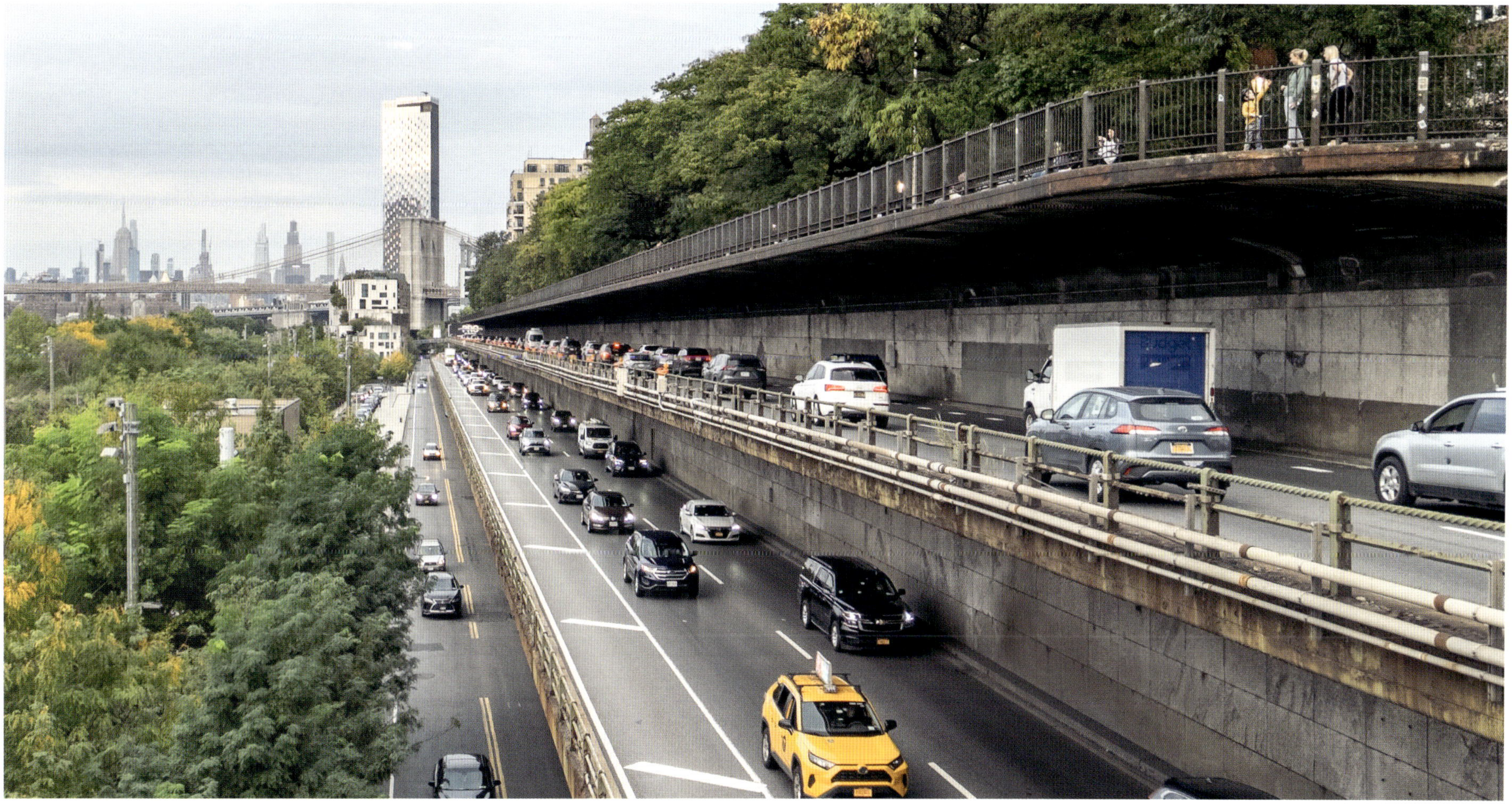

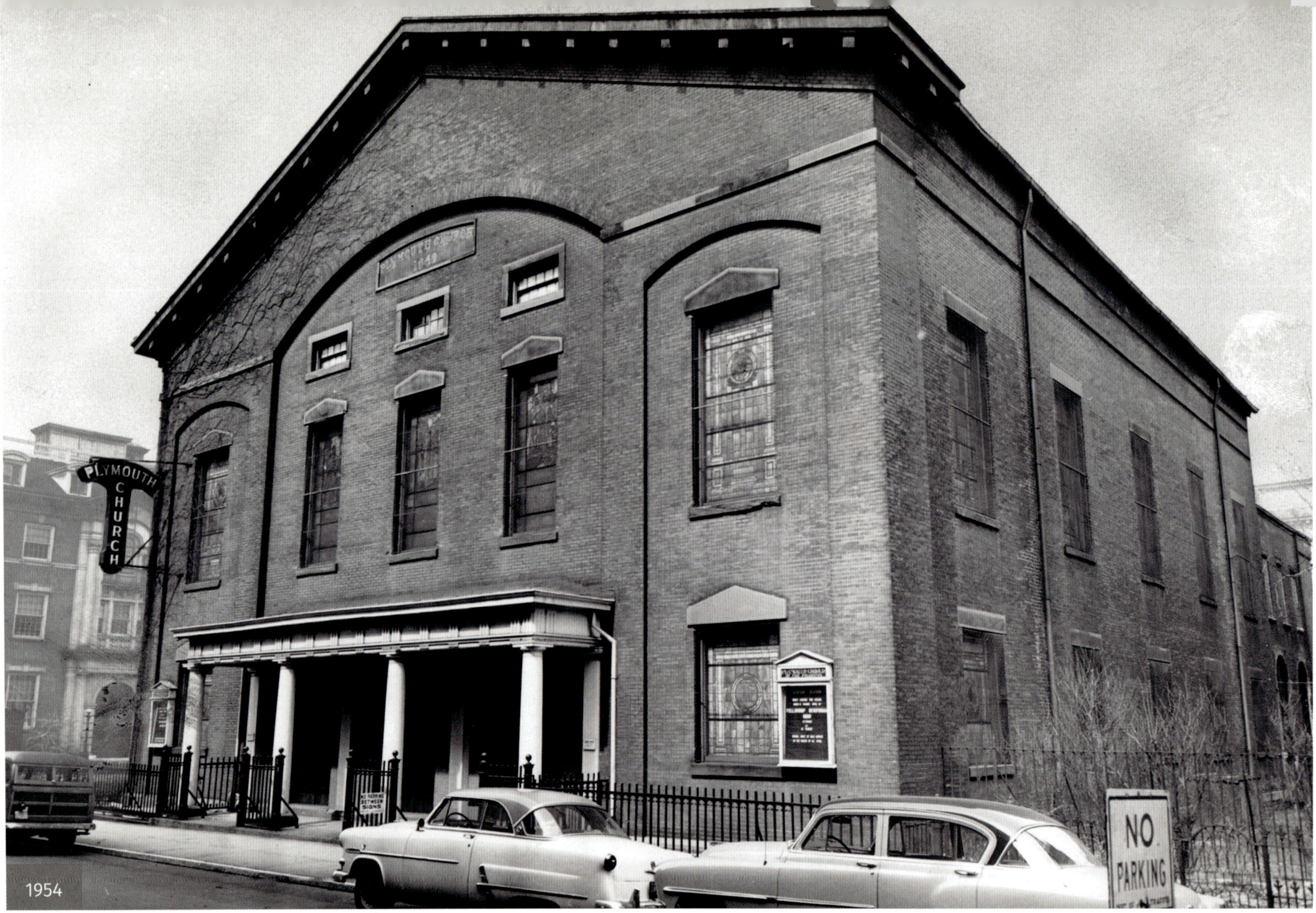

PLYMOUTH CHURCH

A legacy of social justice reaching back to the Underground Railroad

THEN: Plymouth Church of the Pilgrims played a pivotal role in the abolitionist movement in the northeast. Founded in 1847 on Orange Street between Henry and Hicks Streets, its layout was designed by Joseph C. Wells, one of the founders of the American Institute of Architects. Led by founding preacher Henry Ward Beecher, the church served as a bastion for social justice and the abolitionist movement. As part of the Underground Railroad, it provided safe passage for enslaved people escaping to freedom further north. Beecher preached from the pulpit about emancipation, famously conducting mock "slave auctions" to raise funds for individuals to start their lives as free people. The church hosted notable abolitionist Frederick Douglass and writer Mark Twain, and brought a pre-Presidential Abraham Lincoln to Brooklyn for a service and speaking engagement that was moved to a larger location due to interest.

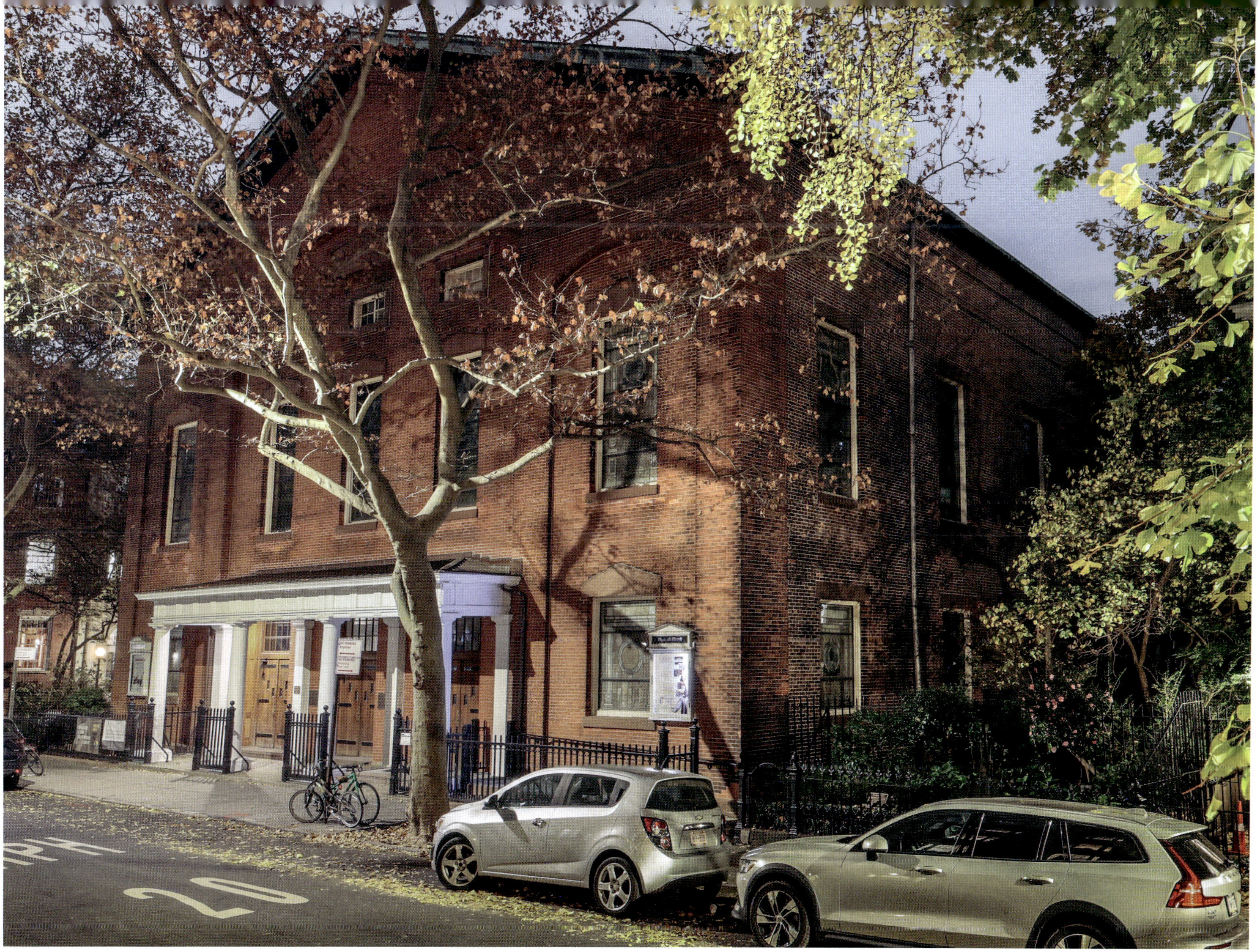

NOW: Plymouth Church merged with the Congregational Church of the Pilgrims in 1934 and was known as the Plymouth Church of the Pilgrims until 2011 when it formally went back to its original name. It has continued to serve as a symbol of Brooklyn's role in the fight for social justice and the movement toward equality in nineteenth-century America. Congregant Branch Rickey is said to have prayed for guidance there before offering Jackie Robinson the Brooklyn Dodgers contract that integrated baseball. The church community has continued to host notable speakers over the years. In February 1963, Martin Luther King Jr. preached a sermon on The American Dream, and Senator Hillary Clinton spoke there in 2001. As part of the Brooklyn Heights Historic District, the church stands relatively unchanged and it is listed on the National Register of Historical Places. The beautiful and mature trees of Orange Street might now hide its deceptively simple architecture, but with its extremely active and community-driven congregation, Plymouth Church looks to stay vital for years to come.

MONTAGUE STREET FERRY

Transportation inspiration for an American classic before the subway came

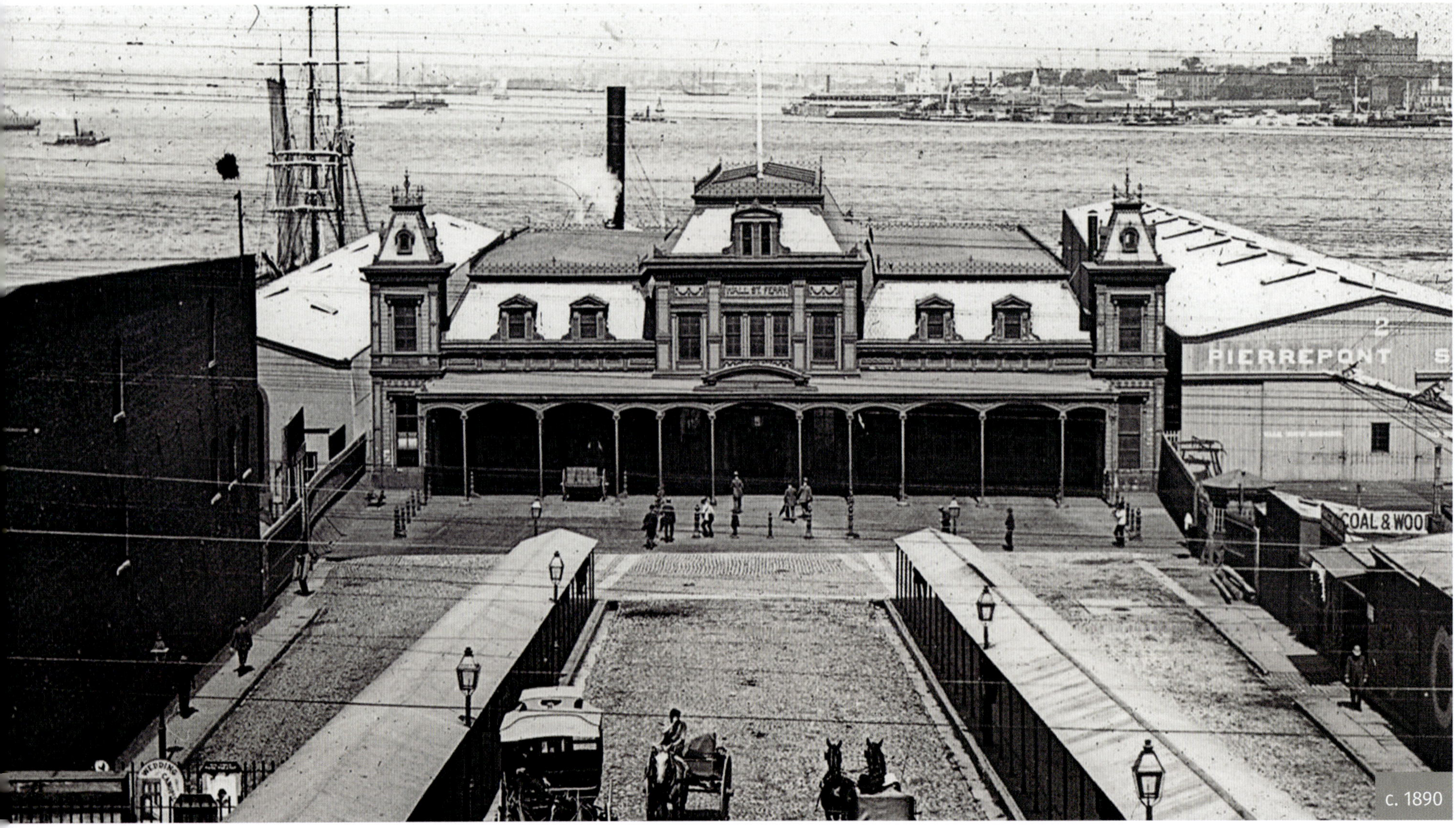

c. 1890

THEN: The Montague Street Ferry in Brooklyn played a crucial role in connecting Brooklyn to Manhattan before the construction of the Brooklyn Bridge. Devised by developer Henry E. Pierrepont, whose family owned most of Brooklyn Heights and operated the Fulton Ferry as well, the ferry service from Montague Street began taking passengers back and forth to Manhattan in 1853. It went across the East River to Wall Street, allowing bankers and businessmen living in the Heights more convenient access than the Fulton Ferry Landing. Passengers used a picturesque path over a viaduct and a small footbridge to get from the street down to the water's edge. The top of the viaduct offered stunning views of the river and the cityscape, and it was this route that was said to have inspired Walt Whitman's poem 'Crossing Brooklyn Ferry.'

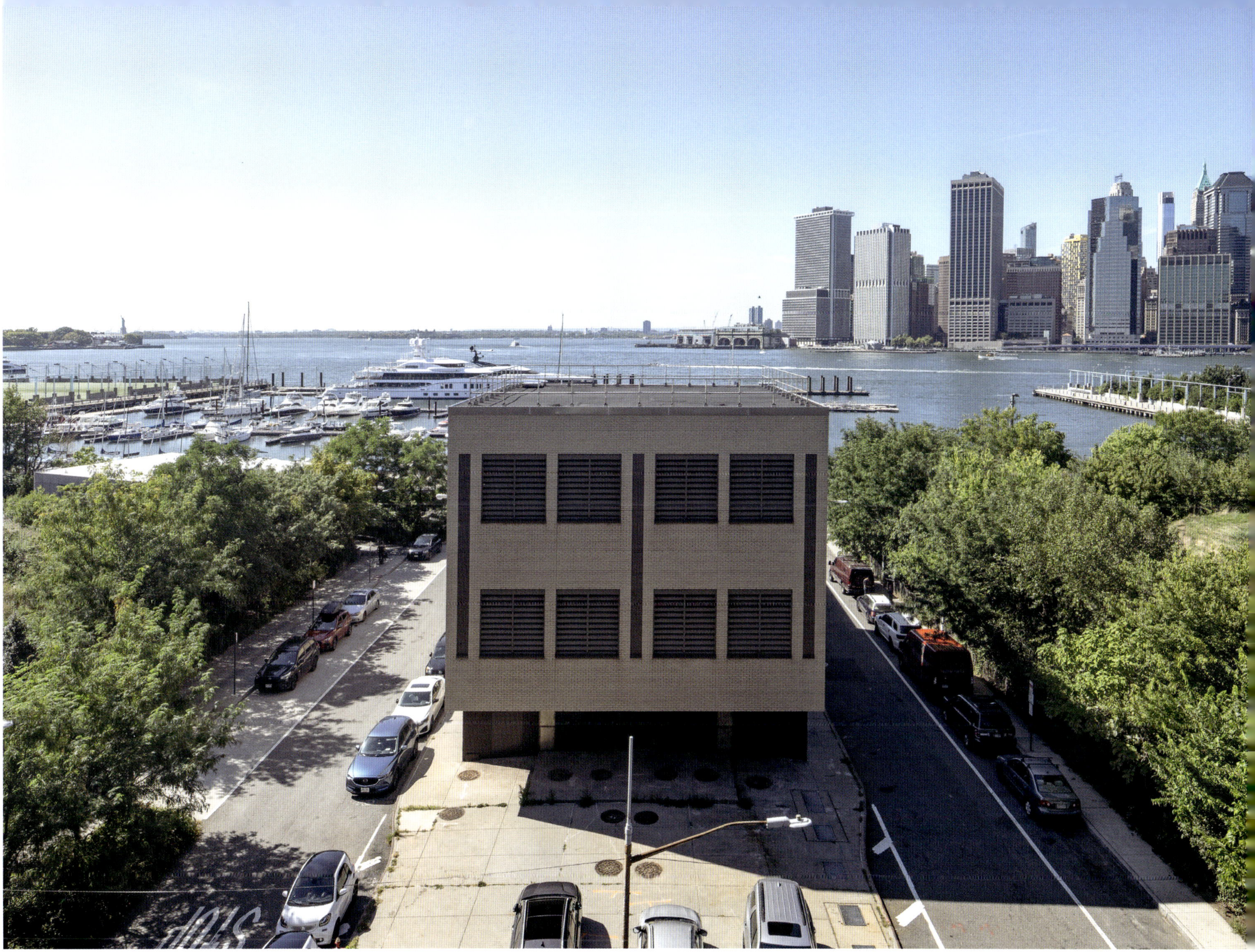

The beautifully designed ferry terminal, shown here in 1890, was already feeling the impact of the opening of the Brooklyn Bridge in 1883—transportation needs were changing and the ferry service had not been profitable for years. In 1912, the subway system reached nearby Borough Hall, and the ferry and the cable cars stayed in business for only a decade more.

NOW: Today, the Brooklyn-Queens Expressway runs where the old footpath was, and a utilitarian air shaft for the subway systems is located where the ferry terminal stood. The landing has been transformed into a part of Brooklyn Bridge Park, offering recreational spaces, cultural events, and the same stunning views of Manhattan that had inspired Walt Whitman so many years before.

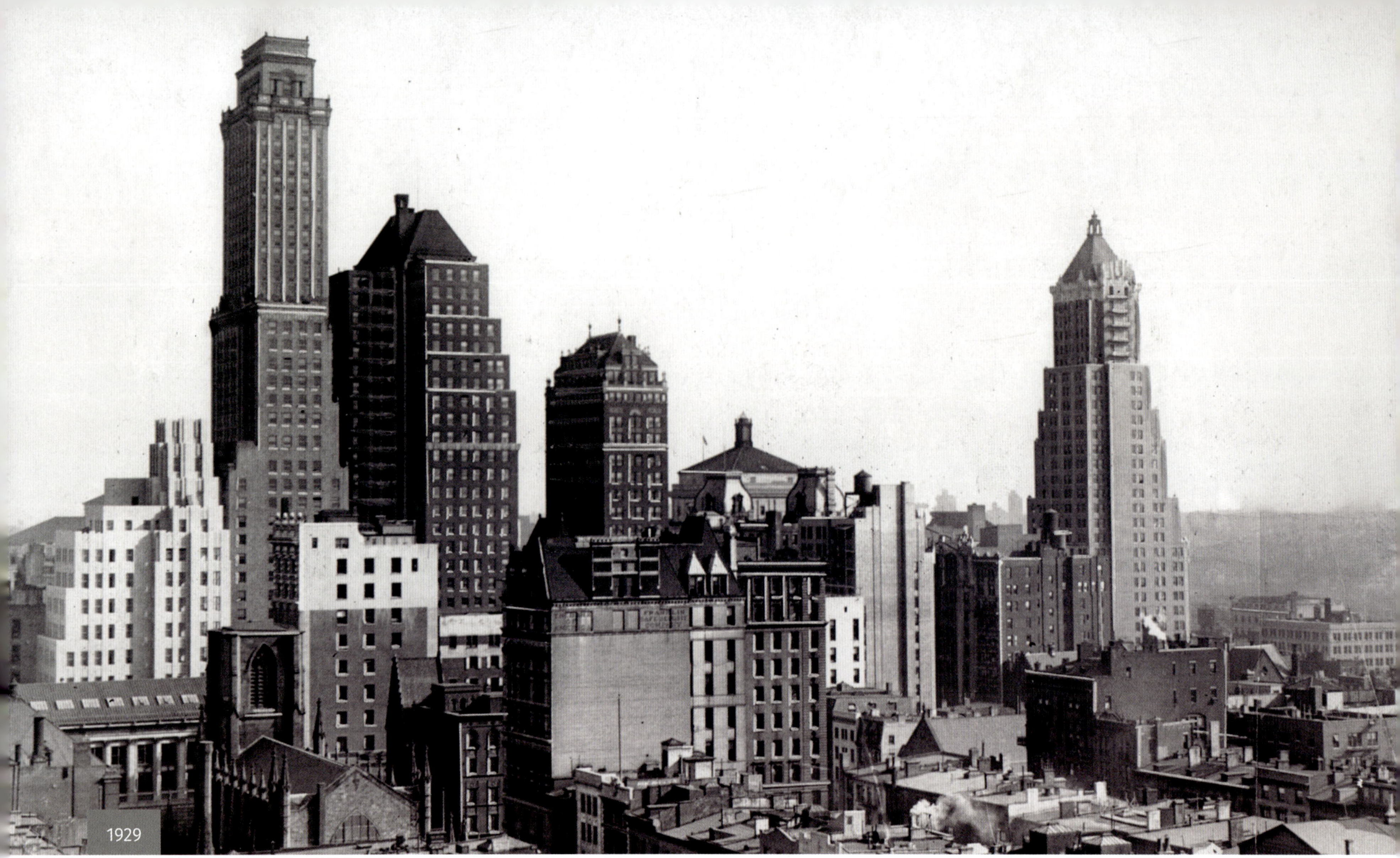

1929

VIEW FROM THE BOSSERT HOTEL, BROOKLYN HEIGHTS

Brooklyn Heights pioneered modern suburbia and historic architectural preservation

THEN: In the early 1900s, Brooklyn Heights, then known as Brooklyn Village, introduced the concept of the modern suburb. Bordered by Old Fulton Street, the Brooklyn Bridge, Cadman Plaza West, Atlantic Avenue and the Brooklyn Queens Expressway, as well as being adjacent to DUMBO, Downtown, Cobble Hill, and Boerum Hill, this neighborhood is a gateway to Brooklyn. Real estate developer and gin distiller Hezekiah Beers Pierrepont and real estate developers John and Jacob Hicks accidentally collaborated on the breaking up of the village, when their competitive plans for laying out streets were ultimately combined in 1816, paving the way for sidewalks, sewers, and water pumps to service the newly designated streets. In 1807, there were only a handful of houses, but by 1890 the neighborhood was fully developed with elegant townhouses, banks, and businesses. In 1909, The Bossert Hotel opened on Montague and Hicks Streets, on a block crowded with brownstones and financial institutions. Built by Louis Bossert, a lumber tycoon, the elegant building was famous for its Marine View restaurant and unparalleled Manhattan views. During and after World War II, the intersection saw increased activity as Brooklyn Navy Yard workers and military personnel frequented the local establishments.

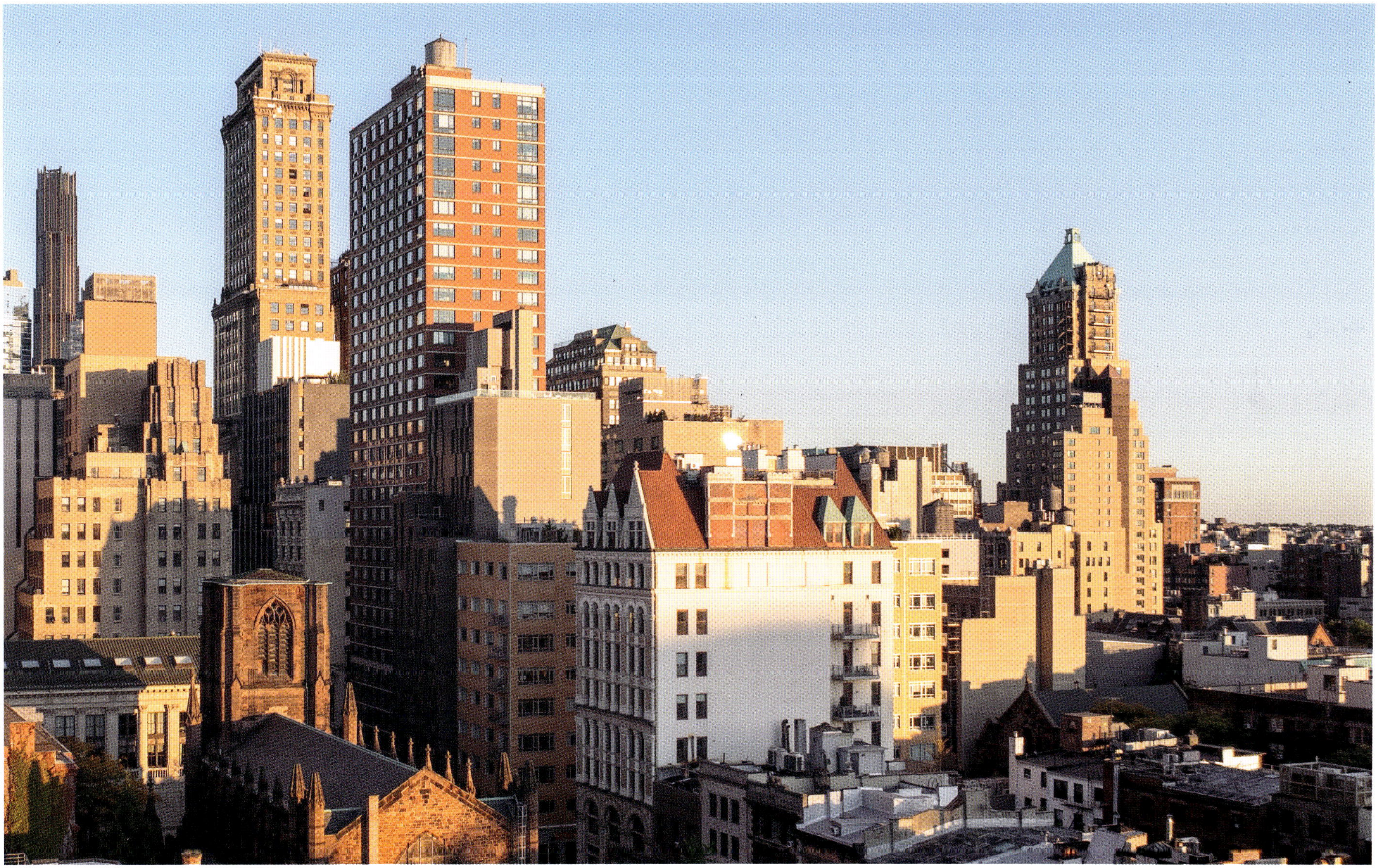

NOW: The Bossert Hotel, which celebrated the 1955 World Series win with the victorious Brooklyn Dodgers, was owned by the large landowner the Jehovah's Witnesses between 1988 and 2012. It is scheduled to open as a hotel again in 2025 after a decade of refinancing and owner swaps. The corner now hosts a mix of cafes, boutiques, and small offices catering to residents and the visitors who come for the area's visual charm. With its commercial character, Montague Street is often referred to as the Main Street of Brooklyn, while Hicks is more residential. The intersection of Montague and Hicks looks remarkably similar to how it did in 1929, with much of the rich architectural detail still visible thanks to a 1965 designation as New York City's first historic district. Due to those protections, the view from the same perspective is largely unchanged, and the lack of significant high-rises helps maintain the feeling of Brooklyn's first village. Even most of the street names are the same, still honoring Pierrepont, Hicks, and other notable residents who helped usher in the Brooklyn residential boom that continues to this day.

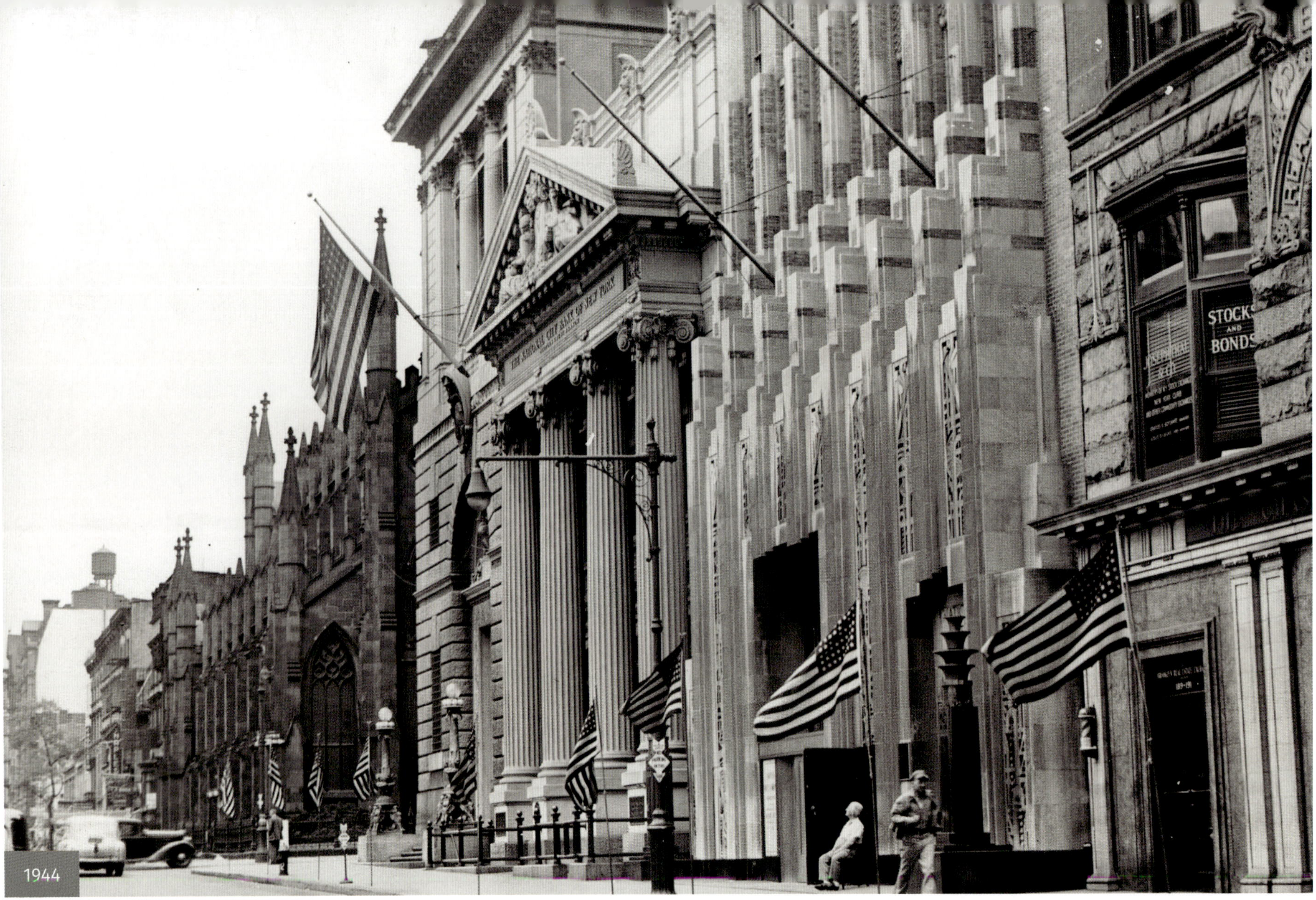

1944

MONTAGUE AND CLINTON, BROOKLYN HEIGHTS

The legacy of "Bank Row" is still intact

THEN: The intersection of Montague and Clinton Streets was an integral conduit between the civic center around Borough Hall and the residential neighborhood of Brooklyn Heights. At the turn of the century, it was known as "Bank Row" due to the large number of financial institutions that stood next to one another. These buildings included the iconic Brooklyn Trust Company building, with its three large 28-ton marble columns and the extensively ornamented triangle pediments designed by York & Sawyer, in the Italian High Renaissance style. Next door to it stood the 1929 high-rise that served as the headquarters for the National Title Guaranty Company, and the Art Deco limestone screens on the lower floors were designed by Rene Paul Chambellan, who also designed the Rockefeller Center. Both of these buildings represented significant investment in Brooklyn and were symbols of affluence and the success of the people who lived there. This intersection hummed with the new electric trolley line that connected residents to Manhattan via the recently completed Brooklyn Bridge and also served as a gathering point for suffragettes, who would often meet at the nearby Brooklyn Women's Club.

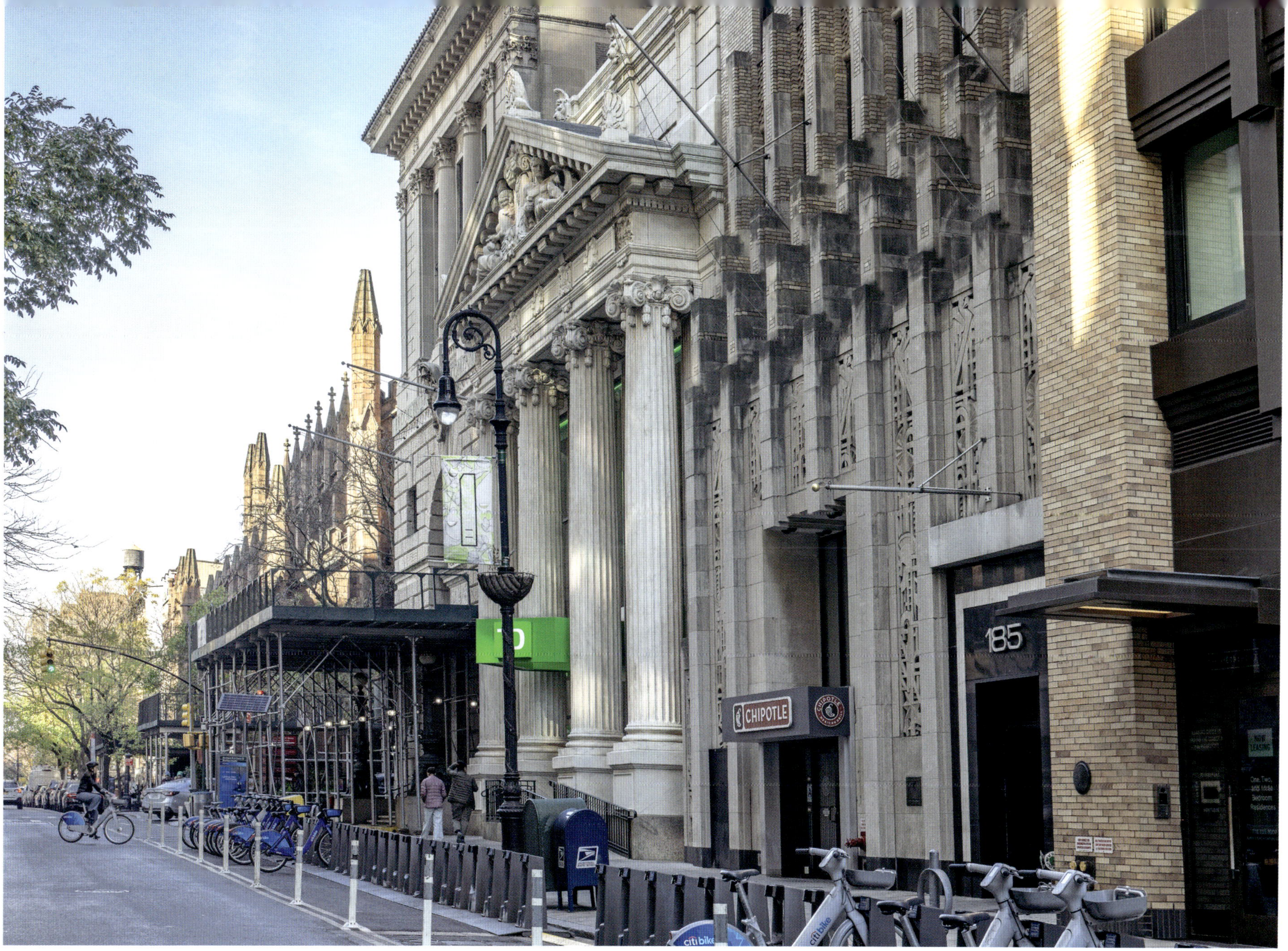

NOW: With so few details changed between the past and modern day, it's easy to understand why the intersection has become a popular spot for architectural tours. Guides highlight original details such as the cast-iron lampposts and bluestone sidewalks that have survived from the early 1900s. The intersection at Montague and Hicks is still a critical junction in the Brooklyn Heights historic district, though many original buildings have been repurposed behind their historic facades. The former Brooklyn Trust Company still inspires awe among visitors, now as a branch of Chase Bank, with the building next door currently housing a Citibank. St. Ann's Church, visible in both images, has served as a continued presence in the community. Around the corner from this site is St. Ann's School, which was affiliated with the church until the 1980s when it became independent. Famous alumni of the institution, including Beastie Boy Mike D and actress Jennifer Connelly, have cemented the location as a cornerstone of the Brooklyn creative scene.

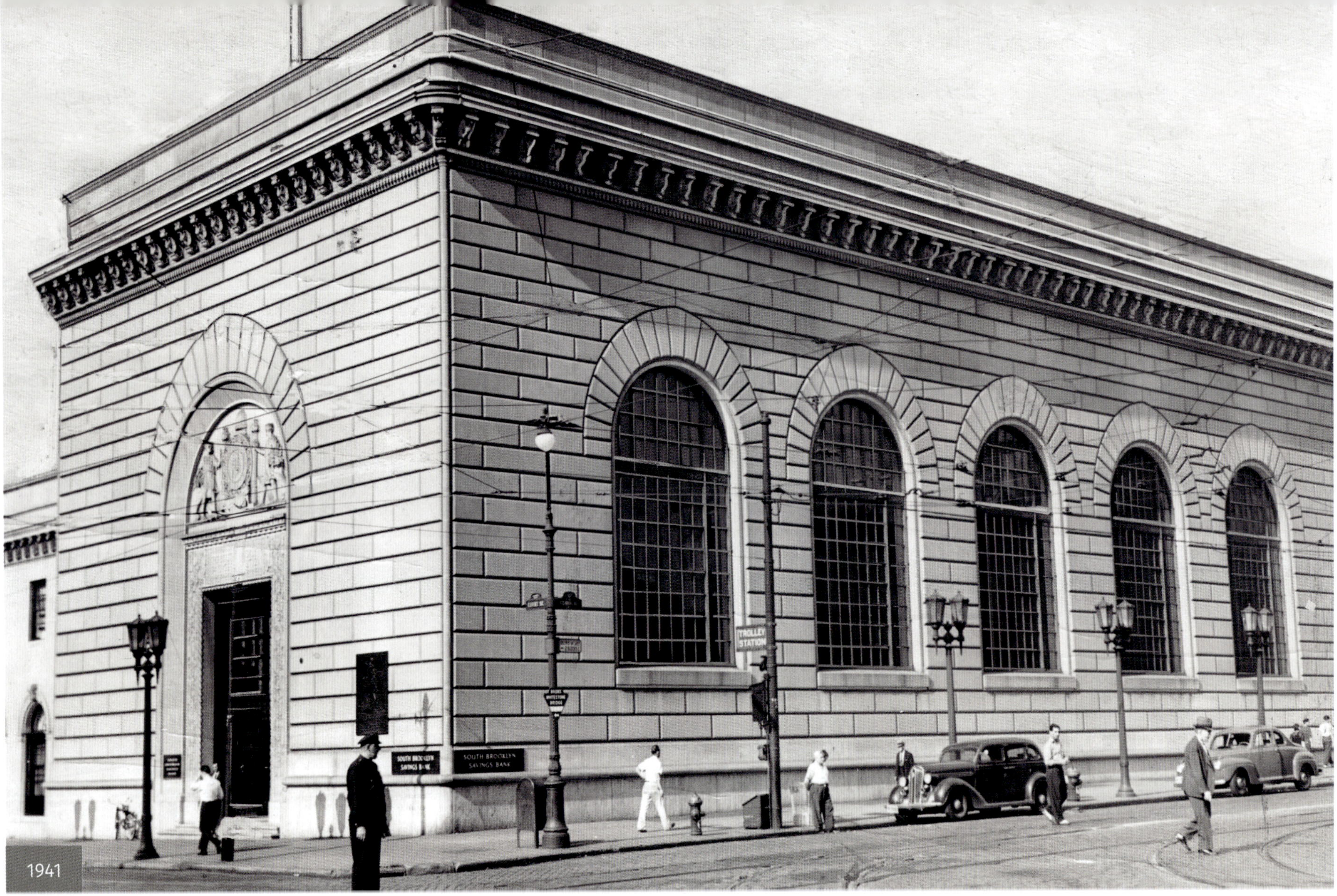

1941

THE SOUTH BROOKLYN SAVINGS BANK, COBBLE HILL

A financial commitment to South Brooklyn

THEN: The South Brooklyn Savings Bank, located at the corner of Atlantic Avenue and Court Street in Cobble Hill, just east of Borough Hall, is tangible proof of how Brooklyn's economic growth led to architectural triumphs in the late nineteenth century. Designed by McKenzie, Voorhees & Gmelin, the architectural firm responsible for the Brooklyn Municipal Building on Joralemon Street. The bank building opened in 1924, and was the third structure to serve as headquarters for the financial institution. The Beaux-Arts style reflected the opulence and optimism of the era, as well as the seventy-five years of the bank's success. The building's Corinthian columns and intricate stone carvings conveyed stability to those who would come to trust the institution with their savings. At the turn of the century, Cobble Hill was a flourishing middle-class neighborhood, home to a mix of Irish, Italian, and German immigrants, as well as native-born Americans. Brownstone row houses graced the tree-lined streets, and the thriving commercial district along Atlantic Avenue and Court Street was the focal point of the neighborhood and distinct from the more industrial parts of Brooklyn. By 1941, the bank had made it through the Great Depression and was providing support to local businesses manufacturing boats and goods for World War II efforts.

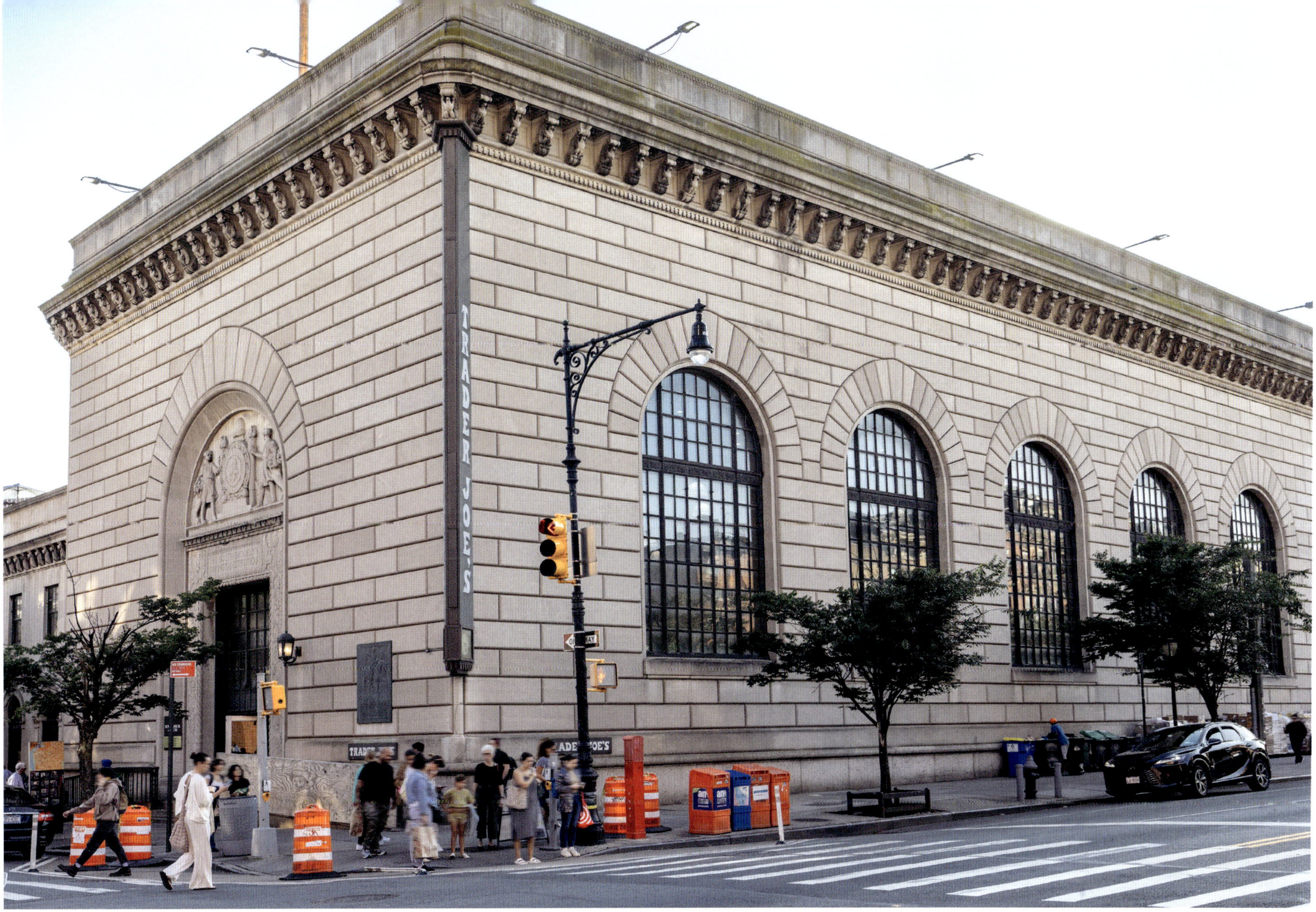

NOW: The bank would change names a few times over the years, but it continued to serve Cobble Hill's financial needs until it sold to Sovereign Bank in 2006. Since 2008, the structure has housed a Trader Joe's, an upscale grocery store that is a better fit for the needs of residents today. Unchanged on the outside, the blending of old spaces with new uses is a key characteristic that seemed to be a requirement for getting support from preservation-minded residents for new projects in the area, like The River Park Development on the former Long Island Hospital site, which includes a mix of restored historic buildings and new construction. Evergreen businesses, like Sahadi's Middle Eastern grocery that has operated there since 1948, and the old-school Italian restaurants on Court Street, stand next to new attractions like The Invisible Dog Center, a hub for contemporary art and performances that opened in 2009. In spite of the new additions, Cobble Hill has maintained so much of its nineteenth-century charm that it's often used as a setting for films and TV shows set in historic Brooklyn, including *Moonstruck* and *The Marvelous Mrs. Maisel*. The upscale boutiques, trendy restaurants, and high property values have drawn a new generation of young professionals from Manhattan. While the demographic makeup has shifted, with a decrease in the working-class and immigrant populations that once defined the neighborhood, Cobble Hill has maintained its distinctive character and strong sense of community.

BOROUGH HALL

The proud civic center gets a twenty-first-century makeover

THEN: In 1848, Borough Hall opened as City Hall, the proud civic center of the City of Brooklyn, which was, at that time, still an independent city and not yet part of New York City. The intersection of Fulton and Court Street was a hub of civic and commercial life, crowded with offices, banks, restaurants, shops, and street vendors. It was busy with pedestrians and horse-drawn carriages, and accessible by the elevated rail line. Multiple newspapers, including the *Brooklyn Daily Eagle* (where Walt Whitman worked as an editor in the 1840s), opened offices here for easy access to local politicians and decision-makers. Architect Calvin Pollard originally won a contest to design the Greek Revival-style structure, but funds dried up soon after the project began, and it was eventually finished by second-place contestant Gamaliel King and included a beautiful cupola on the roof. In 1895, the wood-framed cupola burned down, sending the bell tumbling into the entrance hall. In the momentous year of 1898, Brooklyn merged with New York City, and City Hall became Borough Hall, but the cupola had not yet been restored. By the next year, a new cast-iron cupola once again graced the roofline.

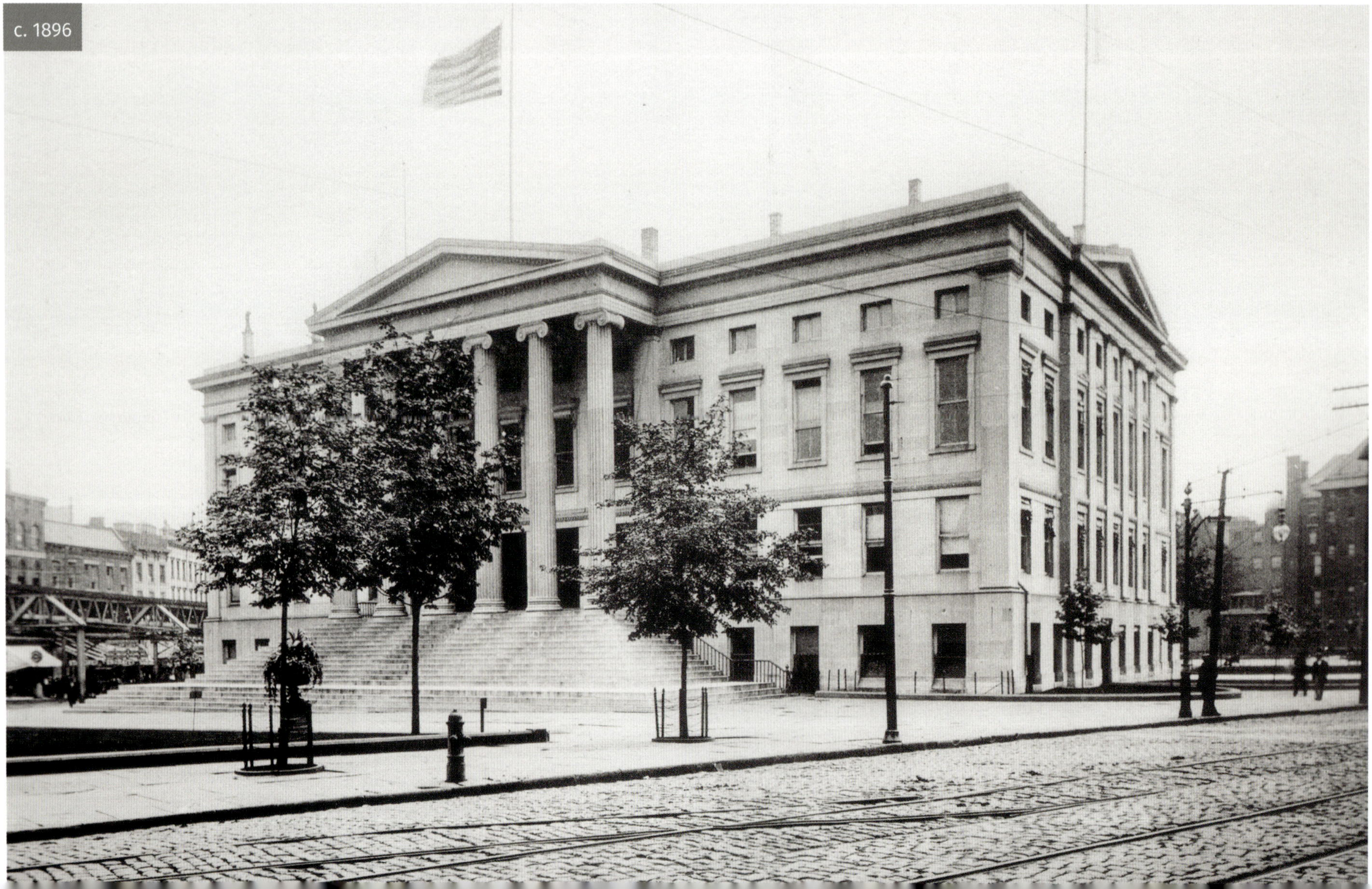
c. 1896

NOW: In the twentieth century, the area went through multiple changes. The rail line and adjacent courthouse were demolished and replaced with new civic buildings and a concrete plaza. The Borough Hall building stayed the same until a full renovation in the Eighties. Today, Borough Hall remains a focal point of Downtown Brooklyn, though everything around it is different. The building itself is now over 175 years old, making it the oldest building in Brooklyn, and it's a protected New York City landmark. It is also the office of the Brooklyn Borough President and serves as a community center for local events. The area around Fulton Street and Court Street has evolved into a dense urban center, with new high-rise office buildings and residential towers reshaping the skyline. The construction of the nearby MetroTech Center in the Eighties and Nineties brought a large-scale office and educational complex to the area. More recently, the development of City Point, a mixed-use complex featuring residential towers, retail spaces, and cultural institutions like the Theater for a New Audience's Polonsky Shakespeare Center, opened in 2013. Despite these changes, efforts have been made to preserve historic elements, including the restoration of Borough Hall's iconic cupola again in 2010. The area continues to serve as a transportation hub, with numerous subway lines converging nearby, echoing its historical role as a nexus of Brooklyn life.

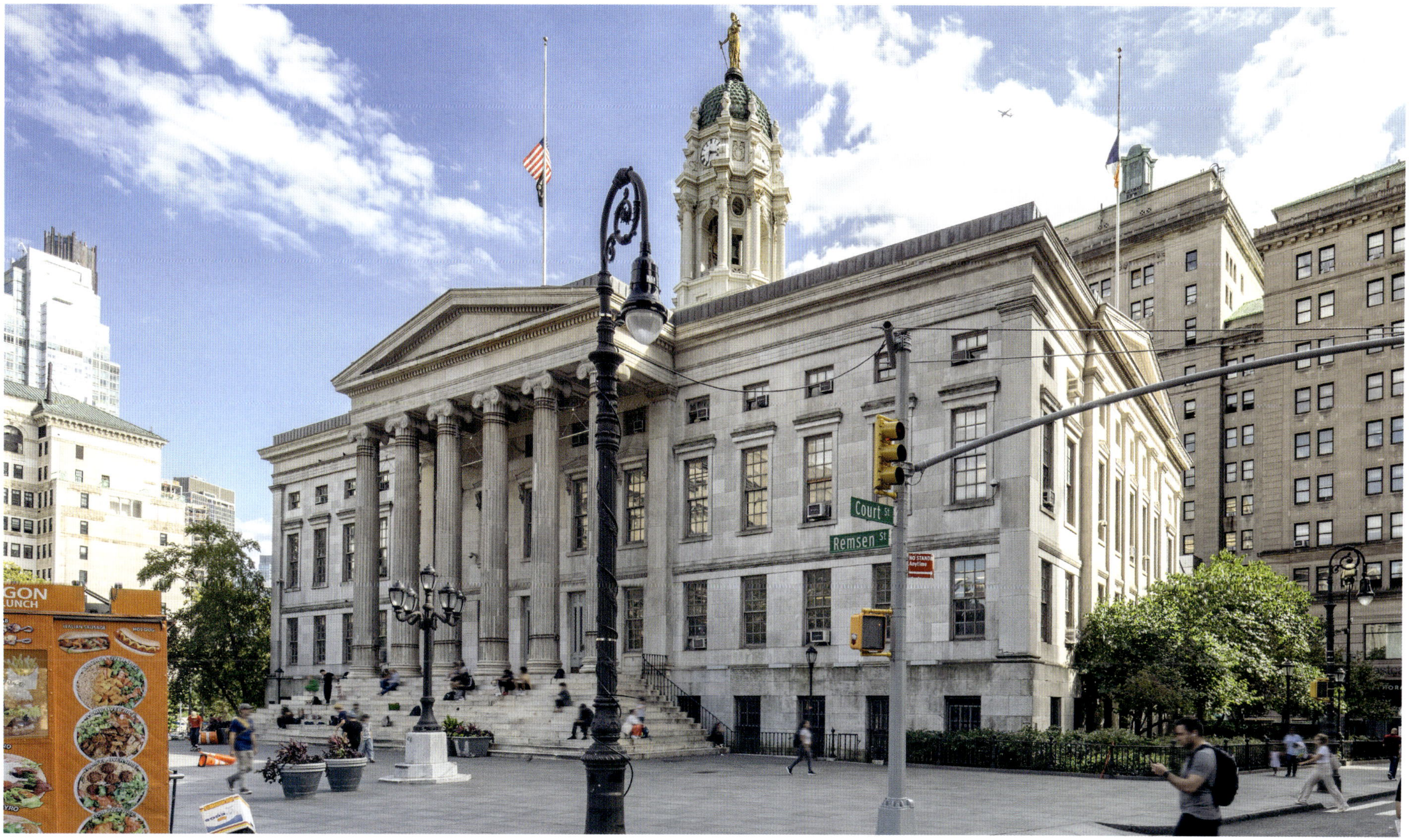

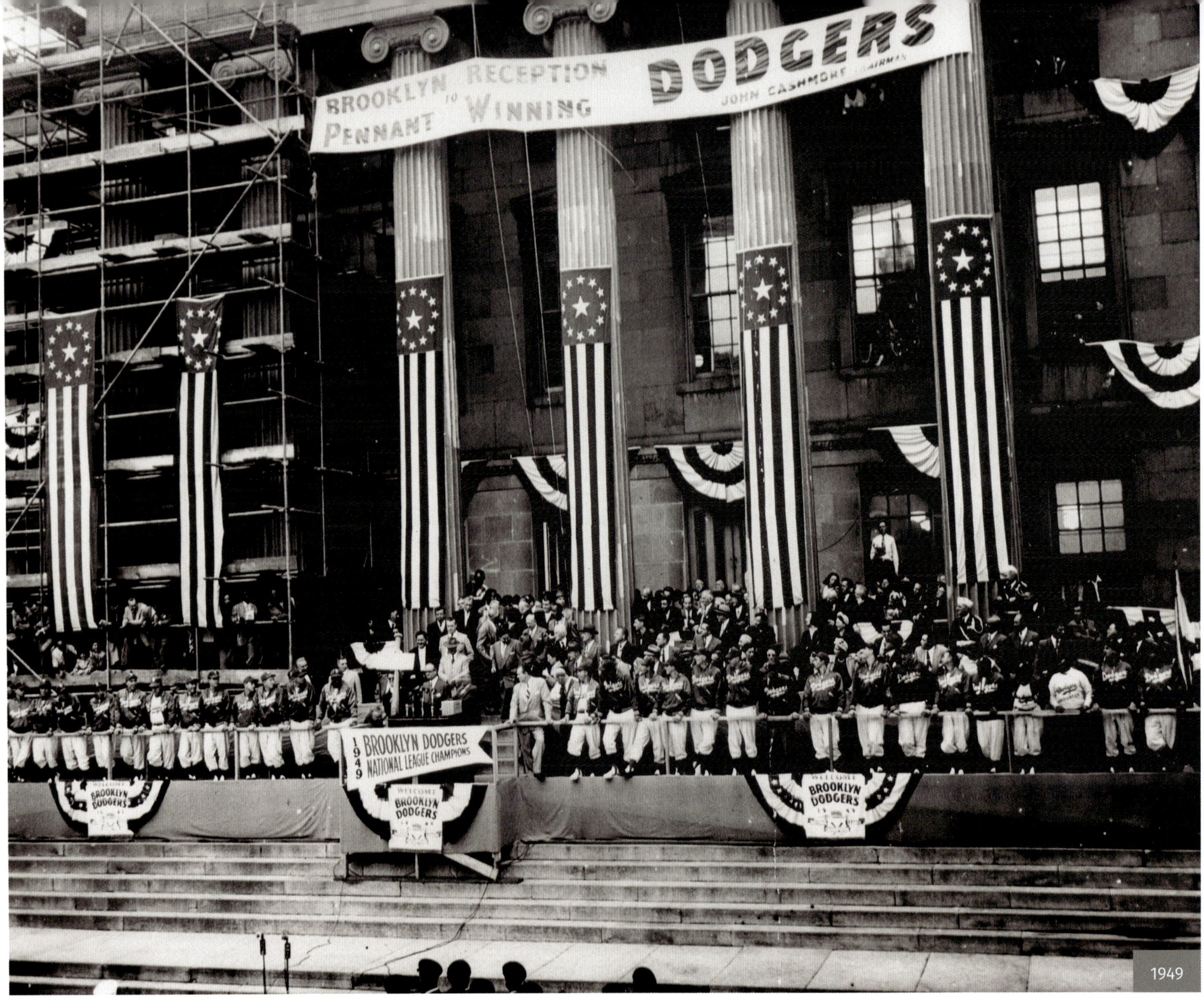

1949

BOROUGH HALL STEPS

From civil rights rallies to skateboarders, these steps have seen it all

THEN: The steps of Brooklyn Borough Hall have witnessed every civil and political milestone for the borough and the country since they were built in 1848. During the Civil War, the steps served as a critical recruiting location for the Union Army. In 1898, there were rallies for and protests against Brooklyn's merger with New York City. In the 1900s, suffragettes fought for women's equal rights there, and the state department sold war bonds and held victory celebrations there after World Wars I and II. There were multiple labor demonstrations held on the steps during the Great Depression. In 1949, baseball's Brooklyn Dodgers won the National League pennant and celebrated there, as seen to the left. The 1949 celebration was particularly significant as it featured Jackie Robinson, who had joined the Dodgers after the desegregation of the league just two years earlier. Two other African-American stars, Roy Campanella and Don Newcombe, joined the team on the steps as part of baseball's first integrated roster.

NOW: Since the Fifties, the steps have continued to serve as the central location for Brooklyn's civic gatherings. More recent decades have seen protests for the Civil Rights movement of the Sixties, the Vietnam War, the AIDS crisis of the Eighties, and more recently Black Lives Matter. It serves as a hub for community-wide celebrations, including Brooklyn Pride, and memorials like the one after September 11, 2001. The Dodgers left Brooklyn in 1957 after failing to secure a new stadium despite years of trying, but the Borough Hall steps remain a Brooklyn institution. On any nice day, you can see dozens of skateboarders of all ages trying out new tricks on and in front of these storied steps.

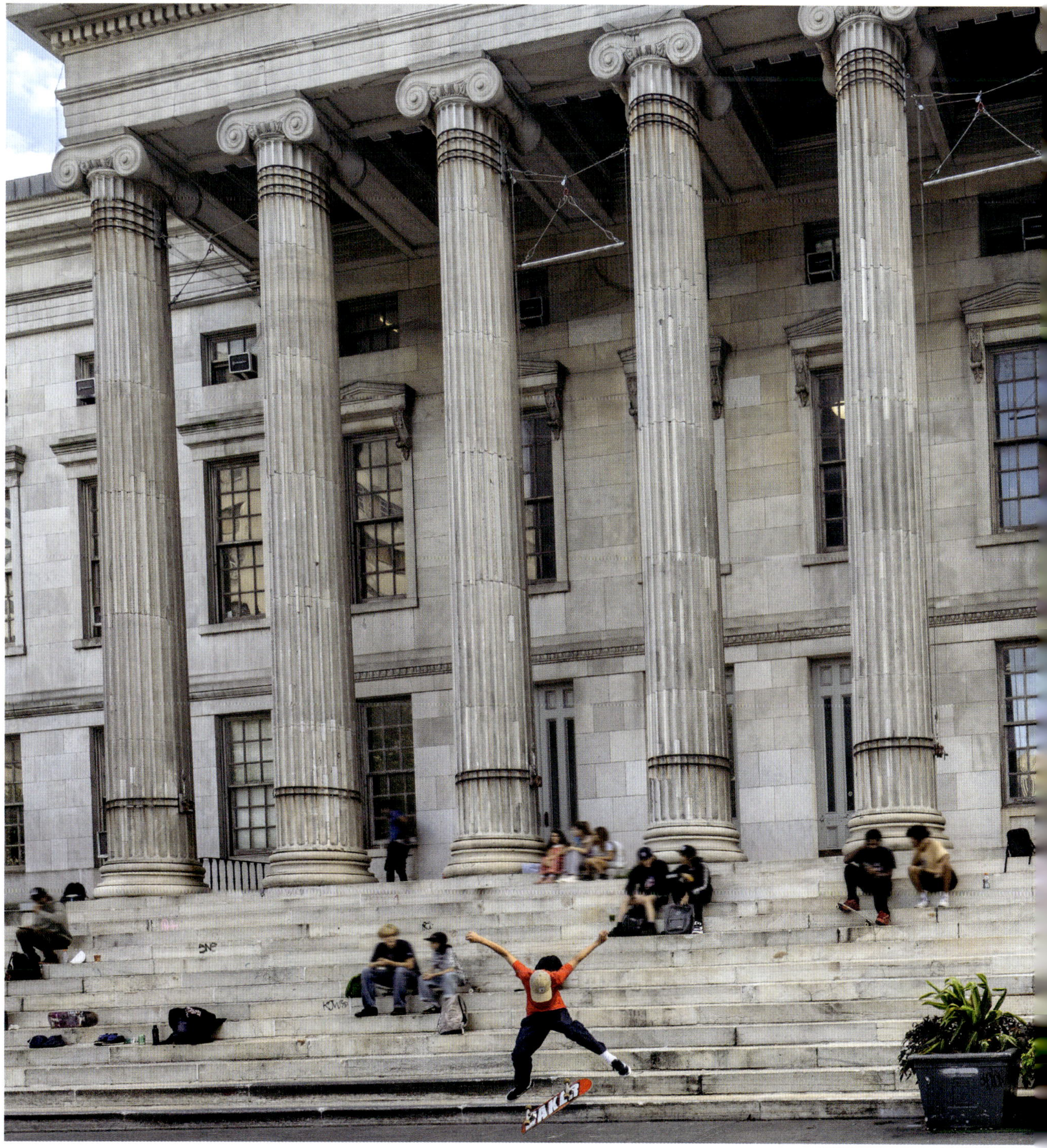

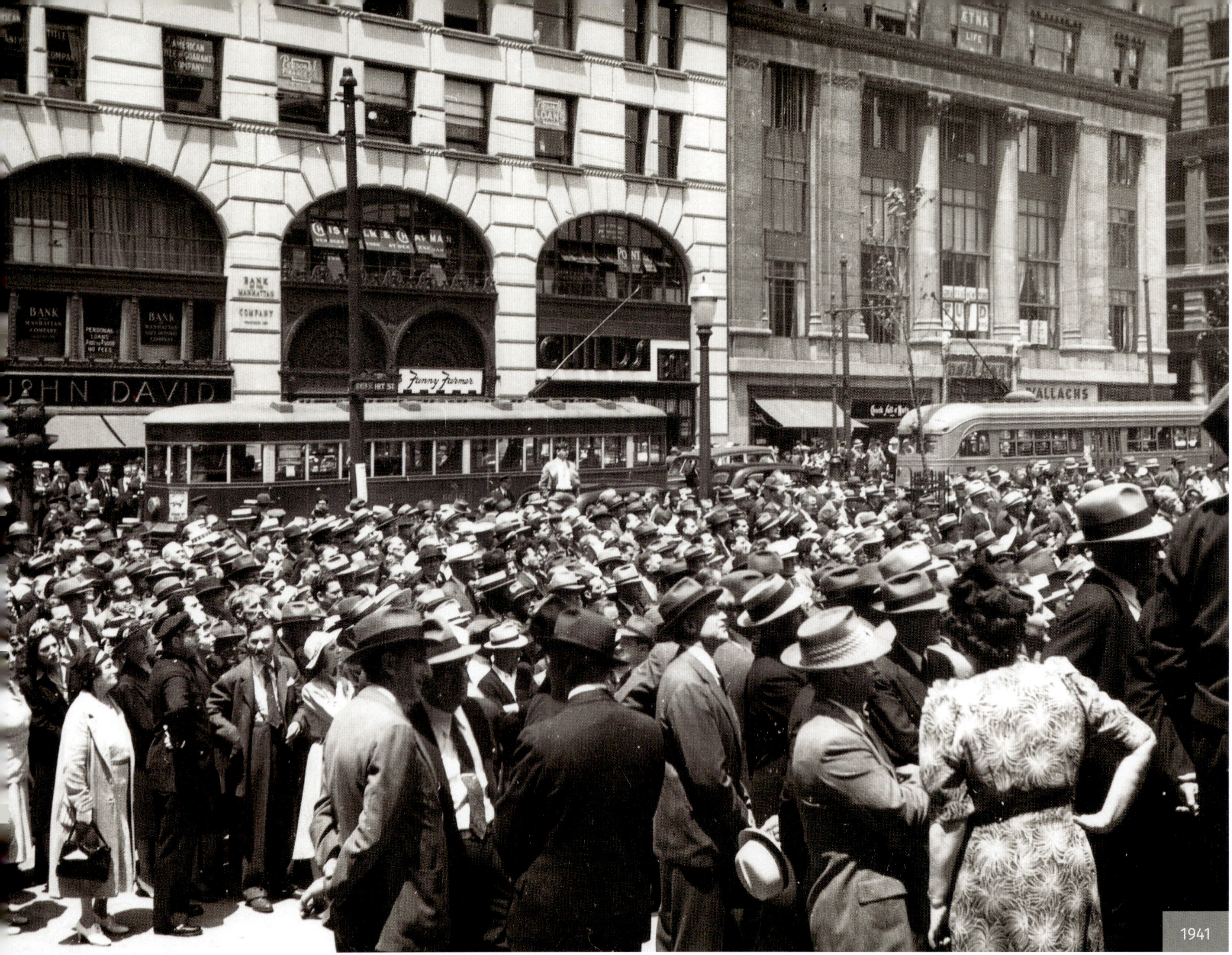

1941

COURT STREET

An important thoroughfare becomes a site for community events

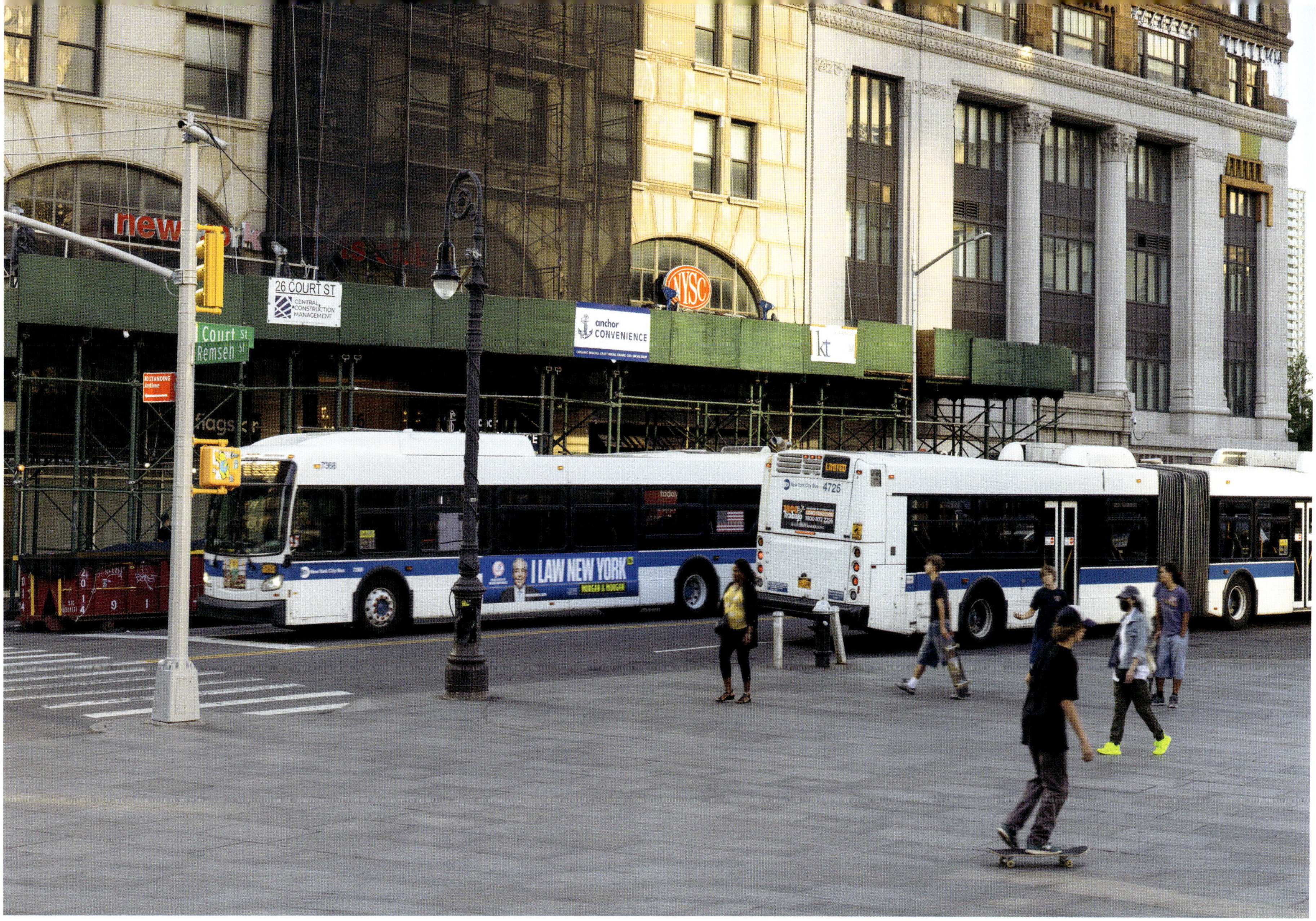

THEN: Court Street was originally named George Street until 1835, when Brooklyn began to plan the city complex that became Kings County Court. It was full of stores and offices that supported the city, and it served as a passthrough to the civic center. It was also a transportation hub to the rest of Brooklyn, with an elevated train stop in the middle of the street. In 1941, locals filled the street to watch the elevated train be demolished. The City of New York had built an underground subway system that was more modern, better for the neighborhoods, and more gentle on the environment—and the elevated trains were slowly disappearing. Opened in 1908, the Court Street stop was an extension of the Lexington Avenue line from Lower Manhattan, and it was the first subway station built in Brooklyn.

NOW: The old office buildings still serve the workers of Brooklyn every day, with some now repurposed as gyms and other amenities. New stores and businesses fill the storefronts, from new cafés to classic Italian bakeries and restaurants. The area around Court Street, near Borough Hall, also serves as one of Brooklyn's most popular sites for festivals, food fairs, and street vendors, and it is an excellent place for anyone to get a small taste of Brooklyn's vibrant culture. The Court Street/Borough Hall station between Montague and Joralemon Street has five subways that connect there, which are all still based on—and use—the original station from 1908, which is still in working order to this day.

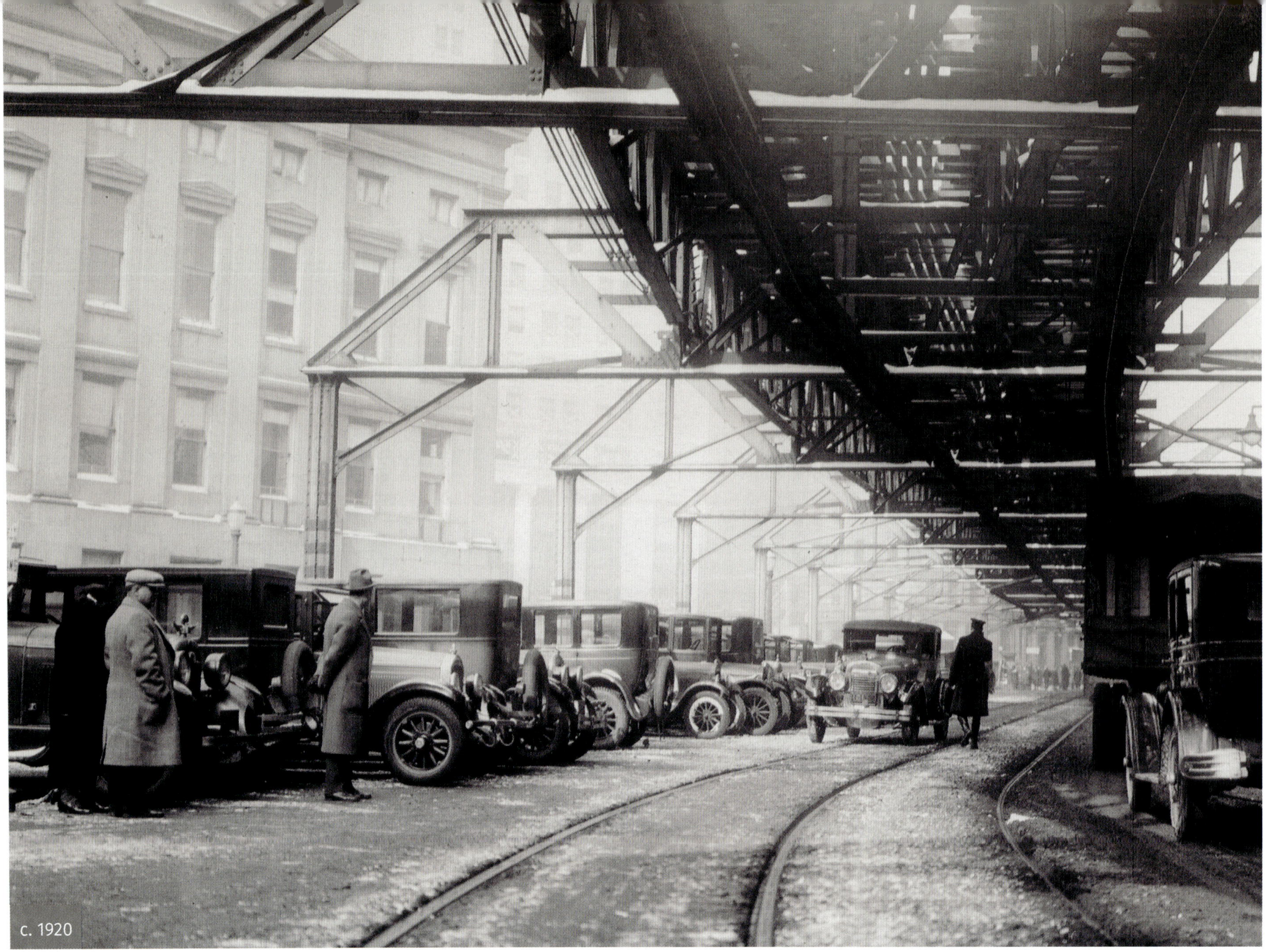
c. 1920

CADMAN PLAZA

Green space preserved from urban renewal projects leads the way for new homes

THEN: The area seen in this 1920s photo, just off Joralemon Street, was defined by the elevated rail line that ran right alongside Borough Hall, just around the corner from its iconic steps. City bigwigs and their visitors parked here for easy access to the civic district, and the offices and businesses that supported it. The structure of the elevated train made for what looked like a dark and shadowy environment, but it was mostly busy and utilitarian.

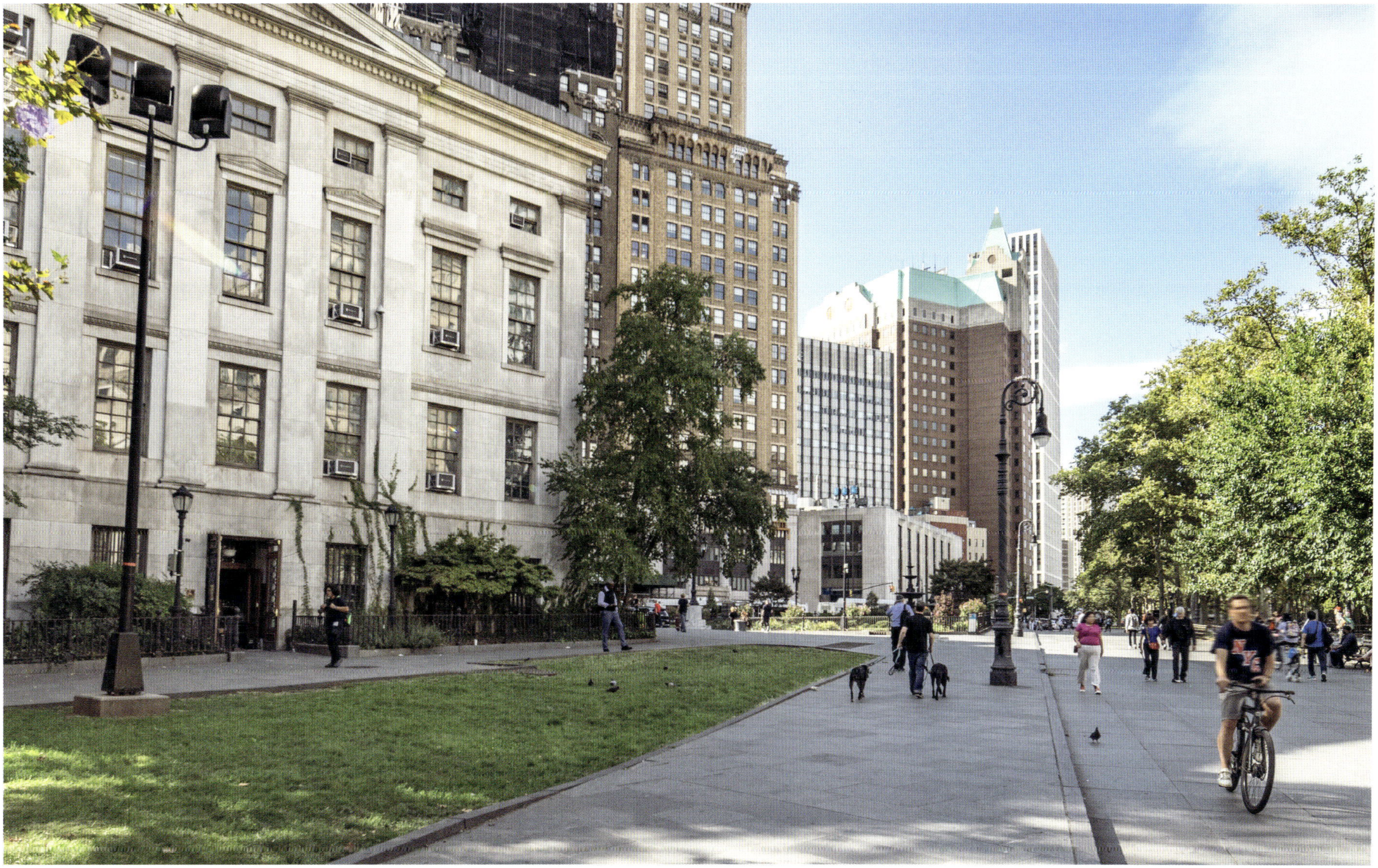

NOW: Today, with the elevated railway gone, the area is now known as Cadman Plaza and it presents a dramatically different landscape. As part of Robert Moses' urban renewal project in the Thirties and Forties, the city purchased or seized much of the land around Borough Hall and transformed it into interconnected urban parks. Combined with the Korean War Veterans Plaza and Walt Whitman Park, this string of green space spans all the way from Borough Hall to the Brooklyn Bridge. The plaza is surrounded by the Roosevelt Federal Courthouse and the main Brooklyn Post Office, and is a popular place for protests due to its proximity to the Brooklyn Supreme Court and the U.S. District Court for the Eastern District of New York, the location of the first ever criminal trial of a former United States President. Condominium skyscrapers are going up on all sides to provide new residences in a space that has been mostly commercial for the past 100 years, taking advantage of the convenient location and multitude of transit options.

MAIN POST OFFICE AND BROOKLYN EAGLE, CADMAN PLAZA

The post office and the newspaper were neighbors for a reason

c. 1950

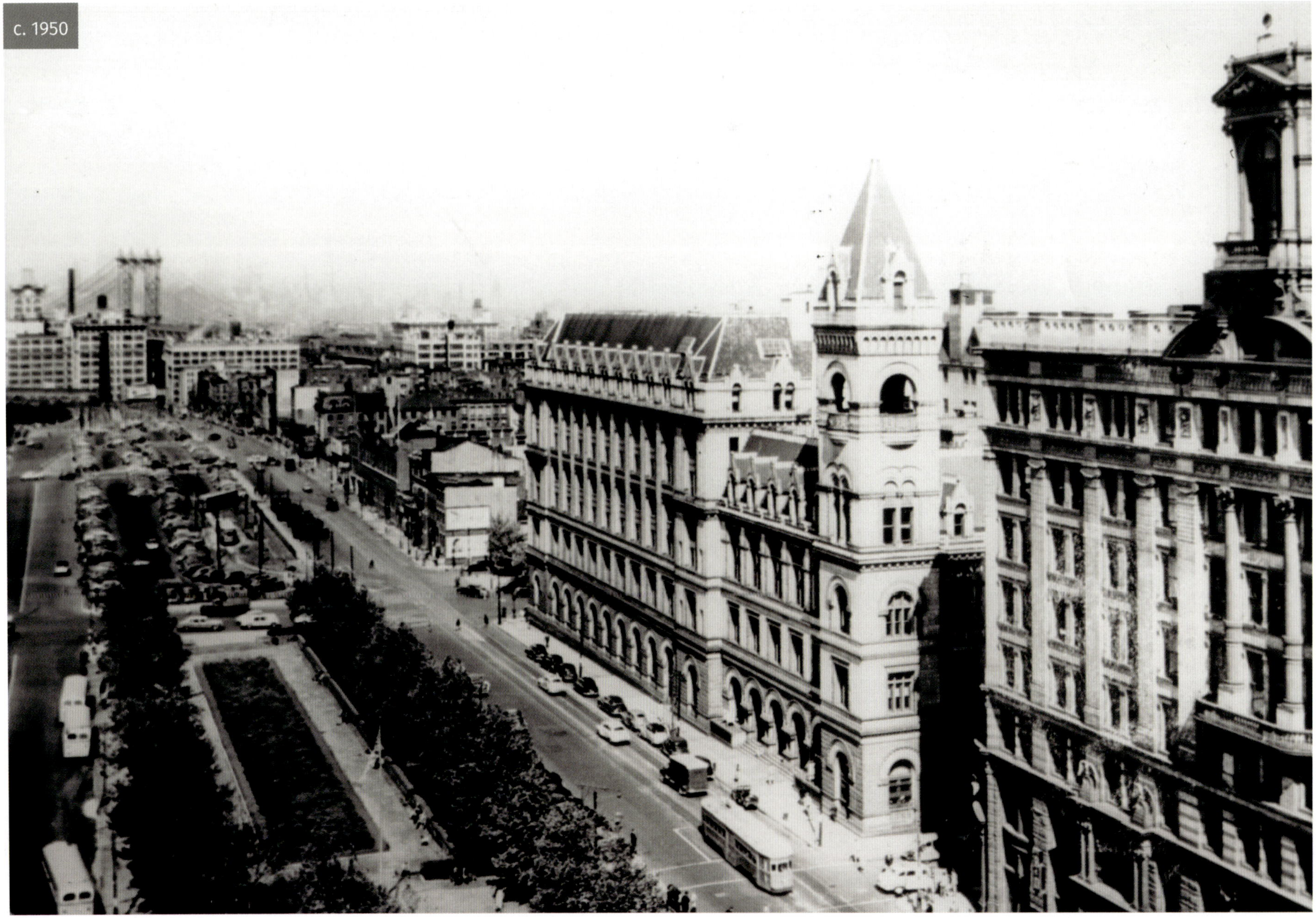

THEN: The Brooklyn General Post Office at 271 Cadman Plaza East (formerly Washington Street) was built between 1930 and 1936 as part of the federal government's Depression-era public works programs. Designed by architects Lorimer Rich and Burt L. Fenner, with consulting architects Louis A. Simon and James A. Wetmore from the U.S. Treasury Department's Office of the Supervising Architect, the monumental Art Deco structure is imposing and grand. The limestone building features various scenes of postal service work in sculptural relief by artist Carl Paul Jennewein. Its Cadman Plaza location was strategic for the proximity to Brooklyn Borough Hall and other civic buildings, and it also meant that it was close to the newspaper district, in particular the *Brooklyn Daily Eagle*. The *Eagle* was Brooklyn's premier newspaper at the time, and newspapers sent subscriptions to readers via mail. By 1950, both buildings functioned at maximum capacity, forming a critical communication center in downtown Brooklyn. The post office was Brooklyn's main postal facility during the post-World War II boom; its vast sorting room covered an entire city block and employed hundreds of workers, bustling with the work of handling the *Eagle*'s large circulation mailings. However, this period marked the beginning of a significant change: the *Brooklyn Daily Eagle* stopped publishing in 1955 after a 114-year run.

NOW: The post office continues to serve as Brooklyn's main postal facility, and the building was added to the National Register of Historic Places in 1974. In 2016, the building was redeveloped as The Postal House, a mixed-use property with apartments built on top of the original structure. The conversion created eighty-seven condominium apartments in the upper floors, while preserving the building's historic Art Deco facade and many architectural details, including the limestone exterior and sculptural reliefs. The grand lobby was restored to highlight its historic features, including the original murals. The former *Eagle* site across the street has transformed since the old building was demolished, providing the neighborhood with modern commercial and residential developments as part of the broader Cadman Plaza complex. The change reflects Brooklyn's evolution from a newspaper and industrial hub to a modern residential and commercial district. While the *Eagle* building is gone, several historical markers and plaques in the area commemorate the newspaper's importance in Brooklyn's history and its relationship with the postal service across the street. The giant eagle statue that flew above it continues to guard knowledge and information, as it's been relocated to the main branch of the Brooklyn Library, where it sits right over the front door.

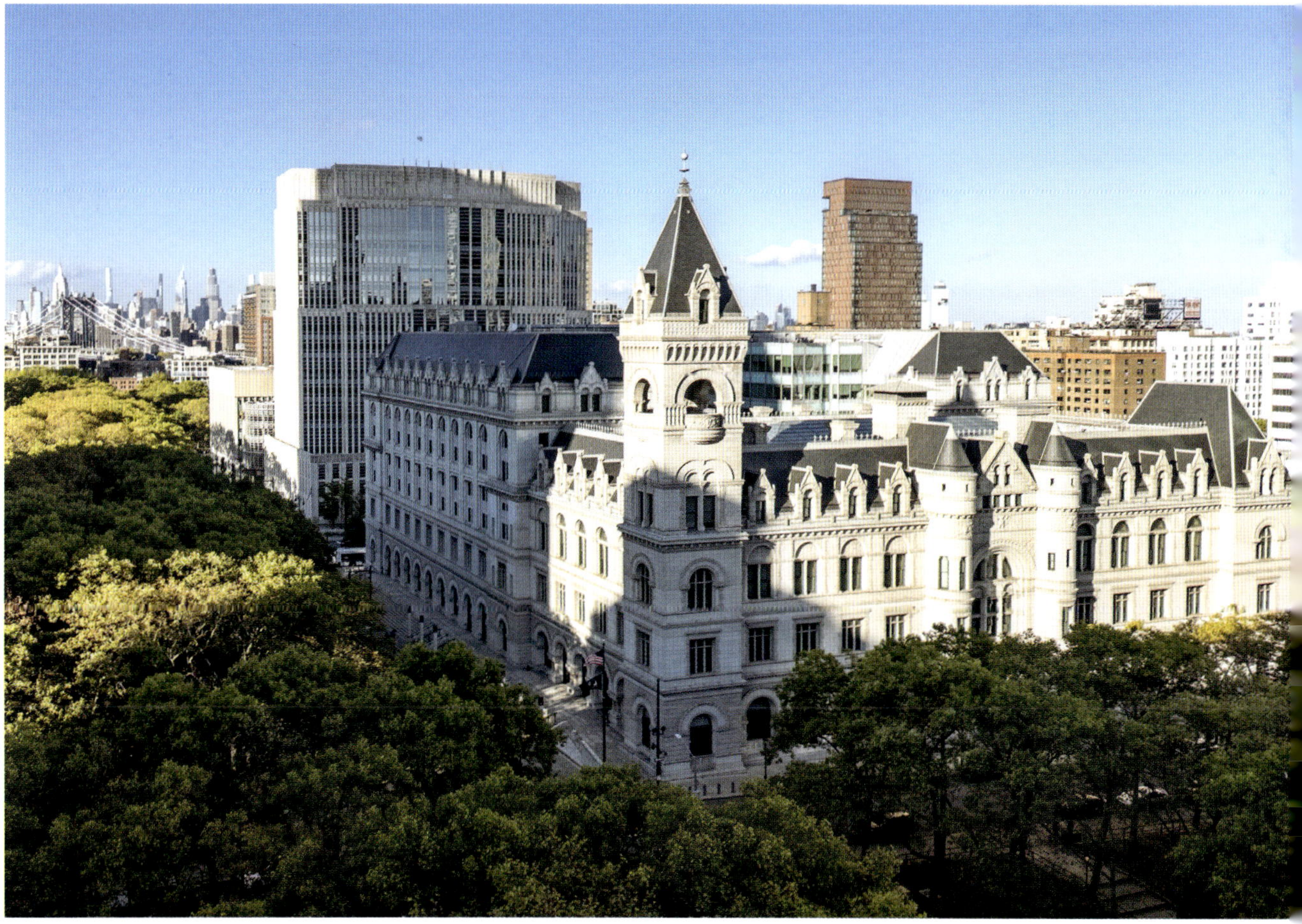

FULTON STREET

The Automat represented Brooklyn's golden age of commerce

THEN: In 1958, the stretch of Fulton Street between Flatbush Avenue and Adams Street was a thriving commercial district. It was the heart of downtown Brooklyn and one of the busiest shopping districts in New York, dominated by large department stores, including A&S (Abraham & Strauss). These multi-level marketplaces offered everything from clothing to home goods, and attracted customers from all over Brooklyn and beyond. Specialty shops, like haberdasheries and millineries, were tucked in between the larger stores. Luncheonettes, diners, and cafeterias catered to office workers and shoppers. The Horn & Hardart Automat, was part of a chain of automated restaurants that put a coin-operated food cabinet between servers and customers, and called it self-service. It was, at the time, considered the height of modernity.

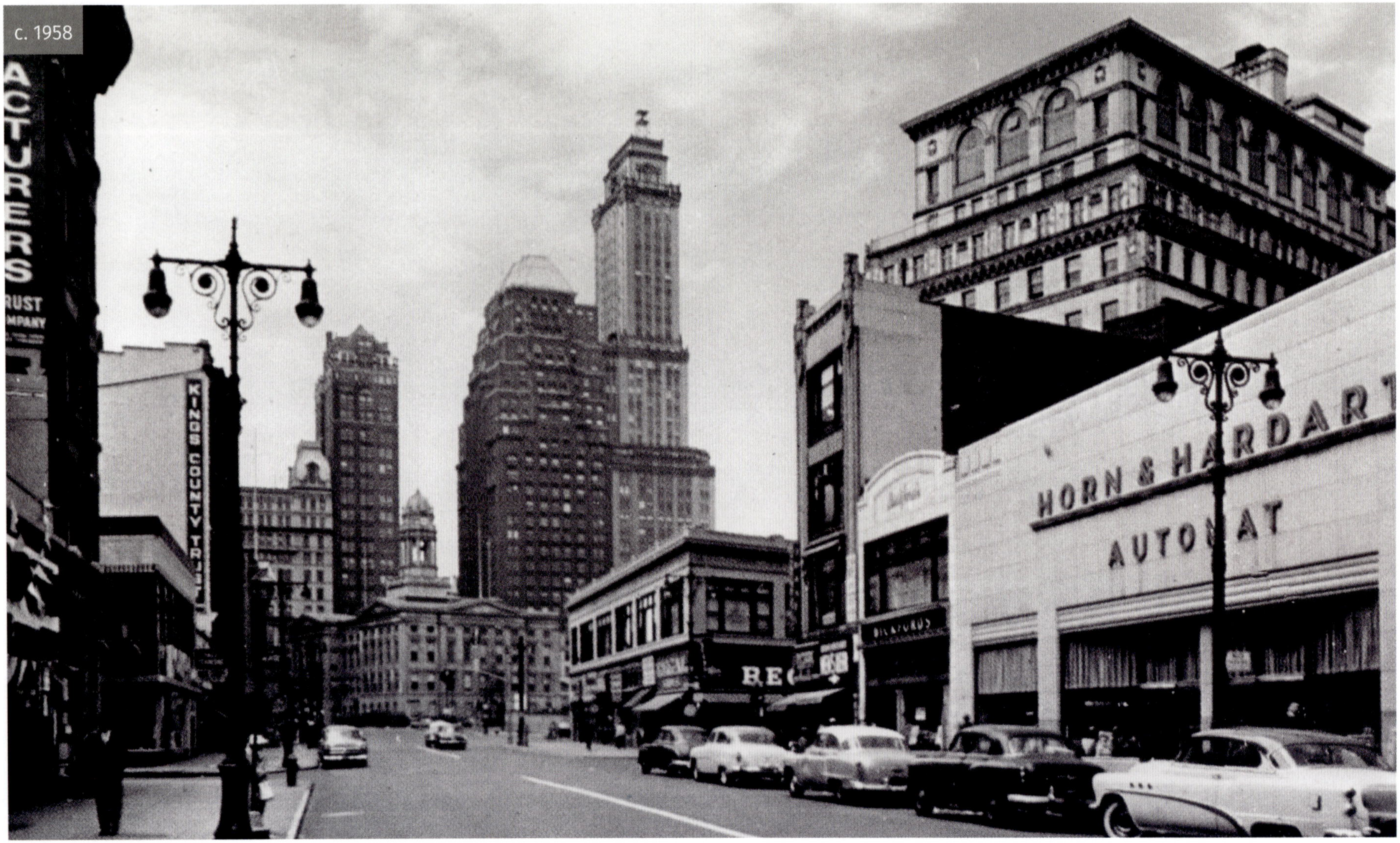

c. 1958

NOW: The Horn & Hardart Automats introduced a new style of dining that felt independent and exciting. It remained a hallmark of the mid-century urban restaurant experience until the Seventies, when only one store remained in Manhattan, and the Fulton Street Automat finally closed. At that time, the city succumbed to pressures from local merchants, who wanted a pedestrian-oriented shopping zone. Today, the intersection of Fulton Street between Flatbush Avenue and Adams Street, the third-largest commercial center in New York, is dominated by the Fulton Mall. Major retailers like Macy's—which took over the former Abraham & Strauss building—anchor the street, alongside a mix of national chains and local businesses. While the names on the windows have changed, Fulton Street remains an integral commercial thoroughfare, maintaining its role as a crossroads of Brooklyn life.

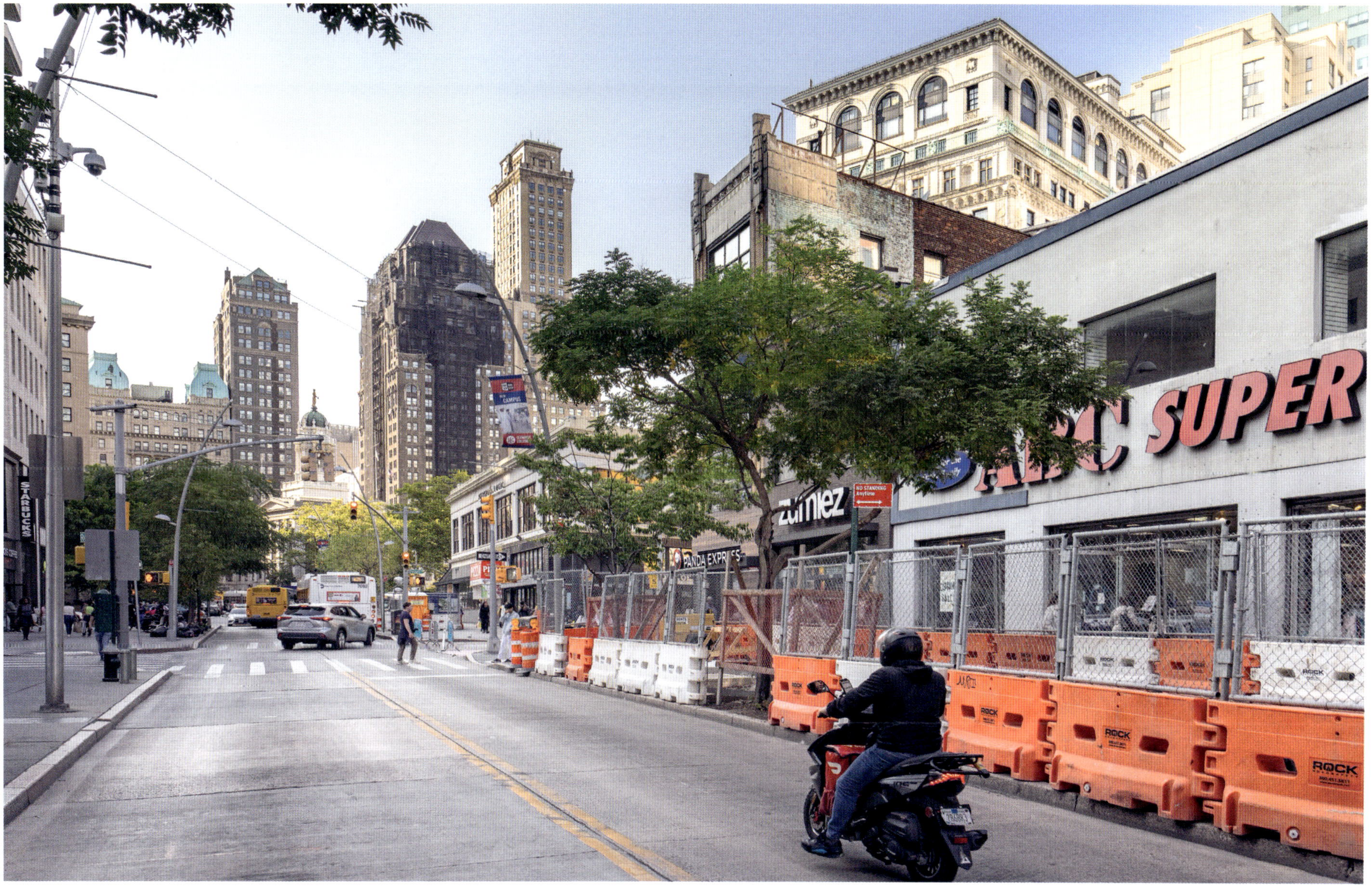

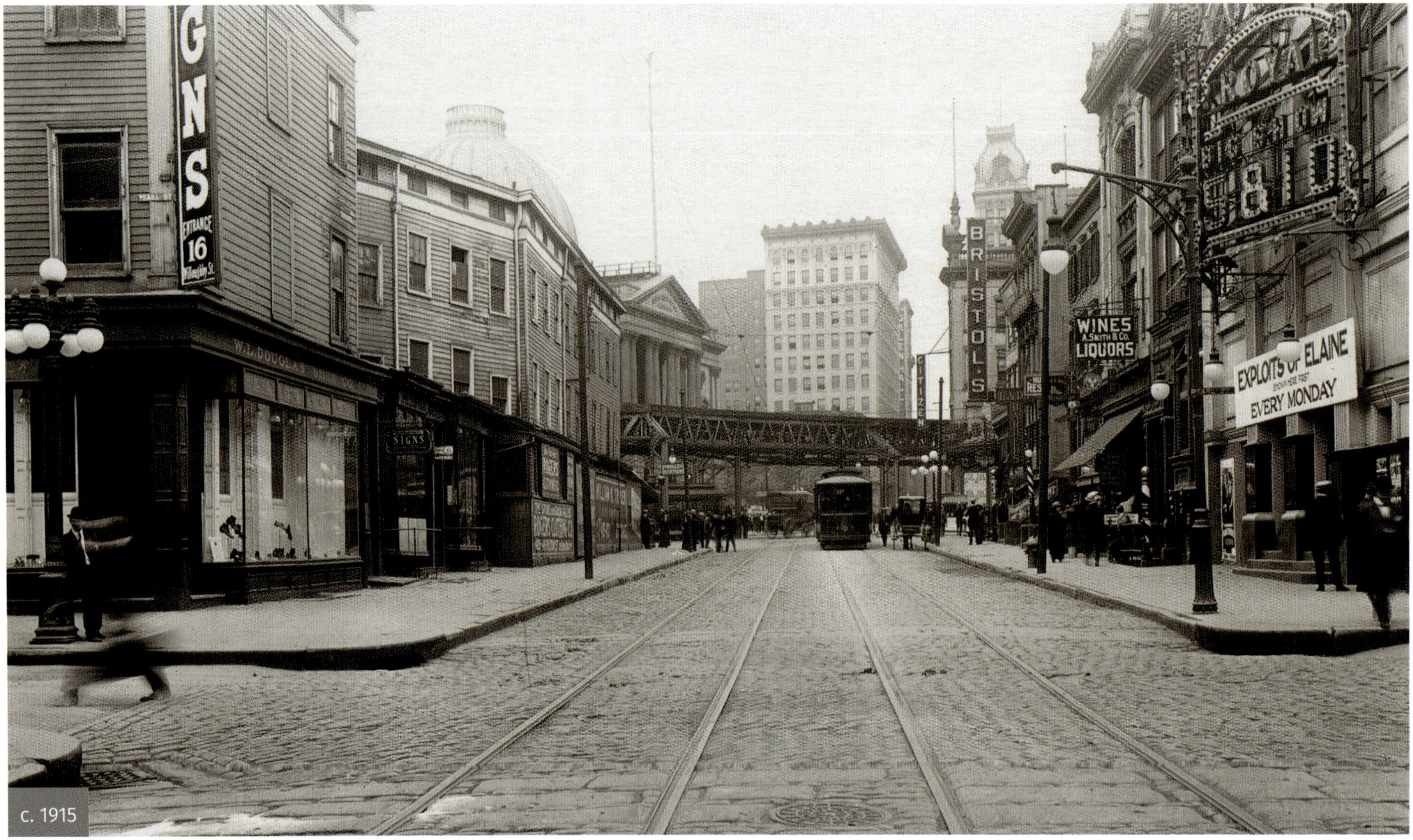

c. 1915

WILLOUGHBY STREET AT THE INTERSECTION OF PEARL STREET

The intersection evolved from local shops to a tech triangle

THEN: In 1915, Willoughby Street was a busy part of the borough's commercial and residential fabric. The area was notable for its blend of modest brick buildings and small stores owned by the people who lived nearby. Trolleys provided public transportation along with horse-drawn streetcars, as automobiles were only just beginning to fill more space on the roads. In the above photo, the Kings County Courthouse dome and portico are visible behind the elevated rail tracks. The Royal Theater was the first Loews theater in Brooklyn. It opened in 1908 with an Italian opera and ten-cent seats, serving vaudeville entertainment and silent films to the neighborhood until it closed for good in 1922.

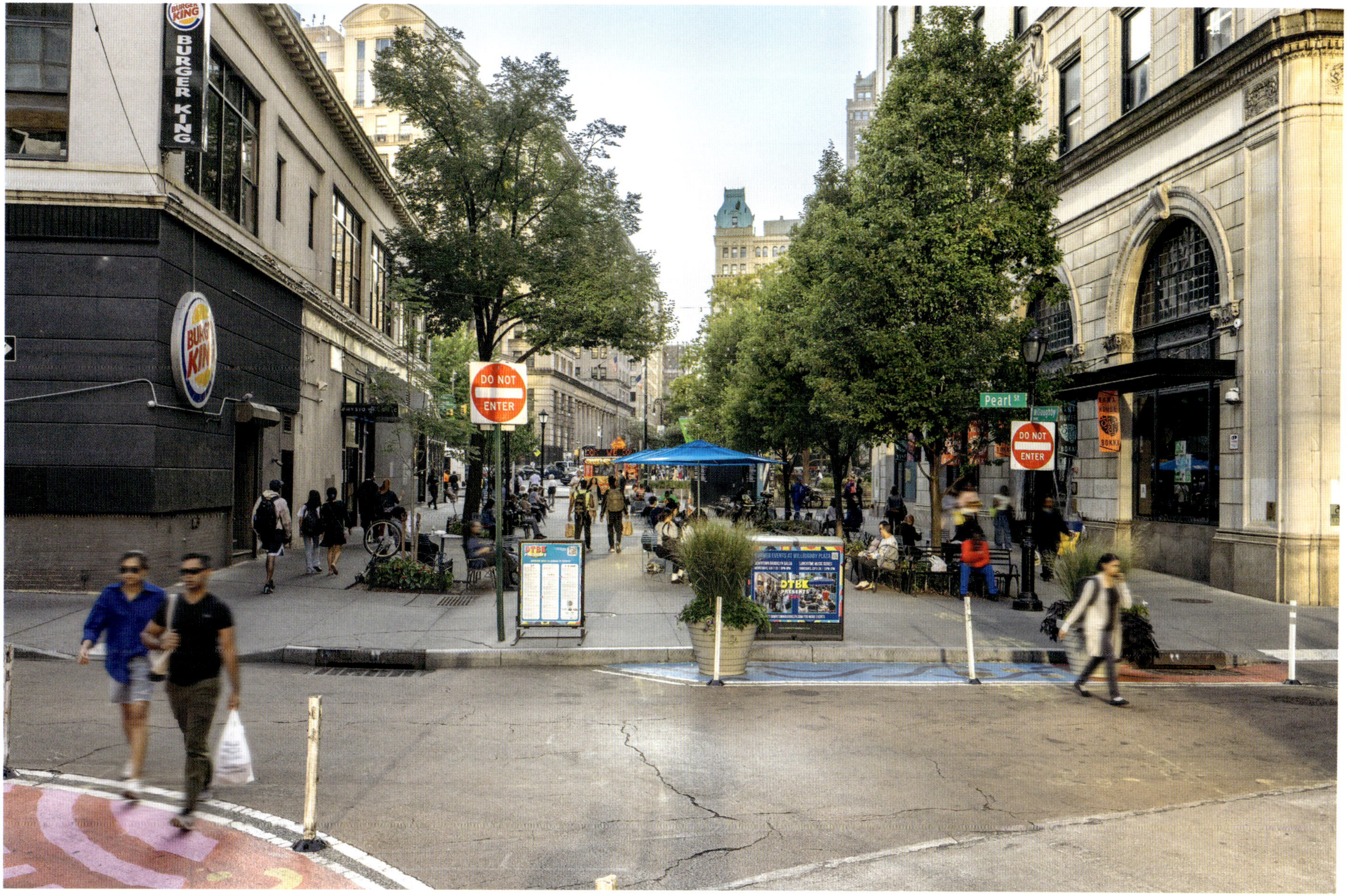

NOW: Today, Willoughby Street near Pearl Street has transformed in step with the rest of Brooklyn. The area is a central point in Brooklyn's Tech Triangle, with many technology and creative companies filling the office space. The area around Willoughby Street has also now become a hotspot for food lovers, with DeKalb Market Hall and many other new restaurants opening in the area to provide people with an incredibly broad range of options. The skyscrapers, trees, and pedestrian zones surround older buildings that have been carefully renovated to maintain their history. International brands fill the storefronts and the office spaces, with new developments such as the Borough Hall Transit Center, and high-rise buildings like the Willoughby Tower, adding to the area's modern dynamic.

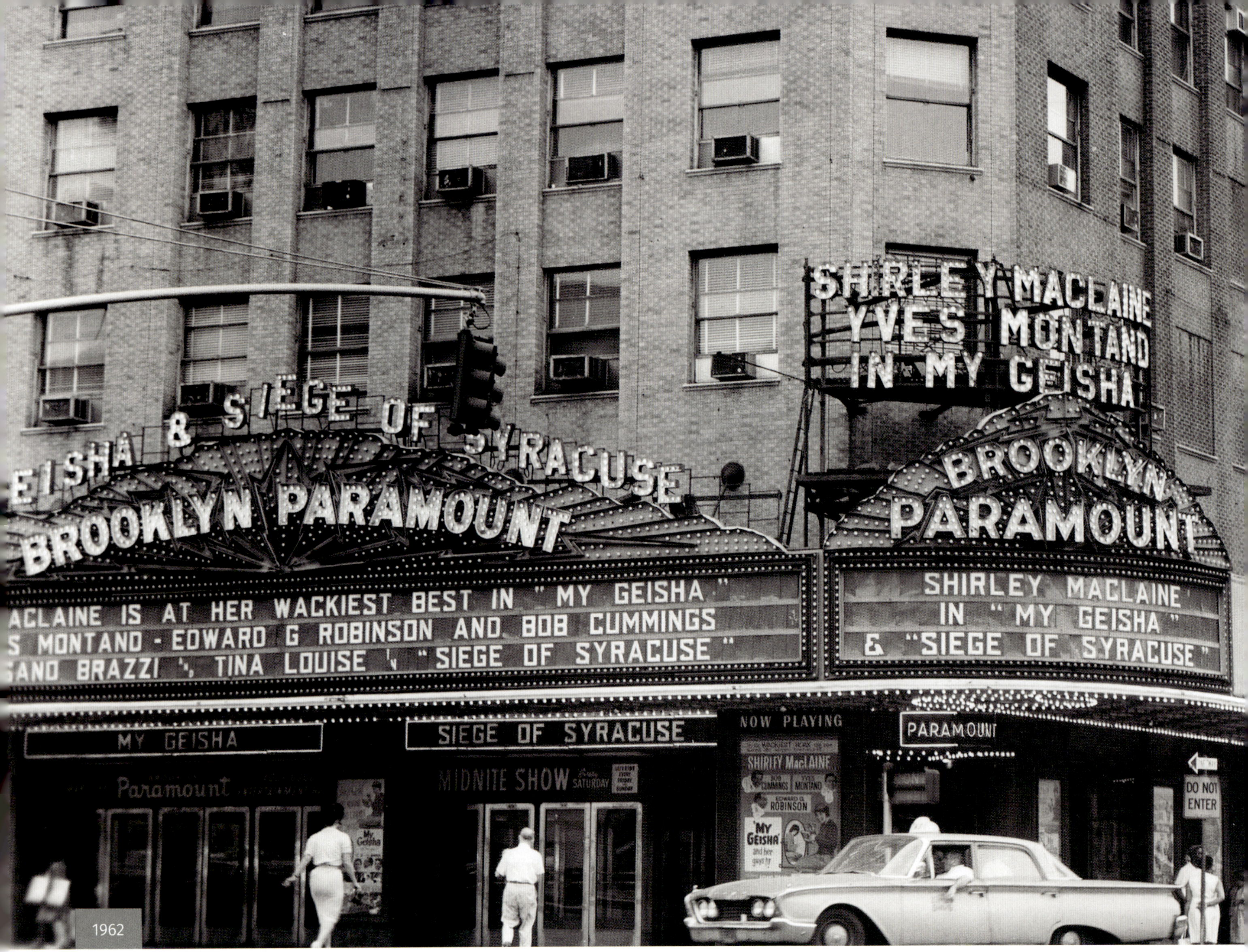

1962

THE BROOKLYN PARAMOUNT THEATER

A neighborhood star that brought jazz to Brooklyn

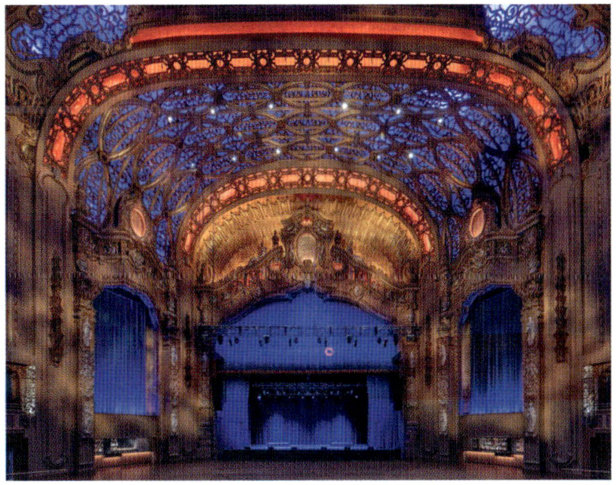

ABOVE: The ornate interior is highlighted with the use of hundreds of individual colored fixtures that can be adjusted by lighting designers for each show.

THEN: The Brooklyn Paramount Theater opened its doors in 1928 and immediately became an important landmark that changed the borough's entertainment scene. Located at the busy intersection of Flatbush and DeKalb Avenues, right down the street from Borough Hall, the building was originally constructed by Paramount Theaters. Theater architects Rapp and Rapp, who designed over 400 theaters nationwide, created a space with red velvet seats for 4,000 under a ceiling of painted clouds. It was designed from the start to be immersive, with a screen and audio system that would bring sound in films to Brooklyn audiences, along with all kinds of new music. Over the years, the Paramount became well-known for musical performances and helped introduce Brooklyn to new music. In 1931, Duke Ellington played there, introducing Brooklyn to Jazz and setting the stage for Dizzy Gillespie, Miles Davis, and Ella Fitzgerald. The Paramount was also known as an early home of Rock-n-Roll. Chuck Berry, Fats Domino, and Buddy Holly played a show there together in the Fifties, and DJ and TV host Clay Cole would launch a Christmas Special there that featured Ray Charles, Chubby Checker, The Supremes, and many others. By 1962, the theater had been sold to Long Island University, who later put in a basketball court and used it for sporting events.

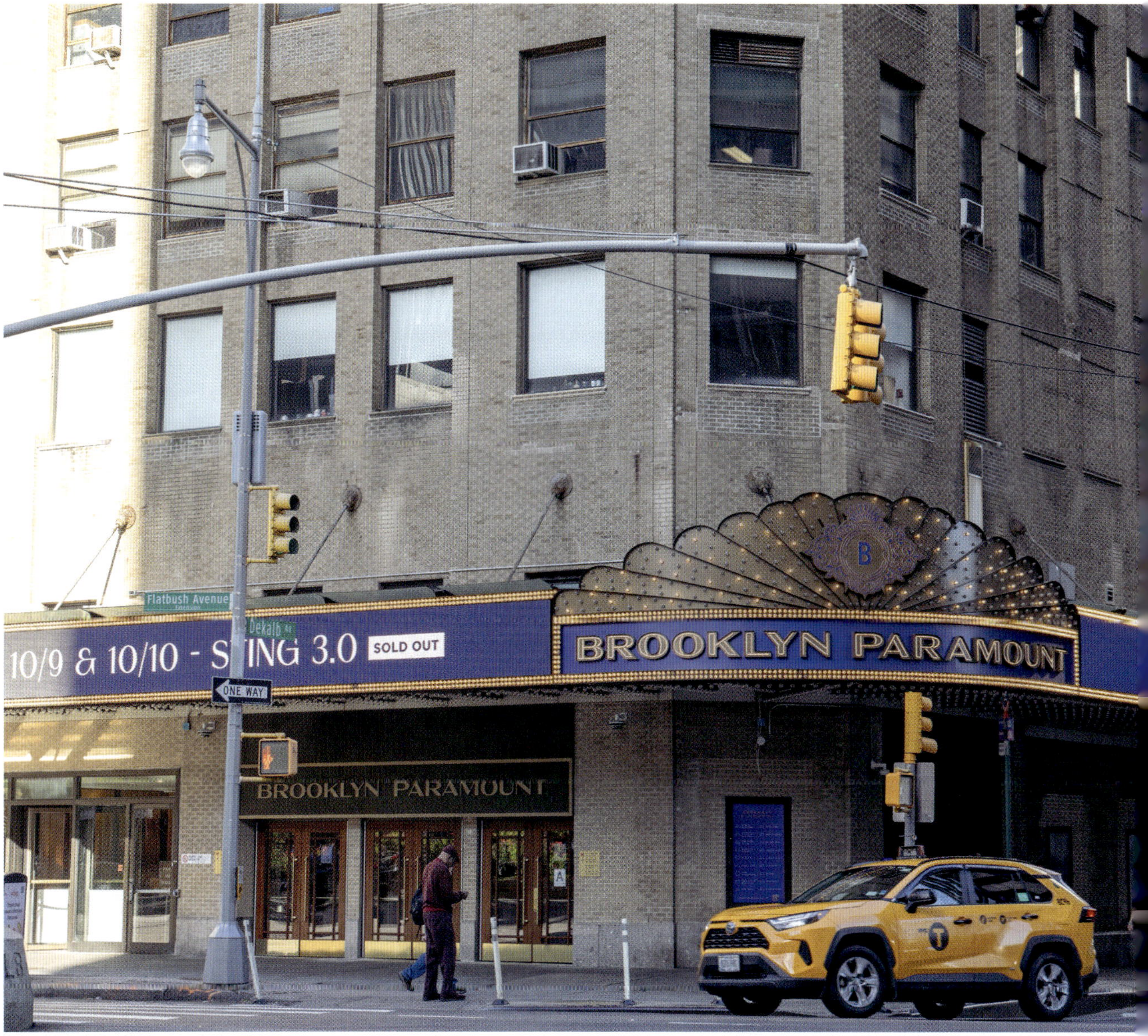

NOW: Luckily, the LIU purchase protected the Baroque ceilings, and the massive Wurlitzer organ that once accompanied silent films was used to rally the crowd at sporting events. The theater served as the home for LIU Blackbirds Basketball until 2005, when it was leased to the company that owns the nearby Barclays Center and the Brooklyn Nets. After eight years and a stalled renovation, concert promotion and ticketing conglomerate Live Nation Entertainment took over the development. In 2024, the Paramount reopened with a stunning renovation and a full calendar of music, including Damian and Stephen Marley, Norah Jones, and Sting.

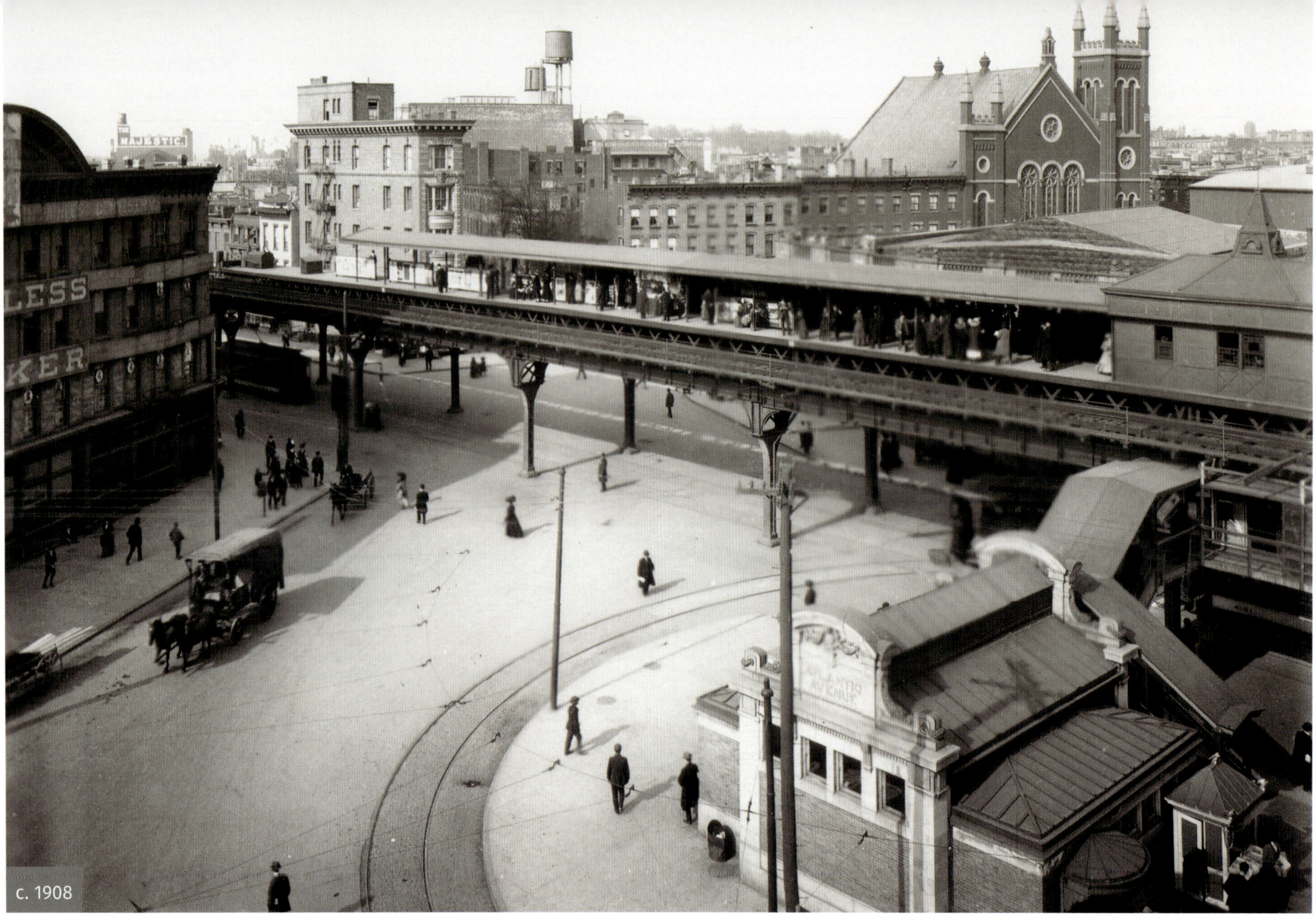

FLATBUSH AND ATLANTIC AVENUES

A transit hub becomes a modern sports and residential complex

THEN: The intersection of Flatbush Avenue and Atlantic Avenue has long been a vital transportation hub and commercial center, linking the local elevated train with the longer-distance Long Island Railroad (LIRR). Flatbush Avenue itself has a history that goes back even further, as it was a previous trail used by the Native Americans—and then eventually the Dutch settlers—as a way to reach the waterfront. The LIRR terminal opened in 1877 and served as the western end of the LIRR's main line, allowing commuters and goods to travel from Long Island to the heart of Brooklyn. The above photo from 1908, featuring an elevated train, a horse-drawn carriage, and the brand new Atlantic Avenue subway station, highlights the juxtaposition of the old and new types of transportation that co-existed at that time. The subway would eventually service enough passengers to warrant removal of the elevated railway in the Forties, which brought in an opportunity for massive change around the bustling intersection.

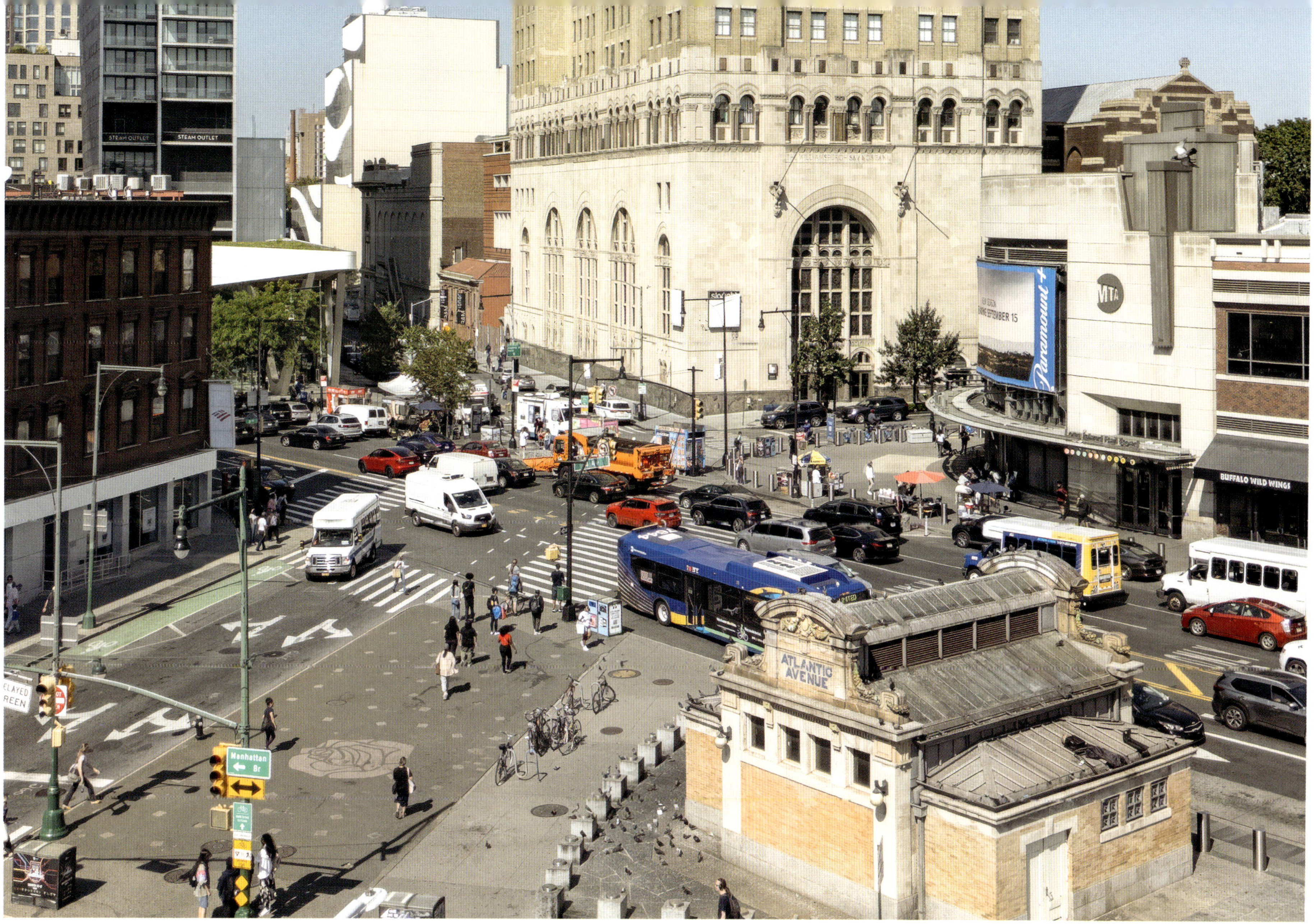

NOW: Today the streetscape is unrecognizable, except for the tiny Atlantic Avenue subway kiosk—though it no longer connects with the very robust subway system still in place underground. High-rise buildings surround the intersection, representing years of debates, as well as the contentious development of the Barclay Center Arena and Atlantic Yards Project. Early proposals for a covered ball stadium began in the Fifties, when the Brooklyn Dodgers owner, Walter O'Malley, wanted to build one at this intersection. The plan was rejected by city planner Robert Moses, and this rejection contributed to the Dodgers moving to Los Angeles. Development plans came and went over decades, highlighting the challenges involved with any redevelopment in a busy and historic urban center. In the 2000s, real estate developer Bruce Ratner proposed the Atlantic Yards Project, which was a massive redevelopment plan centered around a basketball arena. The proposal faced significant opposition due to its scale, potential for gentrification, and the use of eminent domain to acquire properties. It was ultimately scrapped in 2009 due to cost. A more modest design plan was approved in 2009 to include the arena, Atlantic Yards, and a commercial and residential housing development that would be required to have 35 percent of its residential units as affordable housing. The Barclay Center Arena finally opened in 2012, with over 17,000 seats available for concerts, as well as Brooklyn Nets and NY Liberty basketball games. As of 2024, the residential towers are still a work in progress, but the neighborhood is vibrant and still growing.

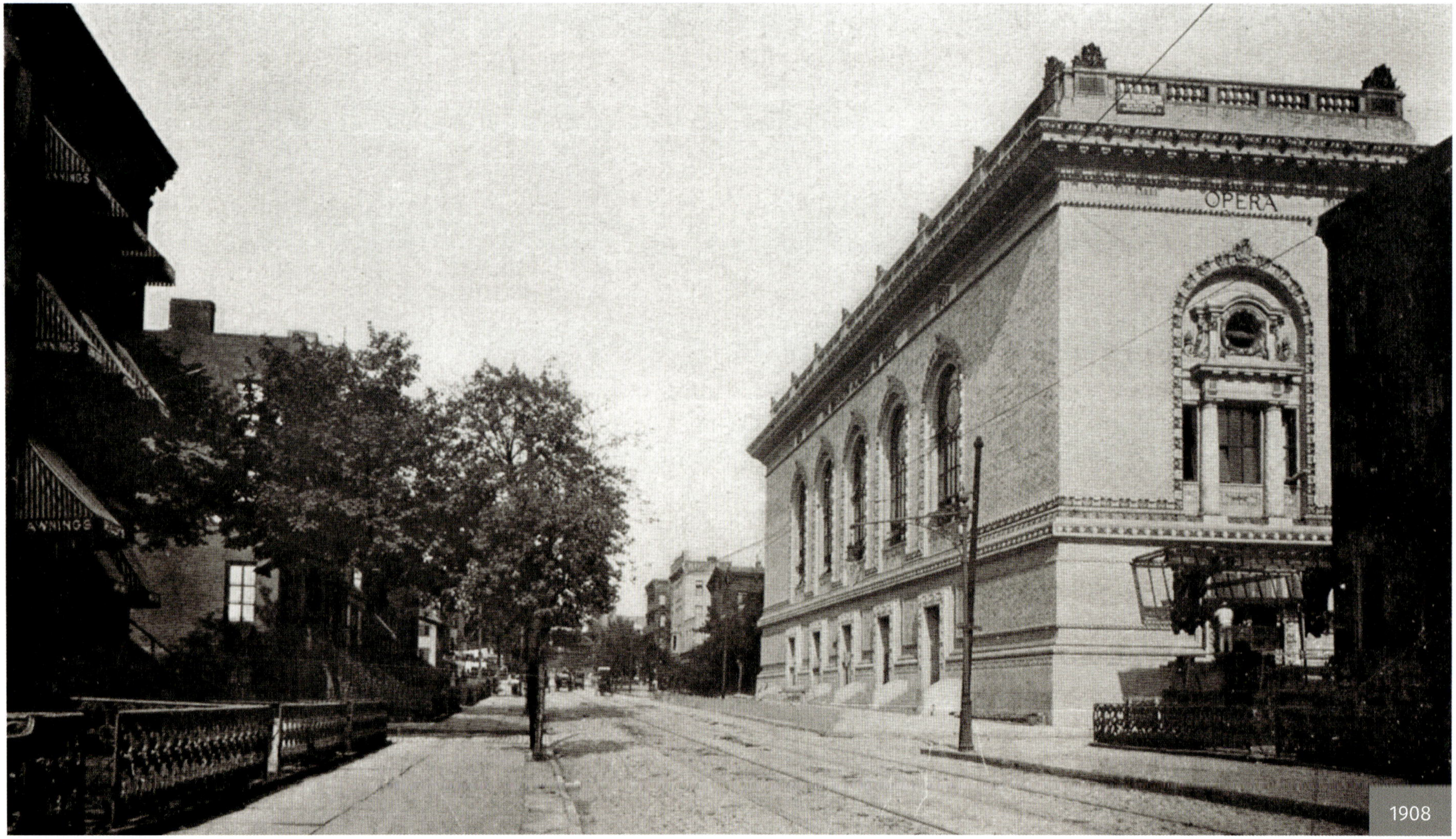

1908

BROOKLYN ACADEMY OF MUSIC

The historic building shepherds in a community built around the arts

THEN: Brooklyn Academy of Music (BAM) was originally located on Montague Street from 1861 to 1905, when the building was lost in a fire. This second location on Lafayette Avenue was strategic, surrounded by the brownstones of well-to-do families, easily accessed from all of Brooklyn by trolley and by the Long Island Railroad further out. Designed by prominent architects Herts & Tallant, it was a grand Beaux-Arts structure that properly reflected Brooklyn's intent to create a premier cultural institution of its time. In 1908, BAM reopened in their new building with an inaugural season that spanned opera, theater, orchestral concerts, and lectures. With its horseshoe-shaped balconies and best-in-class acoustics, the main auditorium was soon renowned as one of the best performance spaces in the country. The academy housed an art gallery and a conservatory of music as well.

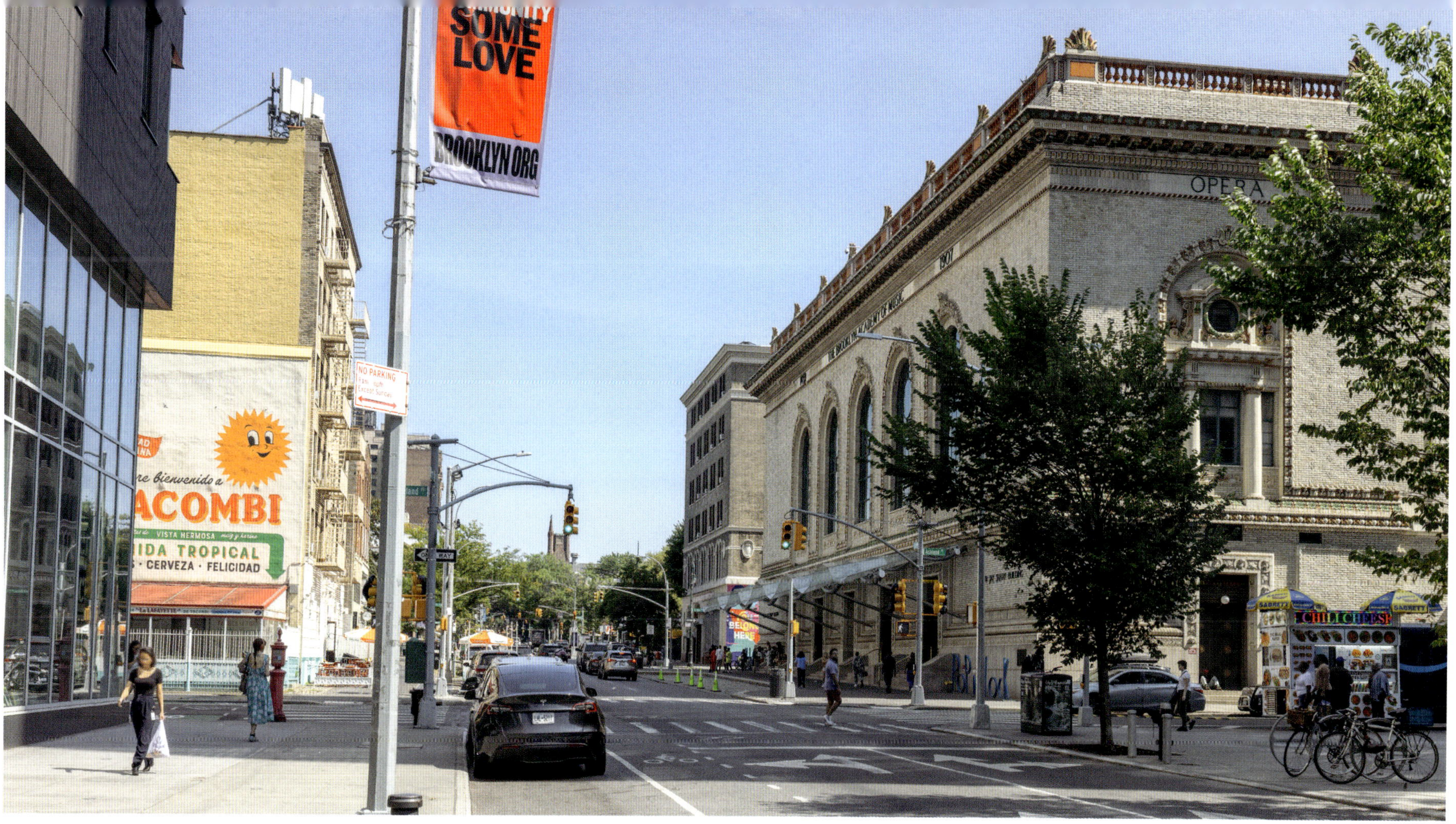

NOW: Today, the Brooklyn Academy of Music is a hub for Brooklyn's ongoing cultural renaissance, and has grown way beyond its 1908 footprint. The Lafayette Avenue main building, once known as the Opera House, has been meticulously preserved, maintaining its turn-of-the-century charm while incorporating modern technology and amenities thanks to a renovation in the Eighties. In 1998 it officially became the Peter Jay Sharp Building, named for a real estate developer and philanthropist who had contributed significantly to BAM's restoration and whose private donations supported arts in the United States, especially when public funds were limited. His contributions helped ensure that BAM could continue to provide high-quality performances, maintain its historic facilities, and expand for future generations. In 1987, BAM added additional venues, including the BAM Harvey Theater, a converted movie house. The BAM Fisher Building, an intimate performance space with 250 seats, opened in 2012. BAM's programming has evolved to embrace cutting-edge performances across disciplines including avant-garde theater and dance, world cinema, and contemporary music. BAM Education partners with schools and organizations to showcase local talent, and BAM Research & Development provides Brooklyn-based artists and companies with rehearsal space, as well as technical assistance for work-in-progress showings and public performances. The BAM Cultural District continues to grow and thrive, attracting new theaters, public spaces, and residential developments to the neighborhood.

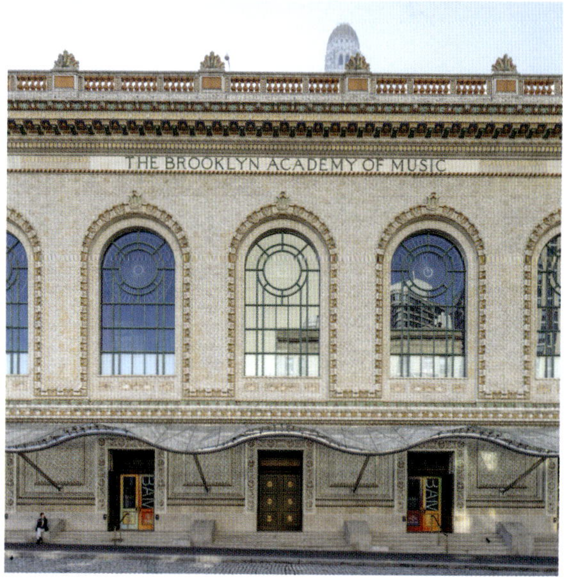

RIGHT: The richly detailed facade features stone carvings of symbols related to the arts.

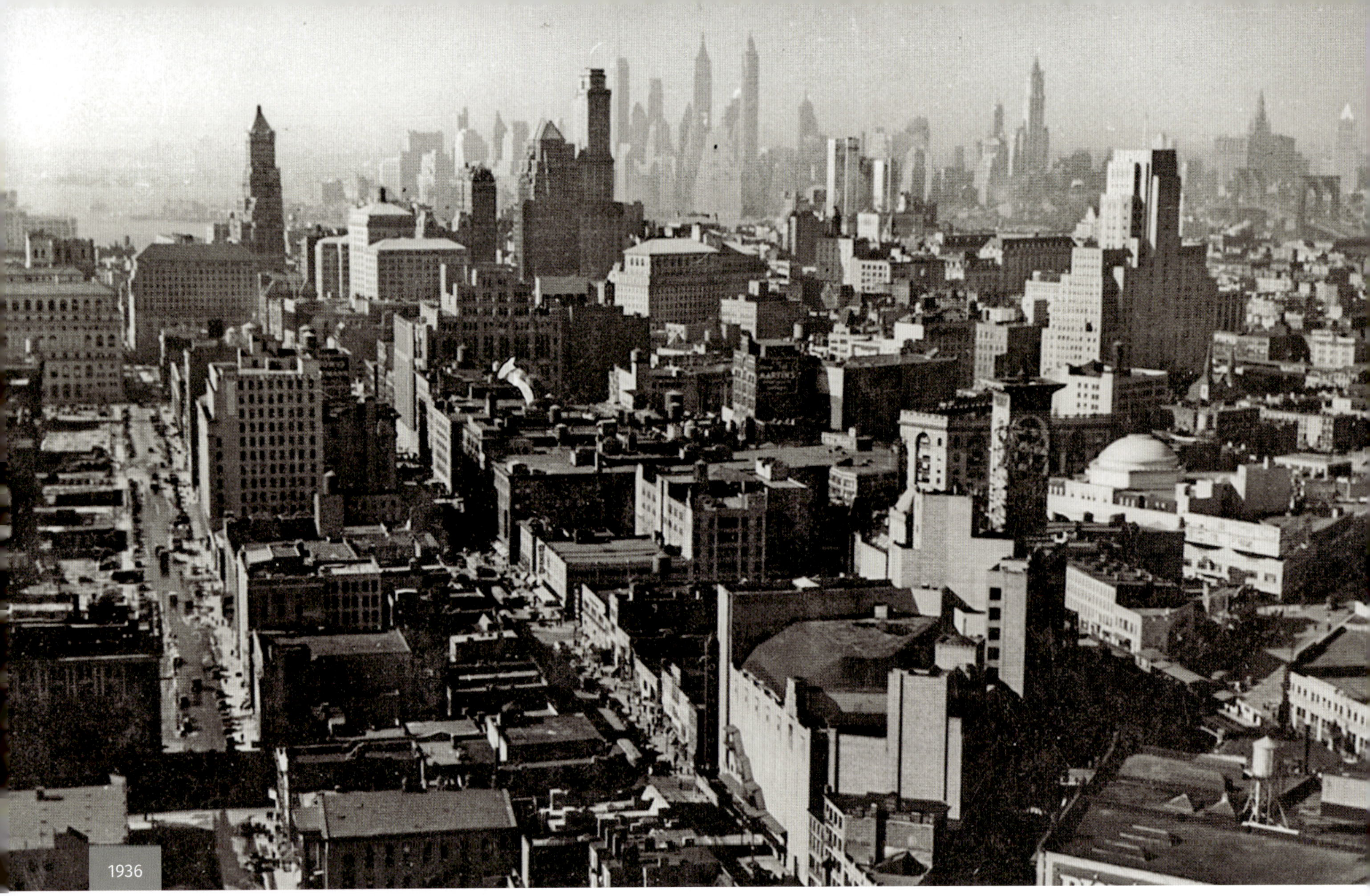

1936

VIEW FROM WILLIAMSBURG BANK TOWER

The skyline spreads to the stratosphere

THEN: Standing 512 feet high, the Williamsburg Savings Bank was once the tallest building in Brooklyn, offering unparalleled views between the building and the East River, and all the way to Manhattan. From here, one could peer over Flatbush Avenue revealing a number of moderate buildings in the urban streetscape. At the intersection of Flatbush and DeKalb, multiple low-rise retail and commercial structures created corridors to the borough that were smaller in scale, compared to Manhattan. The Fulton Street Triangle was a relatively unremarkable retail hub, and Schermerhorn Street stretched through a corridor of quiet brownstones and small businesses. The iconic bank tower was alone in stature but offered a commanding view all the way to Manhattan. Decades of suburban sprawl and fiscal issues, from the Depression through war and the fiscal crisis of the 1970s, caused money to move out of Brooklyn, so building and growth had remained stagnant for decades.

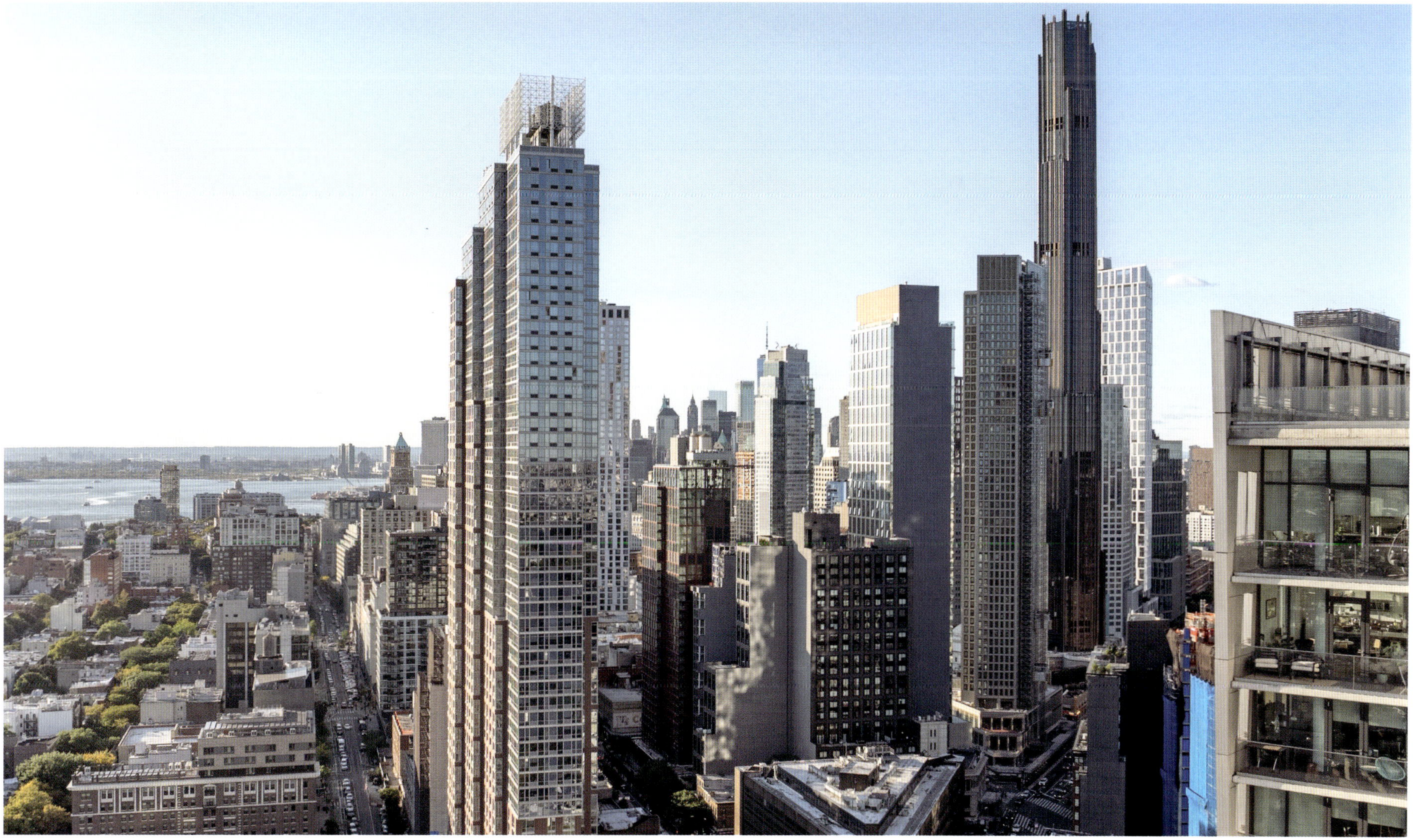

NOW: If Brooklyn was still an independent city in the twenty-first century, it would be the fourth largest in the country. Photographs from the same perspective today offer a dramatically altered urban landscape that rivals many global cities, including Manhattan. The top real estate developers and architects in the world have partnered to create the towers of the new Brooklyn skyline, many of which are visible from the top of the Williamsburg Bank. An early pioneer of this vertical transformation was Brooklyn Point by Extell, with a massive food hall on the lower level featuring many of NYC's culinary delicacies, including the only Brooklyn location of the legendary Katz's Delicatessen. The building was one of downtown Brooklyn's first luxury residential high-rises, setting off a wave of comparable construction. Nearby, SHoP Architects' Brooklyn Tower pierces the sky with its hexagonal form and multicolored facade, dwarfing the domed Dime Savings Bank building that it's built upon and was inspired by. At its feet, The Brook by Witkoff adds another luxury living option to this busy location. Along Schermerhorn Street, 33 Bond Street's bulk reflects the neighborhood's shifting residential character. No longer a modest commercial strip, The Fulton Triangle area now features a cluster of glass and steel towers that have literally raised the borough's profile, confirming Brooklyn's transformation from Manhattan's shadow into a prime real estate destination in its own right.

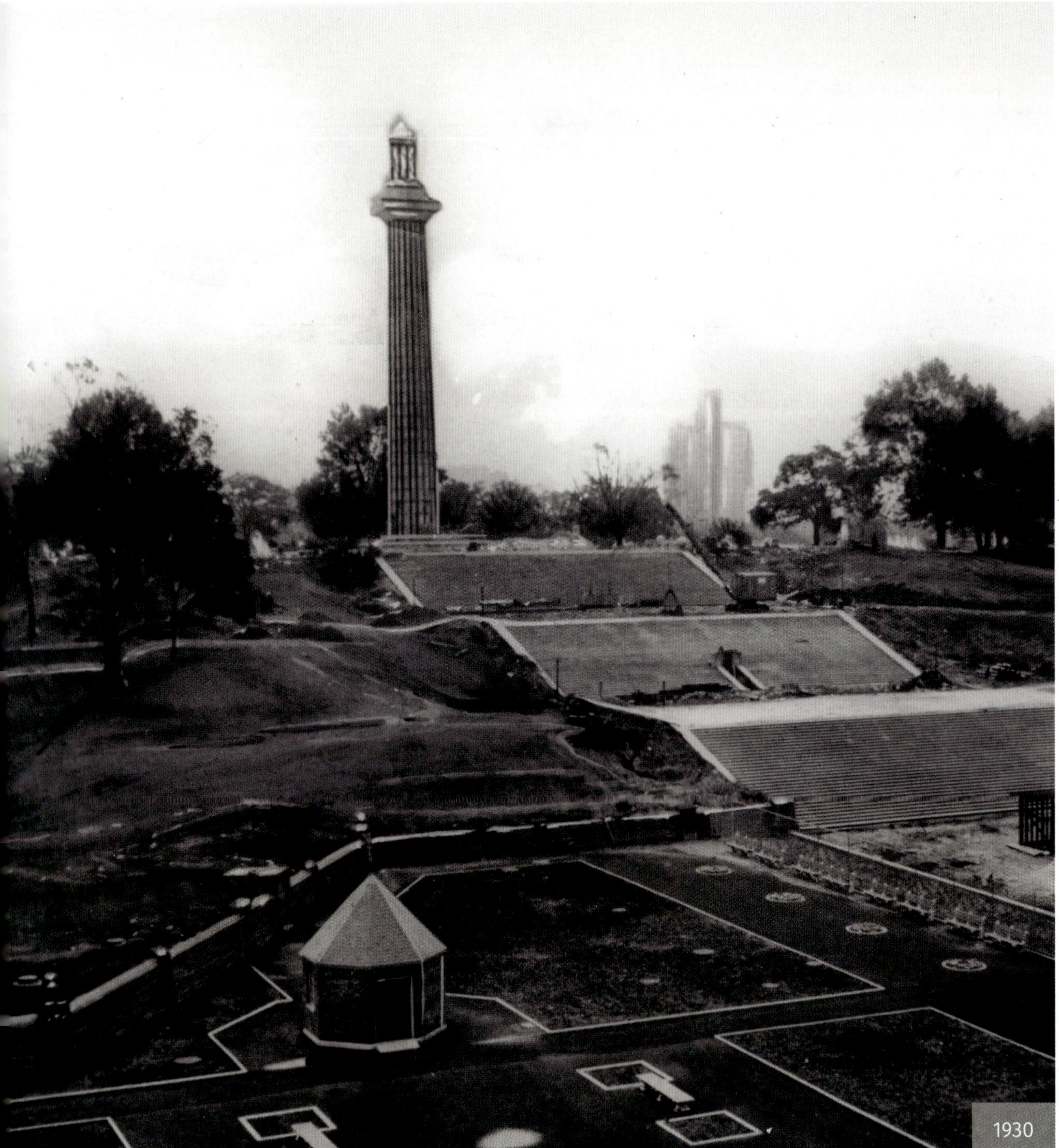

1930

FORT GREENE PARK

Olmsted and Vaux's first Brooklyn park

THEN: Washington Park, renamed as Fort Greene Park in 1897, was established as Brooklyn's first park in 1847. A Revolutionary-war-era fort named Fort Putnam once sat atop the highest hill, and around it Frederick Law Olmsted and Calvert Vaux redesigned the park in 1864 to be a healthy, central space to delight the neighbors. Built after Central, but before Prospect, Washington Park was the first of its kind in Brooklyn, with chestnut trees, lawns for croquet and tennis, walking paths, a military salute ground, and a permanent podium for speakers. In 1908, the Prison Ship Martyrs' Monument was erected to commemorate the thousands of soldiers who died as captives on board British prison ships. The remains of those found washed up near the Brooklyn Naval Yard are interred in a crypt below a monument of a single Doric column that stands 149 feet tall, standing high above a park that truly did service the neighborhood. In 1930, it was a bright spot of refuge during the Great Depression, when stress was high and funds were low, and residents took advantage of the green space further improved by the Works Progress Administration's maintenance and improvements.

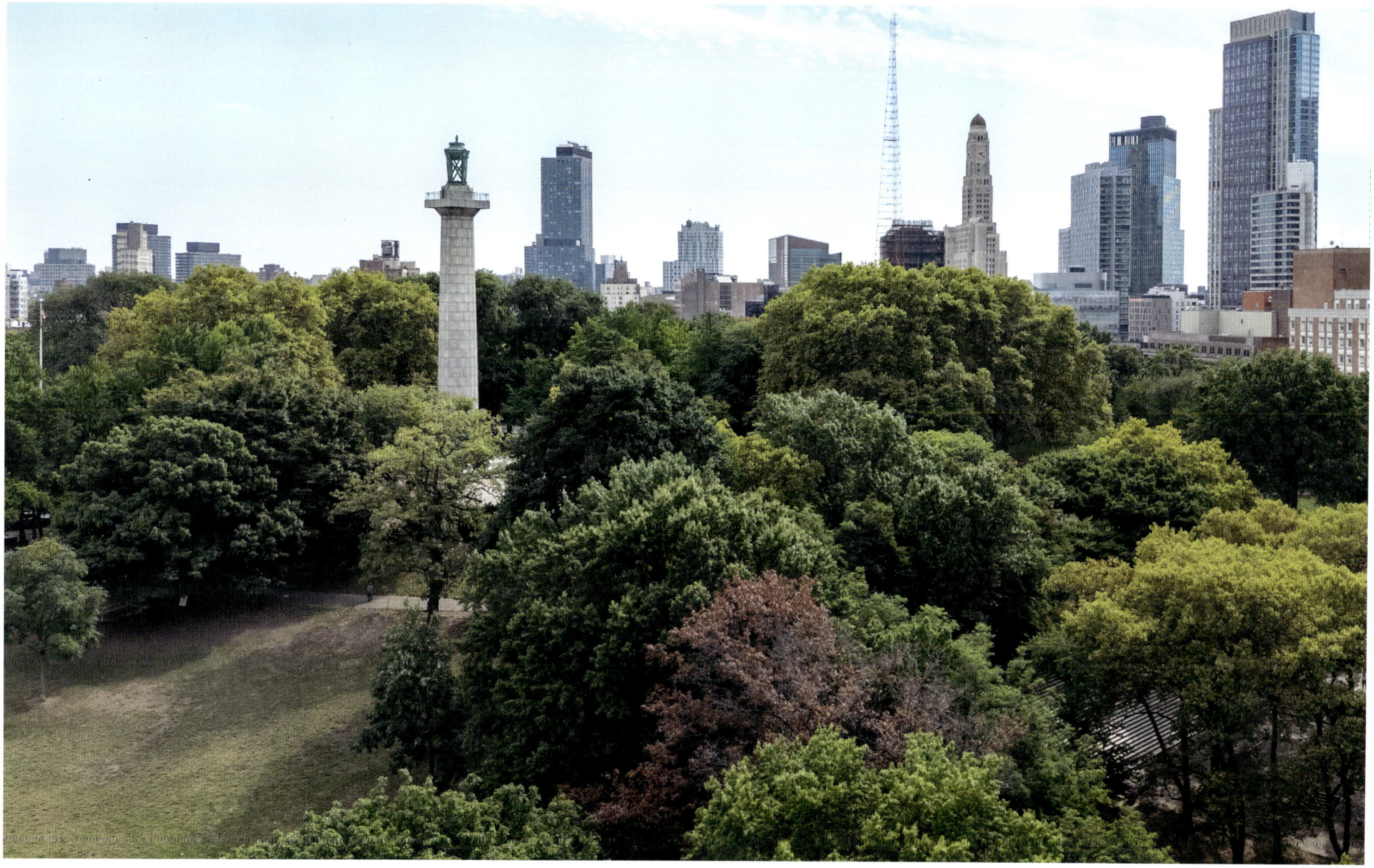

NOW: Fort Greene emerged in the early nineteenth century as a desirable residential district surrounding Fort Greene Park. The neighborhood's elegant row houses were intentionally mixed in with Brooklyn's Academy of Music and the Brooklyn Paramount Theater, making for one of Brooklyn's earliest planned, mixed-use communities. The area has transformed from its military beginnings through periods of urban decline and facility restoration to become a family-friendly neighborhood in the midst of Brooklyn's most important cultural district. Fort Greene Park continues its legacy at the heart of the Fort Greene Historic District. The park has had multiple restorations over the years, including on the monument, the amenities, and the landscape. Since 2006, the Fort Greene Park Conservancy has actively maintained the space, while balancing preservation with contemporary challenges, including increased usage and controlling erosion. With regular farmers markets and community events, the park continues to serve its dual purpose of solemn memorial and community center, even as the area around it continues to gentrify.

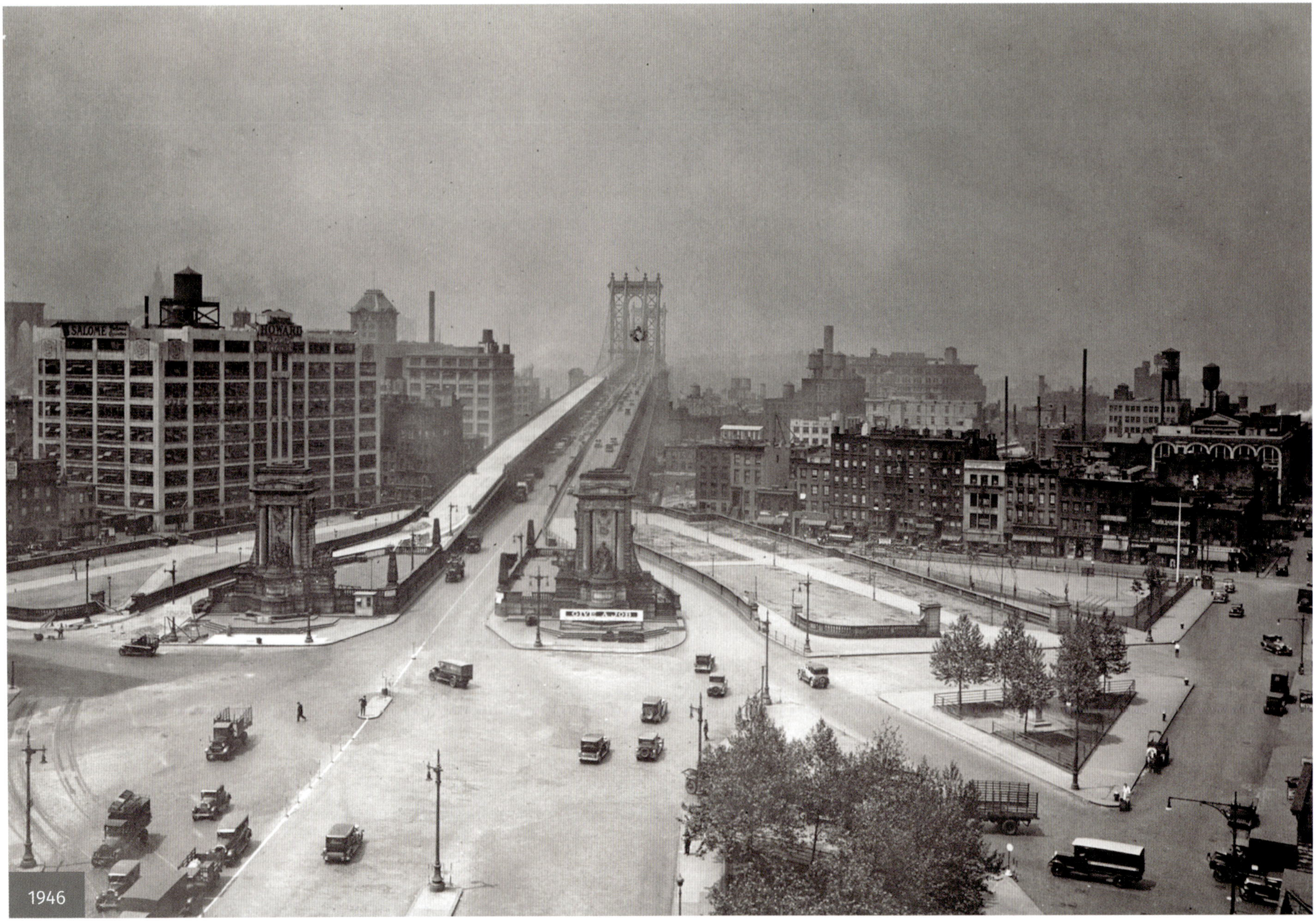

THE MANHATTAN BRIDGE, DUMBO

Down Under the Manhattan Bridge Overpass becomes a destination

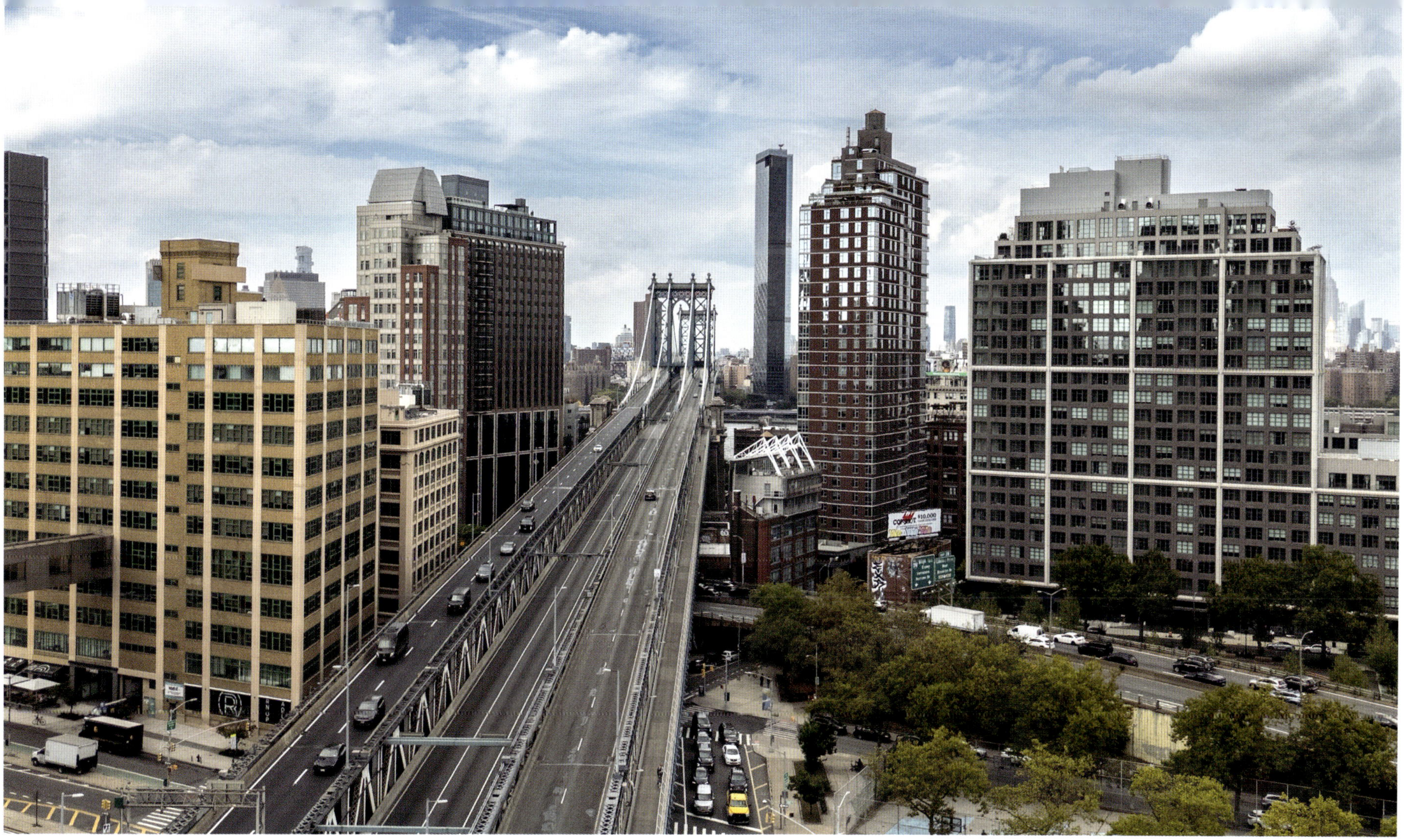

THEN: The Manhattan Bridge opened for traffic in 1909 after seven years of construction, spanning the East River between the tenements of Lower Manhattan and the industrial riverbanks of Brooklyn's waterfront district. As seen in the photo opposite, from the mid-Forties, the Brooklyn entrance encompassed a broad swath of space that funneled streetcars, automobiles, trucks, subways, and pedestrians straight into Brooklyn. It was a heavy load—and the weight of it had the bridge showing dangerous signs of wear and tear as early as 1936. While the bridge had been built with deflection theory, which was revolutionary for the time, it was bending and flexing too much. It was also beginning to lean to one side, because the engineers had failed to accurately predict the impact of the subway load on the outer edges of the structure. The city and its engineers attempted a myriad of traffic-pattern adjustments, which increased congestion without solving the structural issues. By the end of the Forties, waterfront manufacturing had peaked, and the decline left abandoned warehouse buildings along the riverbanks and under the bridge. Even without the pre-war heavy manufacturing, the load requirements on the Manhattan bridge continued to increase, and early repairs did not sufficiently fix them.

NOW: Since the Eighties, more than $1,000,000,000 has been spent on fixing the bridge's initial design flaws and early structural failings. The subway tracks were moved, corroded steel supports were replaced, and the bridge was rebuilt with an innovative damping system to control the bridge movement. The most recent renovation in the 2010s finally allowed for the repainting of the bridge in its original signature blue color. It also included the restoration of the original Carrère and Hastings entrance portals on both sides of the river, with improvements to the arch and colonnade in Manhattan, and additions of safety netting and bike lanes. Today, the bridge is strong and structurally sound, though congestion is still a concern with 450,000 cars and trucks traveling the expanse daily. Over the years of drama with the structure of the bridge, the neighborhood right underneath turned from abandoned factories to artists' lofts. It became known as DUMBO, an acronym standing for Down Under the Manhattan Bridge Overpass. In 2007, it was designated as a historic district, and since then, rapid gentrification has made it one of New York's most expensive and desirable areas.

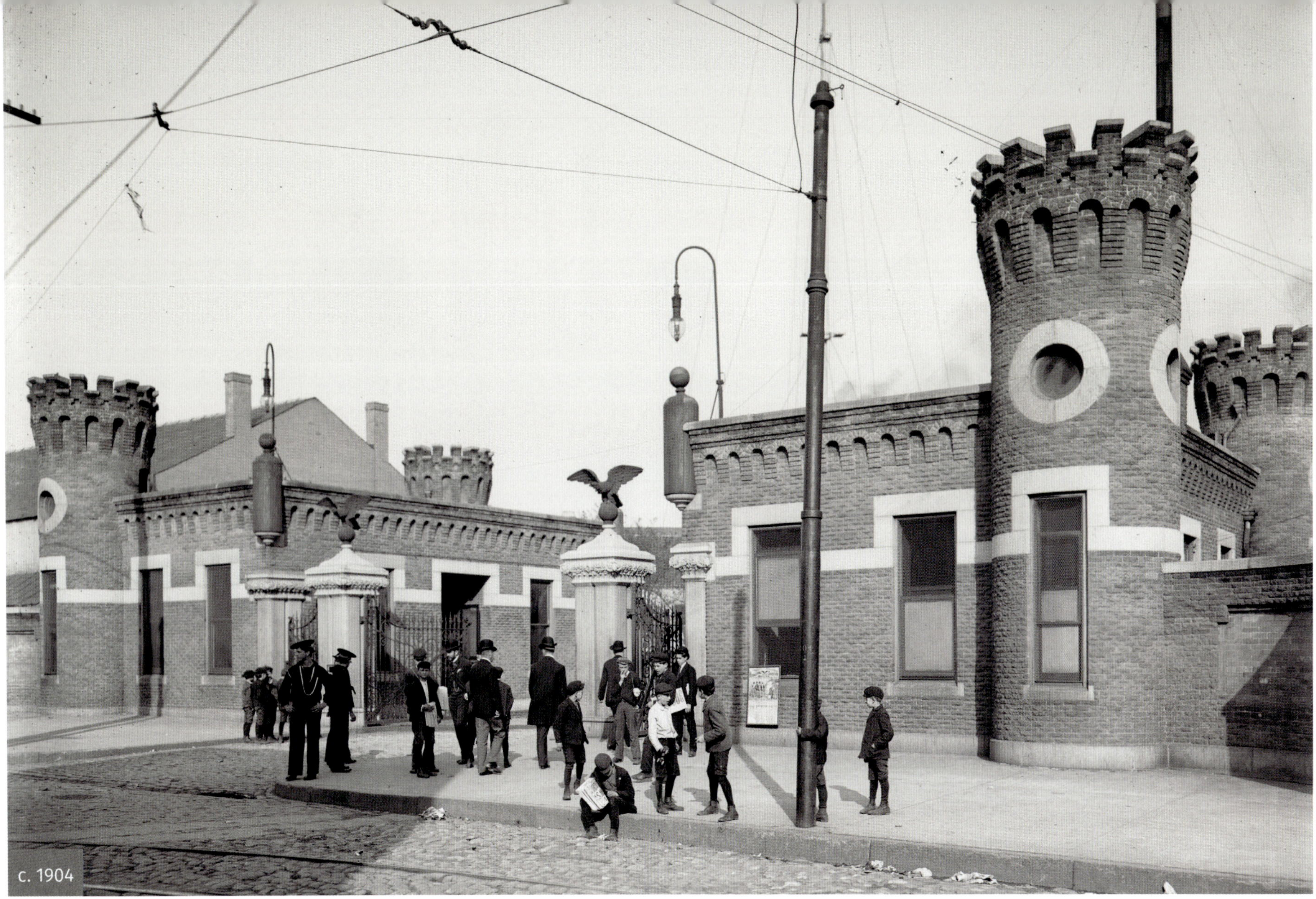
c. 1904

BROOKLYN NAVY YARD

The bustling riverbank center of the country's coordinated maritime concerns

THEN: In 1801, under President John Adams, the United States purchased a forty-acre site surrounding the Wallabout Basin on the East River for the twenty-year-old United States Navy. Selected for its deep waters, protected bay, and proximity to Manhattan, the Brooklyn Navy Yard quickly turned into a powerhouse of activity—converting ships for battle, repairing broken vessels, and constructing boats from scratch. The first ship produced there was the seventy-four-gun *Ohio*, launched in 1820 to deter the slave trade from West Africa. Sixteen ships were assembled there during the Civil War, and 400 more were converted for battle. The USS *Maine* was built there in 1890, and then sank in Havana Harbor in 1898, sparking the Spanish-American War. Though it was technically peacetime, 1904 was a busy time at the yard, with thousands of skilled civilians working alongside enlisted men, as seen in the above photo from the castle-like Sand Street entrance. It was a time of technological transition as

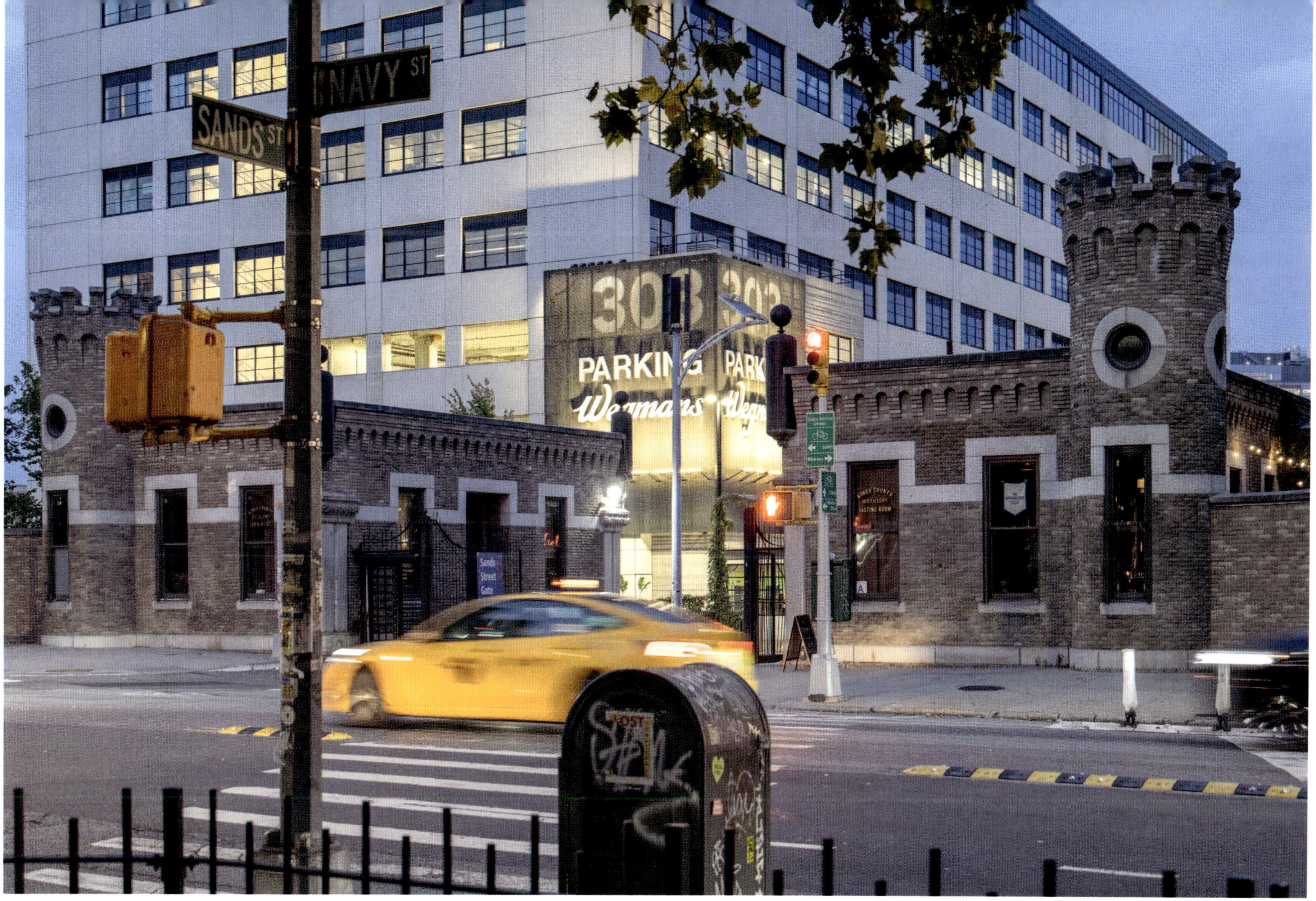

steam-powered ships became the norm and President Theodore Roosevelt—a big believer in naval power—pushed for a stronger and more technologically advanced fleet. The yard grew to be a city within a city, with its own power plant, hospital, and radio station. At its peak, it had 70,000 men and women working around the clock to provide ships and aircraft carriers to U.S. armed forces. The USS *Arizona*, which was destroyed at Pearl Harbor, and the USS *Missouri*, where Japan surrendered World War II to end the war, were both built in Brooklyn. The Brooklyn Navy Yard was a powerful symbol of American strength and exceptionalism, and it contributed greatly to various war efforts until it closed its gates in 1966.

NOW: After the Navy moved out, the Brooklyn Navy Yard transformed into a thriving industrial park, home to over 400 businesses, ranging from traditional manufacturing to cutting-edge tech start-ups. It houses film studios, artisanal food producers, and even a rooftop vineyard. The Brooklyn Navy Yard is still a vital part of the local economy, providing thousands of jobs and business opportunities. There is even a large modern supermarket just through the Sand Street gates. Though the massive warships are gone, the historic architecture has been preserved and repurposed, so the spirit of innovation lives on.

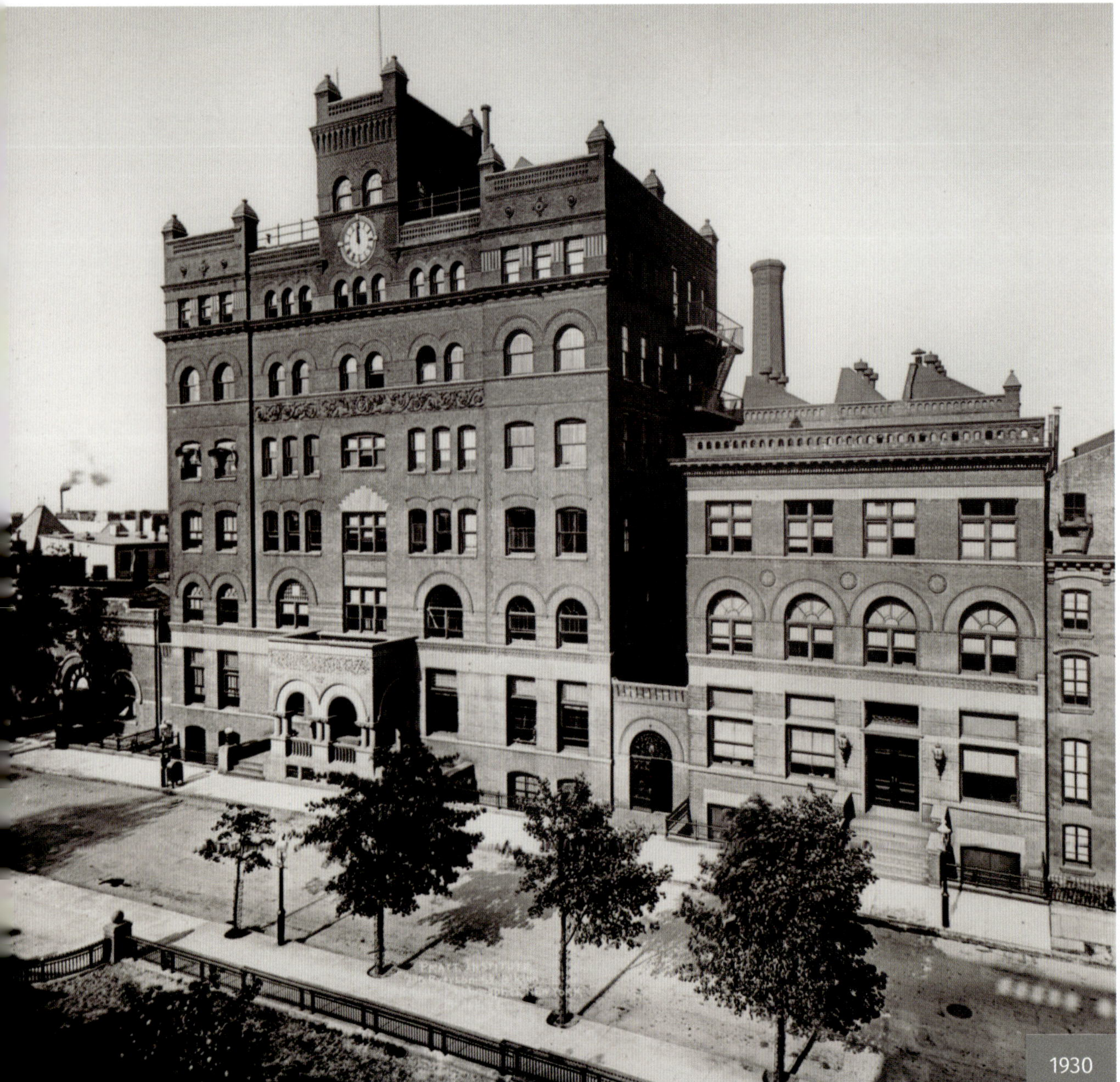

1930

THEN: Founded in 1887, Brooklyn's Pratt Institute was established by industrialist and philanthropist Charles Pratt. Pratt made his fortune in the oil industry refineries that dotted the shores of the East River, establishing Astral Oil Works in Greenpoint in 1867 and selling it to John D. Rockefeller's Standard Oil in 1874. Though he never went to college himself, he used the funds from the sale to open the Institute with the goal of providing practical education and training to the working-class people who had helped to create his wealth. Pratt Institute focused on art, design, and architecture, with an emphasis on both technical trades and higher arts. When Pratt opened the institute, it had twelve students paying $4 per class, per term. Within a year, there were 1,000 students; and five years later, there were over 5,000 enrolled. Students from diverse backgrounds left the Institute prepared for careers in architecture, engineering, mechanics, dressmaking, and furniture making. Drawing was considered the universal language for the school, connecting the various fields of studies, and ensuring that graduates had marketable technical skills. Charles Pratt died in 1891, passing the stewardship of the institution to his sons. In 1897 they opened The Pratt Library for students and the public, becoming the first free library in Brooklyn. In 1900 The School of Science and Technology was the most well-known school and had the largest enrollment of men; however, the Pratt Institute offered courses for women, too, including library science, nursing, home economics, and fashion.

PRATT INSTITUTE

Educating the best and brightest designers, architects, and engineers for industry

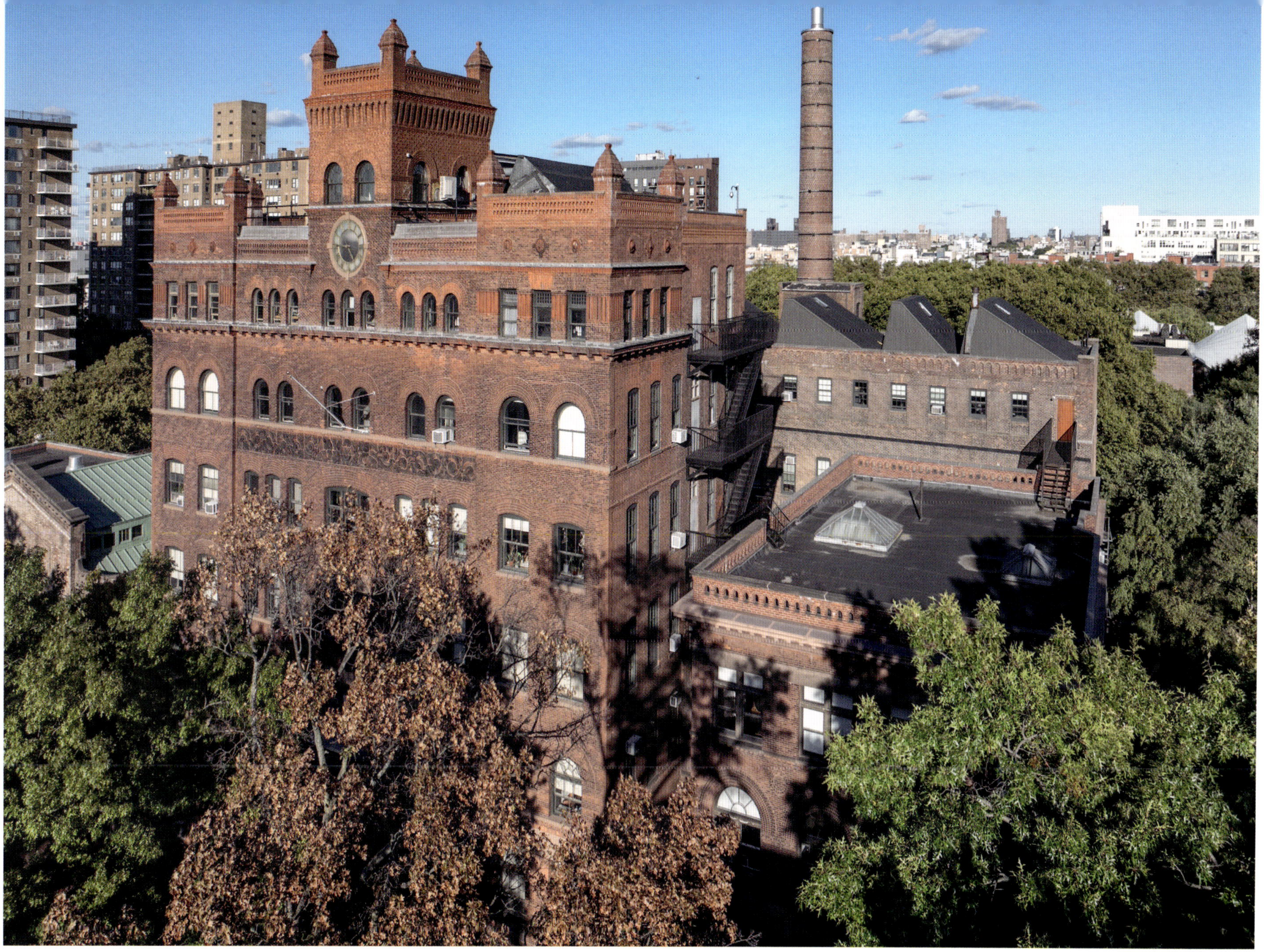

NOW: The School of Science and Technology would remain the most popular area of study at Pratt for the next forty years, as the Institute partnered with the U.S. Government and had its own Student Army Training Corps, teaching engineering skills needed for both World Wars. Pratt students also designed airplanes, uniforms, and buildings, and in 1948 attendance peaked with 6,000 students. The growth was fractured, however, with buildings spread between various streets in Clinton Hill. Thanks to Robert Moses' plan for urban renewal, his clearance of many structures and homes in the area, and the dismantling of the elevated train, Pratt was able to create a true enclosed campus that was closed to automobiles, with a Grand Mall that connected its buildings. Today, the institute offers a wide range of undergraduate and graduate programs across five schools: Architecture, Art, Design, Liberal Arts and Sciences, and Information. It continues to provide new technologies and interdisciplinary approaches to its students.

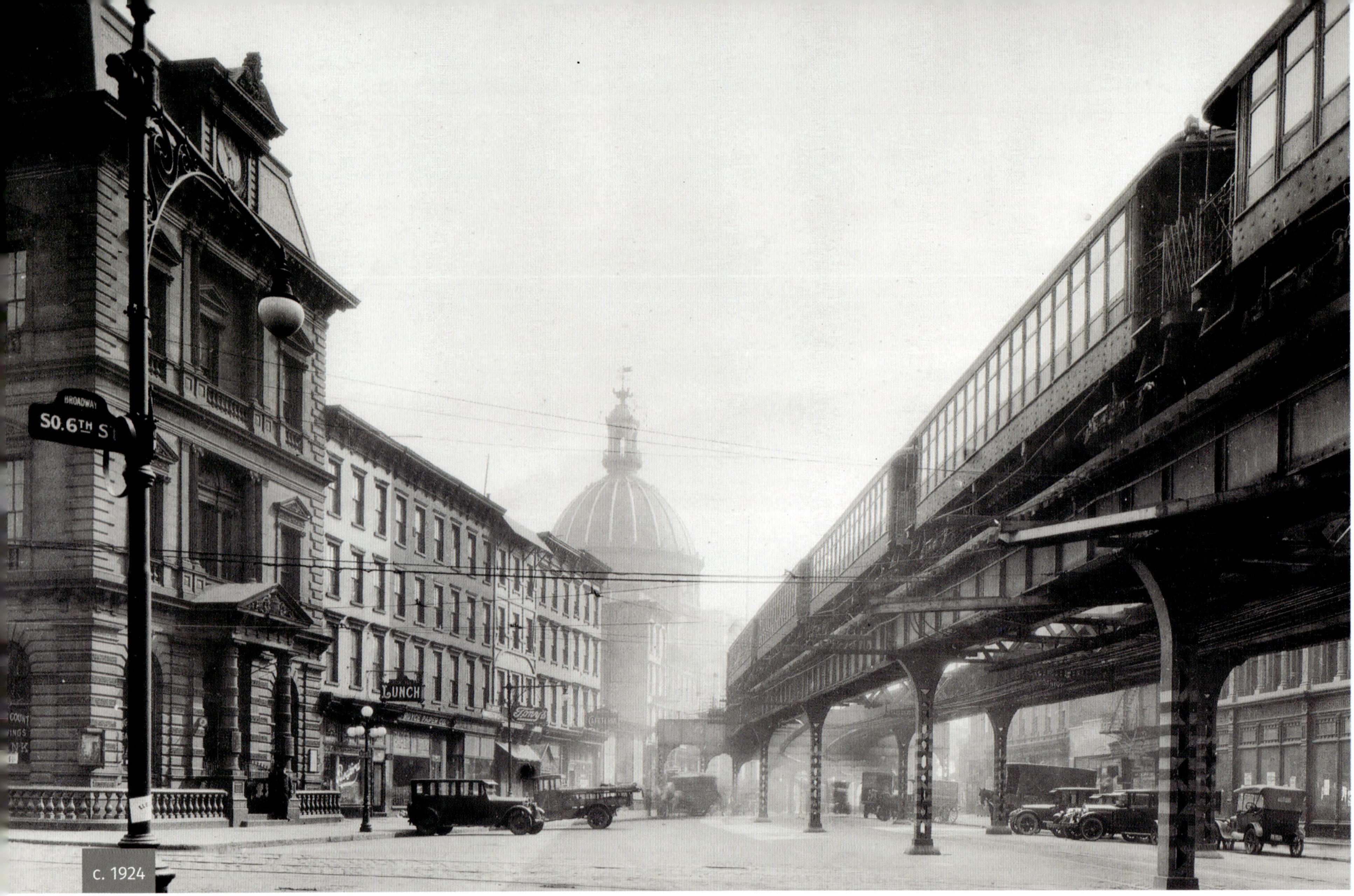

c. 1924

WILLIAMSBURG

Diverse communities have reshaped the once industrial neighborhood

THEN: In the Twenties, Williamsburg was a major industrial and residential area with a diverse population of recent immigrants from Europe—especially Poland and Germany. The new Williamsburg Bridge, opened in 1903, had spurred rapid population growth, bringing large communities of laborers from Manhattan to the garment factories, breweries, oil refineries, and food processing plants that lined the waterfront. The exponential economic growth created a need for local banks, like the Williamsburg Savings Bank, whose impressive dome is visible in the back of this image from 1924. Even at that time, fractures were already starting to appear in the local economy: Prohibition had impacted jobs at the breweries, and unsafe working conditions plagued the sugar refineries and garment sweatshops, which led to significant labor activism. Corning Glass Works and Pfizer Pharmaceuticals, both founded in Williamsburg, moved out of the area for cheaper land and labor.

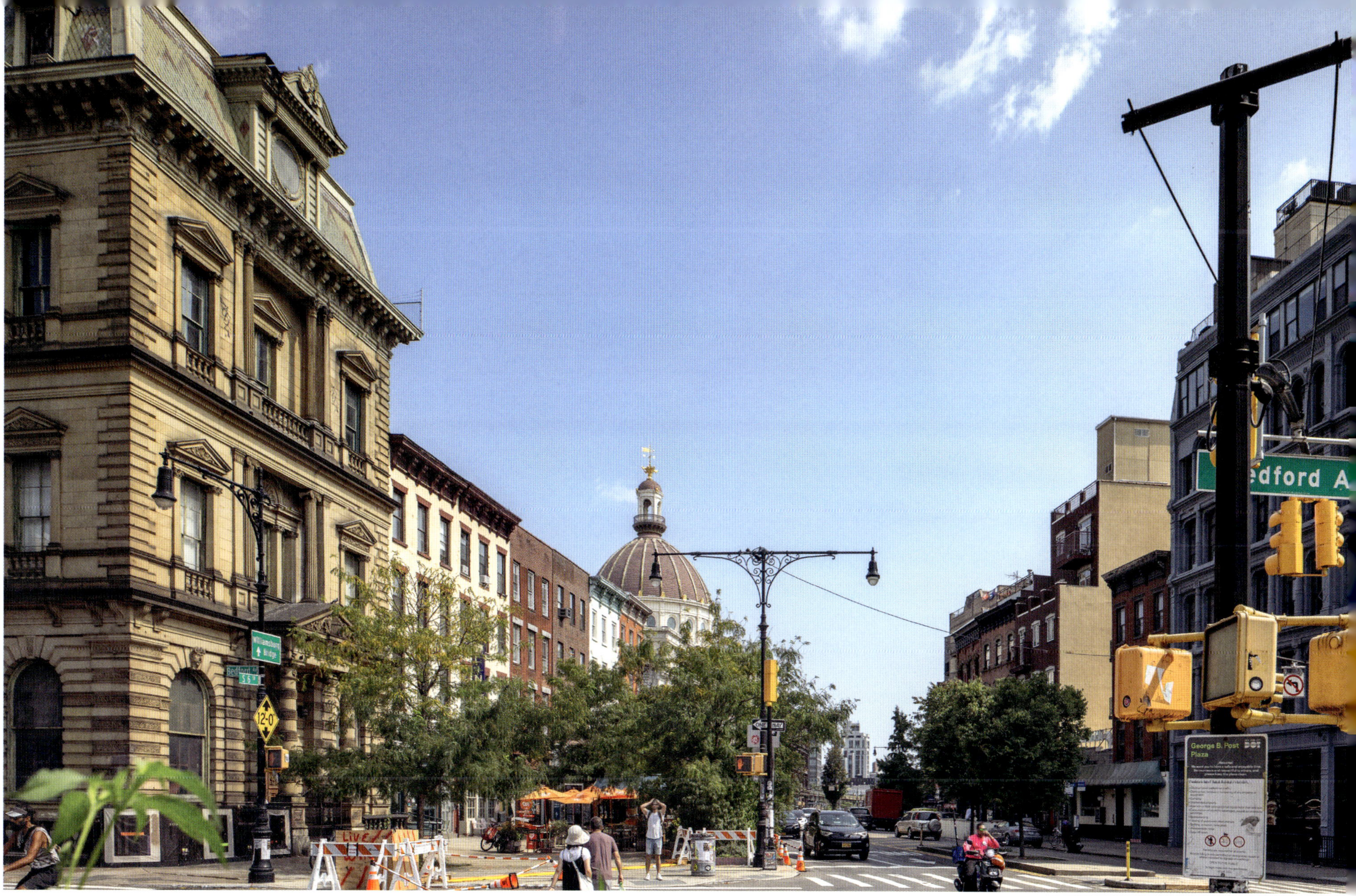

NOW: Williamsburg today still has a network of diverse communities, with each population contributing to the area's unique collective character. The intersection of Broadway at South Sixth Street still features many of the same buildings from 1924. Tensions in Williamsburg largely revolve around gentrification and cultural preservation, as many different populations vie to remain local. Rising rents and property values have displaced many long-time residents, particularly from working-class and minority communities, leading to conflicts over affordable housing, zoning laws, and the changing character of the neighborhood. North Williamsburg—largely composed of young professionals, artists, and creatives—has become synonymous with hipster culture, and has been instrumental in shaping the neighborhood's trendy image. The Latino community—primarily Puerto Ricans and Dominicans with roots going back generations—is centered in the southern and eastern parts of Williamsburg, and there are still pockets of Polish and Italian residents in the northern part. A significant portion of south Williamsburg is home to a large Satmar Hasidic Jewish population with its own schools, shops, and synagogues. They are known for their distinctive dress and adherence to strict religious practices. The Hasidic community, in particular, faces challenges as they seek to maintain their traditional way of life amidst rapid urban change.

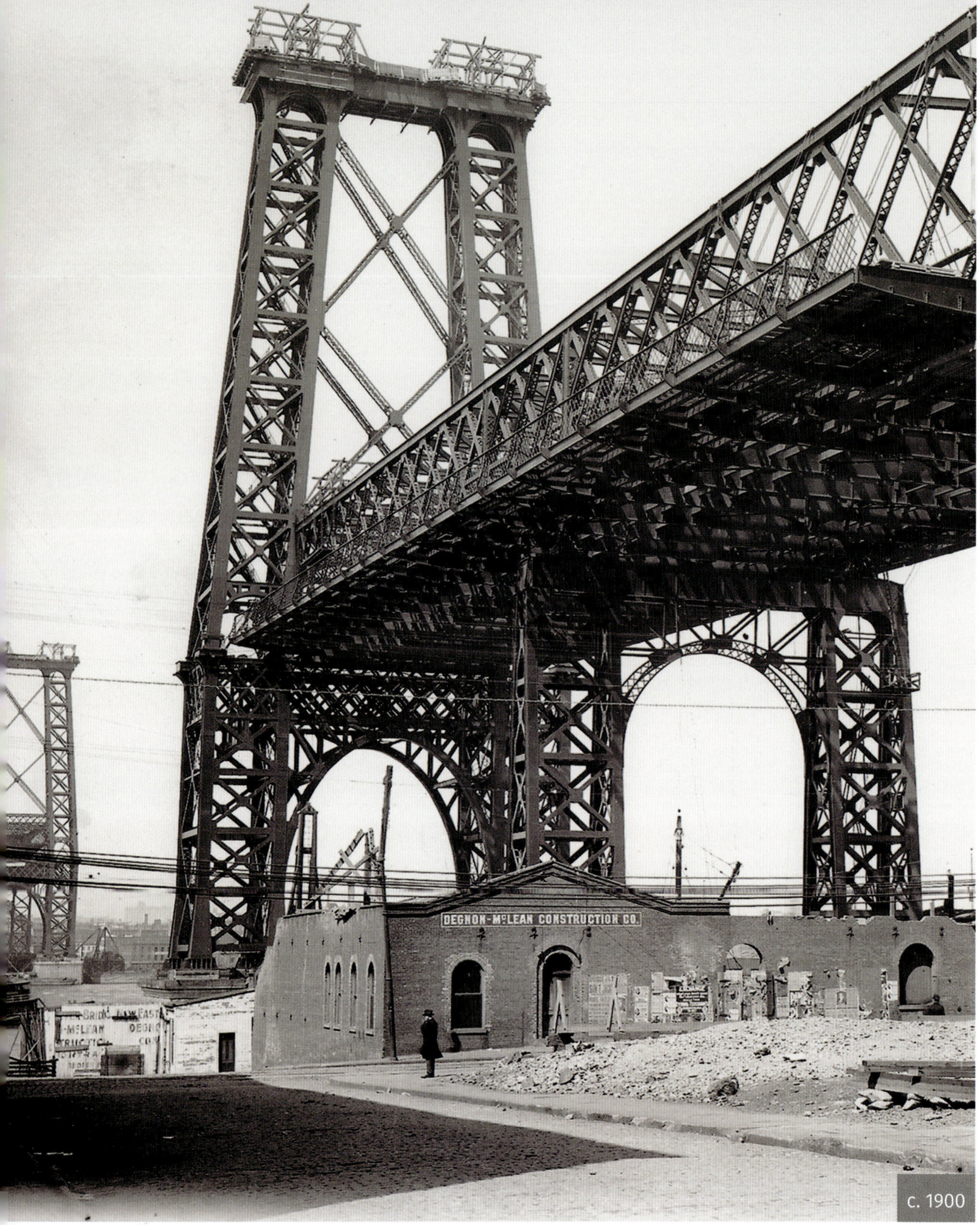

c. 1900

WILLIAMSBURG BRIDGE

A bridge between generations and different communities

THEN: The Williamsburg Bridge held a twenty-year record for the longest suspension bridge in the world. Designed by architect Leon Moisseiff, it was constructed to move passenger vehicles and pedestrians between Manhattan and Williamsburg. Completed in 1903, the Williamsburg Bridge was the second structure to span the East River, and the first suspension bridge with towers made entirely of steel. The bridge provided a direct connection between the tenements on the Lower East Side and the industrial waterfront of Williamsburg. Many immigrants came to Brooklyn for work and stayed for the cheaper housing and better living conditions.

NOW: The Williamsburg Bridge still serves as an important passage between Manhattan and Brooklyn, but the area around it has changed dramatically. Former industrial buildings have turned into condominiums, thanks to a rezoning of the Greenpoint waterfront in 2005, when developers were incentivized to build residential high rises, which then mostly pushed out the smaller buildings. Williamsburg's art scene, once the driving force behind its transformation, is now in a state of flux. Many artists who originally settled in the area for its cheap rents and industrial spaces have been priced out. While it was technologically advanced in 1903, the steel and concrete structure of the bridge fell into disrepair, and the bridge was closed to vehicles briefly in 1988 while a renovation plan was created. Over the years, the bridge has been tagged with a myriad of unique graffiti that is visible from the J, M, and Z subway trains, and the buildings that sit closest to the tracks attract musicians and artists drawn to discounted rents and creative community living.

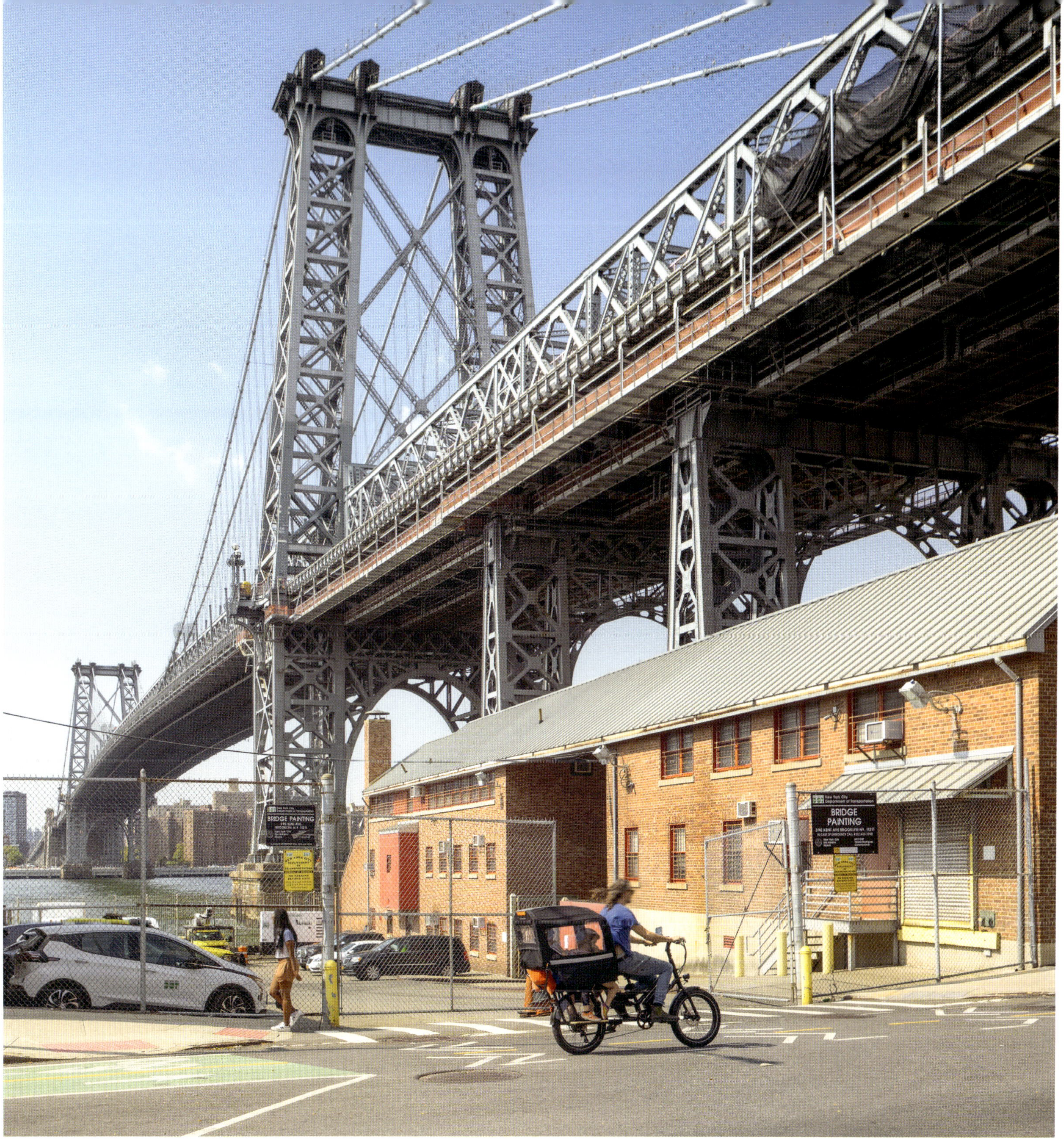
BRIDGE PAINTING
BRIDGE PAINTING

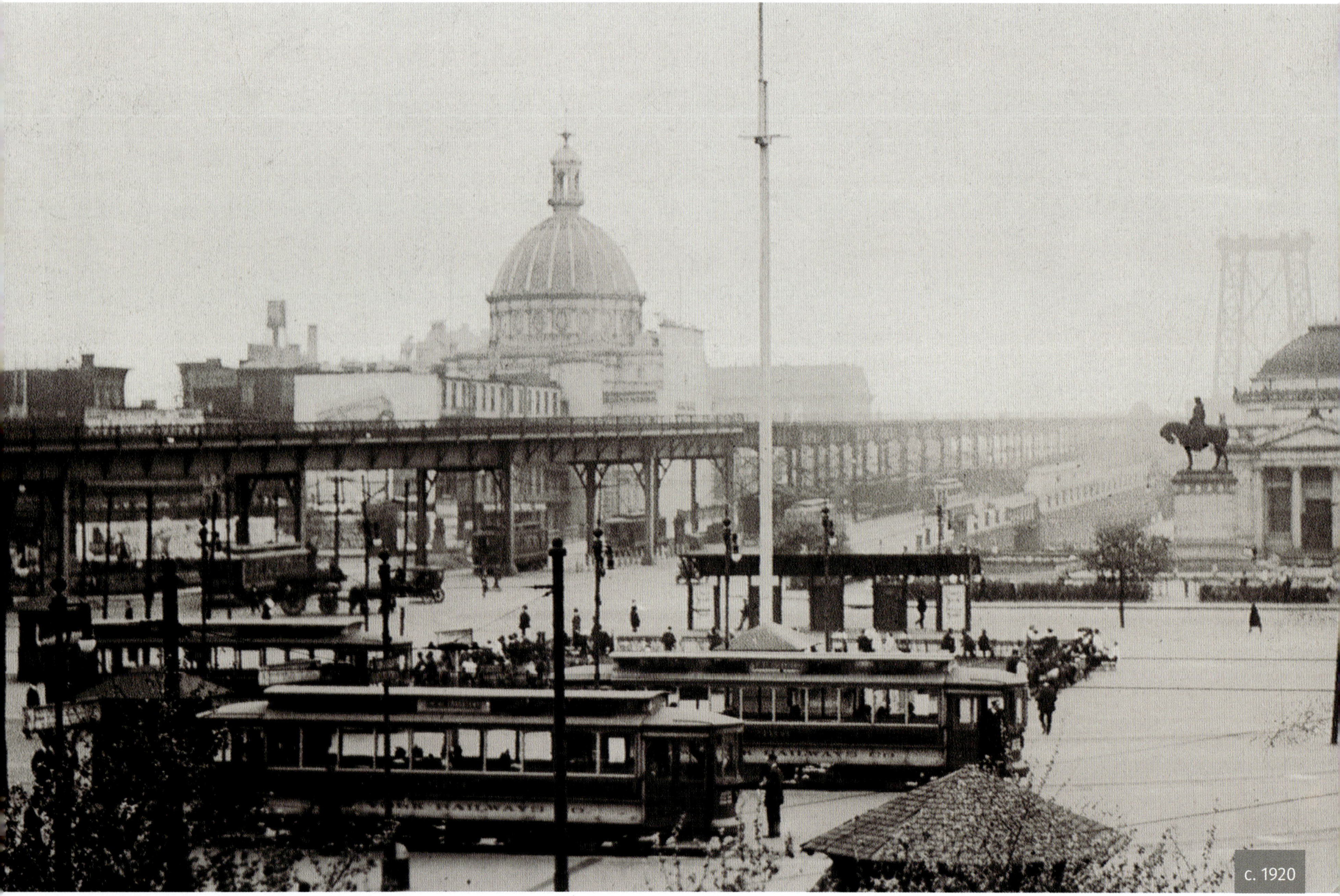

c. 1920

WILLIAMSBURG BRIDGE PLAZA

An evolution from commerce center to modern gathering space

THEN: Shown to the left is the intersection of South Fourth Street at Broadway. In 1920 Williamsburg Bridge Plaza served as a large transportation hub for what would become the most heavily populated part of Brooklyn. Trolleys, street cars, and the elevated train fill the foreground, and there is a statue of George Washington visible before the start of the bridge. The site had been an integral path in the Battle of Long Island in 1776, and in 1950, the city changed the name from Williamsburg Bridge Plaza to Continental Army Plaza to honor the soldiers and the history.

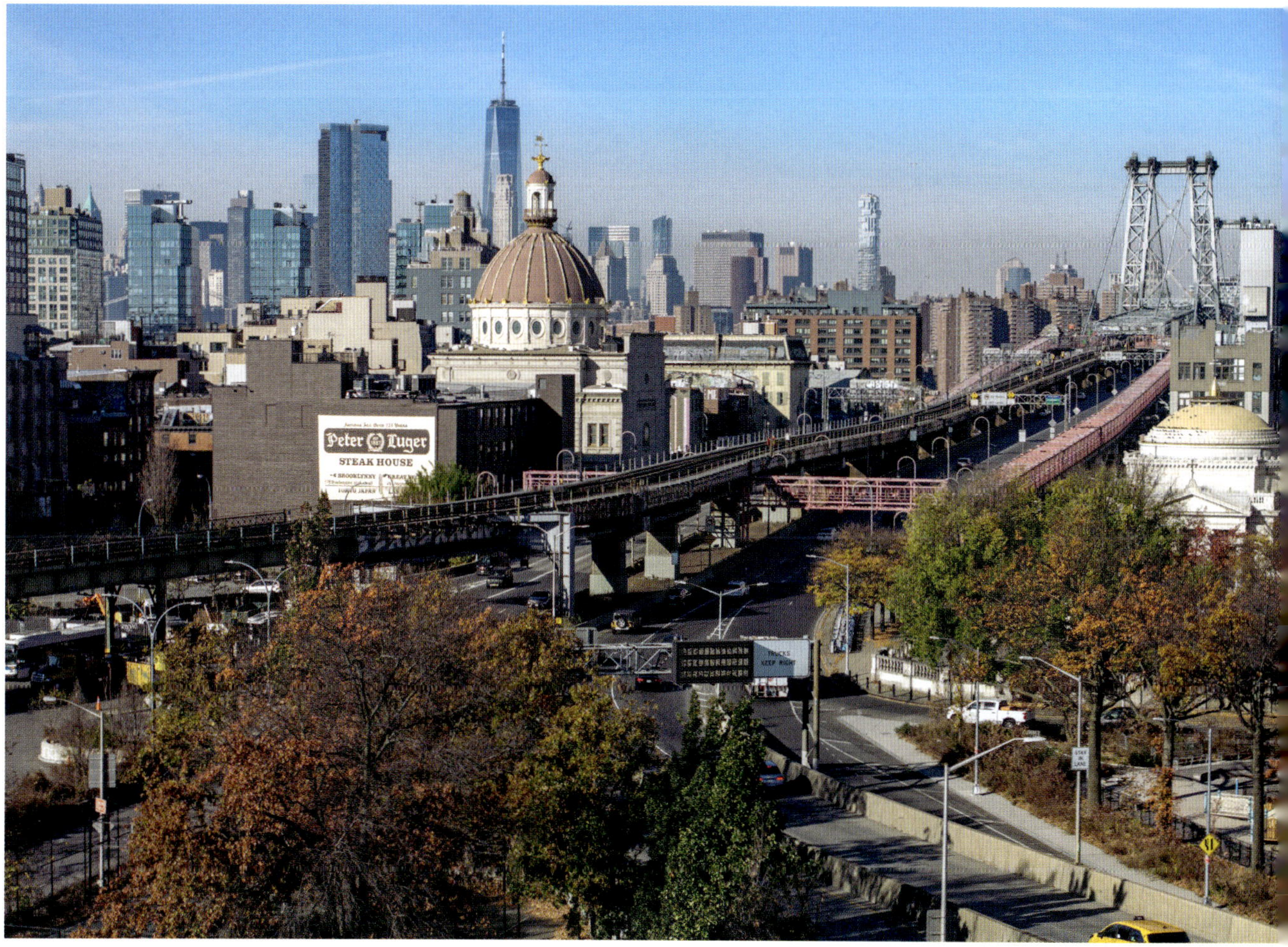

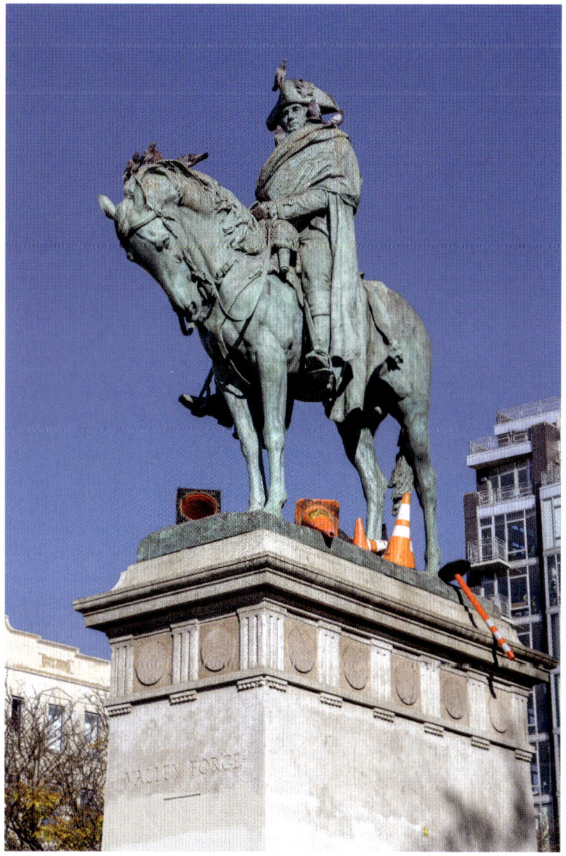

ABOVE: Dedicated in 1906, the bronze figure on horseback is said to represent George Washington humbled by a brutal winter but steadfastly protecting his troops.

NOW: Over the years the plaza has witnessed rallies and protests in parallel to the most important events of the time. There were labor movement rallies in the early twentieth century, Civil Rights Movement protests in the Sixties, and anti-war demonstrations in the Seventies. More recently, there have been immigration reform rallies, Occupy Wall Street encampments, and Black Lives Matter protests. The trolleys have been replaced by buses, and the previously barren streetscape is so filled with trees that the only way to see the Washington statue, the bank, and the bridge at the same time is to get an aerial view like the one above.

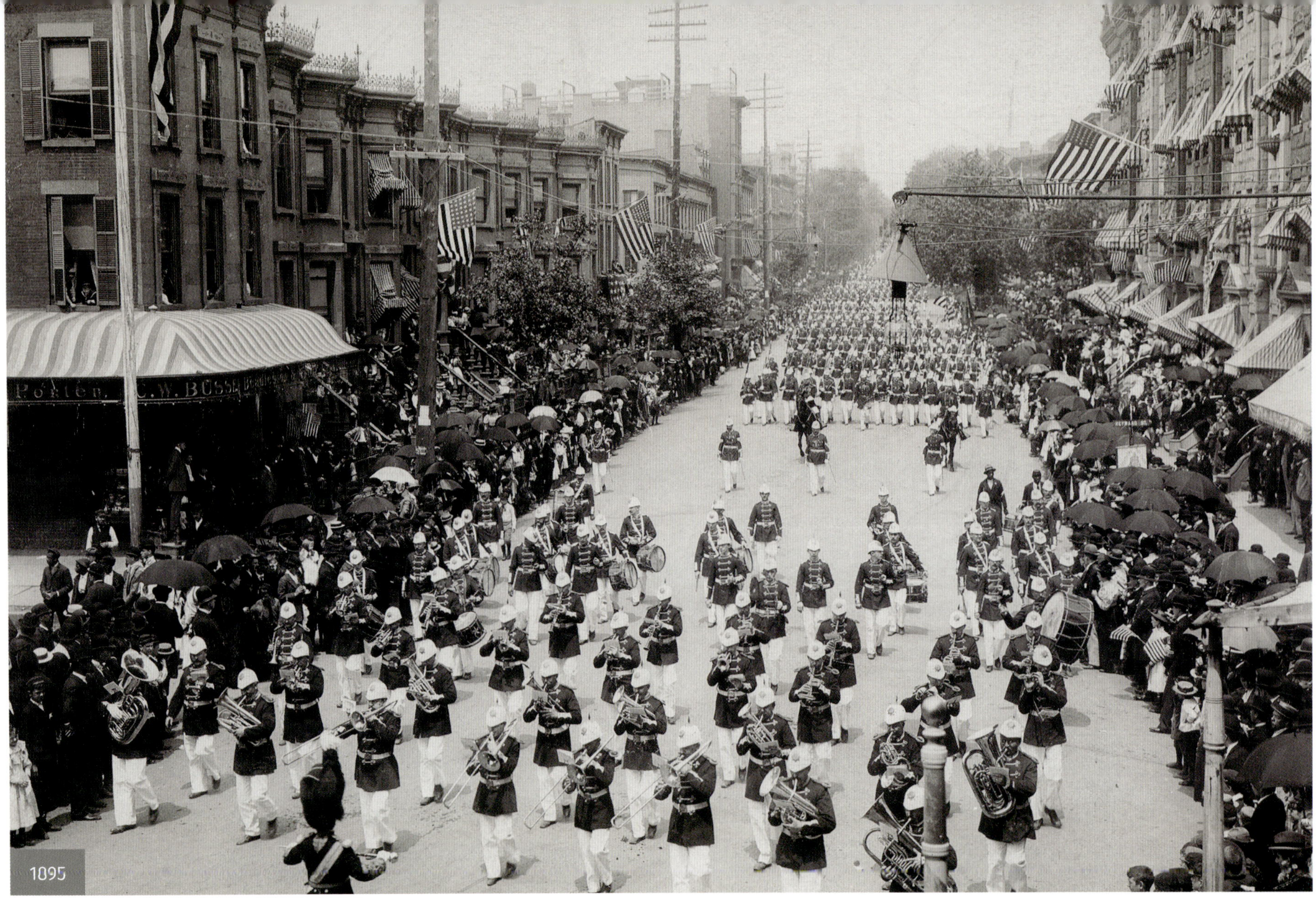

1895

WILLIAMSBURG BEDFORD AVENUE

A parade route runs through ten miles of neighborhoods

THEN: By the late 1800s, Bedford Avenue was already a major thoroughfare in Brooklyn. Beginning at Manhattan Avenue in Greenpoint, it continued for ten miles, over 132 blocks, connecting Williamsburg, Bedford-Stuyvesant, Crown Heights, Flatbush, and Midwood, before ending in Sheepshead Bay. For that reason, it was chosen as the parade route for Brooklyn's annual Memorial Day Parade. In 1895, the intersection of Bedford Avenue and Heyward Street drew large crowds of spectators to watch Veterans of the Civil War march alongside military bands, active militia units, and civic organizations in the holiday parade as it headed south towards the newly erected Soldiers' and Sailors' Monument Arch in Prospect Park. While many Americans believe that Memorial Day was created to honor soldiers lost in World War I, the day was first established in 1868 to honor Union Soldiers who died in the Civil War. After almost thirty years, it had become a significant annual event, and neighborhoods decorated their buildings with flags and bunting, and gathered on sidewalks and stoops to cheer and celebrate.

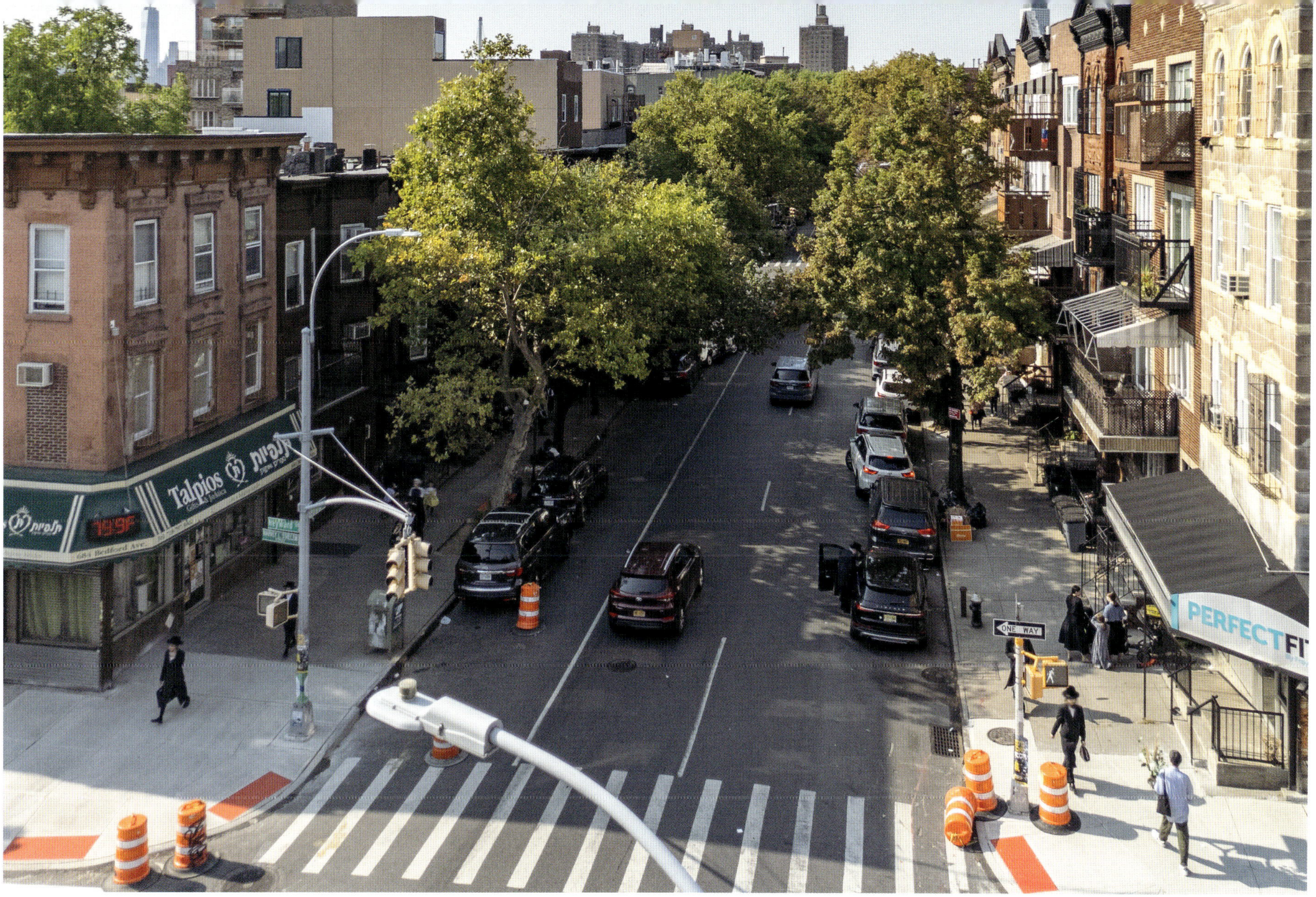

NOW: Today, the Memorial Day Parade still exists, albeit down a shorter route that skips this part of Williamsburg. It has evolved to reflect the changing face of American veterans. Participants from more recent conflicts—including Korea, Vietnam, Iraq, and Afghanistan—march alongside diverse groups, such as Jewish War Veterans, The U.S. Coast Guard, Highlanders, and Bikers of Brooklyn. And though the modern streetscape has changed very little structurally, the intersection now also reflects a dramatic demographic change, as it sits at the heart of the 50,000-person Hasidic Jewish community that began moving to Williamsburg at the turn of the twentieth century. On any given day, men in traditional black hats and coats, and women in modest dress, go about their daily routines. Residential buildings have been adapted to accommodate the large families typical of the community, and grocery stores and restaurants cater to Kosher dietary requirements. The intersection still serves as a gathering point during holidays and special occasions, but the events have changed along with the dynamic nature of Brooklyn's communities and the ongoing evolution of American traditions.

GREENPOINT

Previously Polish neighborhood preserves architectural character with adaptive reuse

THEN: Greenpoint, like all of Brooklyn, was originally home to farms. A true industrial, blue collar neighborhood, at the turn of the century Greenpoint was made up of immigrant families from all of Europe, including Ireland, Italy, and especially Poland. Greenpoint was one of the largest Polish-American communities in all of New York, with countless Polish bakeries, restaurants, and grocery stores. The men often worked on the docks and in the factories, and the women worked in the home, raising their children and frequenting the small local business that lined Manhattan Avenue—including Greenpoint Savings Bank, seen with the Greek columns and dome on the right of the picture.

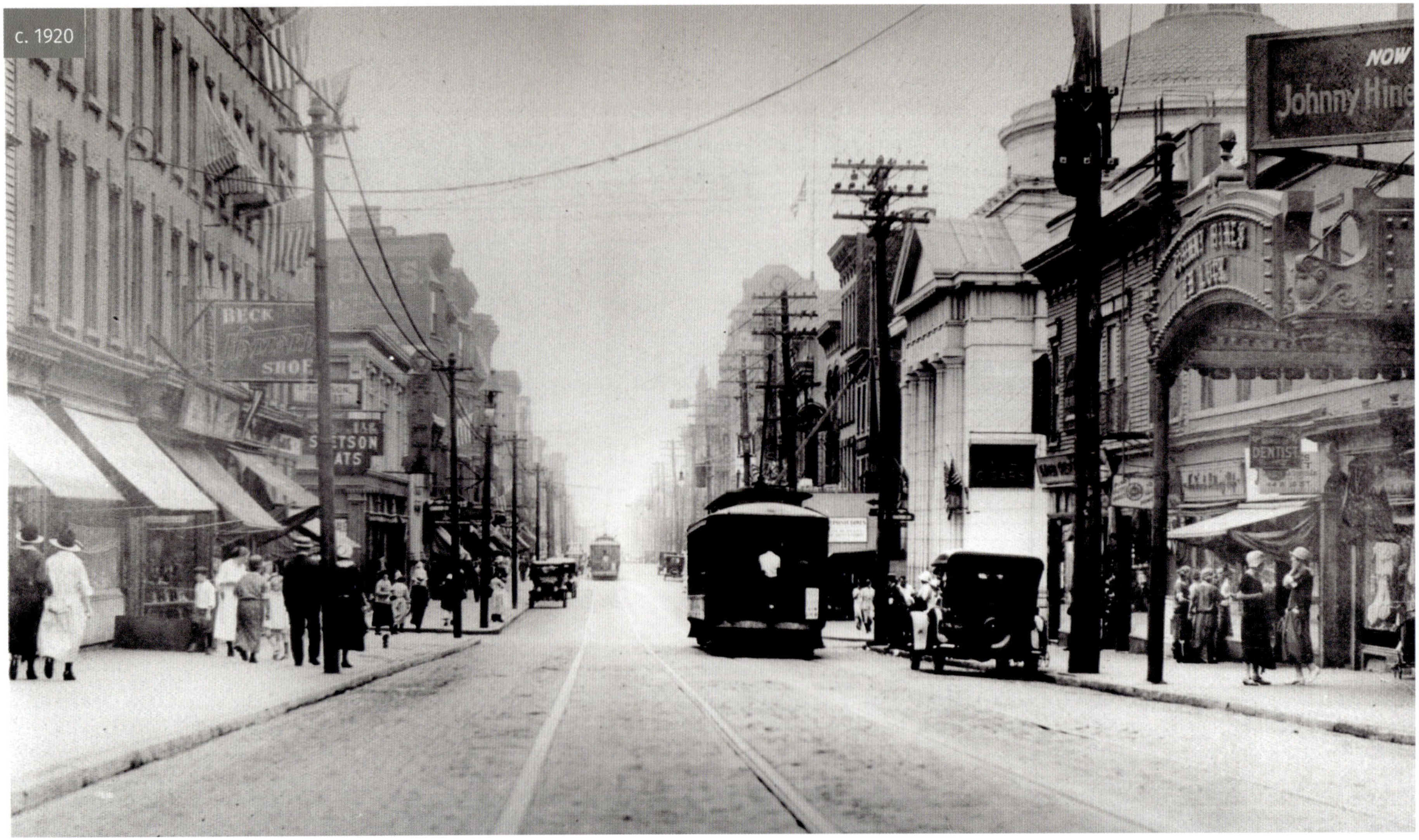

c. 1920

NOW: Today, Greenpoint is a designated historic district consisting of over 300 residential and commercial buildings, built between 1850 and 1900, which have been repurposed to service the modern needs of the neighborhood. This allows Greenpoint to maintain its sense of history amidst the many large-scale developments that have gone up since 2005, when the area was rezoned to allow for higher builds and planned communities, especially along the waterfront. Greenpoint's industrial past has made way for the rise of a new and thriving arts scene, with many of the former factories now home to large art studios and vintage or consignment shops. It has become a magnet for artists, with events like the Greenpoint Open Studios showcasing local talent. As of this writing, the domed Greenpoint Savings Bank is slated to become a cannabis dispensary, a fitting symbol of the modern adaptations of the neighborhood's rich history.

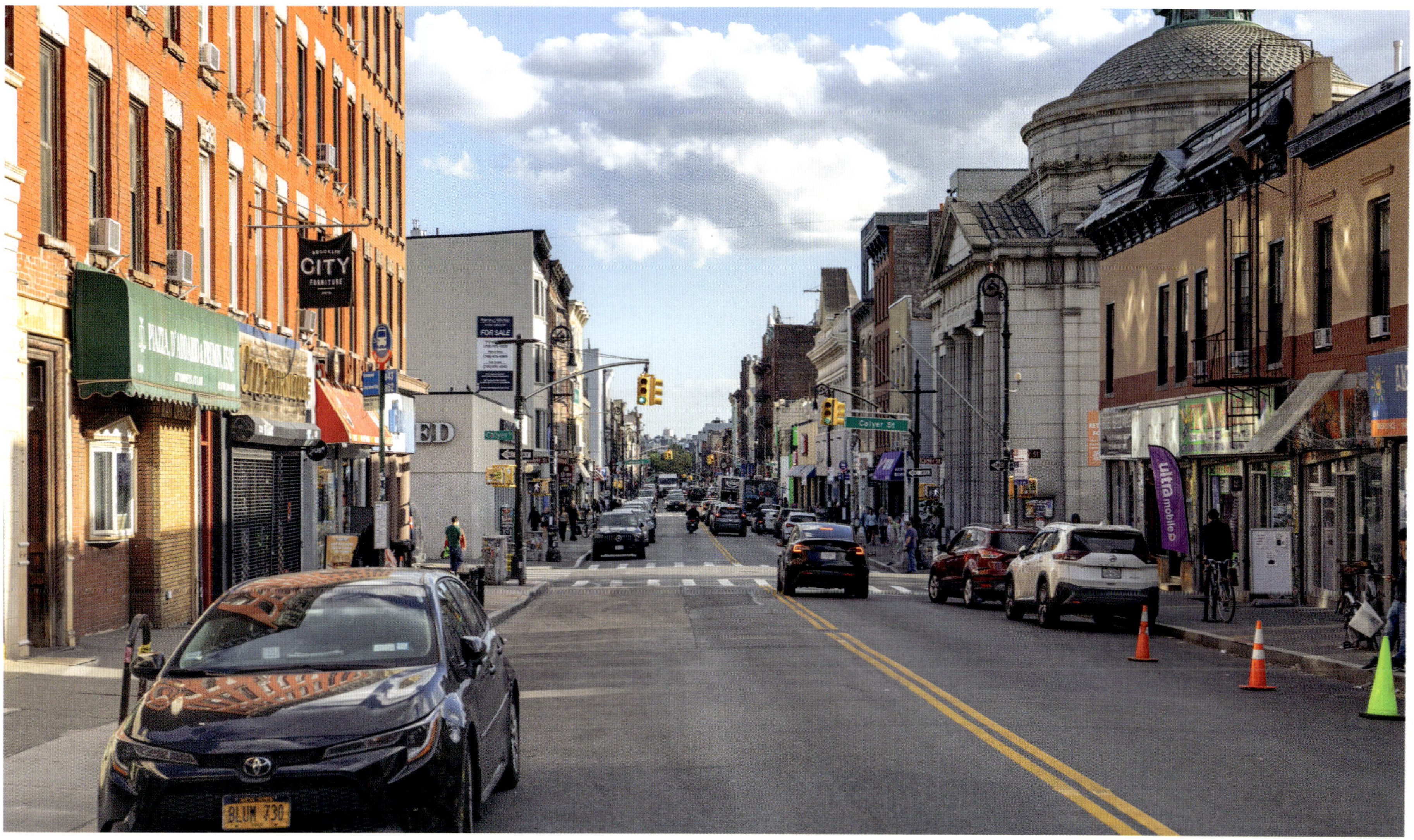

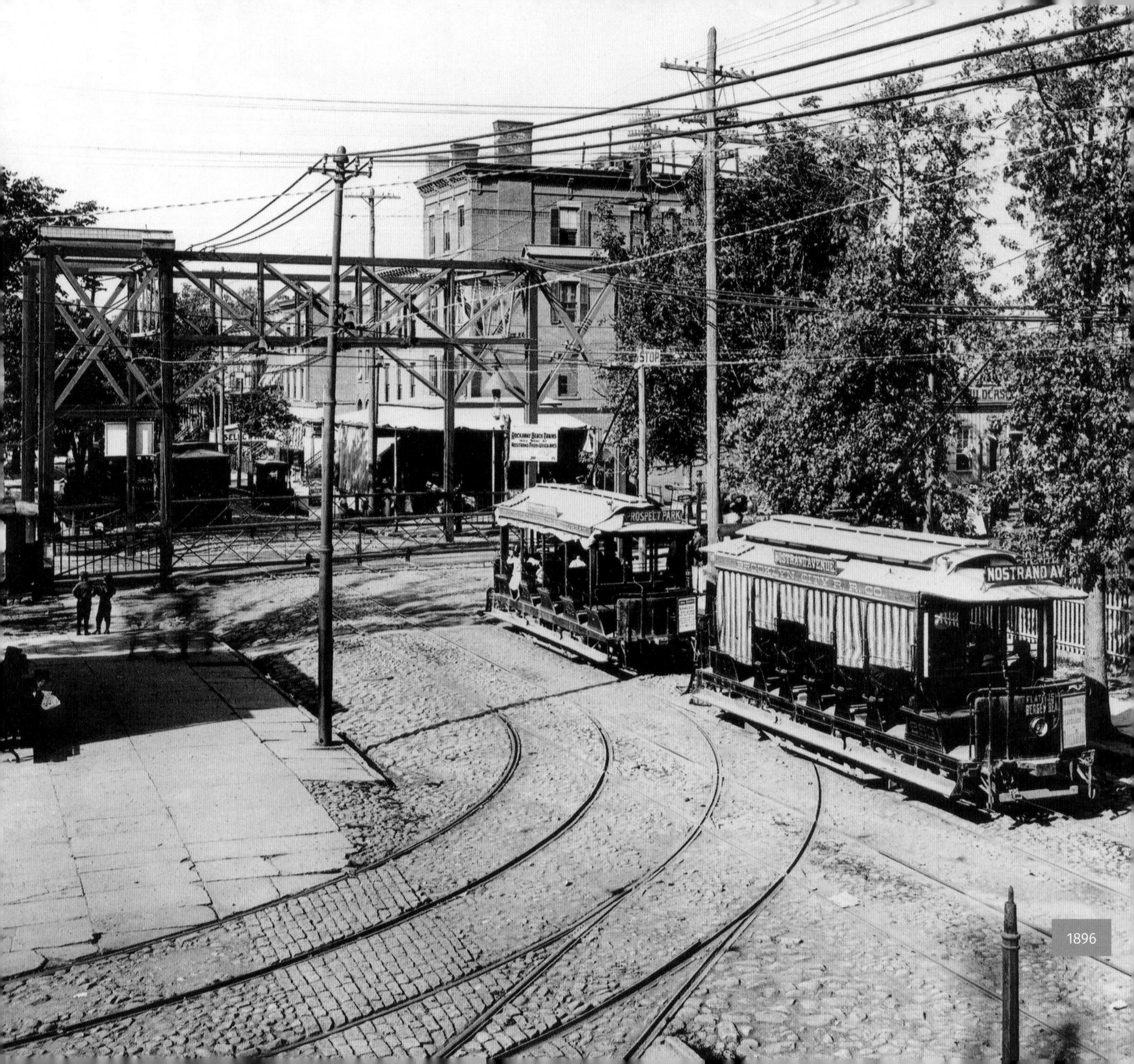
STOP
PROSPECT PARK
NOSTRAND AVENUE
BROOKLYN CITY R.R. CO.
NOSTRAND AV.

1896

BEDFORD-STUYVESANT

An early African-American enclave

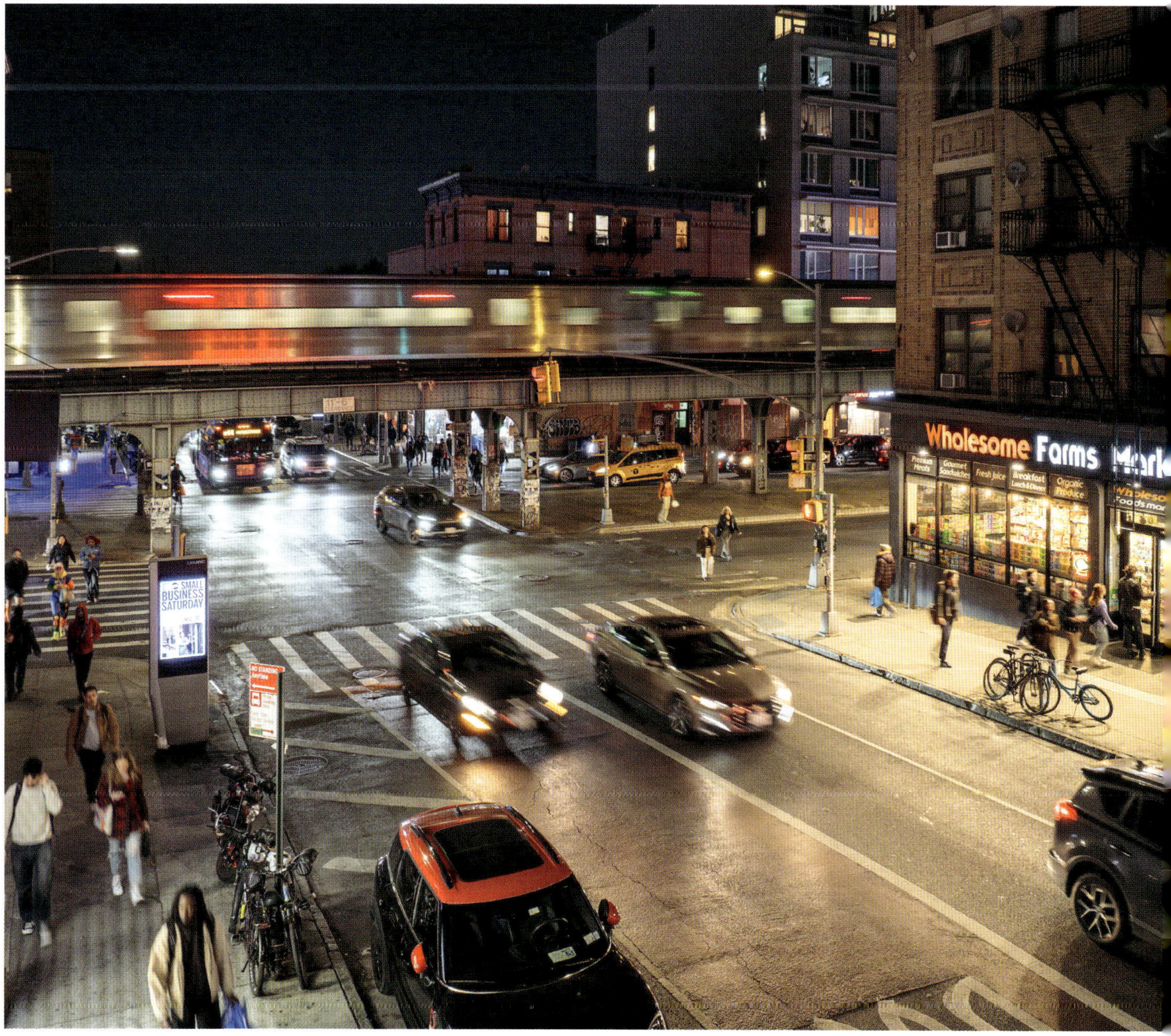

THEN: At its inception around 1638, Bedford-Stuyvesant was part of the Dutch colony of New Netherland, and was one of the original seven villages that would later become Brooklyn. Primarily farmland, the settlement was an instrumental food supplier to the growing population of New Amsterdam. By 1896, the farmland had been turned into a busy urban neighborhood with roughly 88,000 buildings all built before 1900. New, luxurious brownstones reflected the prosperity of the expanding upper-middle class and included high-end decorative details and classical architectural elements such as brackets, cornice banding, and elaborate frieze. Nostrand and Atlantic Avenues were lined with shops and businesses, supported by the trolleys, the Brooklyn City Railroad Line and the Long Island Railroad. In the photo opposite, trolley cars and the railroad station are visible, as is the metal barrier that stops traffic on Nostrand to allow trains to pass, as well as 1243 Atlantic Avenue, a small brick building at the intersection, which is still there today and visible in both photographs.

NOW: While elevated train tracks were being removed all over Brooklyn, the 1930s brought them to this intersection with the A, C and E trains on the Fulton Street subway line, replacing the ground-level tracks of the old railroad and allowing for the unimpeded flow of traffic along the busy Nostrand Avenue. Residents took advantage of the subways, trains, and trolleys available at that time and the location became a major center of Brooklyn's African-American population. Approximately 30,000 people relocated from Harlem for more space and larger housing stock close to the jobs at the Brooklyn Navy Yard. Over the next thirty years, the number of African-American residents increased to 155,000 people, who comprised more than fifty percent of Bed-Stuy. This population boom occurred just before public transportation options diminished without adequate replacements, leaving residents without reliable access to jobs, which led to economic challenges in the neighborhood. In 1967, Senator Robert F. Kennedy joined local community leaders and launched the Bedford Stuyvesant Restoration Corporation, the first grassroots development association in the country. It focused on providing mortgage assistance to help Black families buy homes, and it implemented a plan by architect I.M. Pei to close off streets to make community spaces. It worked, and Bed-Stuy is no longer recognizable as a rundown neighborhood.

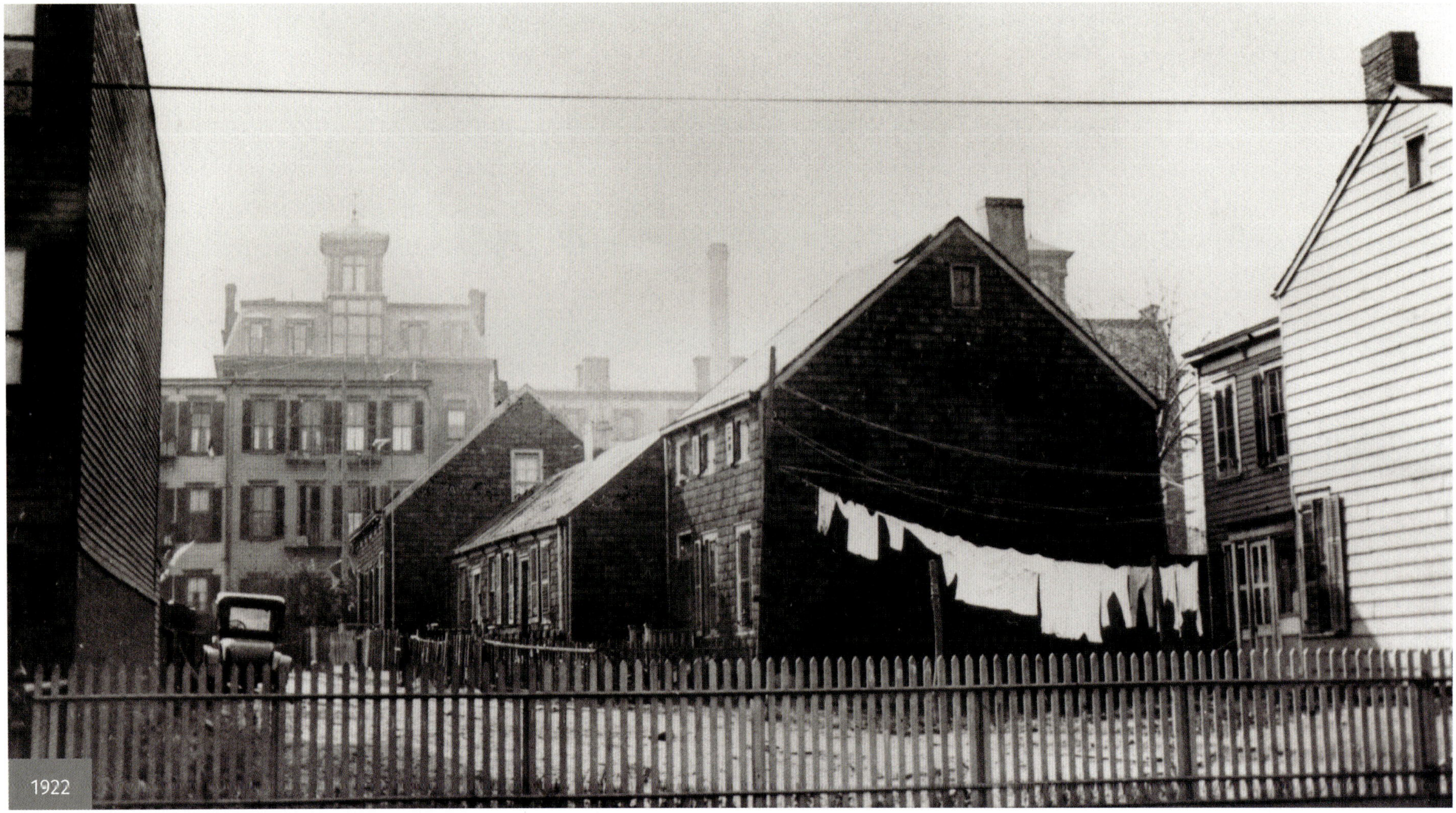

1922

WEEKSVILLE HOUSES

A real-estate opportunity for free African Americans

THEN: The Weeksville Houses in Brooklyn are a collection of historic buildings that represent one of the first free Black communities in the U.S. They're named after James Weeks, a free African-American dock worker who bought a plot of land in 1838, setting the scene for the first village of African-American homeownership. Many African Americans sought to buy land as a way to gain economic and political freedom, and the community became a haven for free-born and formerly enslaved men, with opportunities for businesses, education, and political engagement.

By the Fifties, Weeksville had more than 500 residents, its own churches, a cemetery, an old-age home, and a school, providing social services for its residents through all phases of life. It even had its own newspaper, *The Freedman's Torchlight*. In the 1920s, the modest wood-framed cottages still housed families who were descendants of the original residents, but the rural character of Weeksville eventually gave way to urban development.

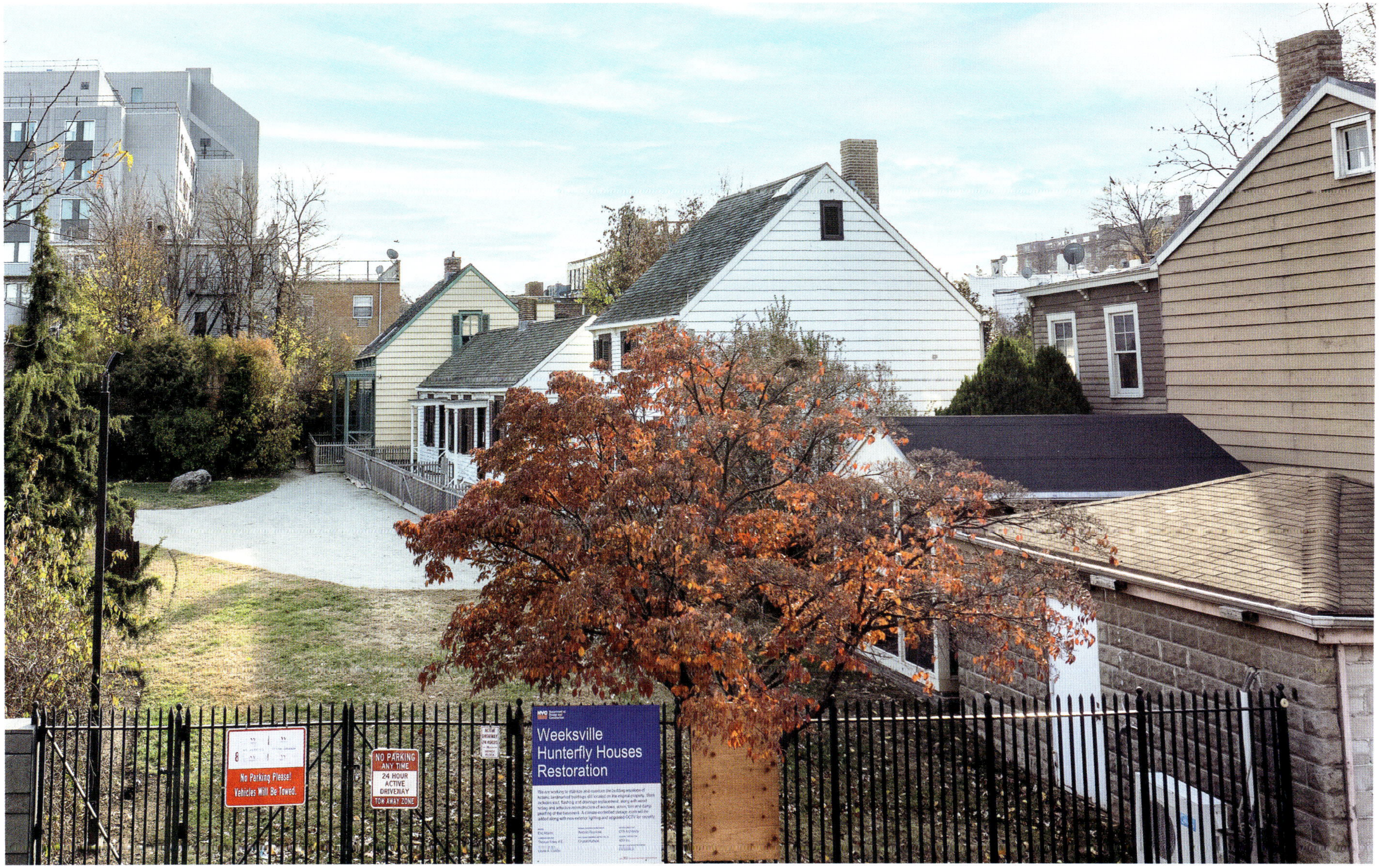

NOW: Weeksville struggled to maintain its character as a self-sustaining enclave for African Americans in the early part of the twentieth century, and it gradually became absorbed into the neighborhood that is today known as Crown Heights. In 1968, during a period of urban renewal, Weeksville was rediscovered and some of the original houses were saved and restored. The Weeksville Heritage Center comprises four Hunterfly Road Houses that have been furnished to reflect different periods of Weeksville history. The Heritage Center offers tours of the houses and serves as an educational institution that offers programs, exhibitions, and events that connect the past with ongoing current concerns, including African-American culture, social justice, and community building. The restoration of Weeksville stands as a powerful reminder of the importance of preserving historical sites for underrepresented communities, so that new generations can understand and appreciate the experiences and the struggles of those who came before them.

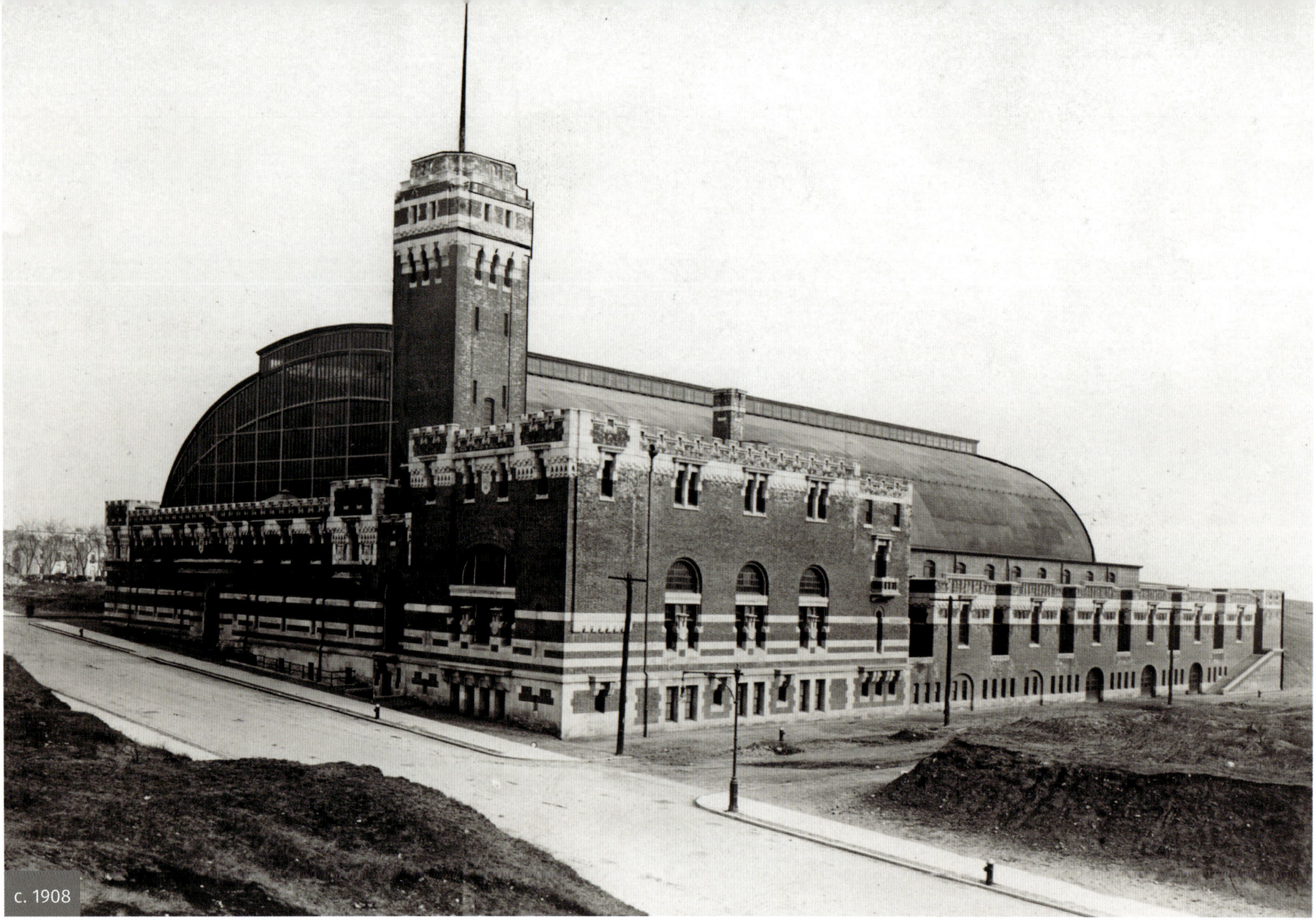
c. 1908

BEDFORD UNION ARMORY, CROWN HEIGHTS

From military fortress to a neighborhood wellness center

THEN: In 1903, construction began on The Bedford Union Armory to house the 23rd Regiment of the New York National Guard. An impressive Romanesque Revival-style building in Crown Heights, designed by architects Pilcher and Tachau, it was completed in 1908 and occupied an entire city block between Union and President Streets and Bedford and Rogers Avenues. The National Guard used the armory for training and as a base for assignments like natural disasters and civil unrest in the city. The centerpiece of the complex was an enormous drill hall capable of accommodating an entire regiment. Administrative offices and storage rooms for weapons and equipment finished off the complex. In addition to serving as a military facility, the Armory was also a place for the community to host exhibitions, sporting events, and social functions. In 1908, Crown Heights was a predominantly upper-class neighborhood, and the Armory reflected the enclave's wealth with appropriate architectural grandeur.

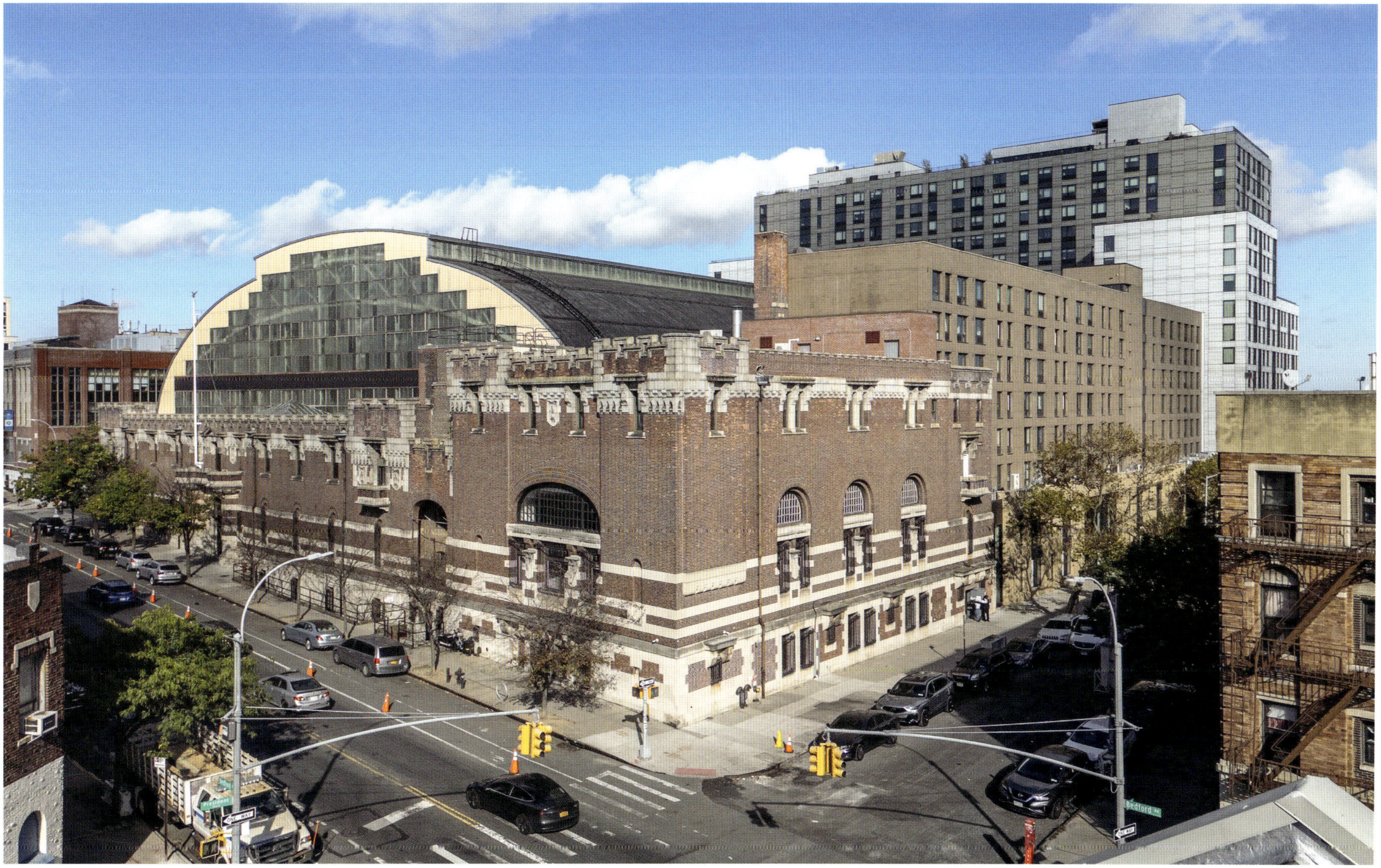

NOW: After the deactivation of the 23rd Regiment, various interested parties submitted proposals for the property. In 2015, a plan to convert the facility into a mixed-use development with 350 housing units and a 45,000-square-foot recreational facility moved forward, despite a lawsuit opposing it in 2017, which failed to derail the project. In 2019, BFC Construction won approval for the project, and construction began. The complex finally reopened in 2021 with an indoor pool, soccer fields, boxing and archery arenas, a fitness center, and dedicated space for local non-profits.

In honor of the Crown Heights Congressman who served from 1983 to 2007, it was renamed the Major R. Owens Health and Wellness Community Center and is New York City's first and largest comprehensive center with medical, emotional, and recreational practices at affordable rates for the Brooklyn community. Two new residential towers were built alongside the Armory, with 400 new units, 250 of which were offered by lottery for affordable housing for the community.

GRANT SQUARE

A "City Beautiful" planned community centerpiece

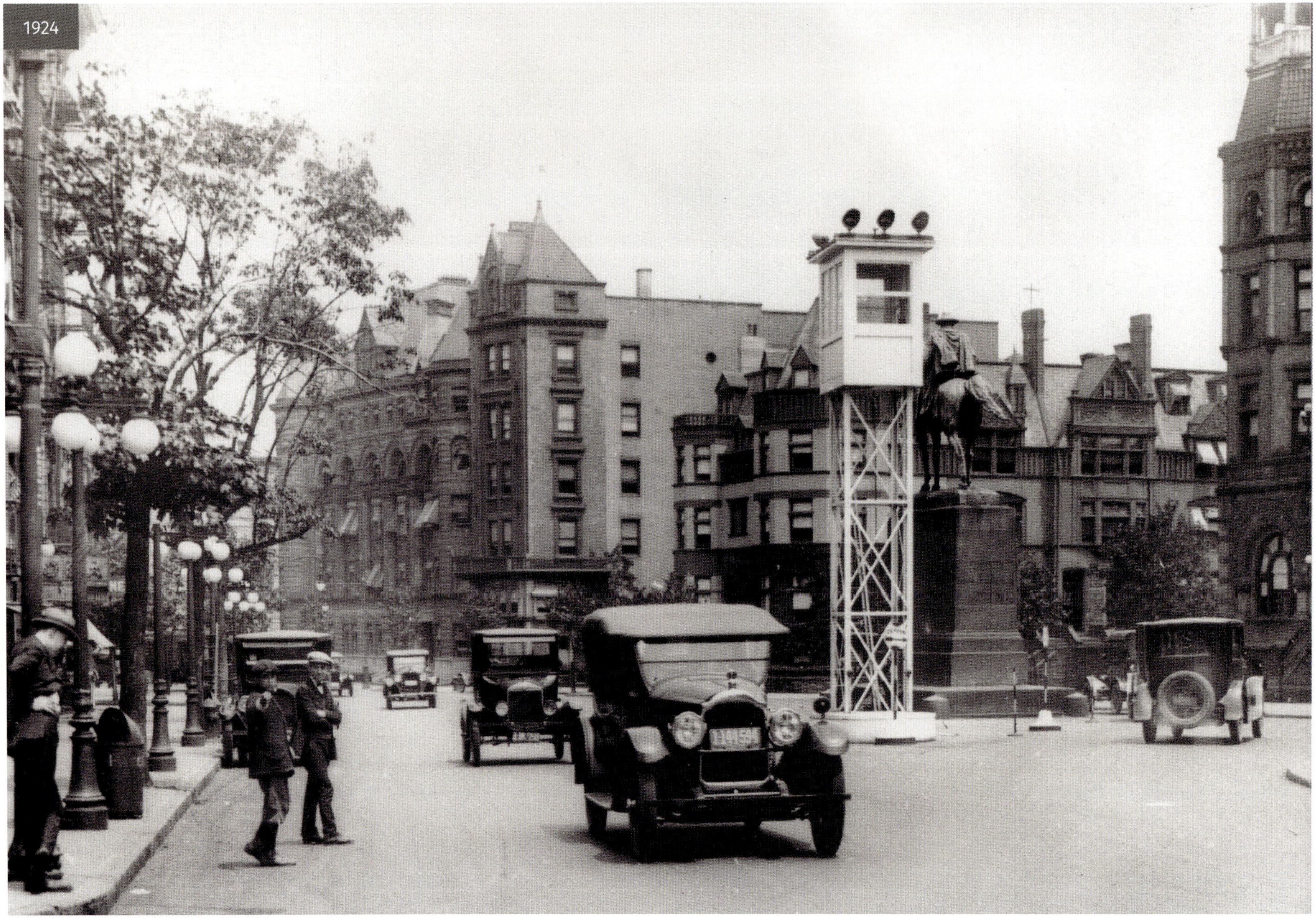

THEN: In 1924, Bedford Avenue near Bergen, Dean, and Pacific Streets was one of the busier intersections in Brooklyn complete with a white towered traffic signal. The square was named after President Ulysses S. Grant, and a statue of Grant on horseback erected in 1896 is still visible in front of the Union League Club. Behind the cub, the Imperial Apartments and the 23rd Armory are visible. Architect Montrose Morris designed the Imperial Apartments in a French Chateau style that appealed to residents who wanted a high-end living space close to the grand homes nearby. The square was a focal point for a development planned during the Seventies' "City Beautiful" movement intended to maintain open areas in urban spaces that were both aesthetically pleasing and functional for events important to the growing community.

NOW: The equestrian statue of Ulysses S. Grant and the buildings on either side of the square are still there. The Union League Club is now a Senior Citizen Center for local residents. The Imperial Apartments, still elegant, are now broken into much smaller units. The Armory is used as a men's homeless shelter run by the New York Department of homeless services. While the grandeur of the Gilded Age remains visible in Grant Square, the buildings have adapted to the current needs of the neighborhood.

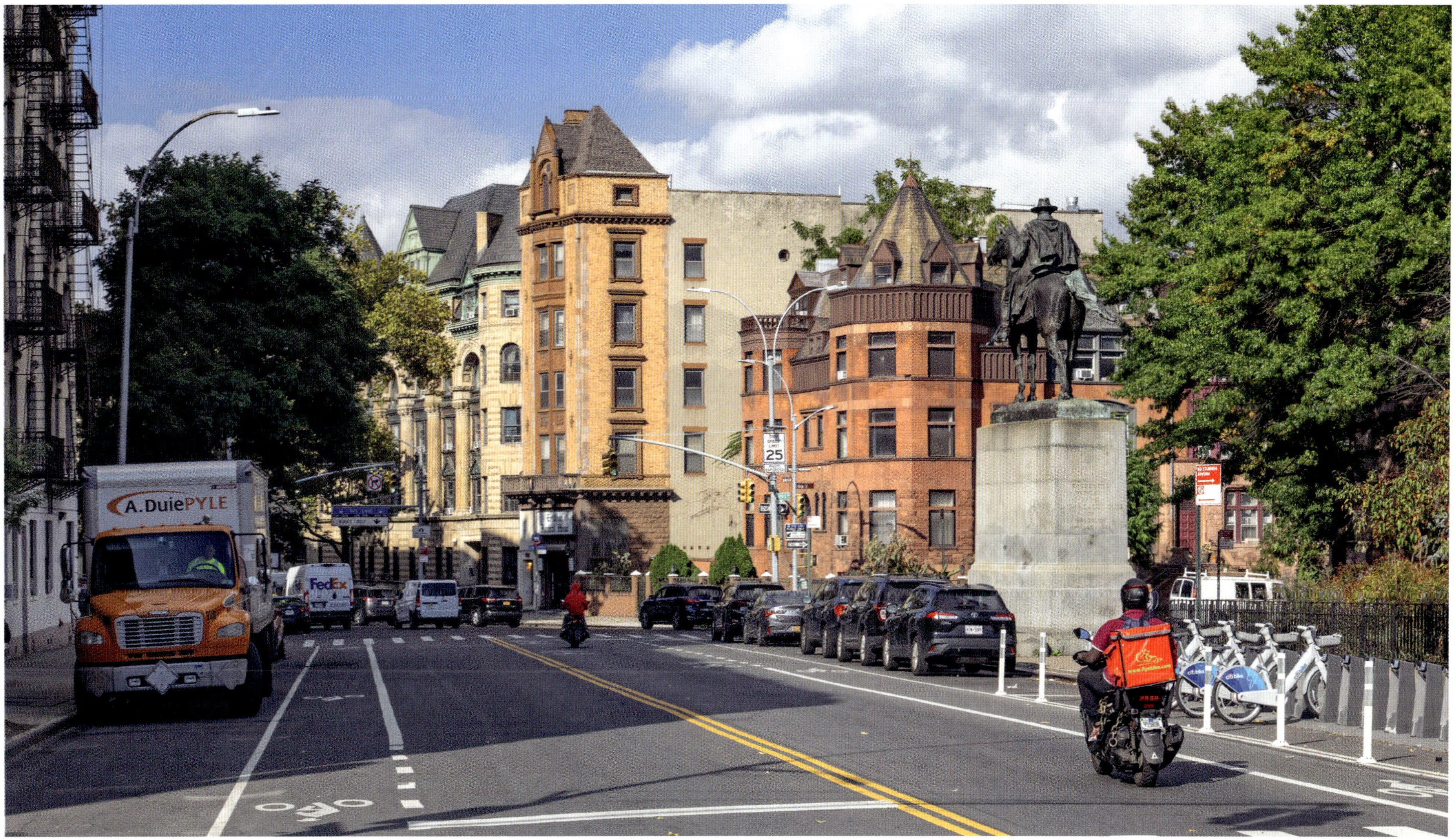

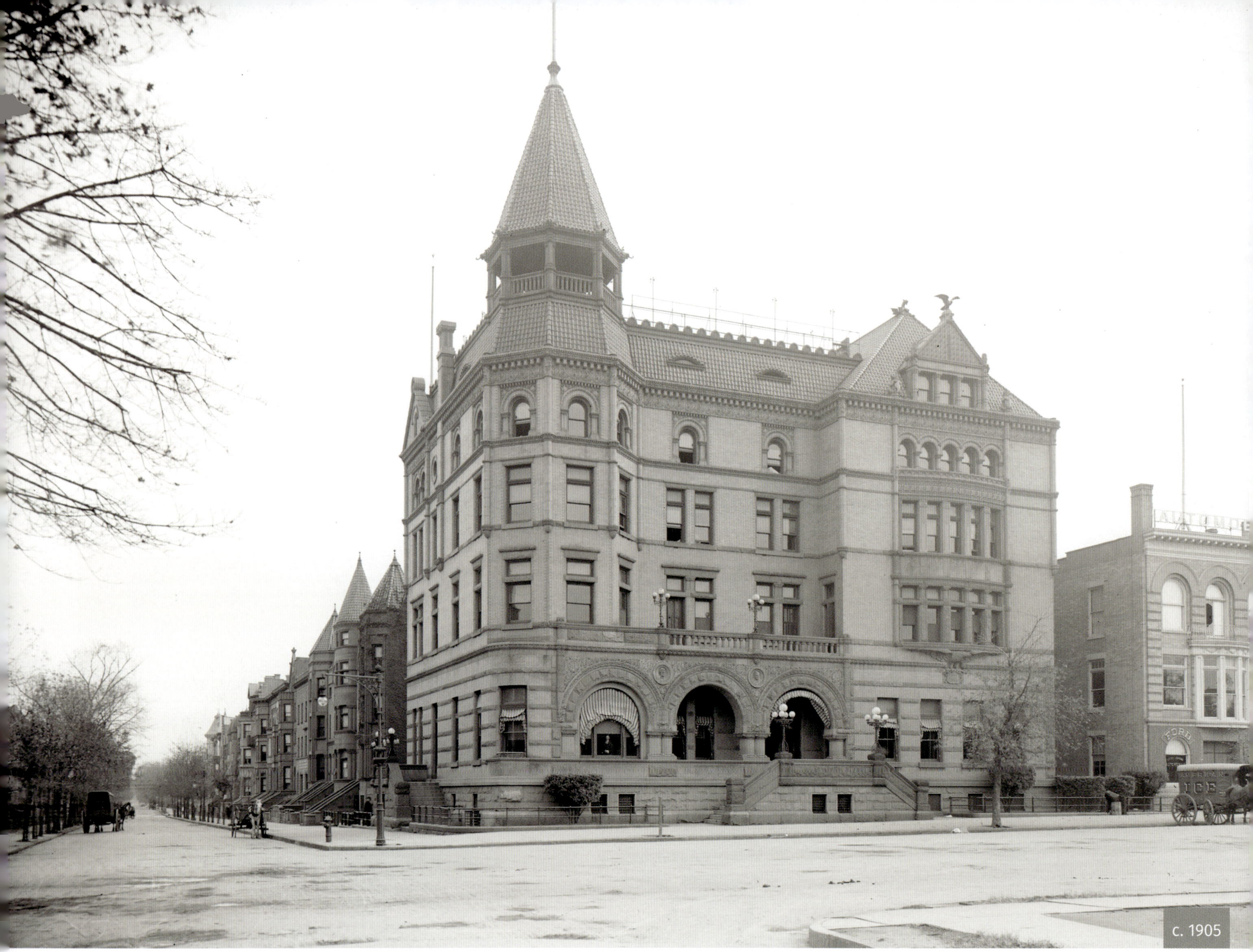

UNION LEAGUE CLUB

A Gilded Age institution built to rival Manhattan social clubs

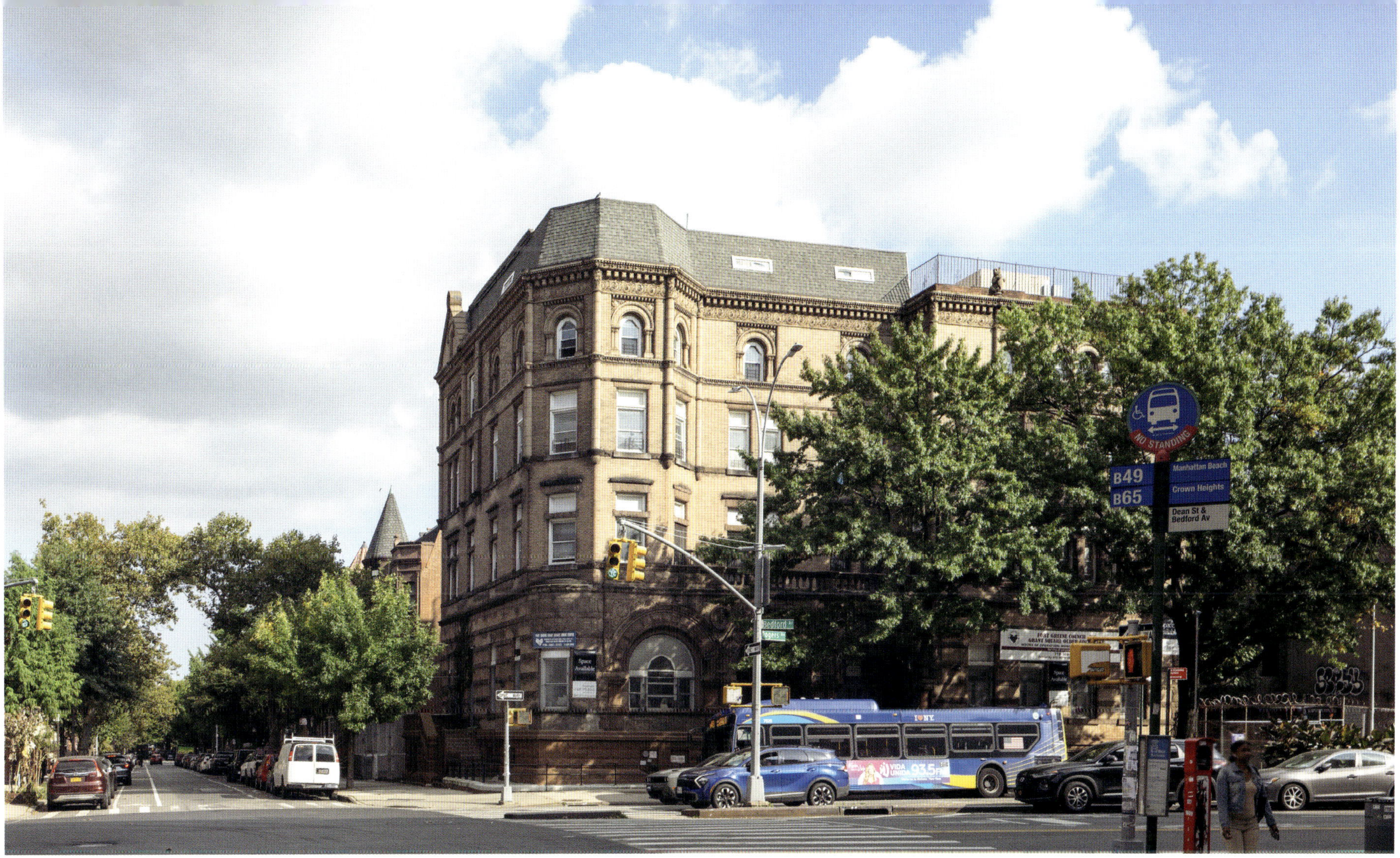

THEN: In the late 1800s, architect Peter Lauritzen was finishing plans for the new Union League Club of Brooklyn, a Romanesque Revival building designed as a gathering place for prominent citizens. Businessmen, politicians, and cultural figures who recently moved from Manhattan to Brooklyn wanted an upscale social club to rival those across the East River. The Union League Club first opened in 1890 on the corner of Bedford Avenue and Dean Street, just down the street from the fashionable mansions of St. Mark's Avenue. The founding membership roster includes the names of men who were already powerful in their communities, who used the club to meet and make the deals that would build the Brooklyn they wanted to see. When it opened, the club was one of the most technologically advanced buildings in the city. While most homes were just transitioning from gas, the club had its own power plant and generator in the basement. In addition to a meeting hall, dining rooms, a ballroom, a library, and guest rooms, it had a shooting range and even a bowling alley in the basement. City power brokers selected politicians and closed deals for real estate and development in the smoky club rooms for decades.

NOW: Today the building facade looks similar, though it's missing the corner tower, a bust of Abraham Lincoln, and the grand eagle that once guarded the second-floor windows. A statue of Ulysses S. Grant still stands out front, the last of its Civil War iconography. In 1914 the building sold to a Jewish organization called the Unity Club, and it operated as a school until the Seventies. Currently, the once exclusive social club houses a senior center, and the building's architectural significance is recognized, protected, and appreciated by local historical societies as part of the Crown Heights North Historic District, a group of over 1,000 buildings.

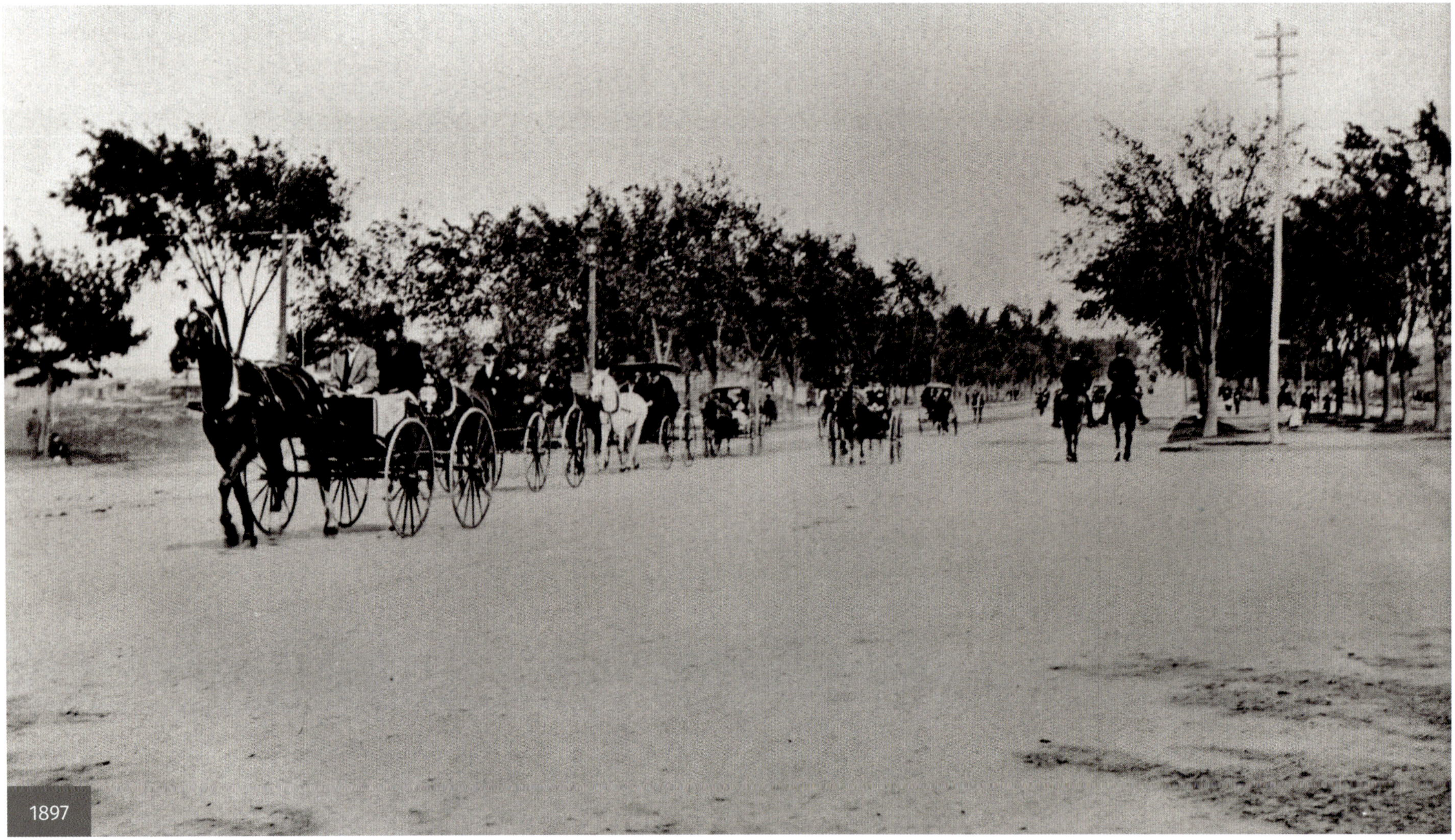

EASTERN PARKWAY

A visionary plan grows into the cultural heart of Brooklyn

THEN: In 1860, trailblazing landscape architects Frederick Law Olmsted and Calvert Vaux conceived Eastern Parkway as Brooklyn's grand boulevard, creating America's first parkway plan. After their successes with Central Park and Prospect Park, they conceptualized an innovative multi-use transit corridor to connect Prospect Park to the more eastern parts of Brooklyn. Their innovative design delineated different lanes for types of traffic, with dedicated paths for pedestrians, service vehicles, and the horse-drawn carriages featured above. The parkway's construction began in 1870 and reached significant completion by 1874. Tall trees and open spaces drew many residents, who enjoyed pleasure drives along the wide road. When Brooklyn officially became part of New York City in 1897, Eastern Parkway played a crucial role during the transition period, spiking a significant construction boom which created elegant new apartment buildings and brownstones, attracting wealthy residents who sought the prestige of a parkway address.

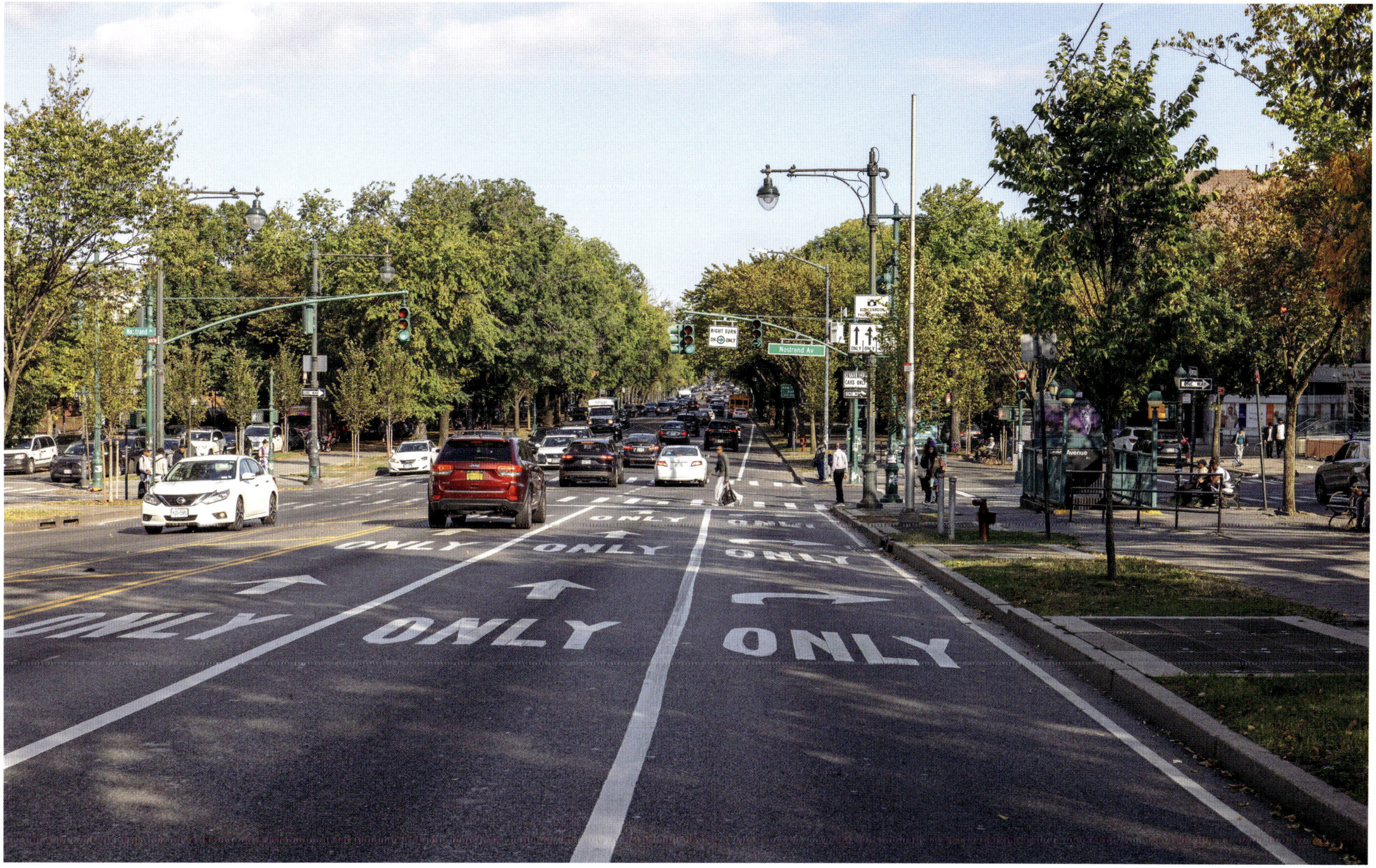

NOW: Today Eastern Parkway is a vital artery of Brooklyn, although its character has evolved significantly from Olmsted and Vaux's original vision. The parkway's unique formation of separated lanes and pedestrian paths persists, but the horse-drawn carriages have been replaced by cars and trucks. Traffic patterns and urban development have shifted the road from a "pleasure drive" to a major thoroughfare, and the 2.2-mile boulevard is the link between several different neighborhoods, including Crown Heights and Prospect Heights. The parkway is home to some of Brooklyn's most important cultural institutions, including the Brooklyn Museum, established in 1895; the Brooklyn Botanic Garden, which opened in 1910; and the Central Branch of the Brooklyn Public Library, completed in 1941. Modern preservation initiatives have worked to protect the parkway's heritage, replanting trees and reinforcing pedestrian promenades. In 1978, the thoroughfare was designated as a New York City Scenic Landmark and in 1983 it was added to the National Register of Historic Places.

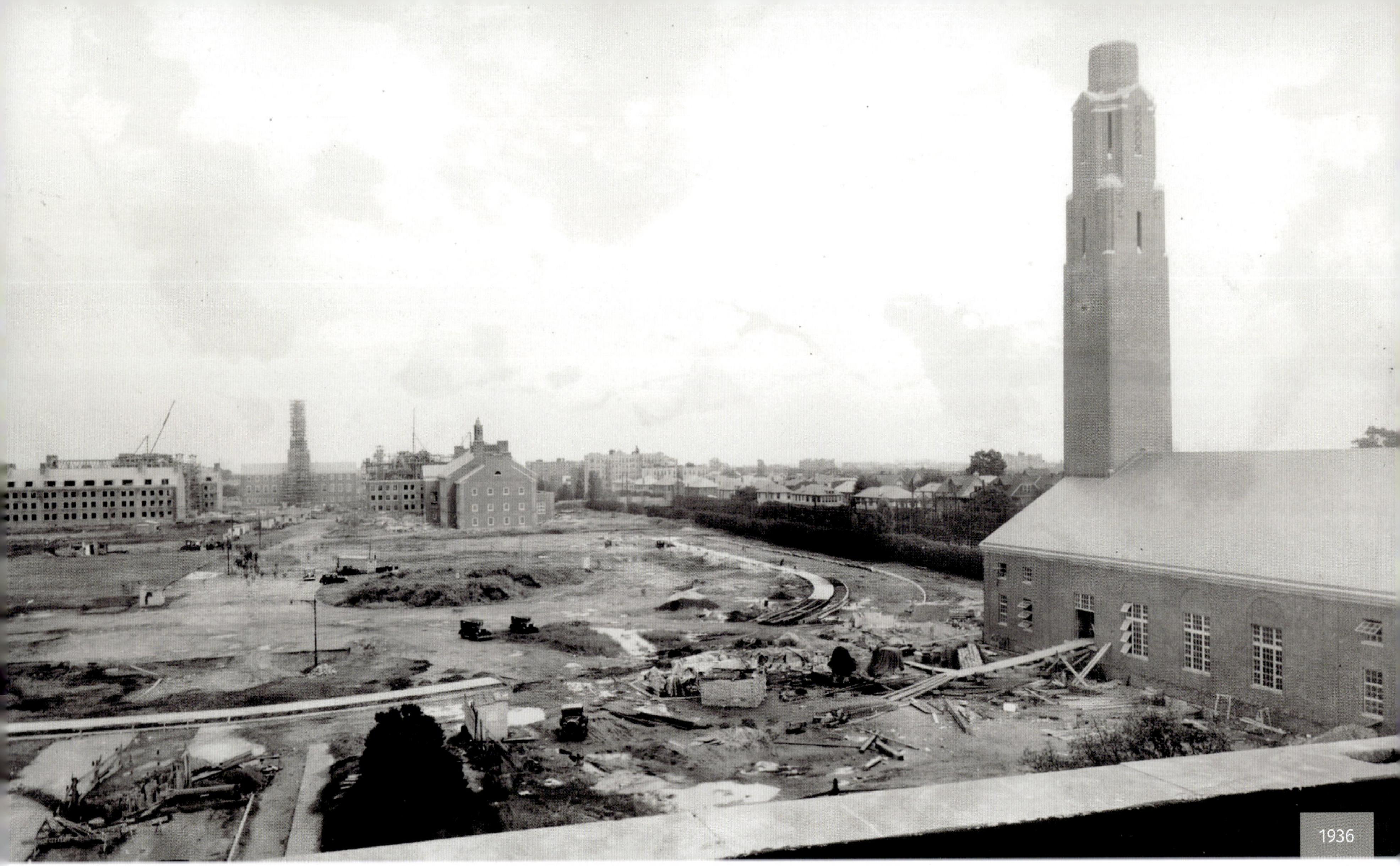

1936

BROOKLYN COLLEGE, MIDWOOD

Free education provided a path to prosperity for qualified pupils

THEN: Brooklyn College was founded in 1930 by order of the New York City Board of Higher Education when it authorized the combination of the Downtown Brooklyn branches of Hunter College, a women's college, and the City College of New York, a men's college. They became Brooklyn College, the first coed liberal arts college in New York City. Classes were divided by gender until junior year, and all students had to pass a difficult entrance exam in order to get accepted. In 1936, the college built a brand new school in the Midwood section of Brooklyn, trading a disjointed downtown experience for twenty-six acres on the site of an old horse racing track.

The Georgian-style campus was built as a Public Works Administration project during the Great Depression in the neighborhood of Midwood. The college immediately impacted the neighborhood, offering a free education to any student who could pass the entrance exams. In 1936, Midwood was a Jewish neighborhood and many first- and second-generation students of European descent took the opportunity to get an education that they otherwise wouldn't have been able to afford after coming to America to escape the war.

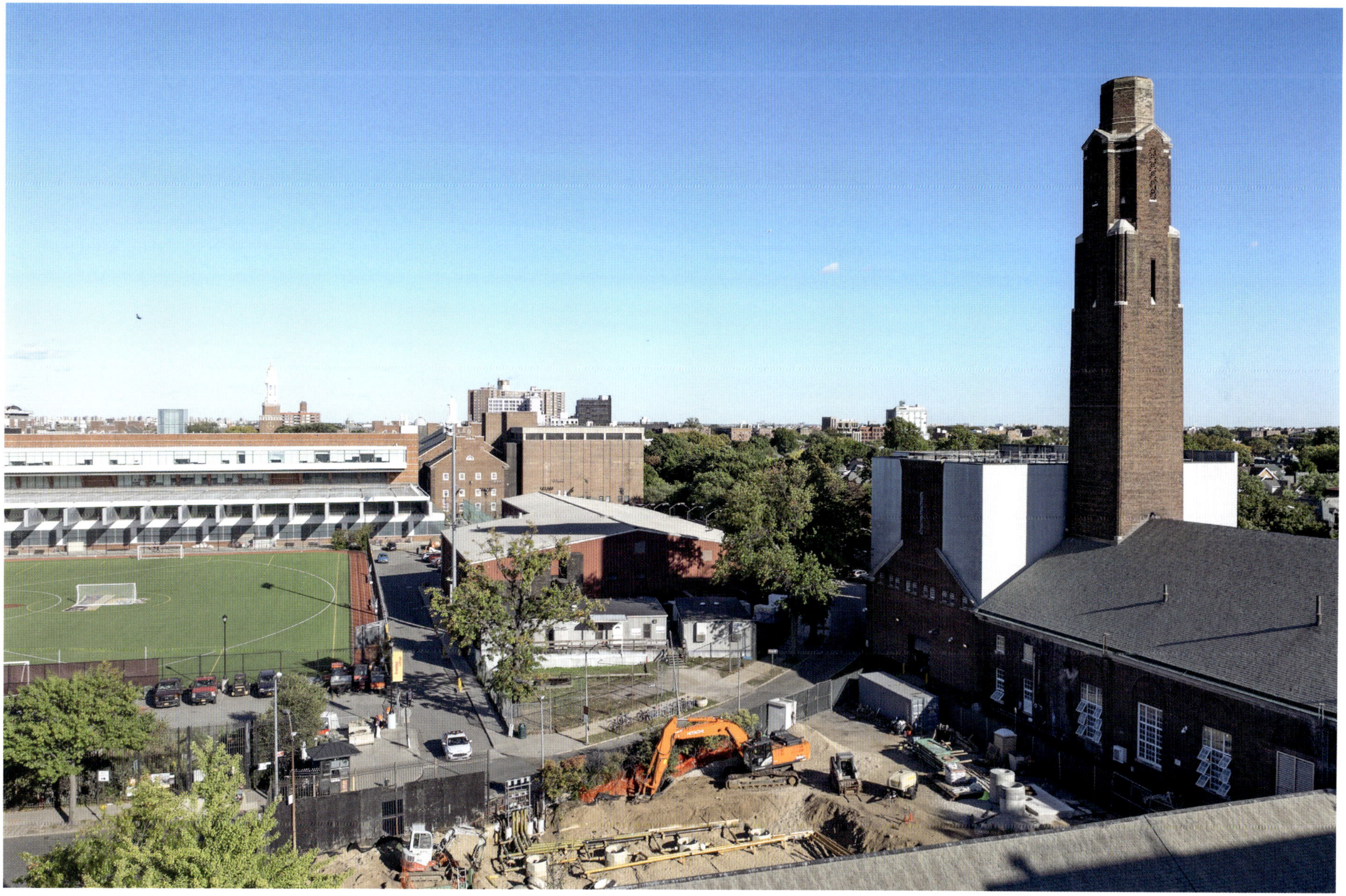

NOW: Since opening, Brooklyn College has grown from 8,000 students to 18,000. The college has added numerous modern facilities while maintaining its core architecture, like LaGuardia Hall, which was still being built when the campus opened in 1936. Since then, the Midwood neighborhood has transformed into a more diverse community, with Orthodox Jewish, South Asian, and Caribbean populations all living together and taking advantage of the vital educational institution. Over the years, Brooklyn College has graduated many notable alumni, including senators, Supreme Court Justices, Nobel and Pulitzer prize winners, and Emmy and Oscar winners as well. Shirley Chisholm, Ruth Bader Ginsburg, Bernie Sanders, Mel Brooks, Don Lemon, Itzhak Perlman, and Dr. Ruth Westheimer all received degrees from Brooklyn College.

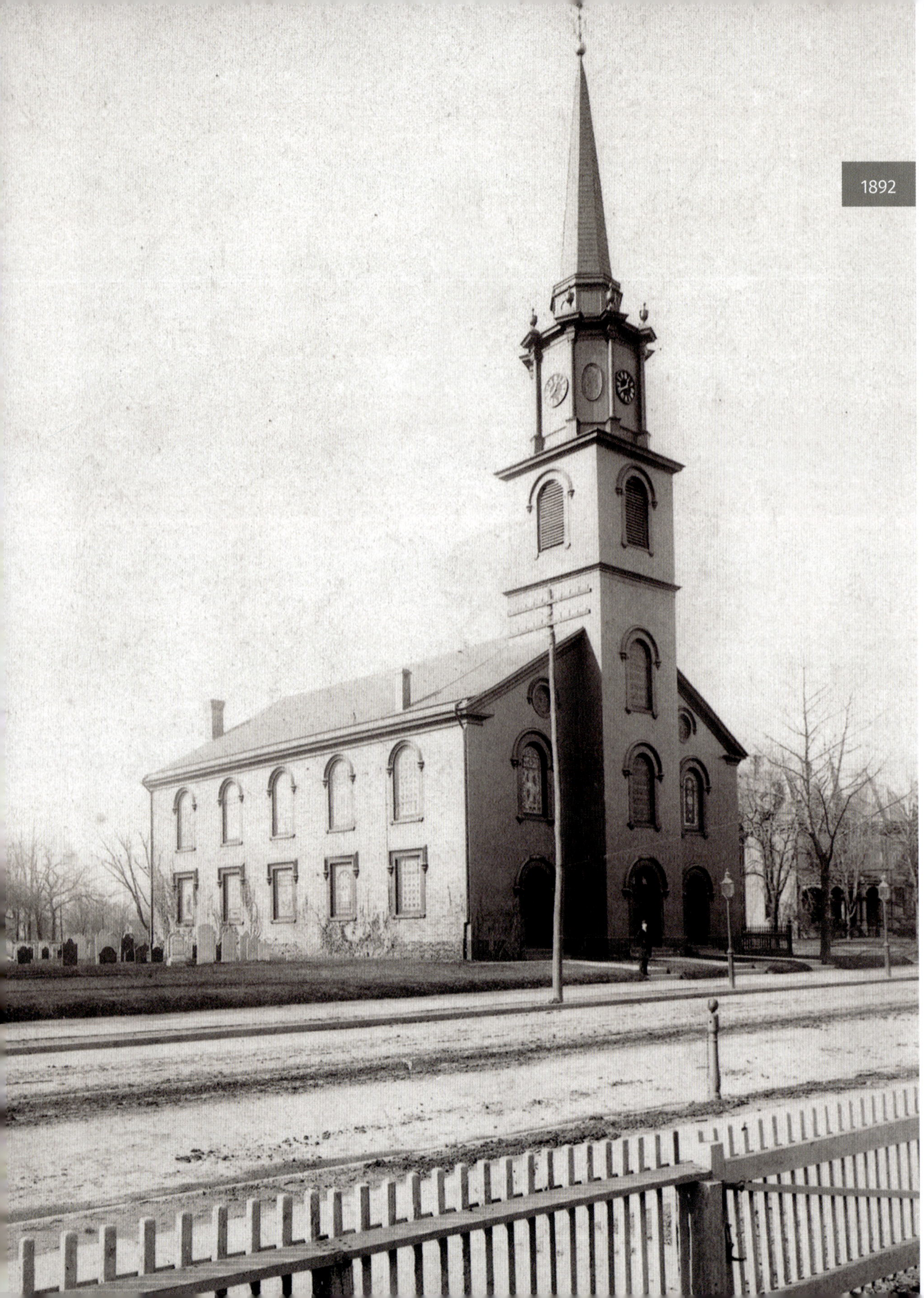

1892

FLATBUSH REFORMED DUTCH CHURCH

A link between Dutch colonialism and current civil justice

THEN: The Flatbush Reformed Dutch Church was built when Flatbush Avenue was still farmland, serving as a foundation of the Flatbush community since its founding in 1654. Established under Governor Peter Stuyvesant, it served Dutch settlers in the town originally known as Midwud. The building, which is visible in pictures throughout the nineteenth century, was completed in 1796 and was the third building on the compound. It includes a cemetery with graves of Revolutionary War soldiers who died in the 1776 Battle of Long Island, as well as the founding families of Flatbush. In 1800, the church was integral to helping Midwud transition to Flatbush, as the area went from farmland to suburbia. By 1892 the church was celebrating more than two centuries, and its thriving congregation dedicated to preserving Dutch heritage installed Tiffany stained-glass windows as a sign of its prosperity and modernity, while still serving an increasingly diverse community. Over the years, church leaders served as schoolmasters, historians, medics, and even grave diggers, involved in the entire lifecycle for those in the community.

NOW: Flatbush Reformed Dutch Church stands as a beacon of history and a tangible link to the area's colonial past. It is the only open space on what is now Flatbush Avenue and the intersection of Church Avenue, a vibrant urban landscape of restaurants, stores, offices, and high rises, crowded with people living and working nearby. The church has been refurbished over the years, as recently as 2022, with updates to the steeple, doors, and windows, making the stained glass visible from the street. Today, it still serves the community with weekly worship, and offers a tangible place to reflect on the changes in Brooklyn, while still living and breathing as a small piece of what life was like here in the seventeenth century.

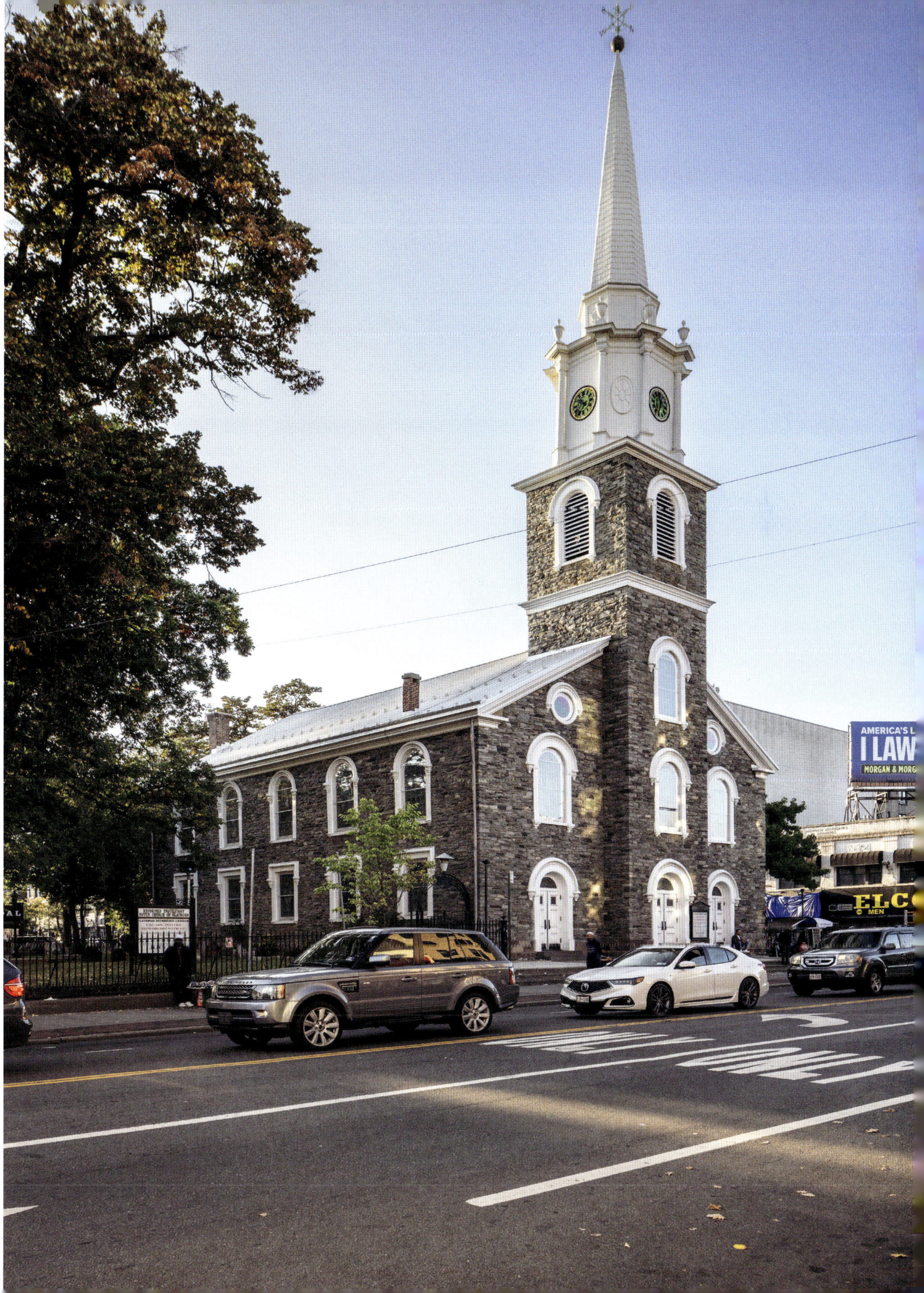

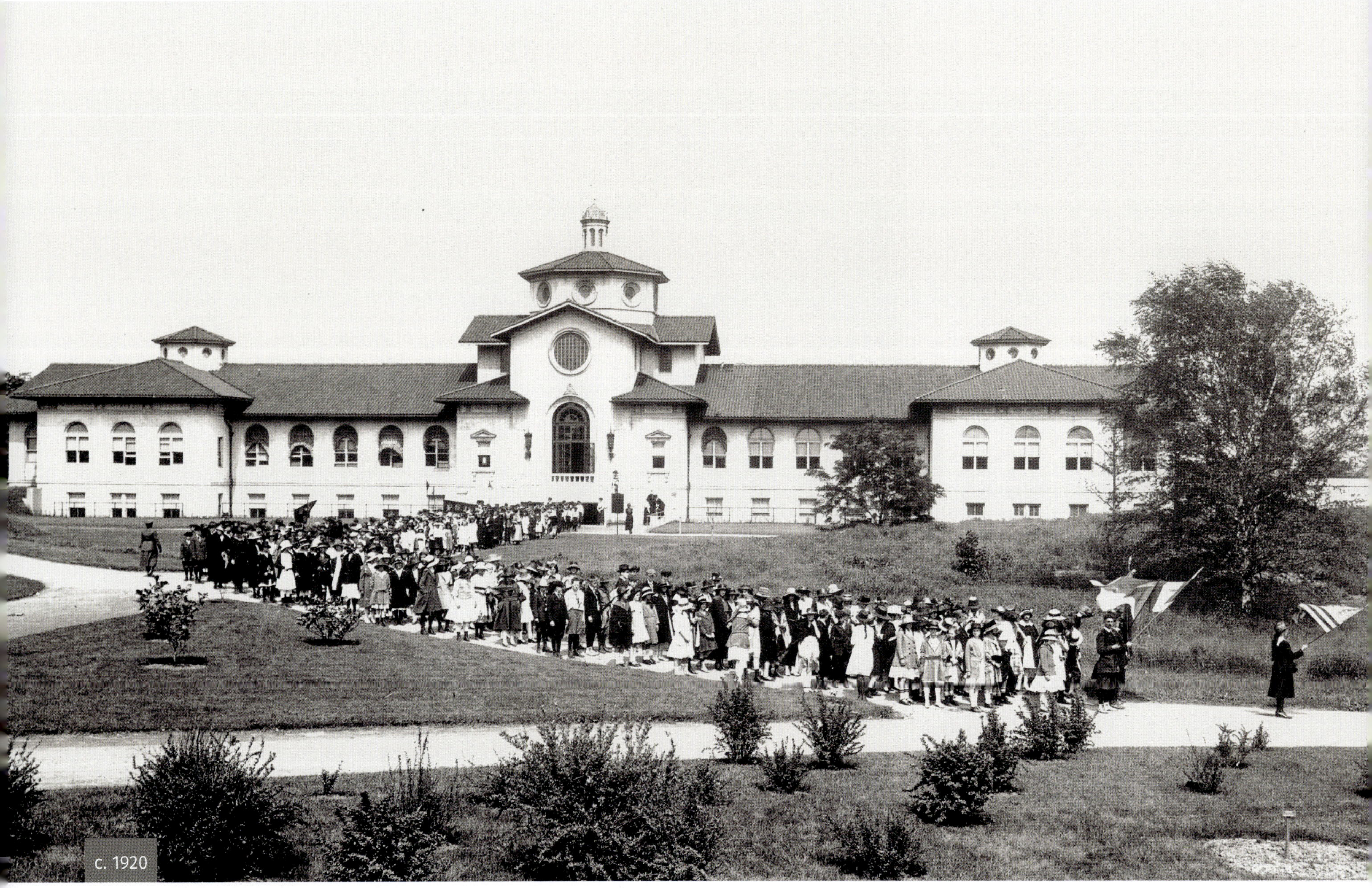

BROOKLYN BOTANIC GARDEN

A public conservatory and educational center provides four seasons of growth

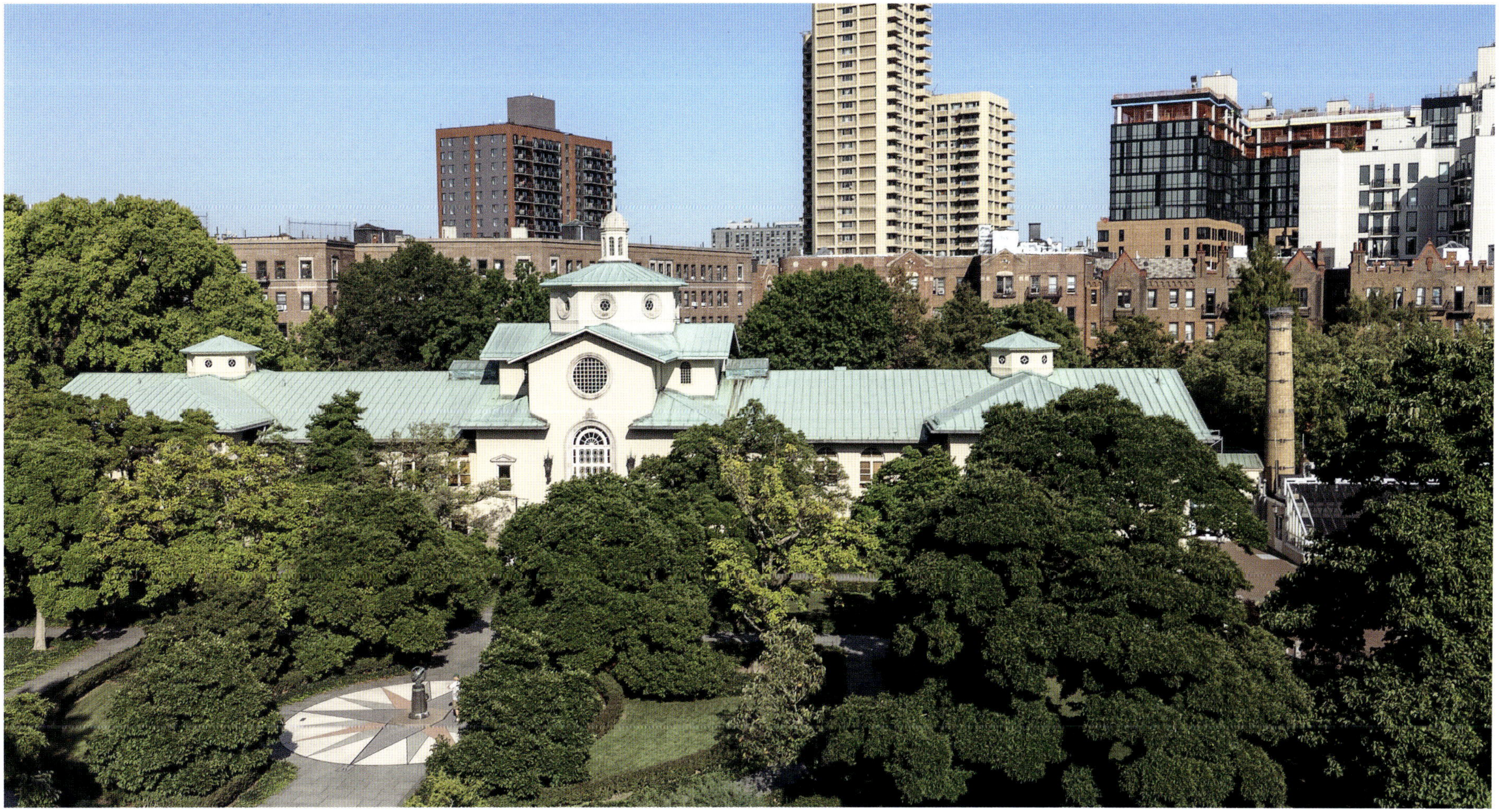

THEN: In 1897 New York State passed legislation to reserve thirty-nine acres of land (which had been carved out for Prospect Park but not yet developed) for the designation of a botanical garden. Brooklyn Botanic Garden opened in 1910, as a public conservatory and arboretum, with a site plan laid out by landscape architects the Olmsted Brothers (sons of Frederick Law Olmsted, designer of the adjacent Prospect Park, along with Calvert Vaux). The garden shares a border with Eastern Parkway, another Olmsted and Vaux project. In this picture from 1920, school children can be seen attending horticulture class in the Tuscan Revival-style Laboratory Building (as it was then known), designed by renowned architectural firm McKim, Mead & White. Educational programs aimed at the community were also responsible for helping Americans make "victory gardens" to grow their own food during World War I.

NOW: Trees cover the formerly bare lawn, making a photo like the one from 1920 impossible. Magnolia Plaza has replaced the grassy knoll from the Twenties: magnolias were first planted on this plaza in 1933 and since then have bloomed every spring – just one of the Garden's specialized tree collections, which include cherry trees and tree peonies. The botanic garden is also home to one of the first ecologically themed native flora gardens; a fragrance garden; the Steinhardt Conservatory, which includes a Bonsai Museum that has many trees over 100 years old; and a Trail of Evolution that details the complex evolutionary history of plant life on Earth. The garden still boasts a robust educational program, offering numerous horticulture, nature, and gardening classes for all ages. The Botanic Garden still run workshops for all ages on biodiversity and ecology, which teach about the wonderful plant life all around Brooklyn.

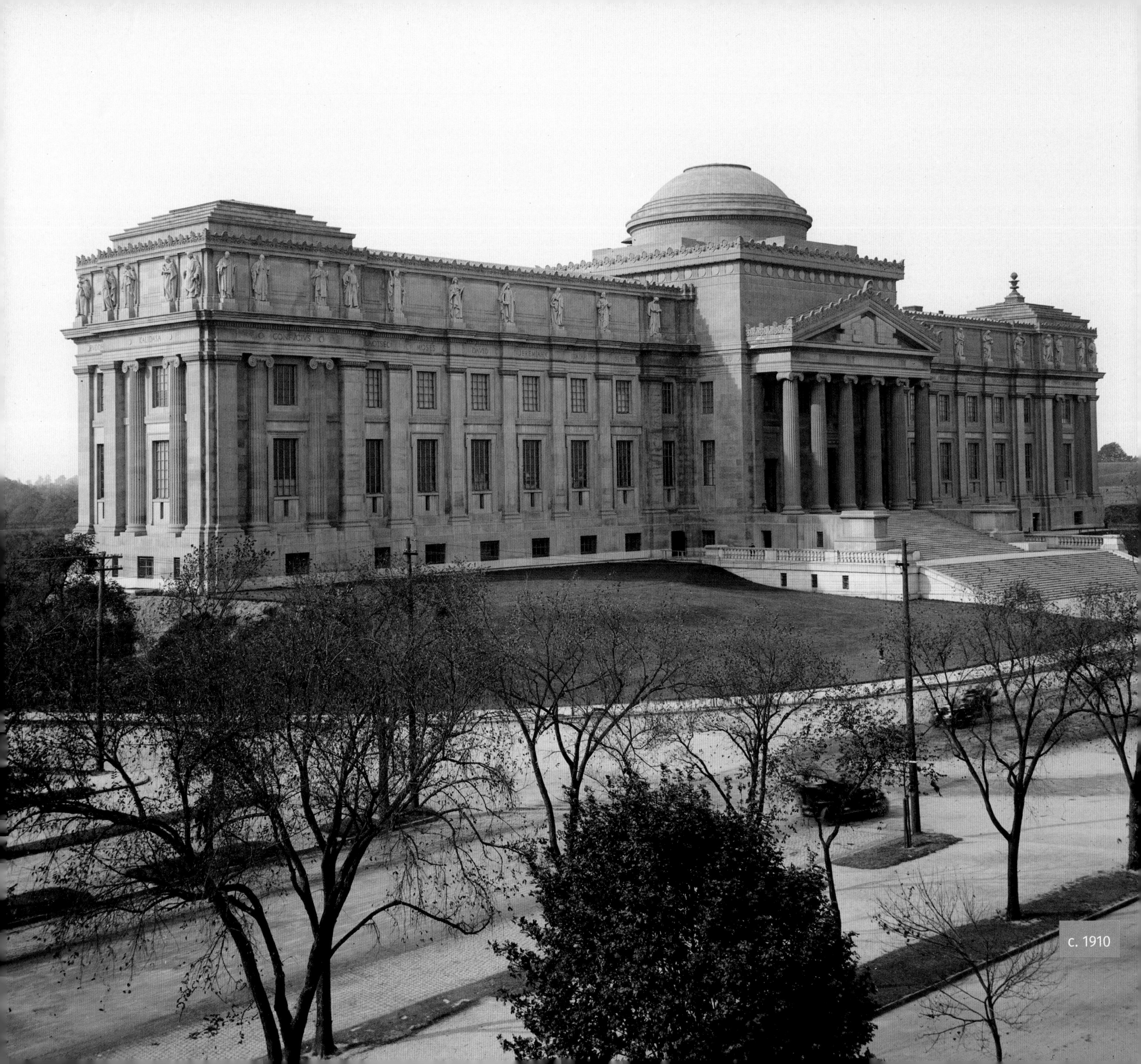

c. 1910

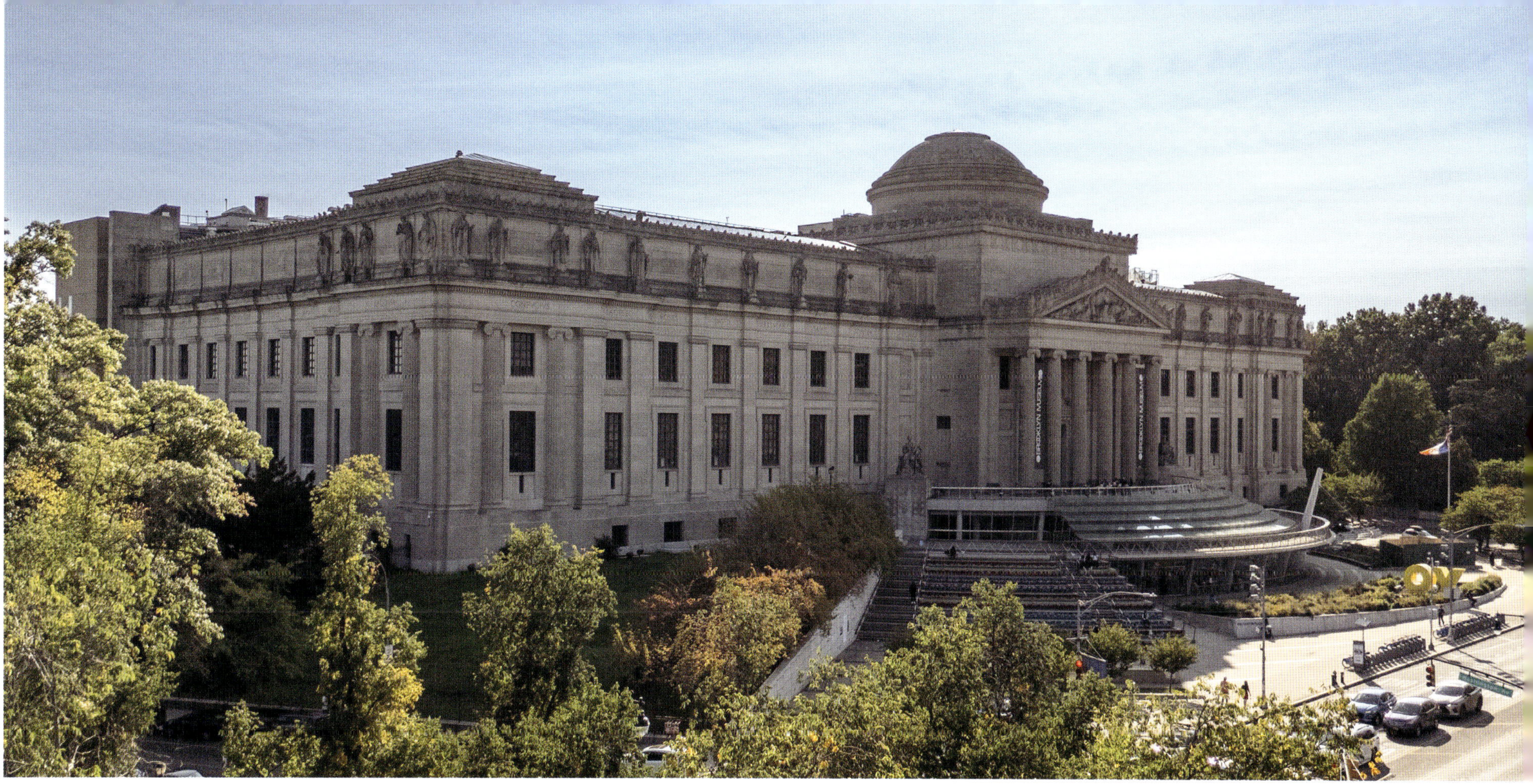

BROOKLYN MUSEUM

An apprentice library becomes home for socially relevant art by marginalized creators

THEN: The Brooklyn Museum started in 1823 as the Brooklyn Apprentices' Library Association, established by Augustus Graham and other prominent citizens to provide educational opportunities for young tradesmen. In 1841, it reorganized, expanded its mission to include the arts and sciences, and was renamed the Brooklyn Institute. It stood next to Prospect Park on Eastern Parkway, which was rapidly changing and becoming a fashionable residential area between Crown Heights and Prospect Heights. McKim, Mead & White, the architects known for creating the White City at the 1893 Chicago World's Fair (and who went on to design the original Pennsylvania Station, Manhattan Municipal Building, and many other grand Beaux-Arts masterpieces), were tasked with constructing the largest building of its kind. It was completed in 1897. In 1910, when this historic photograph was taken, the museum was known for its impressive collections of Egyptian artefacts, and significant American and European paintings, as well as collections of architectural elements and period rooms. One of the most important exhibits of the time was the Tissot collection of paintings representing the life of Jesus Christ, which was acquired in 1900.

NOW: The Brooklyn Museum name change occurred in 1926, soon after the subway connected the location with the rest of Brooklyn and New York. Today, the museum houses 500,000 objects, focused on educating a broad audience. It frequently features exhibits promoting cultural diversity and artists from underrepresented demographics. It has also become known for provocative and socially relevant exhibitions, which engage with current issues and reflect the vibrant, multicultural character of the surrounding neighborhoods—and Brooklyn as a whole.

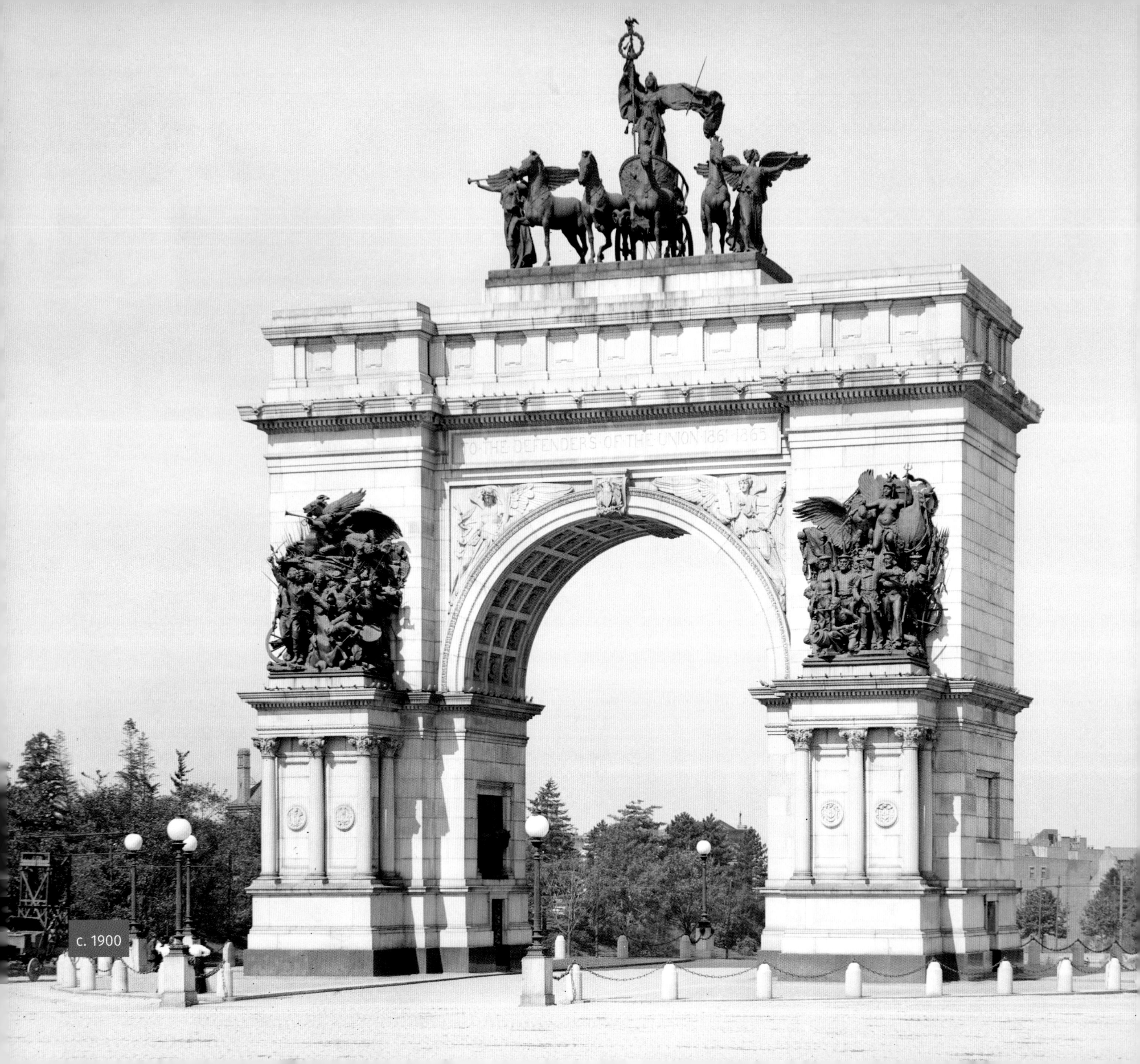

c. 1900

GRAND ARMY PLAZA

An intentional gateway becomes a vital community center

THEN: Grand Army Plaza is a public plaza that frames the entrance to Prospect Park. Park designers Frederick Law Olmsted and Calvert Vaux, who also designed Central Park, intended it to be a physical and visual transition, separating the busy streets of Brooklyn from the serenity inside the park. The original design called for wide open space, sidewalks in the shape of a Georgian cross, and a single fountain. By 1892, there was a statue of Abraham Lincoln. The huge dome between the statue and the arch was a fountain that lit up at night with colored lights, drawing an audience from all over Brooklyn. The Soldiers' and Sailors' Arch, a grand monument dedicated to Union soldiers from the Civil War—designed by John H. Duncan and featuring many impressive bronze creations by Frederick MacMonnies—would soon be completed. In 1915, the city built subway stations under the plaza, and the electronic fountain was removed. The Bailey Fountain opened in 1932, when philanthropist Frank Bailey built the three connected fountains in tribute to his wife. The Abraham Lincoln statue was relocated to another location, replaced with a bust of John F. Kennedy.

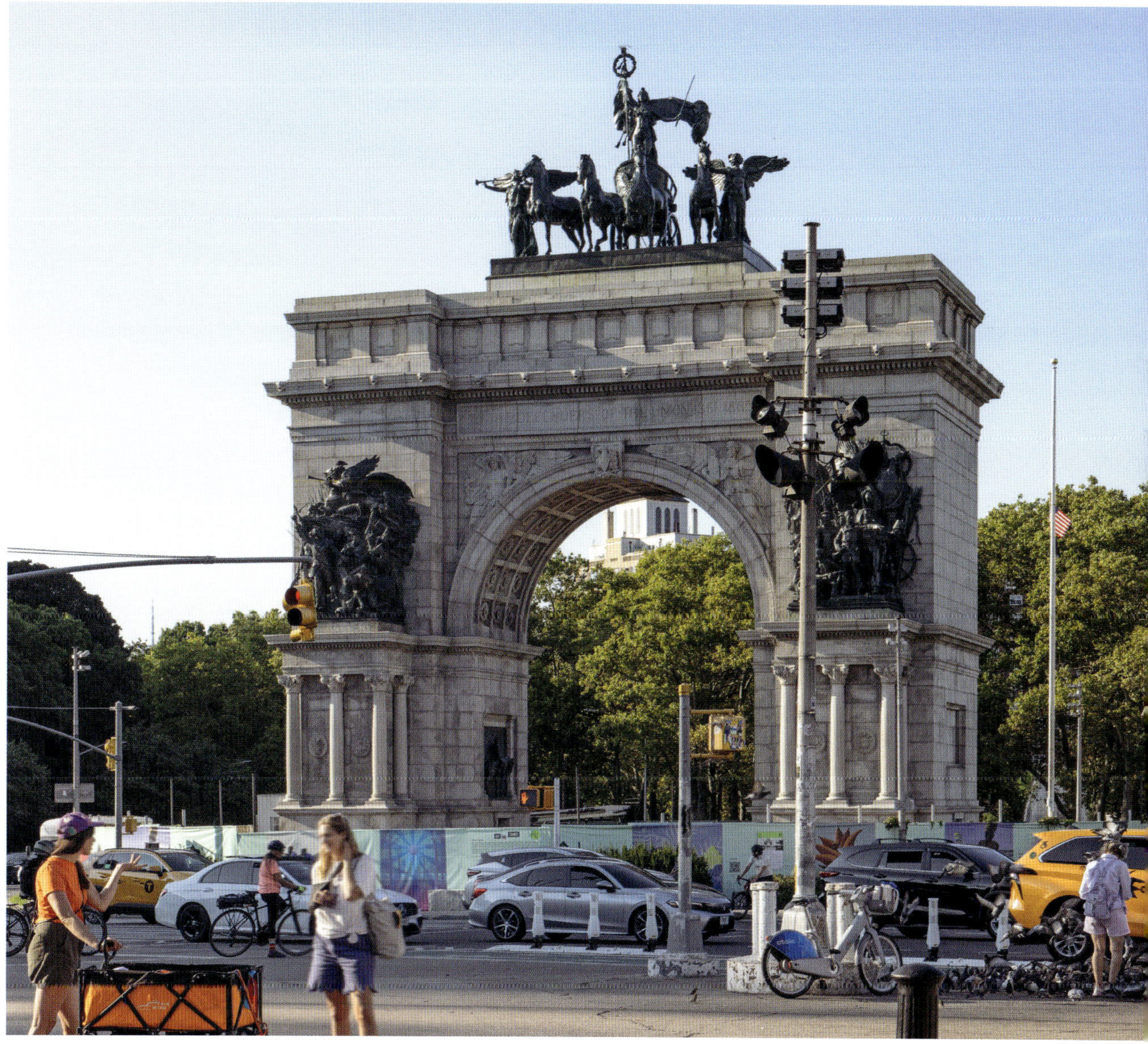

NOW: Today, nine different streets link at the Grand Army Plaza, and the city is working to transform the traffic patterns to cut down on car and bus traffic. It is the home of one of Brooklyn's biggest farmers markets on Saturdays, showing this plaza's continual commitment to serving its local community members.

But, as it did in the American Revolution when it served as a critical path between developed Brooklyn and the open space beyond, it still functions as a graceful transition from the bustle of urban life to a place of quiet contemplation.

BROOKLYN PUBLIC LIBRARY (MAIN BRANCH)

A thriving community resource that was well worth the wait

1913

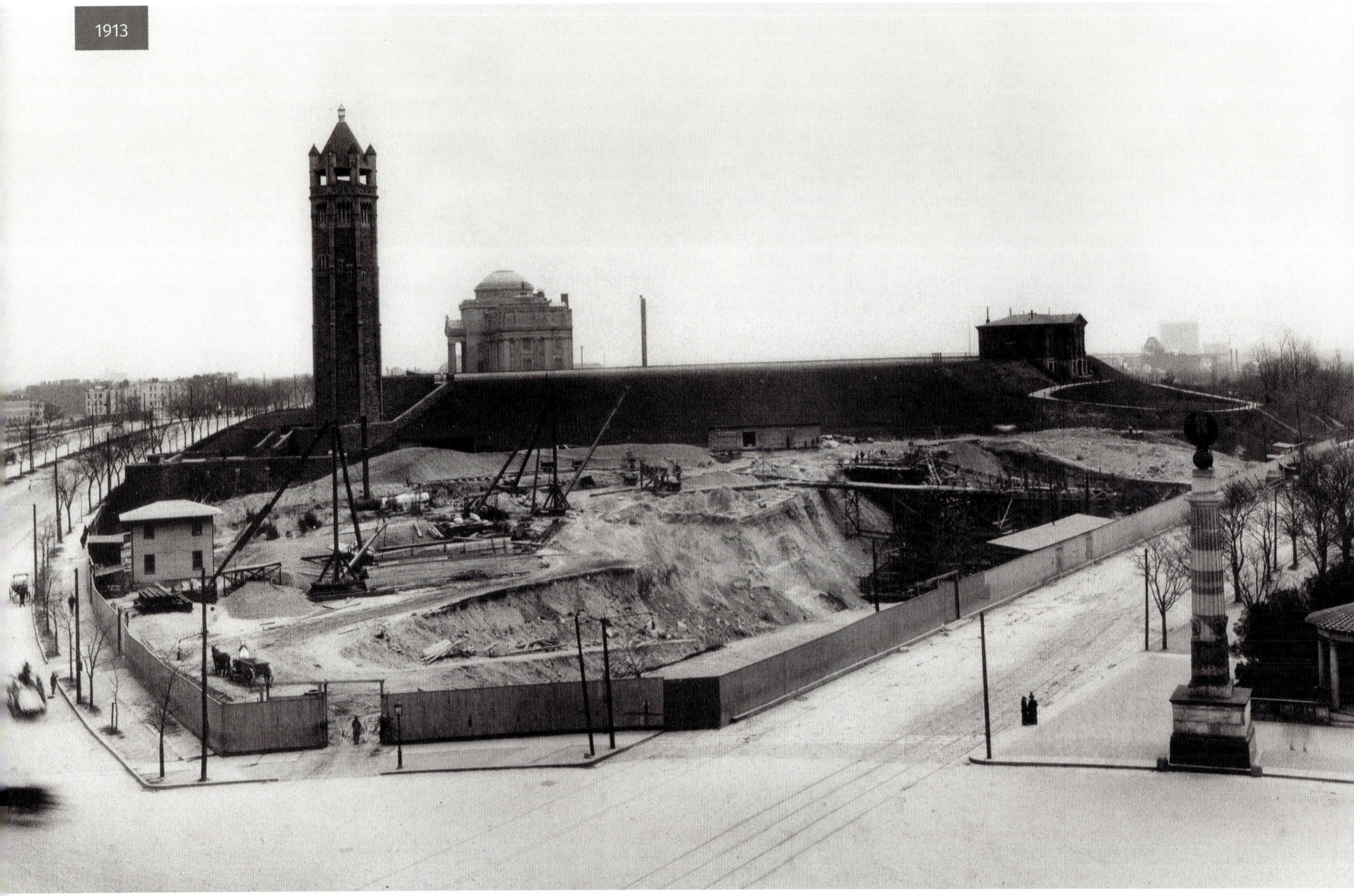

THEN: The main branch of the Brooklyn Public Library, officially known as the Central Library, broke ground in 1912 as part of the City Beautiful movement, and the expansion of public libraries in the early twentieth century led by Andrew Carnegie. Although this library was not part of the Carnegie movement, the construction was part of the broader national impetus to expand access to information and education for the public. In spite of the national prioritization and Brooklyn's interest in a grand monumental structure, the library wouldn't open until after World War II and the image here shows the building still under construction. The building was eventually completed in 1941 by architect Raymond F. Almirall, with a limestone facade and an impressive fifty-foot-high entrance portico completed with Art Deco styling.

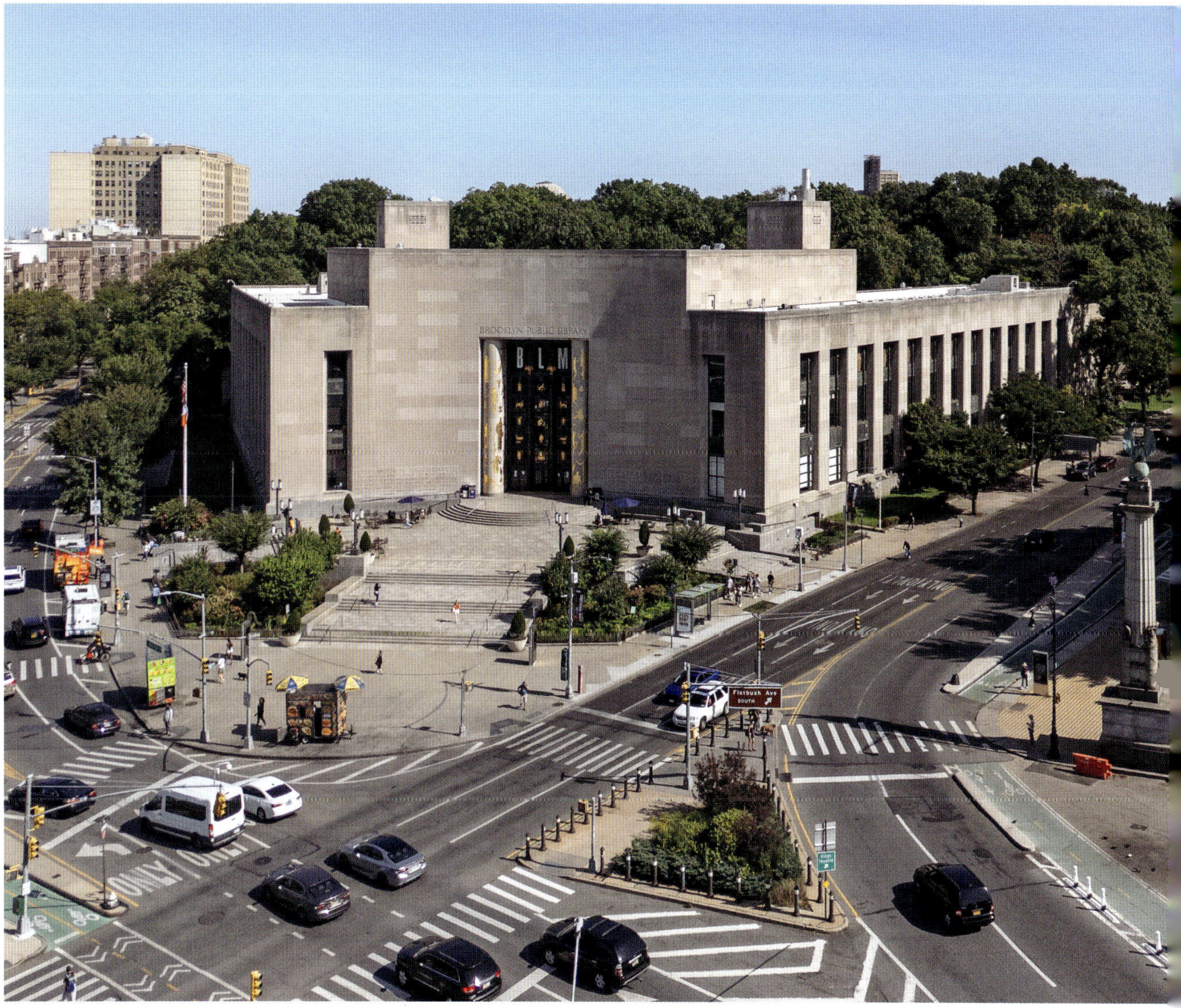

BELOW: This eagle was 'flown' from the demolished Brooklyn Eagle building to stand guard over the entry to the library, where the archives of the newspaper are now housed.

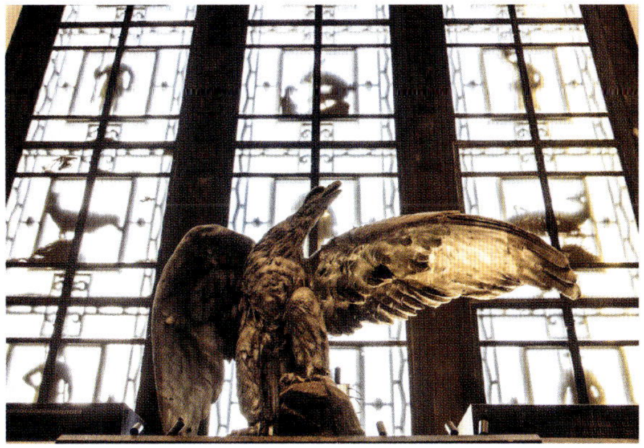

NOW: The Central Library is still an important part of the fabric of Brooklyn. The building underwent a renovation in 2021 and holds 1.7 million materials, including over 33,000 books, 1,600 archival collections, and 50,000 photographs. Current offerings include computer labs, digital resources, and Wi-Fi access for all visitors. There are special collections like the Brooklyn Collection, which preserves the borough's history, as well as a business and career center, which offers resources for job seekers and entrepreneurs. Open spaces inside offer author talks and educational programs for children and adults, and the outside has also been renovated with outdoor seating and performance space, making the open book design even more open to all.

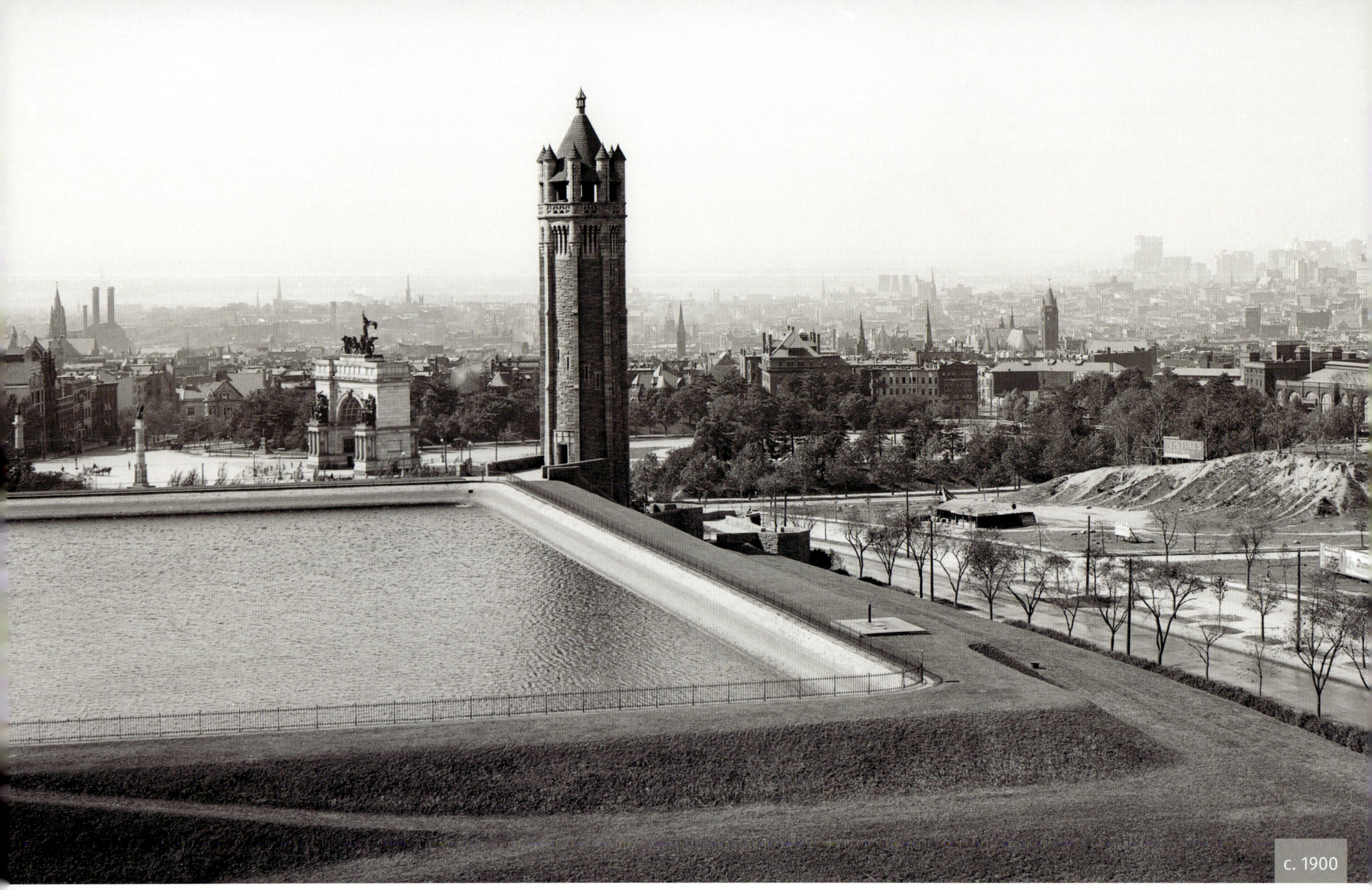

c. 1900

MOUNT PROSPECT RESERVOIR

The once vital water source made way for the library

THEN: The Mount Prospect Reservoir was a critical component of Brooklyn's early water supply system, built in 1856 to distribute water through the pipes and pumping stations to Brooklyn homes and businesses. Designed by engineer James P. Kirkwood, the reservoir was located on Mount Prospect, because this second-highest point in Brooklyn provided an ideal elevation for the gravity-fed water distribution system required. Fed by the Ridgewood Reservoir and various streams and ponds on Long Island, the Mount Prospect Reservoir originally had a capacity of about twenty million gallons. By 1868, the increase of people and industry required more output, and the reservoir was expanded to hold 150 million gallons of water. In 1891, a magnificent Romanesque-style pumping station known as the Brooklyn Waterworks was built to meet demand, and an eighty-two-foot pink-granite water tower followed soon after in 1900 near the new Grand Army Plaza Arch.

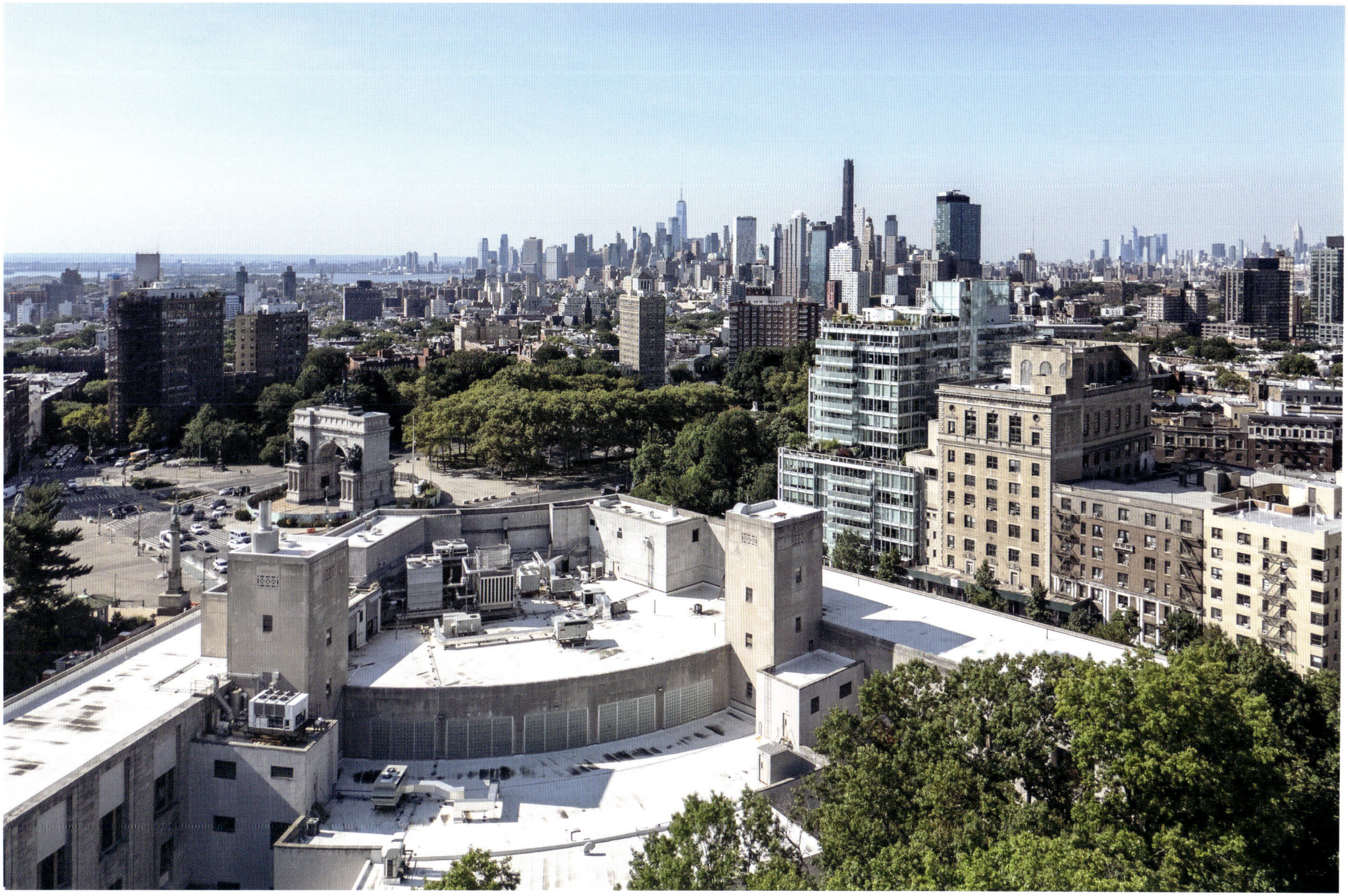

NOW: In spite of the technological advancements, the water supplied by the reservoir failed to meet the growing city's needs, and New York City looked beyond the Mount Prospect Reservoir to avoid a water crisis. It was eventually decommissioned and drained in 1940, and the city developed Mount Prospect Park and the main branch of the Brooklyn Public Library on the land.

Today, the original hill and walking paths are still part of the grounds so visitors can walk in the steps of history. As is visible in the photo, Mount Prospect Park still offers the same clear views of the Grand Army Plaza Arch, Brooklyn, Manhattan, the New York Harbor, and New Jersey, just like it has since the Revolutionary War.

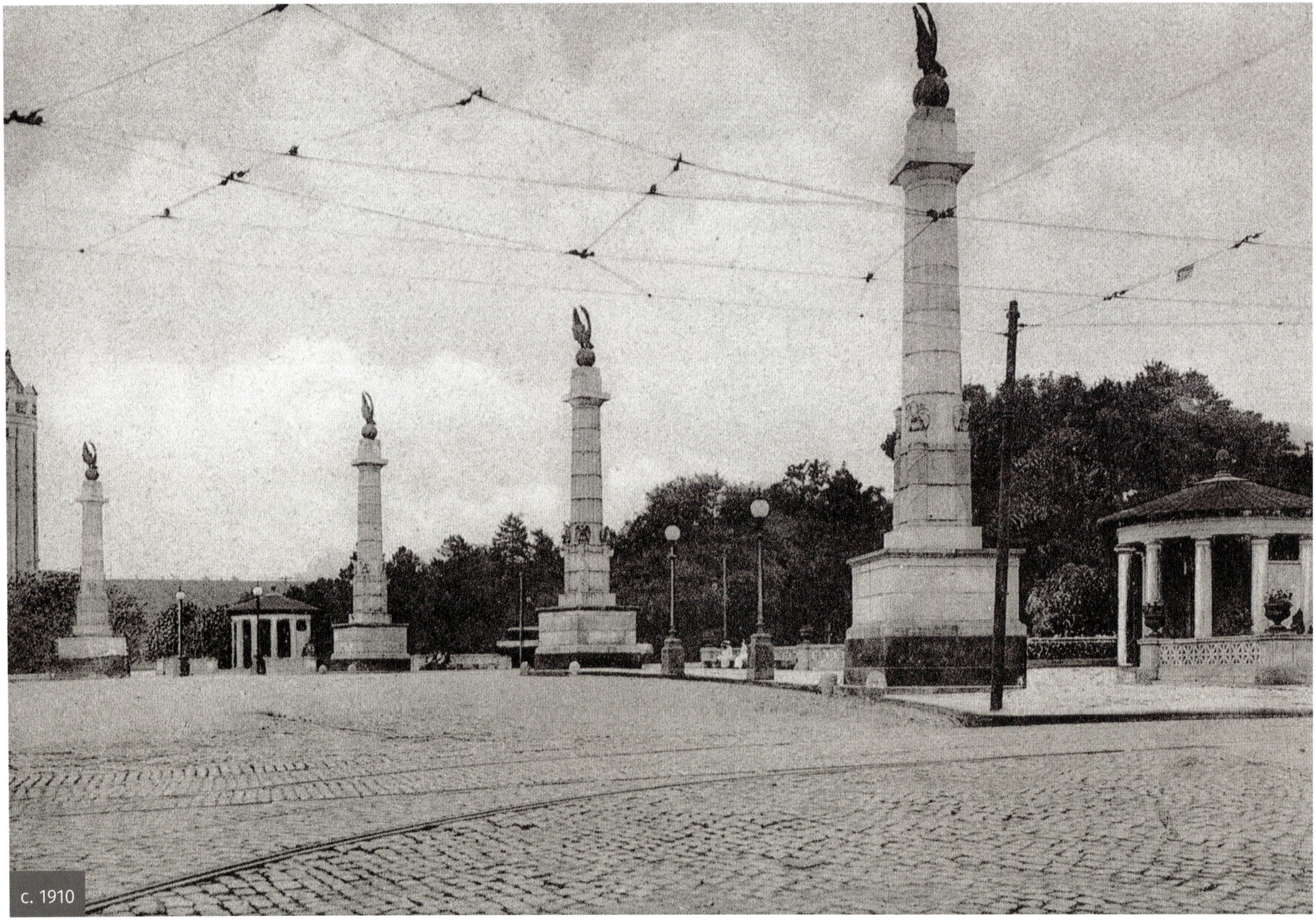

c. 1910

PROSPECT PARK ENTRANCE

A natural entrance evolved along with the community's needs

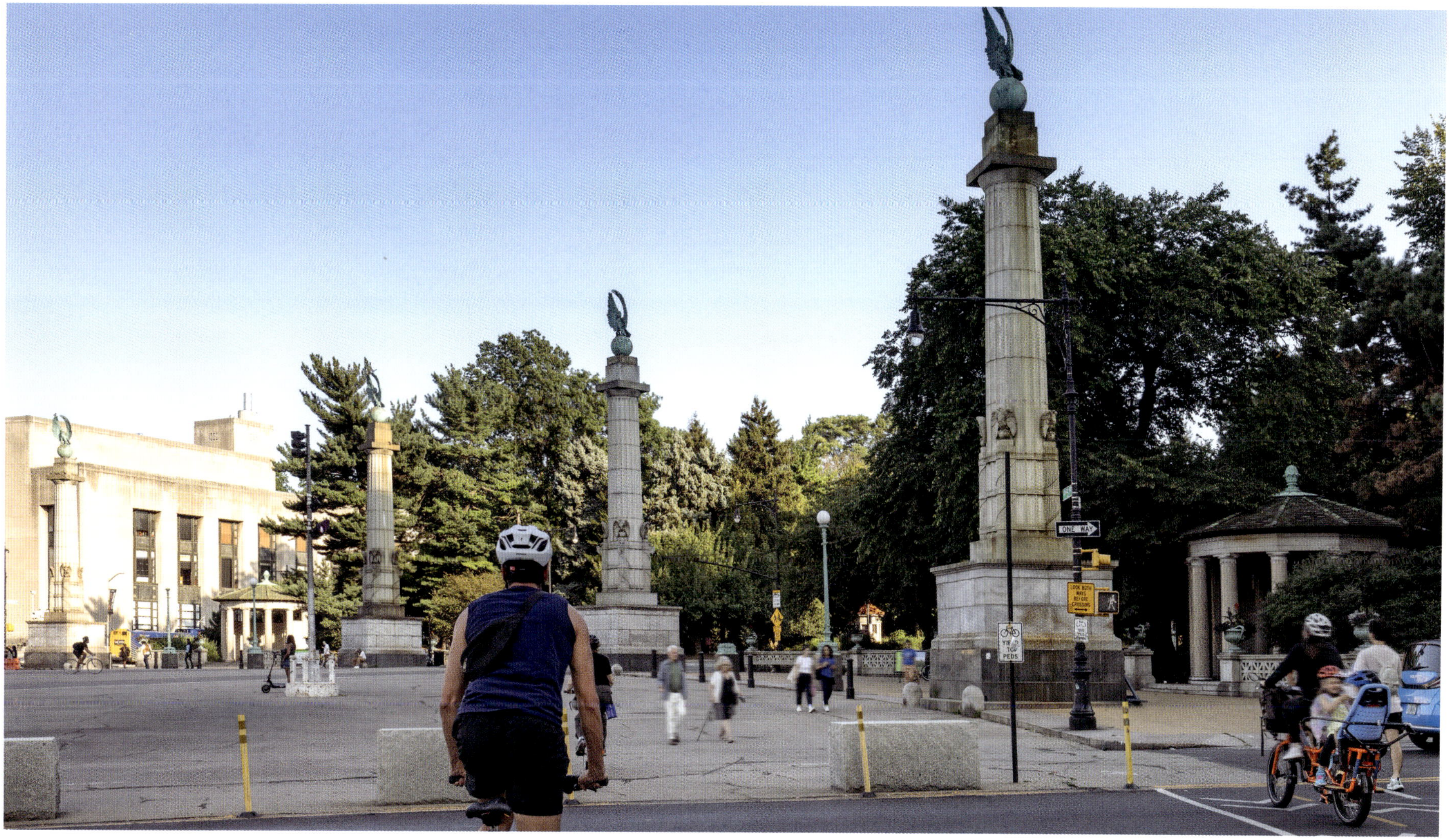

THEN: When Prospect Park first opened in 1867, the main entrance at Grand Army Plaza was a broad, tree-lined, naturalistic approach, which exemplified the Olmsted and Vaux philosophy of pastoral landscapes within urban environments. By 1910, there was a growing trend towards more formal, classical designs in public spaces, and creating a grander entrance to the park was a way to highlight Brooklyn's sophistication and importance after the consolidation with New York City in 1898. City planners sought to create a more impressive environment, and so they added four 54-foot marble columns topped with bronze eagles for a symbolic, patriotic touch. The renovation was part of a larger project that added more structure for the traffic around the entrance to the park.

NOW: Today, the columns remain and the eagles serve as sentinels for the Soldiers' and Sailors' Arch. While the entrance generally serves as a traffic circle, it closes to cars twice a week for a farmers market, bringing fresh produce and local goods into the neighborhood.

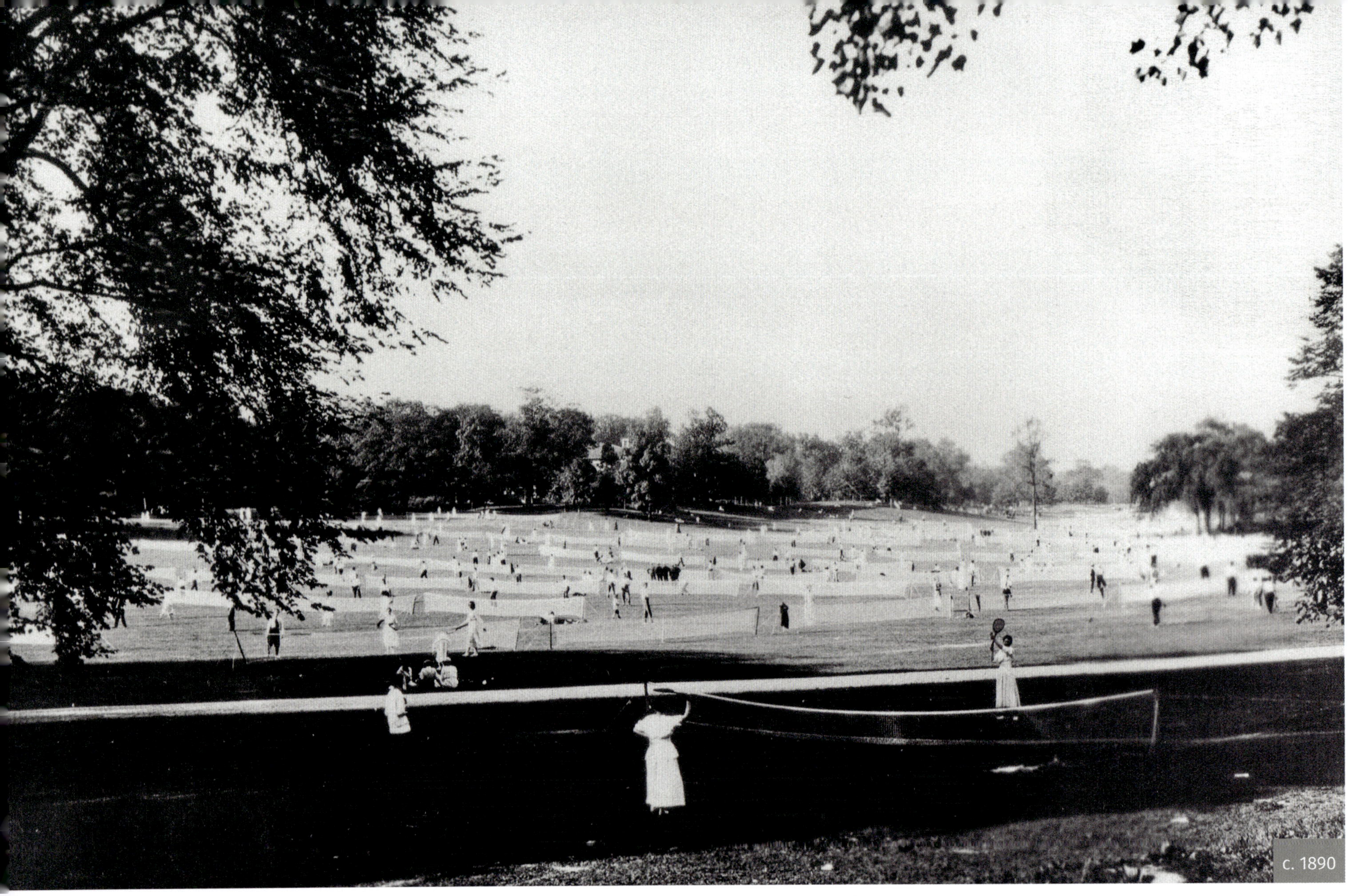

c. 1890

PROSPECT PARK LONG MEADOW

A center for play for many generations in the open space of Prospect Park

THEN: The ninety-acre Long Meadow, free of hills, streams, trees, or buildings, was an essential central feature envisioned by Olmsted and Vaux in 1867 when they designed Prospect Park. The juxtaposition of vast open space in the midst of Brooklyn was intended to provide urbanites with a taste of countryside tranquility. In the late nineteenth century, a lawn tennis craze gripped the city, and by 1910 there were 300 grass courts marked out on the meadow. This mile-long stretch of grass was the longest unbroken meadow in an urban park in the United States. However, this large grassland required a substantial army of groundskeepers who maintained the fields with horse-drawn tractors, as well as a large flock of gentle sheep who helped with the upkeep and accepted affection and treats from children who came to the park to play.

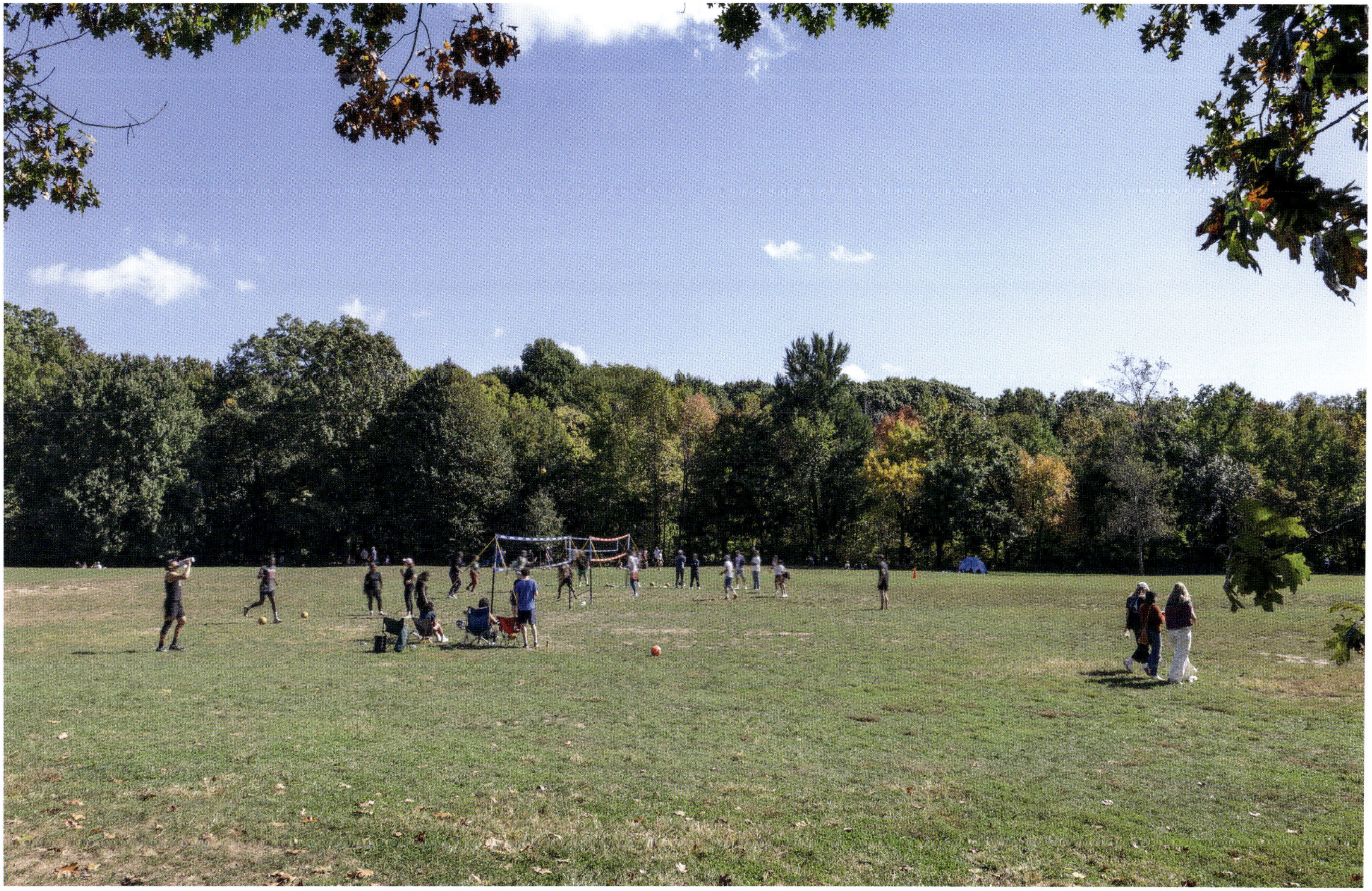

NOW: The combination of recreational use and rural aesthetics perfectly captured the designers' passion to provide locals with the best of both worlds. And as Brooklyn has built up around it, the open space has become even more significant to the lives of Brooklynites now. Today, picnickers and sunbathers have replaced the sheep, while volleyball, spike ball, hacky sack, and kan jam players fill the grass, with people constantly adapting the space to suit their preferred activities. Jogging and walking paths surround the area. Parts of the meadow are intentionally planted and managed to increase the biodiversity of the area and better equip it to handle its ecological responsibilities. But one thing remains constant: the open nature of the meadow allows for spontaneous play and community interaction, exactly as Olmsted and Vaux envisioned.

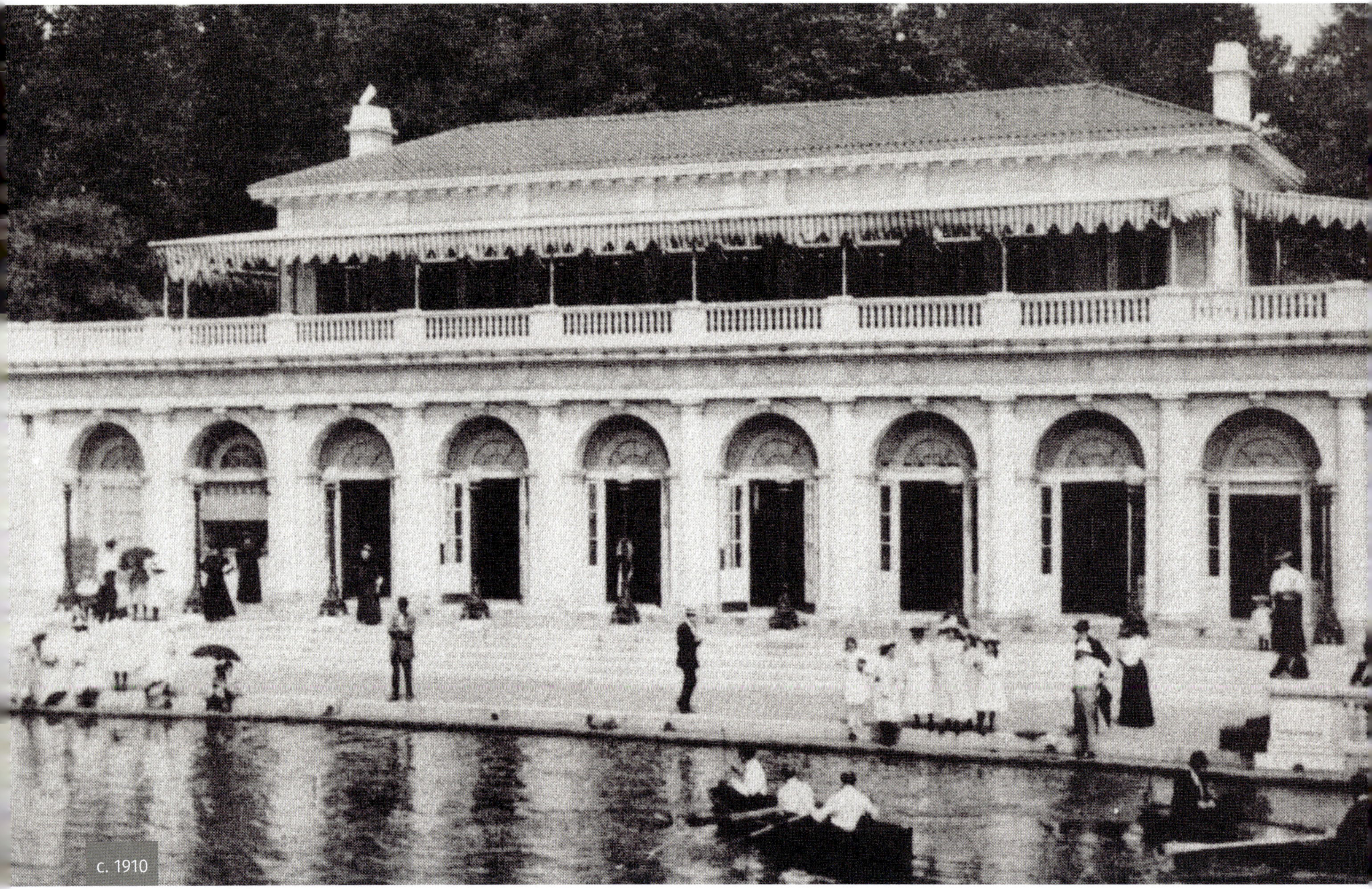

c. 1910

PROSPECT PARK BOATHOUSE

Historic boathouse transforms into an Audubon Center for nature education

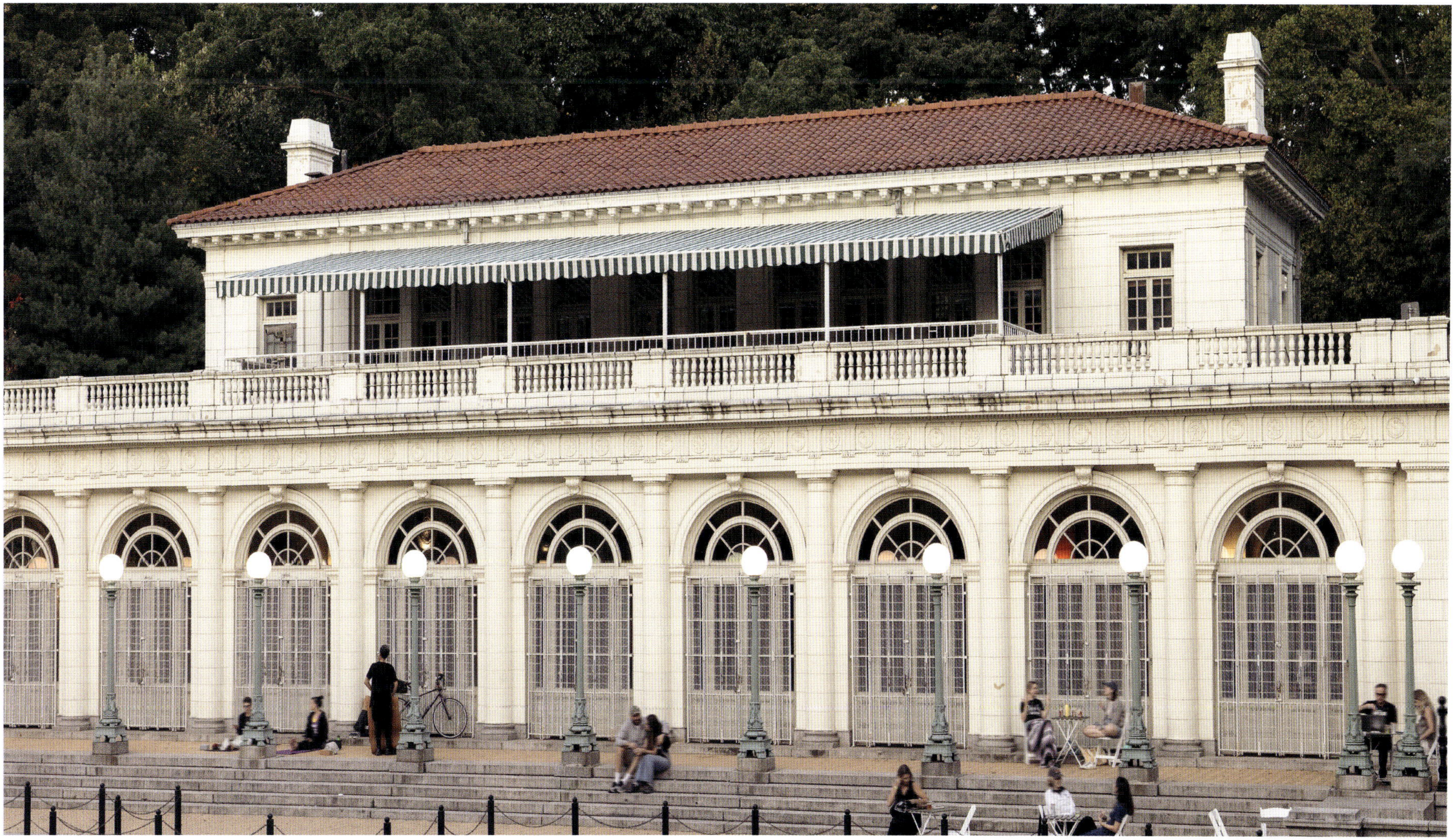

THEN: The Prospect Park Boathouse was built in 1905 by Helmle, Huberty and Hudswell, a prominent Brooklyn architectural firm also responsible for the Tennis House (in the park) and Greenpoint Savings Bank. Their work favored the Beaux-Arts style, which was popular at the turn of the century, and they designed the boathouse in that style, with ornate terracotta details and grand arches. By 1910, the boathouse had become a popular attraction for Brooklynites to rent rowboats to explore the sixty acres of man-made waterways in the park, and then enjoy refreshments when they returned. The boathouse was almost torn down in the Sixties, but thanks to fast action from conservationists, the boathouse was made a Historic Landmark in 1965, and then officially added to the National Register of Historic Places in 1972.

NOW: Today, over a century later, the Prospect Park Boathouse continues to be a favorite landmark within the park, though its function has evolved. After falling into disrepair in the mid-twentieth century, the building was restored in the Seventies and then again in 1999. Now, it's available for special-event rental and has become a popular wedding venue. It also serves as the Audubon Center at the Boathouse—the first urban Audubon Center in the nation—where visitors come to learn about the park's birds. Interactive exhibits on bird watching, ecology, and conservation offer educational and ecological programming to nature enthusiasts and local schools and families. While boat rentals are no longer available directly from the boathouse, the building's stunning architecture remains a draw—especially the terrace, which offers stunning views in every season.

PROSPECT PARK CONCERT GROVE

A Victorian concert space develops into a venue for diverse cultural enrichment

THEN: Developed in the 1870s, the Prospect Park Music Grove was designed as a formal, European-style garden and performance space within the larger, more naturalistic park. Landscape architects Olmsted and Vaux envisioned the space as the artistic center of Prospect Park—a cultural focal point and elegant setting for outdoor concerts and socializing on the edge of a lagoon. The Concert Grove Pavilion, also known as the Oriental Pavilion, anchored the area and served as a restaurant and meeting place. This view from 1880 shows the main terrace near the lagoon, where musicians played on Music Island and the sound carried over the water and through the park. Just beyond the steps and along the terrace is a sculpture garden with a musical theme. Busts of classical composers, including Ludwig van Beethoven, Wolfgang Amadeus Mozart, Carl Maria von Weber, and Edvard Greig, still stand proudly along with a statue of Abraham Lincoln that was moved from Grand Army Plaza.

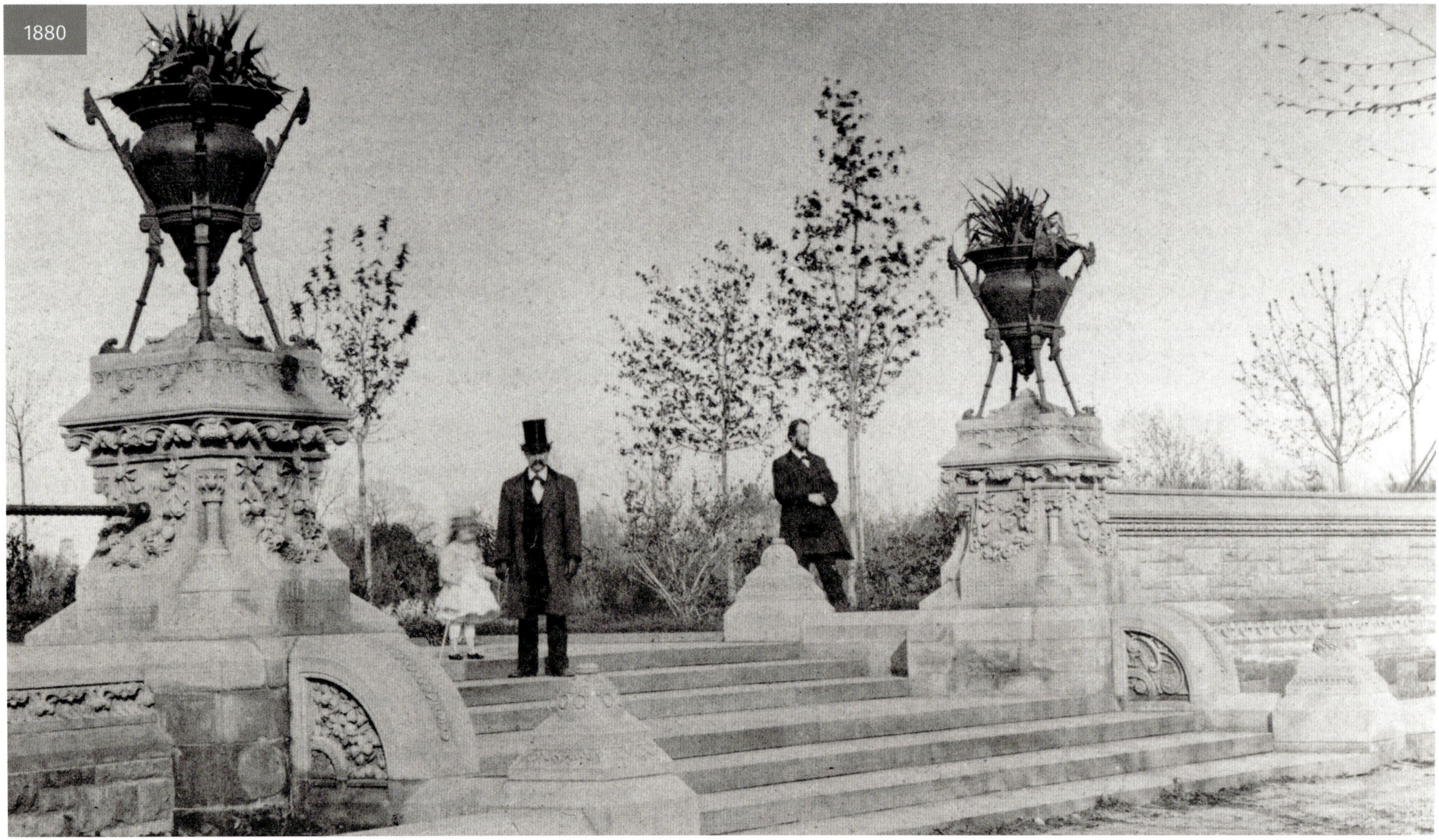
1880

NOW: The Concert Grove Pavilion was destroyed by fire in 1974 and was refurbished in 2021 when pandemic heath practices made every possible outdoor space prime real estate. The Prospect Park Alliance secured $2,000,000 in funding and worked diligently to bring back every original detail, including intricate wooden molding at the eaves, and terne-coated stainless-steel roof shingles. The Prospect Park Alliance was awarded an Excellence in Design designation for the restoration of the Concert Grove Pavilion. Today, the area still provides a center for culture and connection within the park. Offerings include exercise classes, movies, and food festivals. Local skateboarders have also adopted the area, sharing it happily with visitors who come looking for many kinds of cultural enrichment, which go far beyond the music first envisioned for the space.

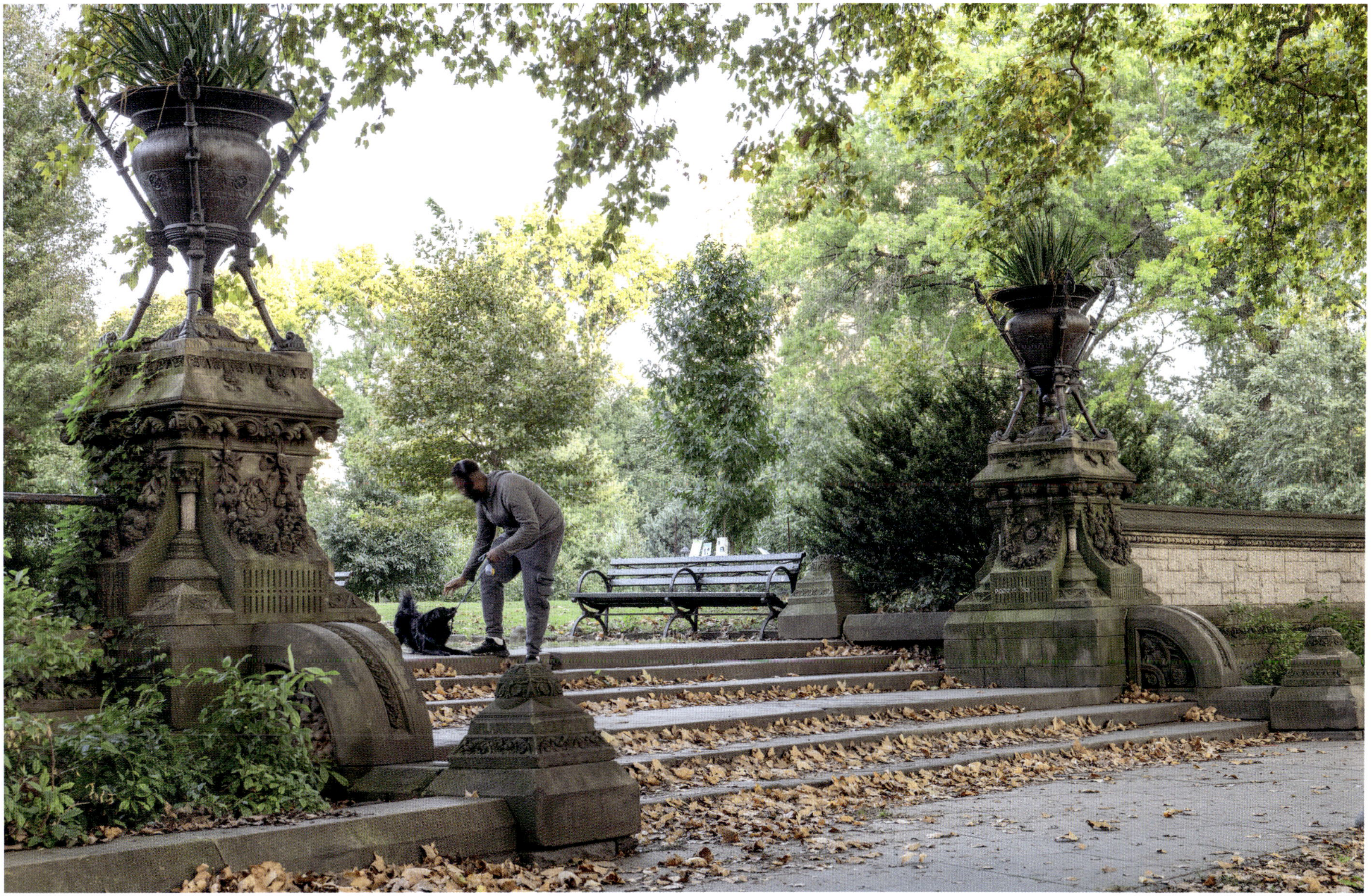

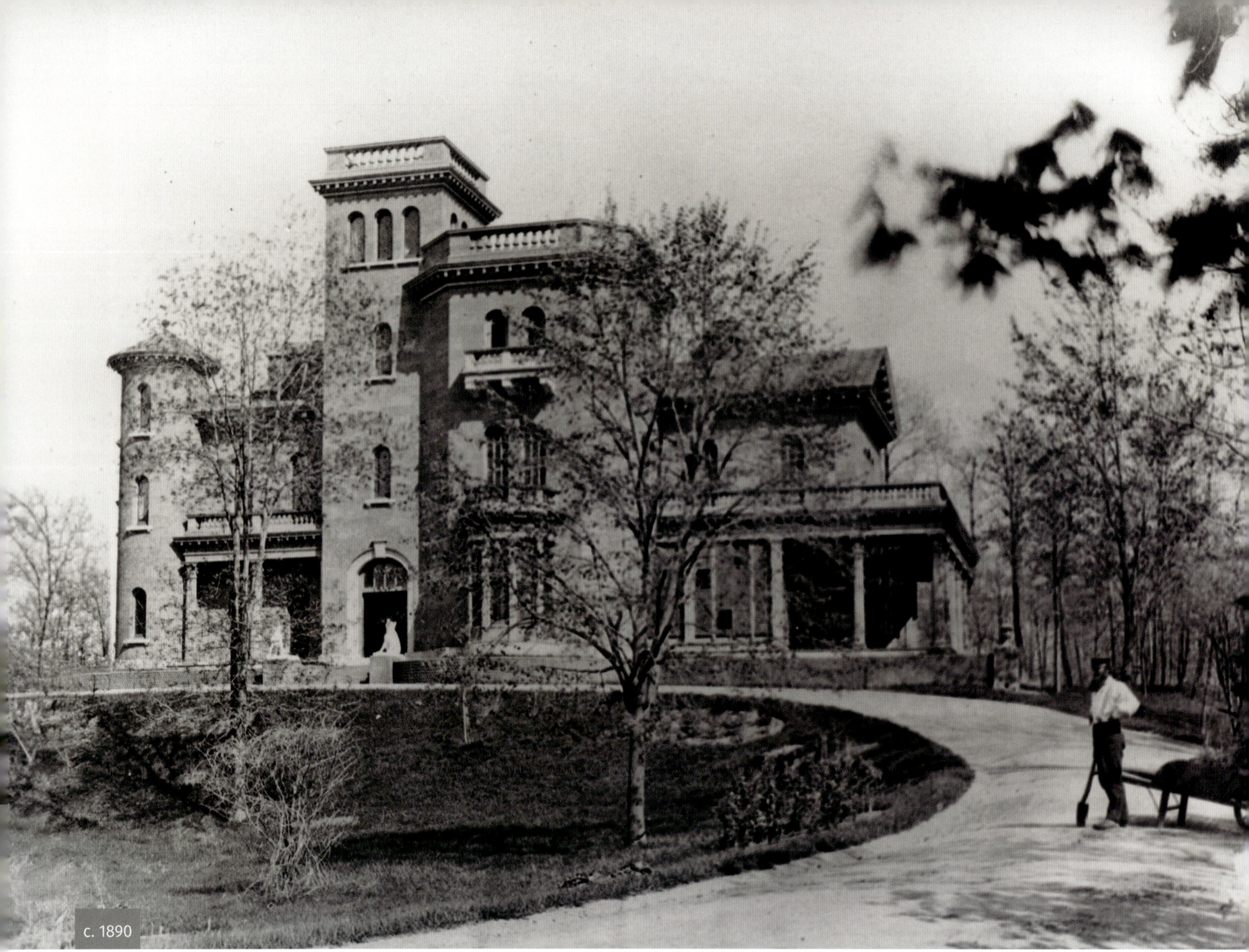
c. 1890

LITCHFIELD VILLA

This formerly private home now houses the Prospect Park Alliance

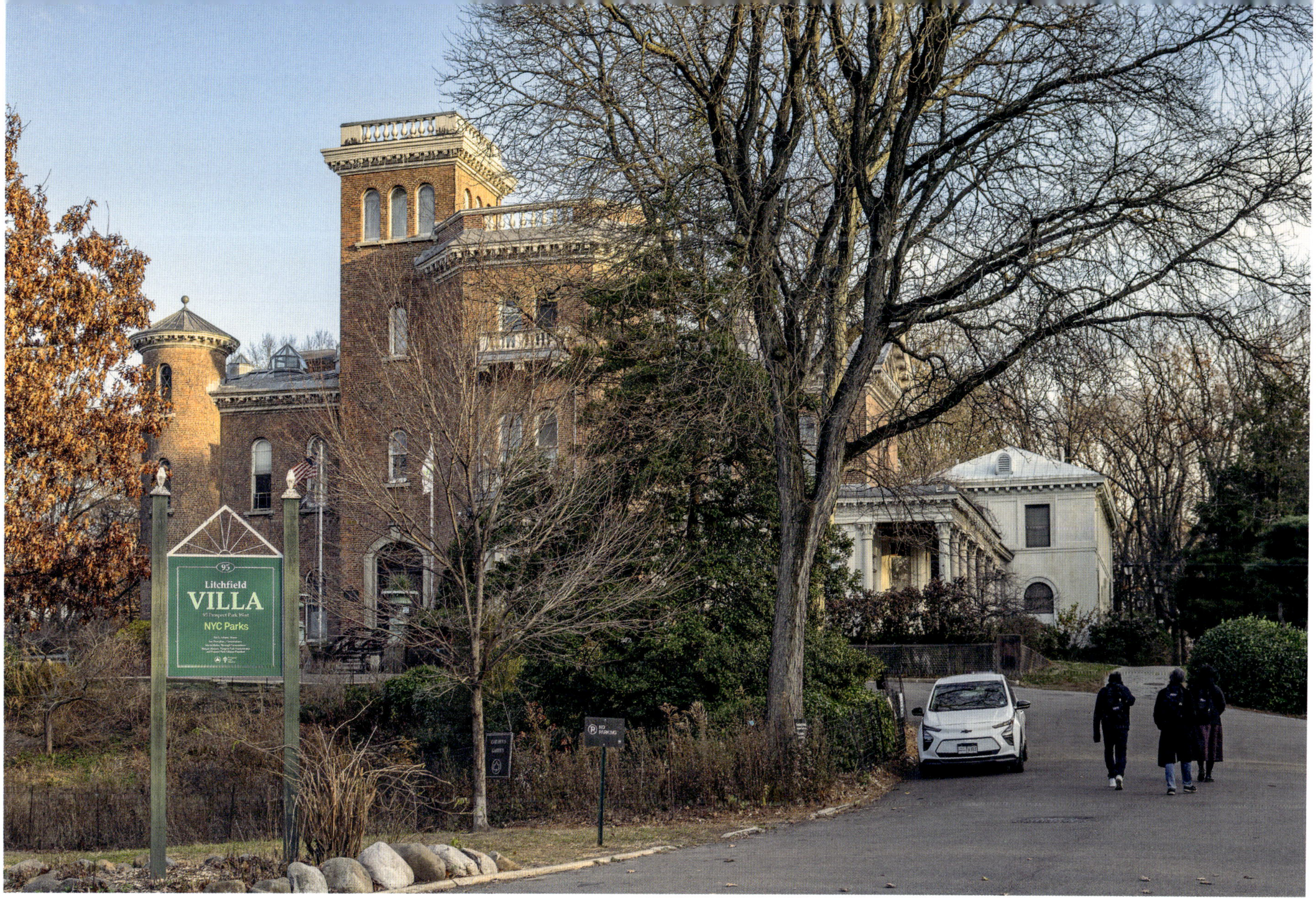

THEN: This Italianate mansion, built between 1854 and 1857, was a country estate for railroad and real estate developer Edwin Clark Litchfield, who is credited with creating the Park Slope neighborhood when he bought the parcel of land that sloped down below his property and subdivided it for new homes. The villa was designed by the architect Alexander Jackson Davis, and represents the style popular at the time—in fact its unique features make it one of the best examples of that style in the United States. When Prospect Park was created in the 1860s, the villa remained separate, then in 1883 the family sold it to the city of Brooklyn. Over the decades, the building has served various purposes, including headquarters for the park administration and a local police precinct. While the interior is not often open to the public, the asymmetrical design, prominent tower, and ornate detail take visitors back in time.

NOW: After facing potential demolition in the mid-twentieth century, Litchfield Villa was restored in the Seventies. Today, it stands as one of the few pre-park structures within Prospect Park, and is listed on the National Register of Historic Places. It serves as the home for the Prospect Park Alliance, the organization that cares for the park, and is still an ongoing part of the community, serving as the park's current main information center.

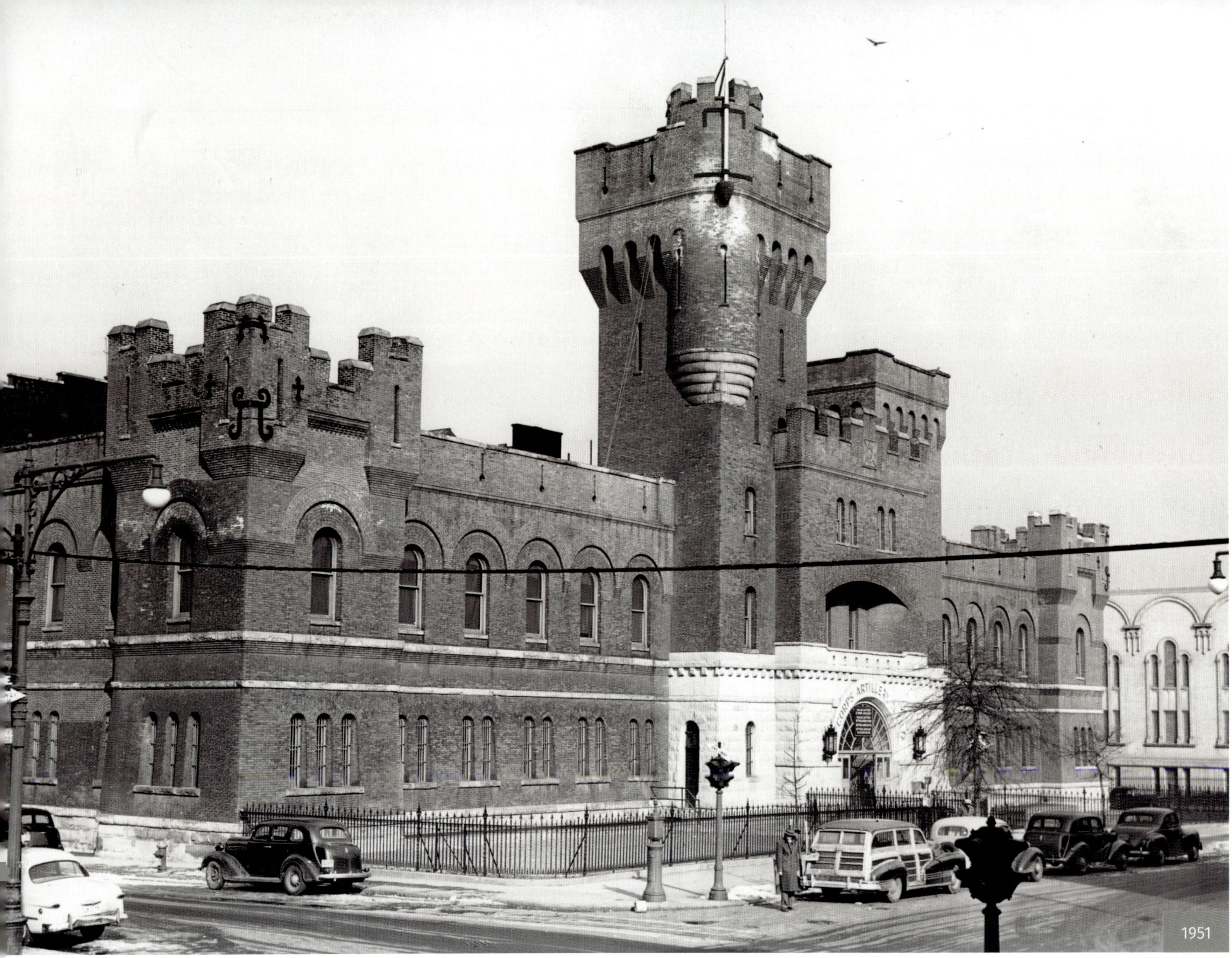

1951

PARK SLOPE ARMORY

Military marvel makes a magnificent municipality center

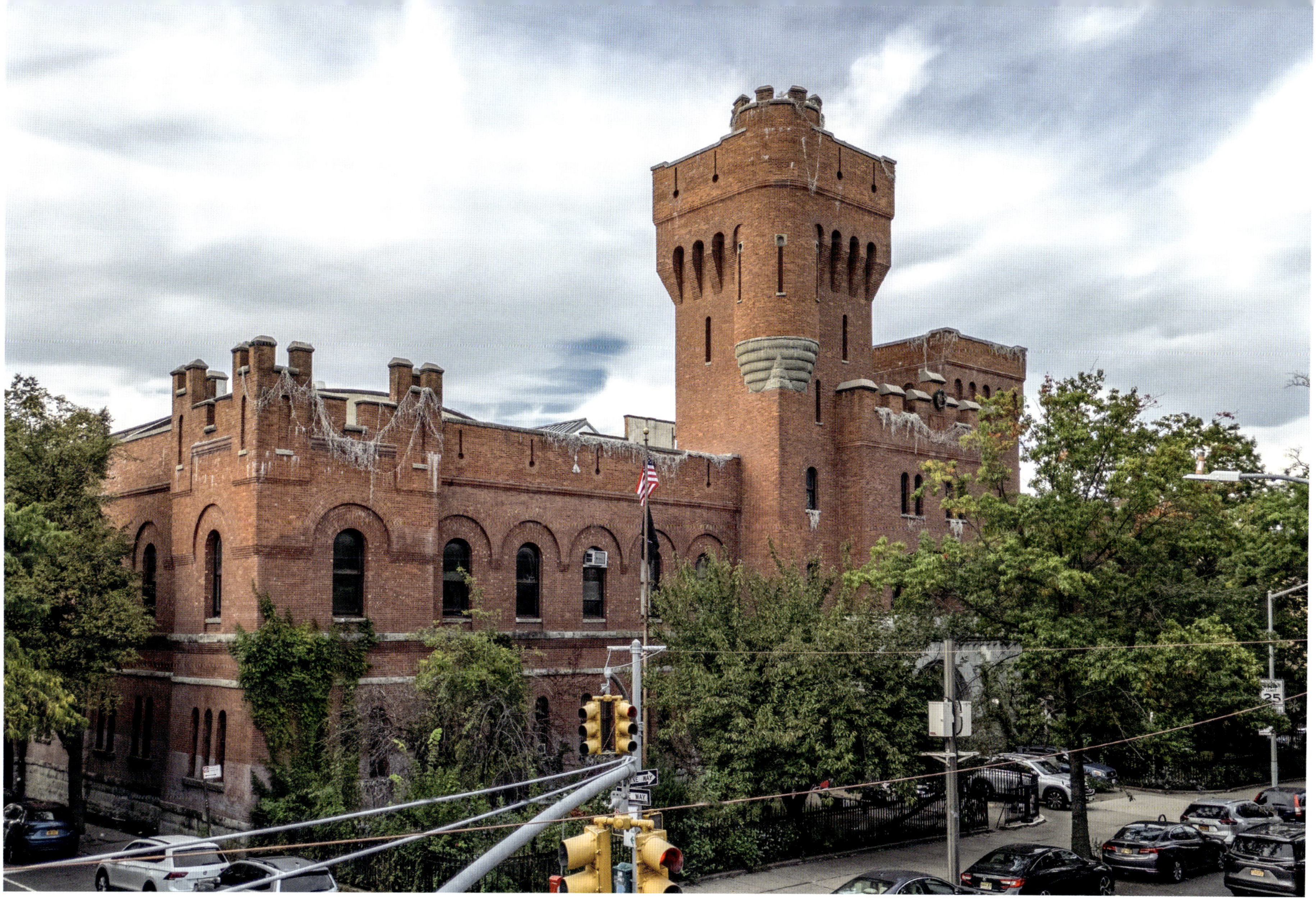

THEN: Constructed between 1891 and 1895, the Park Slope Armory was built at a time when New York City needed facilities to serve as military strongholds for potential civil unrest. It was also known as the 14th Regiment Armory after the National Guard unit with the same name. Designed by William A. Mundell in the Late Victorian style, the imposing brick structure filled an entire block between 7th and 8th Avenues and 14th and 15th Streets in Park Slope. The fortress-like structure had parapet walls, turrets, and a 70,000-square-foot drill hall that could fit the entire regiment for training. During the Cold War era, the Armory was prepared to serve as a fallout shelter and an emergency response center. In 1951, the Armory was still in use by the National Guard, and occasionally by the Brooklyn Dodgers who held practice there when it was too wet to be outside.

NOW: Though the National Guard maintained a presence in the Park Slope landmark until 1994, its use tapered off, beginning in the Eighties when the dormitory in the garrison was put into service as a shelter for unhoused women, a purpose it still serves today. Over the years, it has provided staging space for the Macy's Thanksgiving Day Parade balloons, and filming locations for a number of movies, including *Goodfellas*, *Donnie Brasco* and *Meet Joe Black*, but without a consistent plan or programming it fell into disrepair. In 2008, Councilman Bill de Blasio began lobbying for repurposing the space. He wanted to create a dual-purpose facility that would serve as a community recreation center and would continue to provide shelter services. In 2010, after a $16,000,000 renovation, the Park Slope YMCA officially opened as a full-service fitness center in the former drill hall.

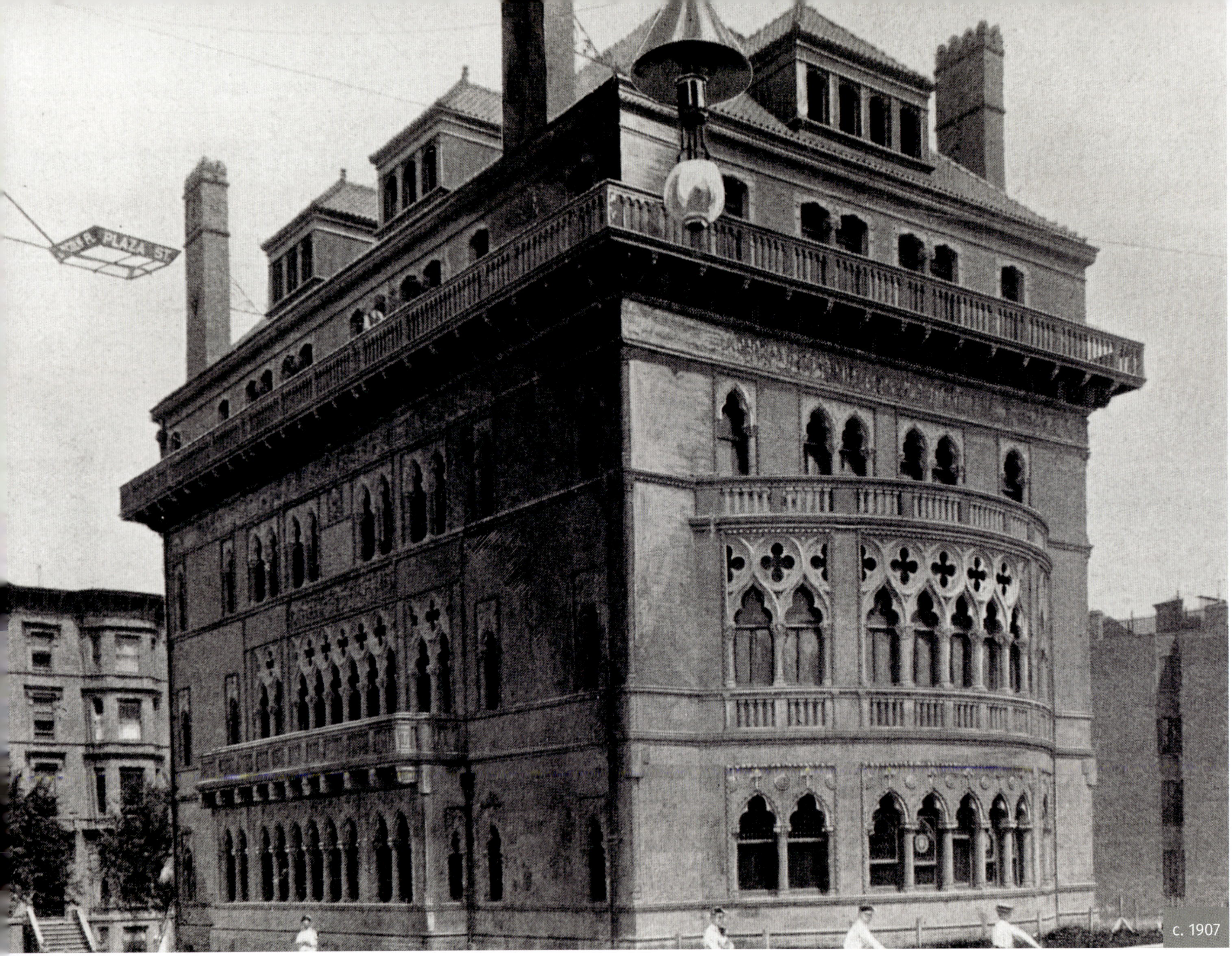

MONTAUK CLUB

A Gilded Age gathering place transformed into new housing

THEN: Montauk Club was built in 1889 in Park Slope, and was designed by architect Francis H. Kimball in the Venetian Gothic style, with magnificent classic brownstone brick and stained-glass windows. In 1907, at the time of the photo opposite, it served Brooklyn's wealthiest businessmen and politicians as an exclusive gentlemen's club, hosting celebrities and even presidents, including Grover Cleveland and Dwight D. Eisenhower. It was a central hub for Brooklyn's movers and shakers who went there to socialize in the grand dining room, billiards rooms, bowling alley, and library. The club was well known for lavish parties, political gatherings, and cultural events.

NOW: Today, the Montauk Club building still stands at the corner of Eighth Avenue and Lincoln Place, right near Grand Army Plaza, and serves as a testament of the architectural grandeur of Brooklyn's past. While it no longer functions as a private social club, the building has been repurposed (and mostly preserved) as luxurious condominiums, allowing residents to live in an important piece of Brooklyn history.

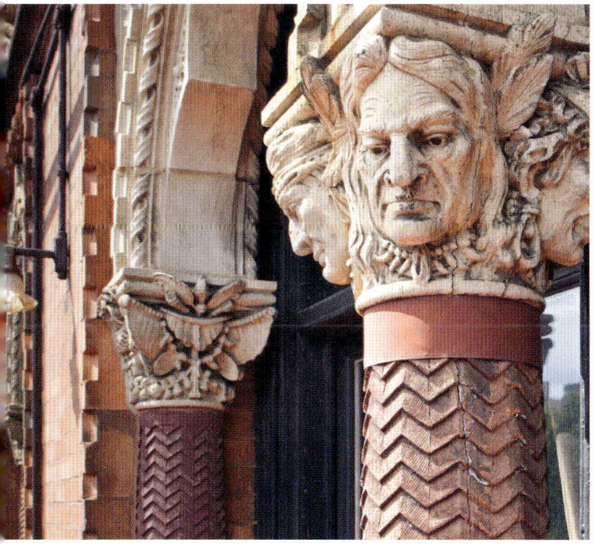

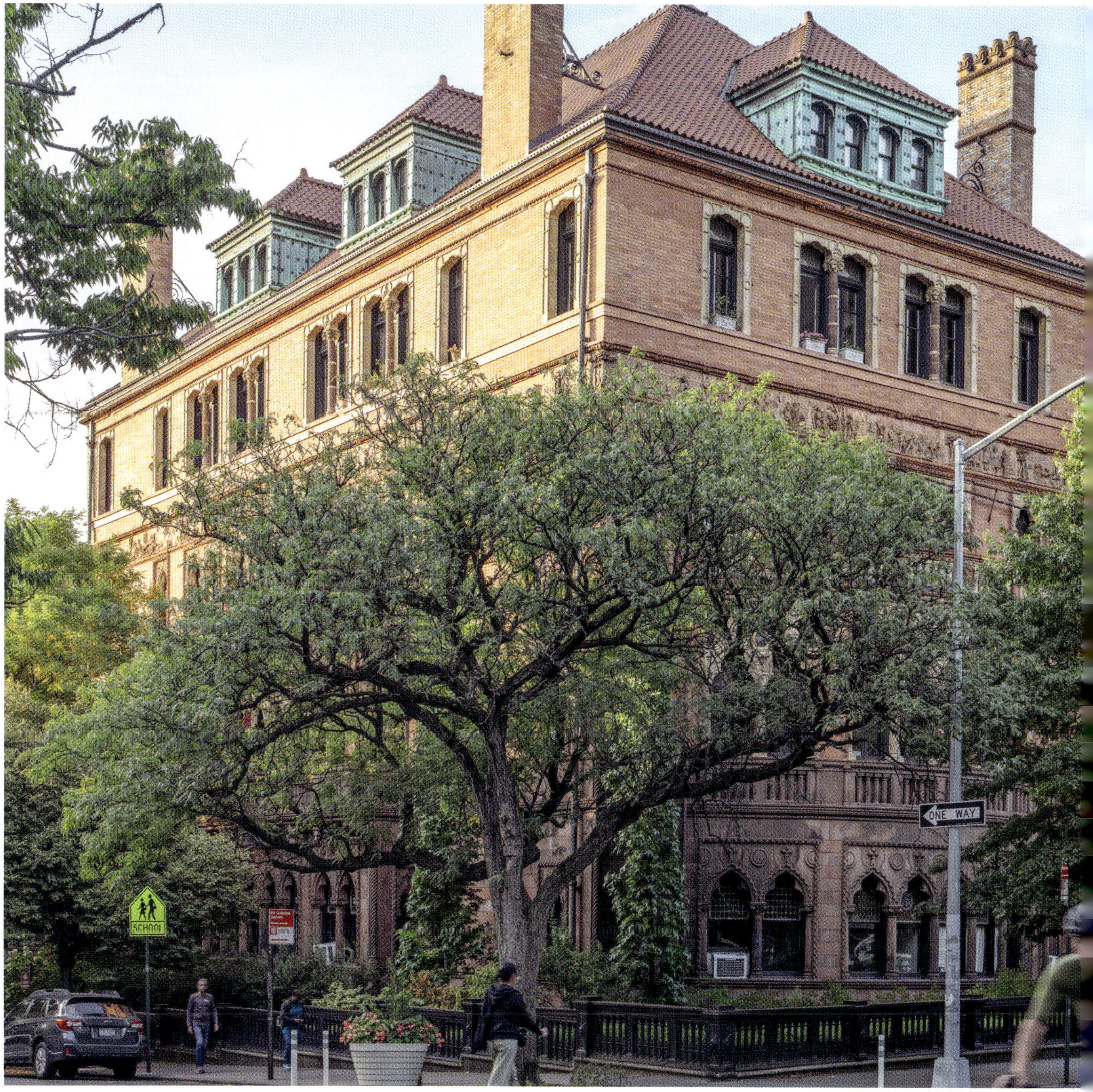

LEFT: The club was named after the Montauk Tribe of Long Island, and Native American themes are featured in the details of its terracotta decorations and designs.

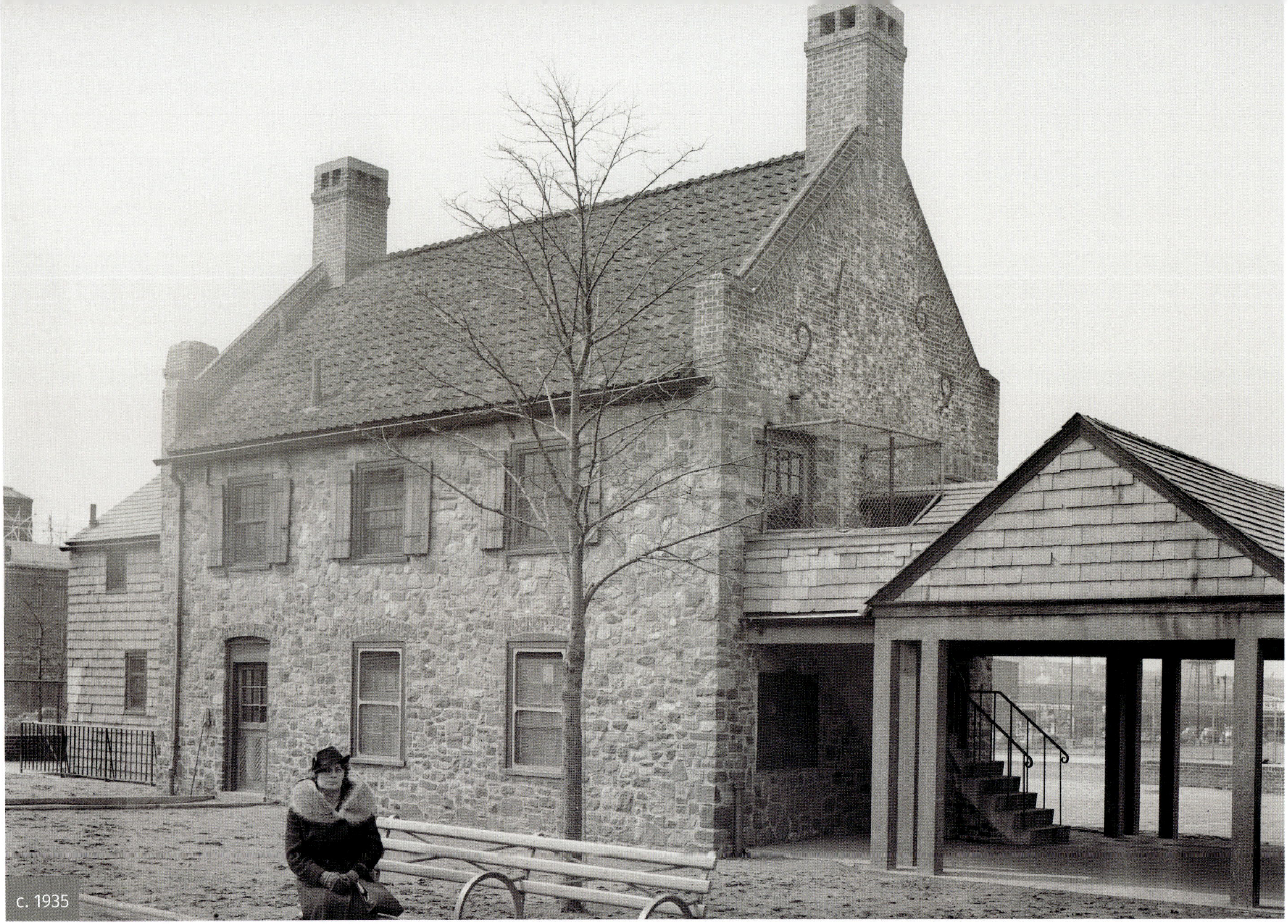
c. 1935

OLD STONE HOUSE

A home of battles and baseball becomes a playground and history center

THEN: The Old Stone House, visible here from 1935, was a replica of the Old Stone House originally built in 1699. The house was part of the site of the Battle of Long Island, an integral fight that was crucial to American victory in the Revolutionary War in 1776. American troops fought a bloody battle, successfully delaying the British army, allowing General George Washington and a significant portion of the Continental Army to escape capture via the Gowanus Creek to the East River and Manhattan. Many lives were lost here and are believed to be buried on or around the grounds. Between 1776 and the late 1800s, the original house remained a private home, and it began to decline as Brooklyn modernized and built a public park around it. In the 1890s, the baseball team the Brooklyn Superbas (who later became the Brooklyn Dodgers)

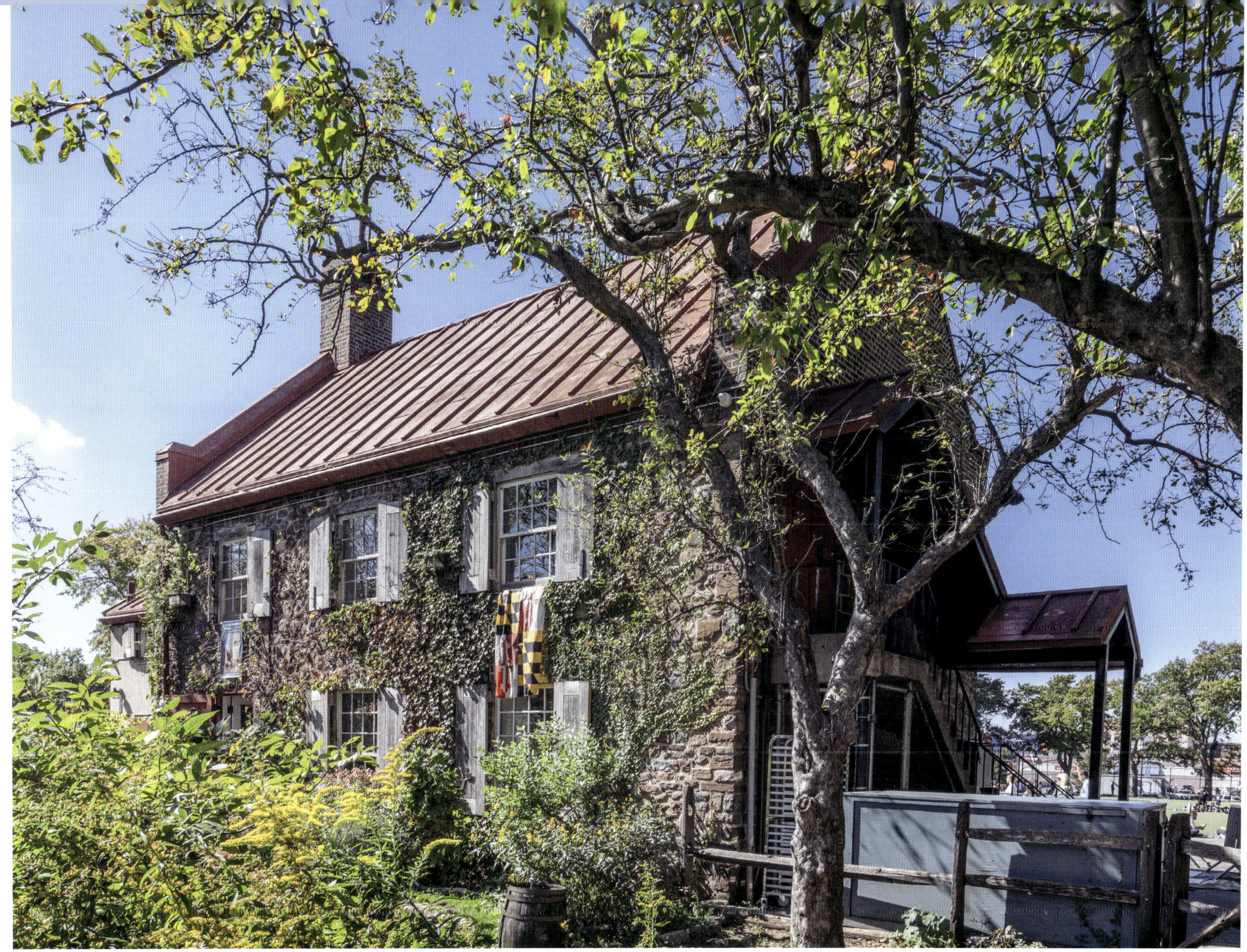

played in the park and used the building for their clubhouse, before it was demolished in 1897. Before its demolition, historians recognized the importance of the site, and they salvaged and stored some of the original stones to be used in the replication built in 1933.

NOW: This replica still stands on the side of the J.J. Byrne Playground in Washington Park on Third Street between Fourth and Fifth Avenues. Today it serves as a non-profit historical center, with exhibitions on the history of the property and the battle fought on the grounds, as it hosts various community events and educational programs.

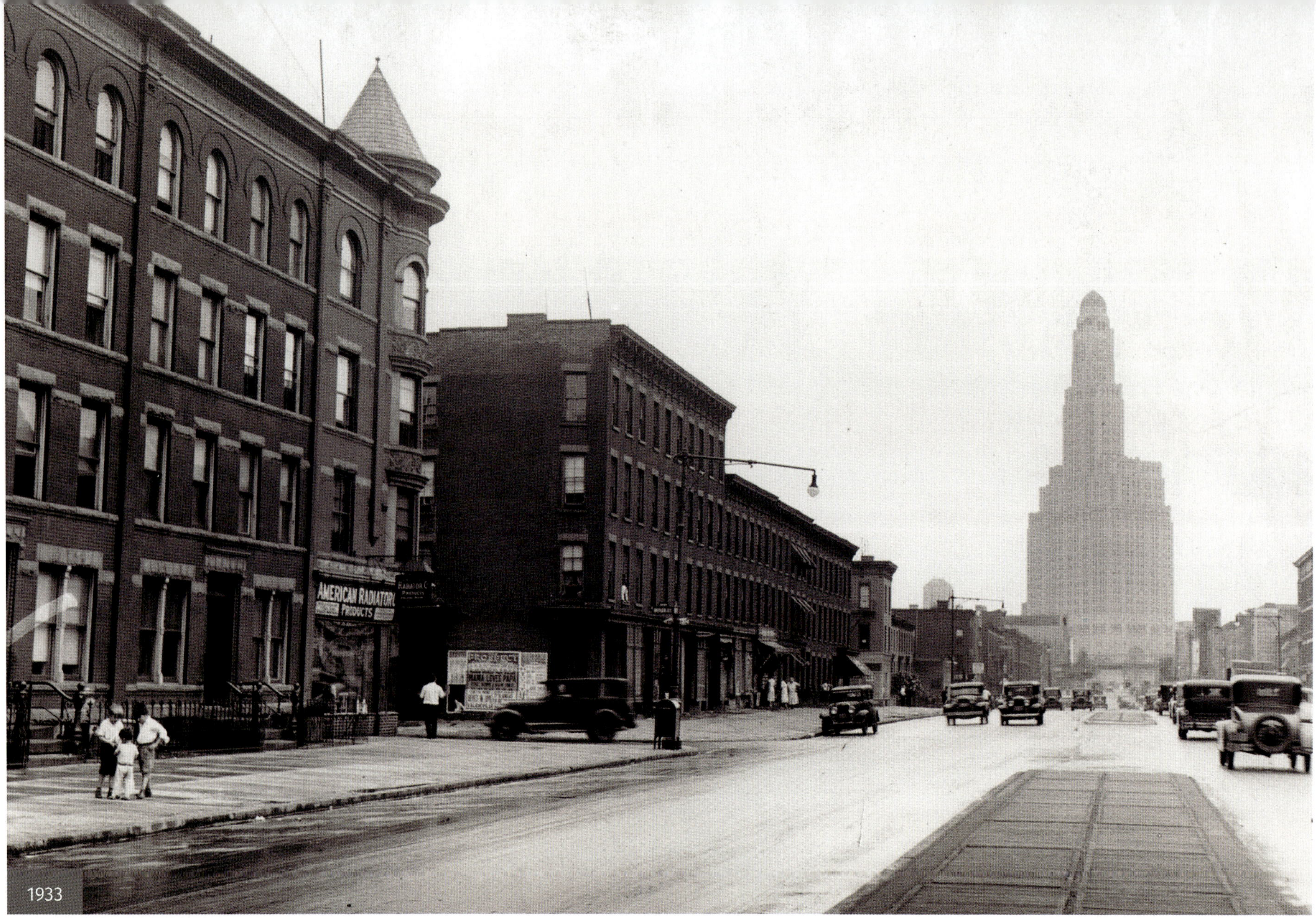

1933

FOURTH AVENUE AT BUTLER, SOUTH PARK SLOPE

The South Park Slope transformed from working-class homes to luxury towers

THEN: For much of the last century, South Park Slope was a working-class neighborhood comprising a mix of small row houses and multi-family apartment buildings near the edge of Gowanus Canal. In 1933, Fourth Avenue and Butler Streets were home to a mix of Irish, Italian, and Polish immigrants who worked along the waterfront in shipping and manufacturing. The area was conveniently well served by multiple public transportation options, with trolley cars and a subway stop for what is now the R line opening in 1915. The gold-dome and four-faced clock tower of the Williamsburg Bank Tower is visible in the distance, at the end of the avenue. Opened in 1929, at 512 feet tall it was the highest building in Brooklyn and would remain so for decades. Housing not only the bank but so many dentist offices, it became known as "the Mecca of dentistry."

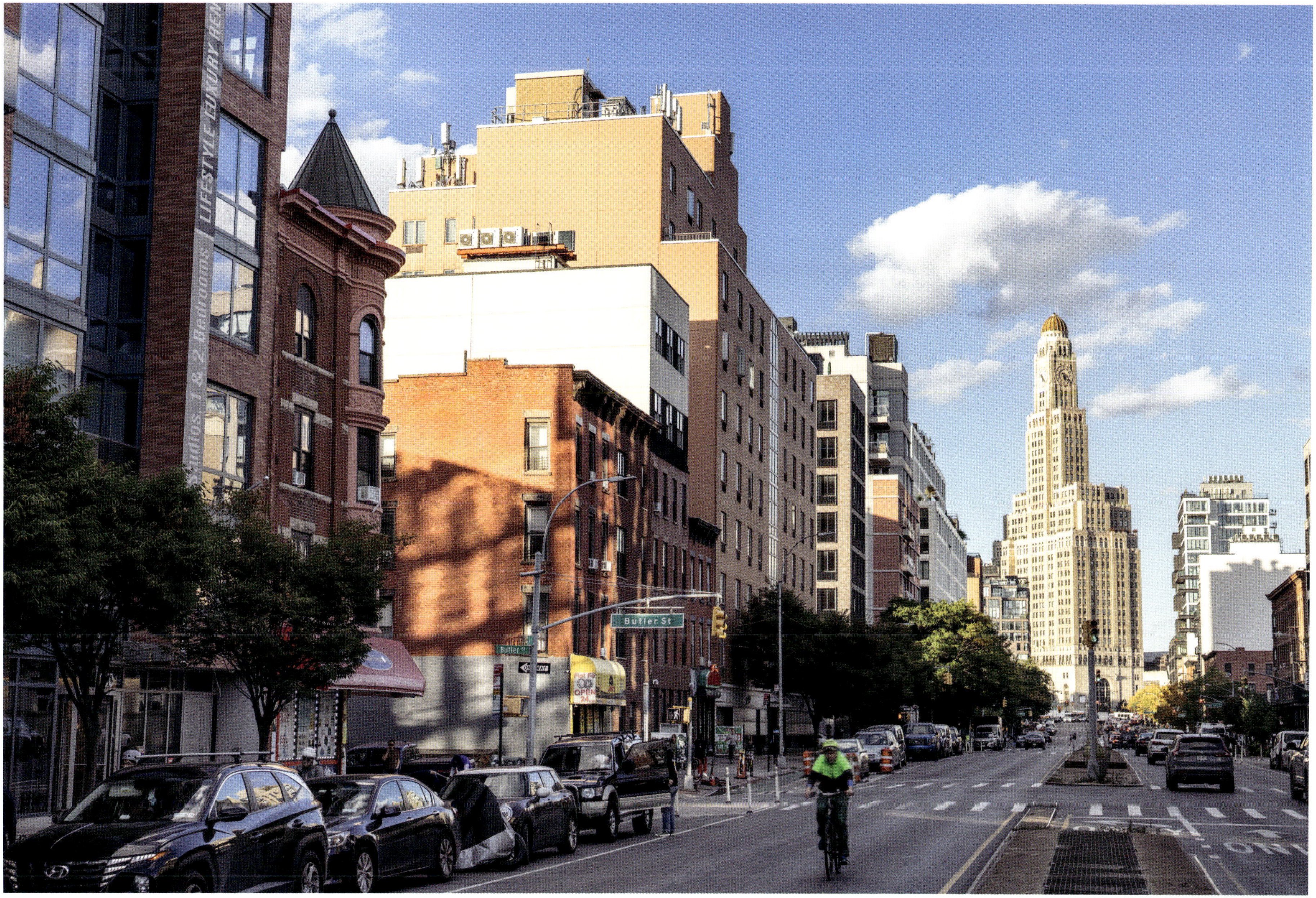

NOW: In 2006, the Williamsburg Savings Bank Tower was converted into condominiums called One Hanson Place. Residential life in the neighborhood has become more affluent, with young families drawn to the area for its proximity to Prospect Park. Fourth Avenue has seen a great deal of buildings converted into new housing options and residents support multiple commercial corridors along Fifth and Seventh Avenues, where high-end coffee shops, boutiques, and restaurants reflect the new demographics. These changes in South Park Slope have impacted Gowanus too, which is shifting to a high-end residential neighborhood.

CARROLL STREET BRIDGE, GOWANUS

The bridge that connected Gowanus

1912

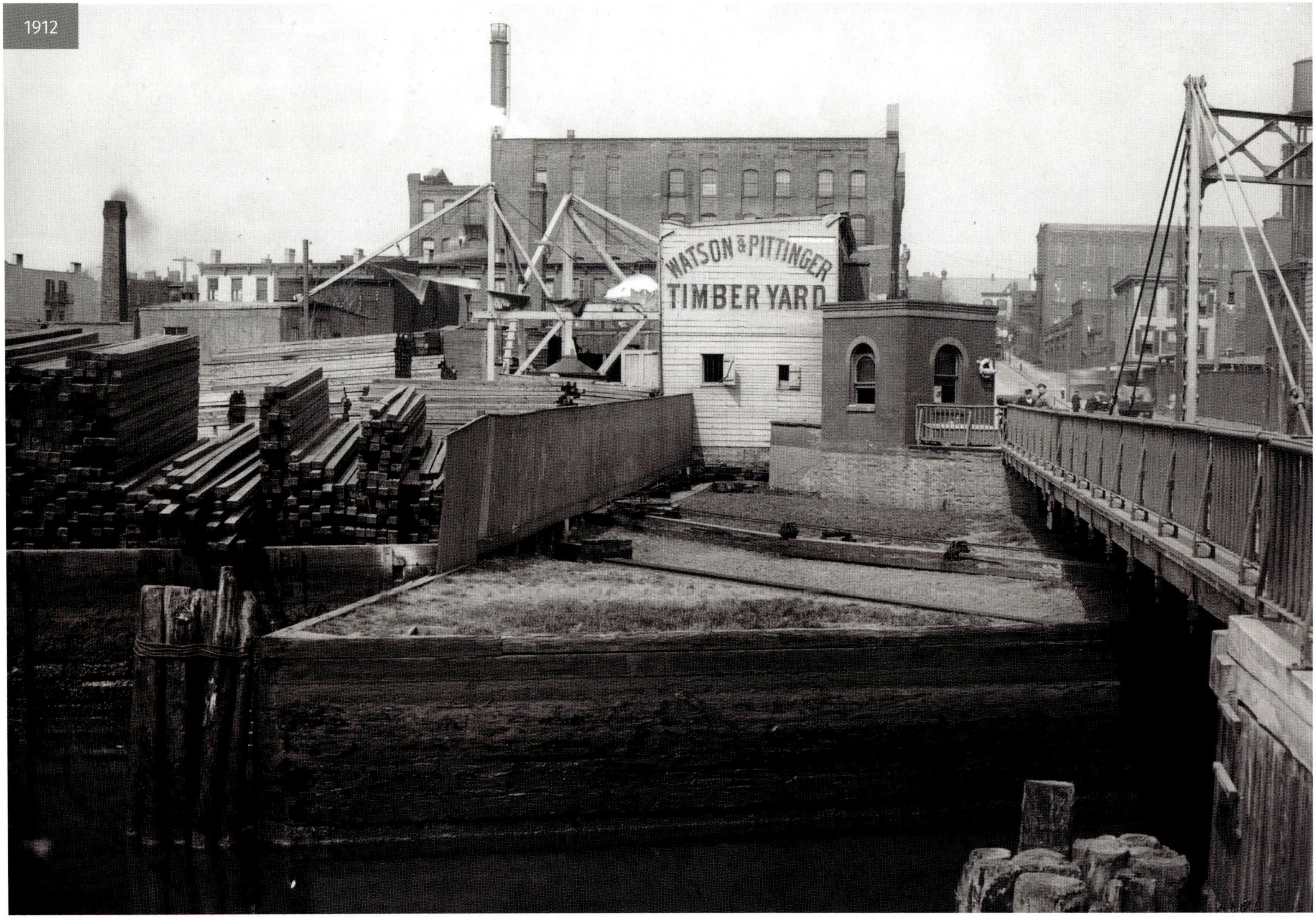

THEN: The Carroll Street Bridge, which spans the Gowanus Canal in Brooklyn, is one of the oldest retractile bridges in New York, and one of only four that are still in the United States. When the Gowanus Canal was completed in the 1860s, it transformed the area into a central pathway for Brooklyn's booming shipping and manufacturing industries. Factories, warehouses, and mills filled the canal's banks, producing raw materials (like coal and oil) and manufactured goods (like chemicals and building materials). Constructed in 1889, the bridge eliminated long detours and allowed larger shipments of freight to cross the canal. The positive impact on the economy of South Brooklyn was immediate, boosting industrial expansion and shortening the commute for workers seeking opportunities a little further from home. The bridge supported the area's transformation from marshy farmland to a dense urban neighborhood, which also allowed for residential growth. The bridge's unique design allows it to roll horizontally on wheels, manually controlled by the engineer working in the small brick engineer's hut visible in the image from 1912.

NOW: Between World War I and II, 6,000,000 tons of cargo would be produced and trafficked over the canal each year. What was once a symbol of progress was designated as a superfund site in 2010. A century of unregulated dumping of industrial waste and sewage polluted the water and air, and after a few decades of ill-fated attempts at cleaning up, the City of New York finally began to remediate it in 2013. The clean-up aims to restore the canal's ecological health and improve the quality of life for the residents in the surrounding neighborhood. Its proximity to Park Slope and the robust clean-up have led to a surge in development, with large-scale residential towers incorporating the old factories into designs for waterfront homes, stores, and restaurants. Today the bridge remains, turned permanently to the left, serving as a permanent open channel for new residents and businesses who want to settle by a healthier, more desirable Gowanus Canal.

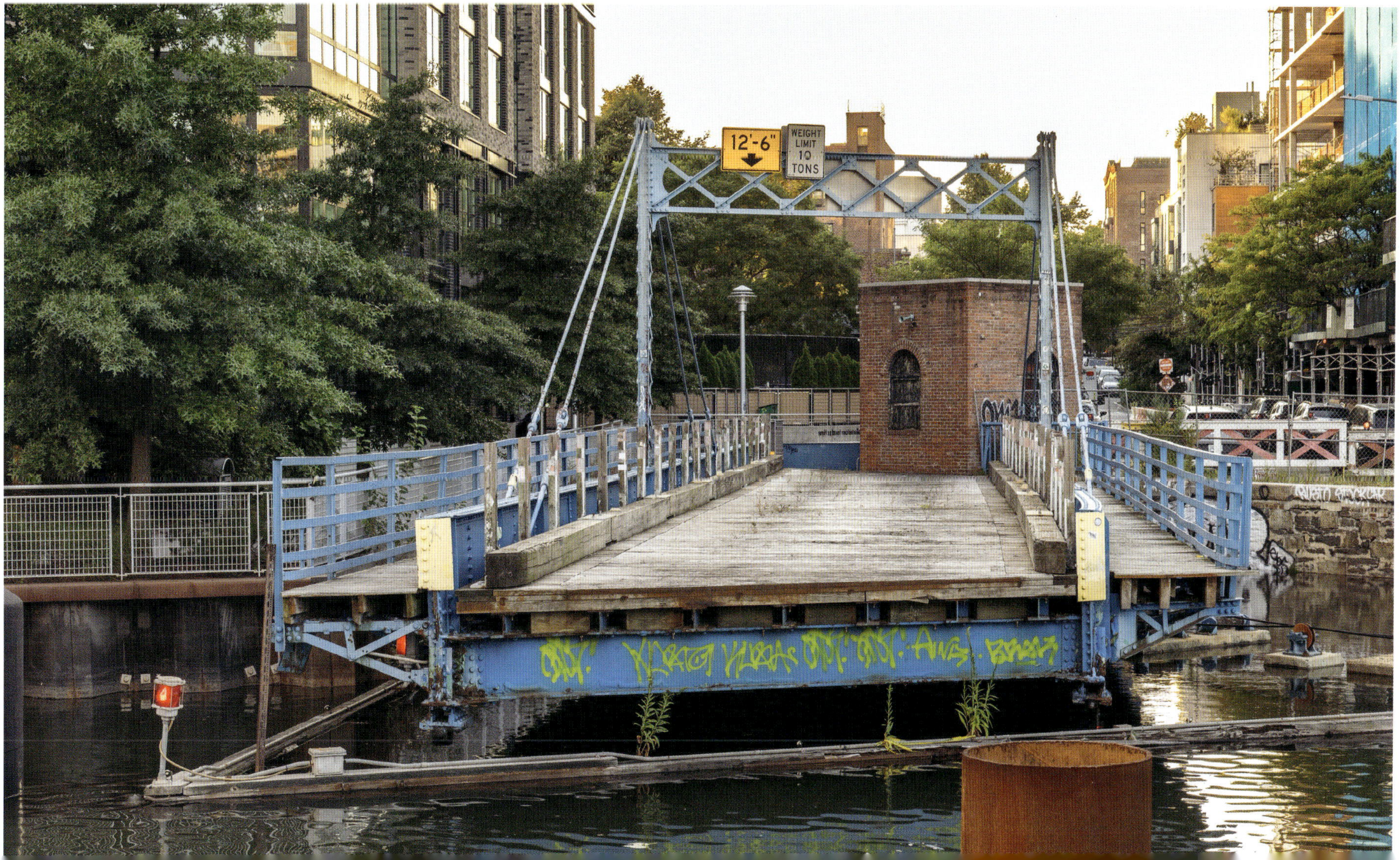

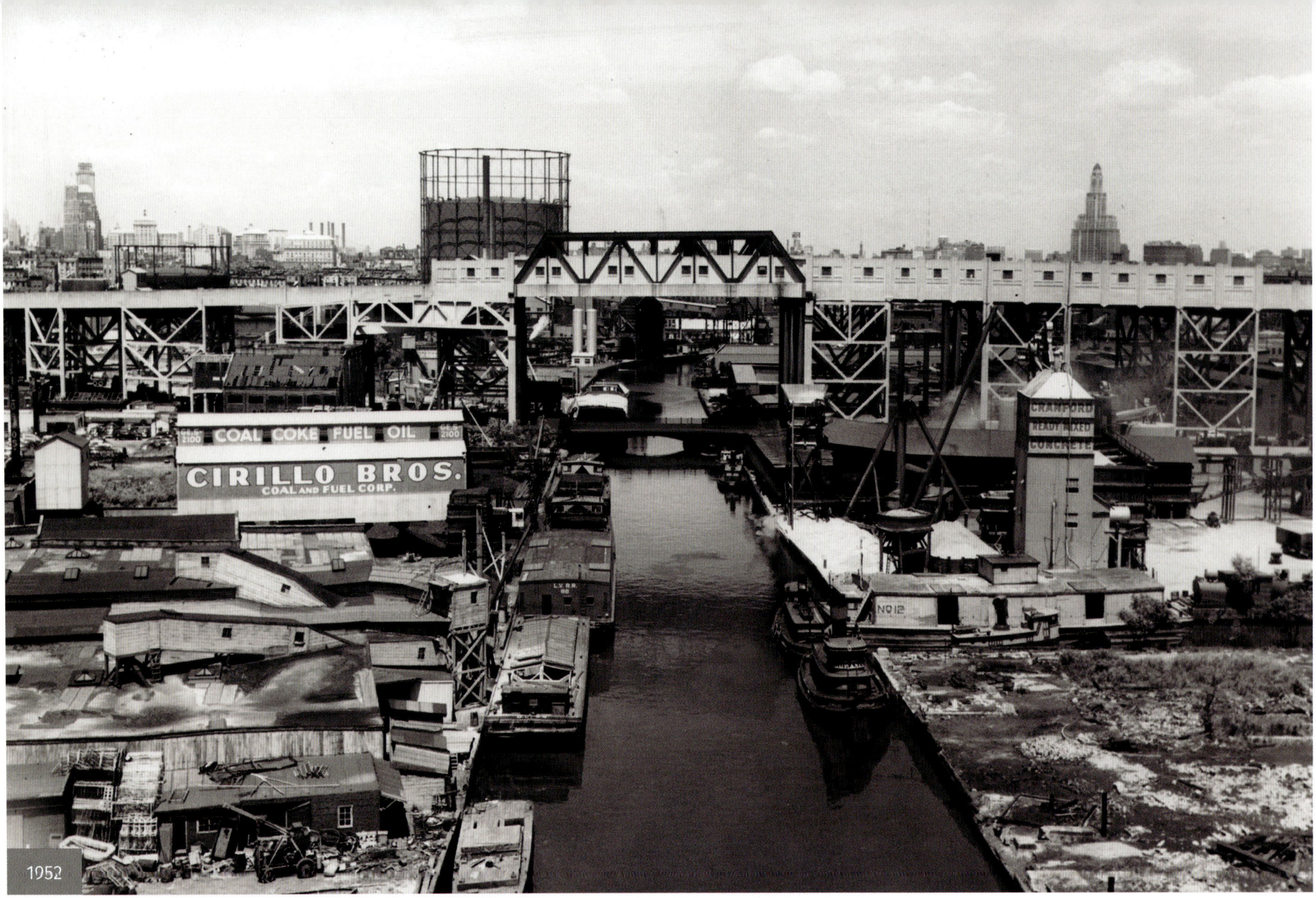

GOWANUS CANAL, VIEW OF DOWNTOWN BROOKLYN

From modern marvel to mid-century mess

THEN: The above photo from 1952 captures the Gowanus Canal at the end of its industrial high point, busy with the commotion that drove the Brooklyn economy for decades. In the earliest days, the canal was a marshland tidal estuary, used by the Canarsee tribe for fishing and hunting oysters. Early Dutch settlers drained the marshland for farmland in the seventeenth century. By the mid-nineteenth century, the natural waterway became the Gowanus Canal, an integral part of Brooklyn's industrial landscape and a vital waterway for the Industrial Revolution from the moment it opened in 1869. Factories, warehouses, and mills were built along the banks, producing a broad spectrum of goods, including coal, oil, and chemicals. In 1952, barges and tugboats lined the shore, surrounded by the warehouses, silos, and smokestacks they serviced, and signs hinted at the problems to come. A combined sewer system discharged wastewater directly into the head of the canal, turning it into a polluted cesspool that impacted the environmental and economic health of the neighborhood for years.

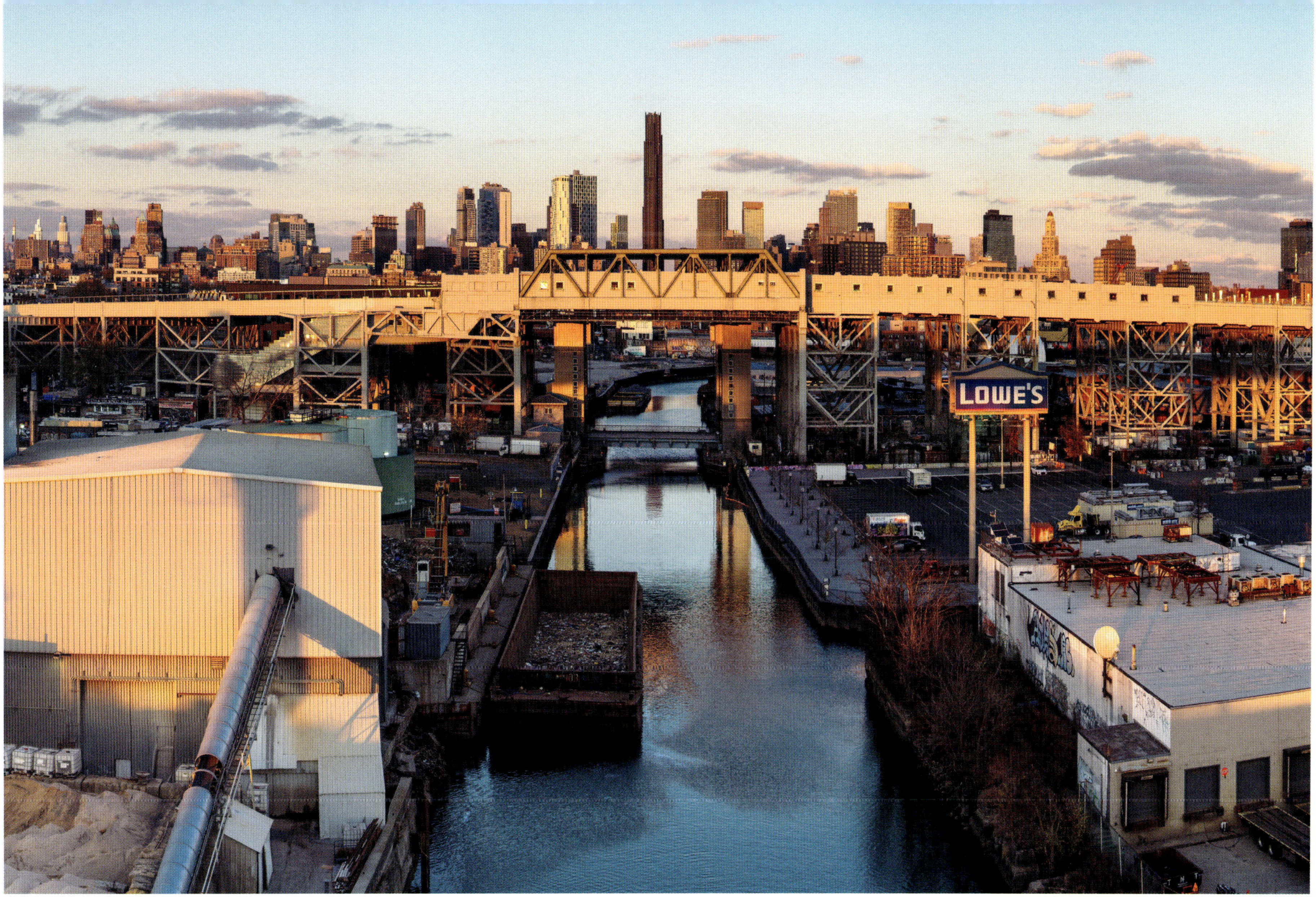

NOW: In 2010, the Gowanus was declared an Environmental Protection Agency Superfund site, and work began to clean up the water and the land surrounding it, and many of the factory and warehouse buildings on the river banks have already been converted for residential and commercial use. The elevated subway station, visible in the distance, still services the neighborhood and it gives a unique vantage point to the Gowanus and the skyscrapers springing up in the distance. The canal and the remediation highlight the challenges of industrial legacy and urban transformation.

Since 2006, the Gowanus Canal Conservancy has become the environmental steward for the neighborhood. Headquartered in the Old American Can Factory, the organization works to educate the politicians and the public on best practices for rejuvenating the canal, while spearheading grassroots initiatives to sustain the growing green infrastructure and nurture the ecological systems that are finally coming back to Gowanus.

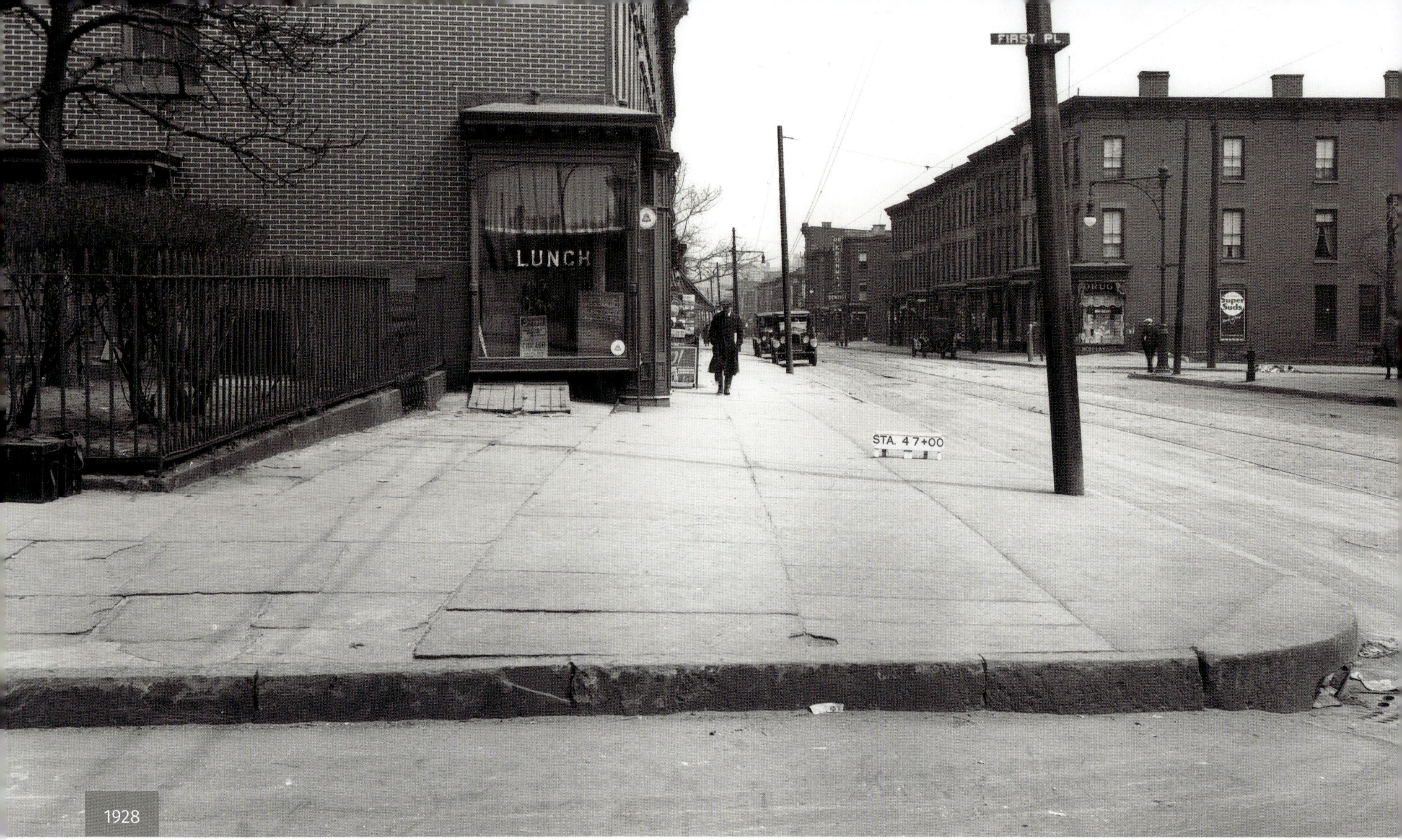

SMITH STREET AT 1ST PLACE

An 1846 design mandate creates charm for centuries

THEN: Brooklyn's Carroll Gardens neighborhood was named after Charles Carroll, the only Catholic to sign the Declaration of Independence—and whose name was already attached to Carroll Street and Carroll Park, the third-oldest park in Brooklyn. Originally called South Brooklyn, and considered part of Red Hook, it comprises approximately forty blocks adjacent to Cobble Hill, Boerum Hill, and Gowanus. The area stands out from its neighbors with unique garden blocks that are deeper than those of nearby neighborhoods, due to an 1846 law that declared that the homes along 1st, 2nd, 3rd, and 4th Places would have front gardens that were 33½ feet. While the area was initially settled by Irish immigrants, a significant wave of Italian-Americans in the late nineteenth and early twentieth centuries would shape the neighborhood's culture and is still evident today in the local businesses, numerous social clubs, and mutual aid societies that served the tight-knit community. St. Mary Star of the Sea Church, founded in 1851, was a central fixture of community life. In 1928, local businesses thrived along Court and Smith Streets, offering everything from fresh produce to handmade pastas and dental services, as seen in the above picture. The elevated train line running along 3rd Avenue was still in operation, connecting the neighborhood to other parts of Brooklyn and Manhattan, and bringing residents to work at blue-collar jobs along the industrial waterfront.

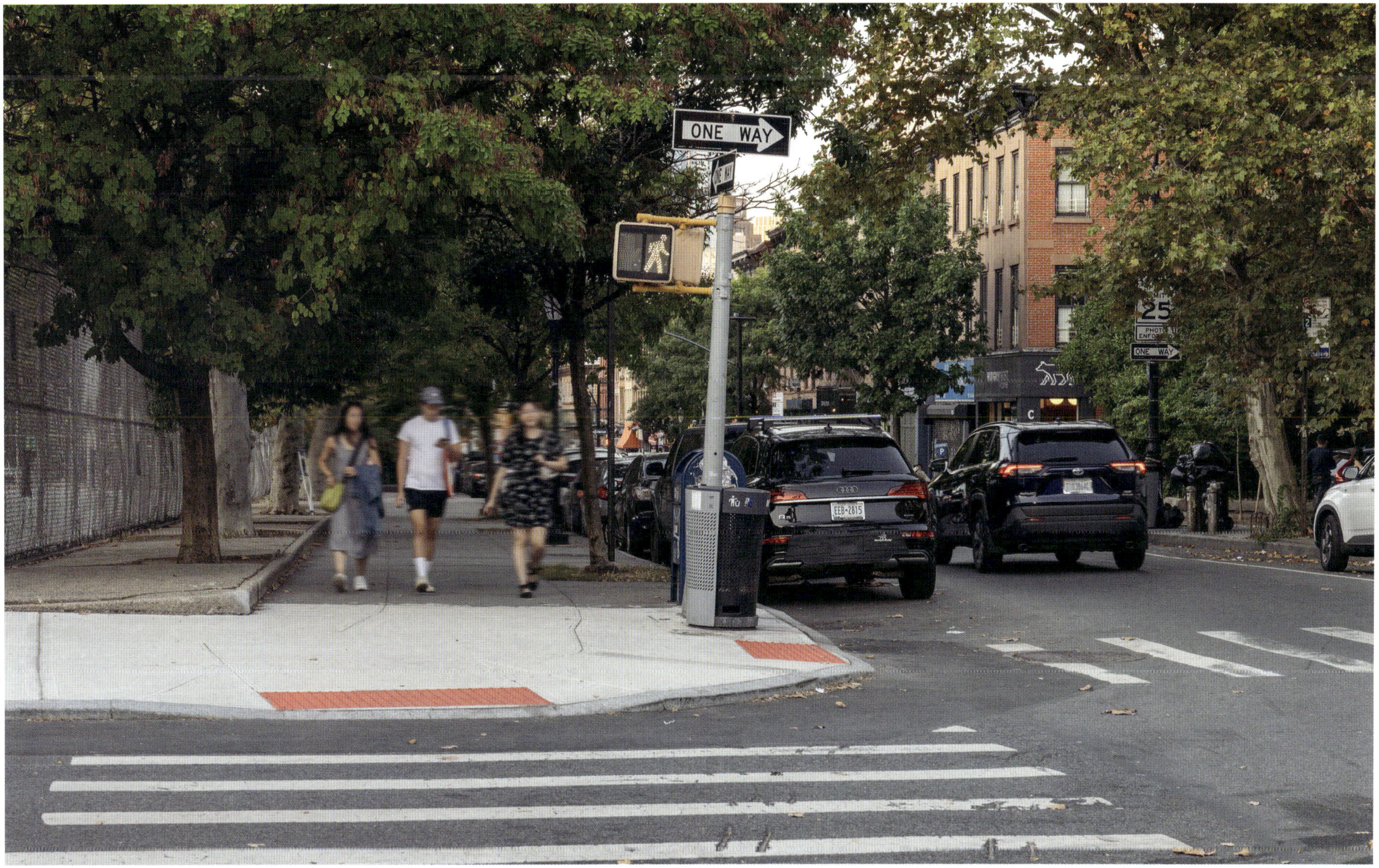

NOW: Carroll Gardens remained a relatively stable working-class area, with strong family and community ties helping residents weather economic hardships through the Great Depression. In the late twentieth century, the Italian-American population declined dramatically from fifty-two percent in 1980 to twenty-two percent in 2012, although it remains an important part of the area's cultural fabric. Residents can still be found speaking various Italian dialects while playing bocce in the parks, and long-time establishments like Caputo's Fine Foods and F. Monteleone Bakery continue to serve the community. The neighborhood has also become known for its diverse culinary scene, with trendy restaurants and artisanal shops lining Court and Smith Streets, a number of which are operated by a large community of French immigrants who have moved into the neighborhood, impacting the demographics once again with a weekly mass in French at St. Vincent de Paul Church, and a dual language immersion program at one of the neighborhood schools.

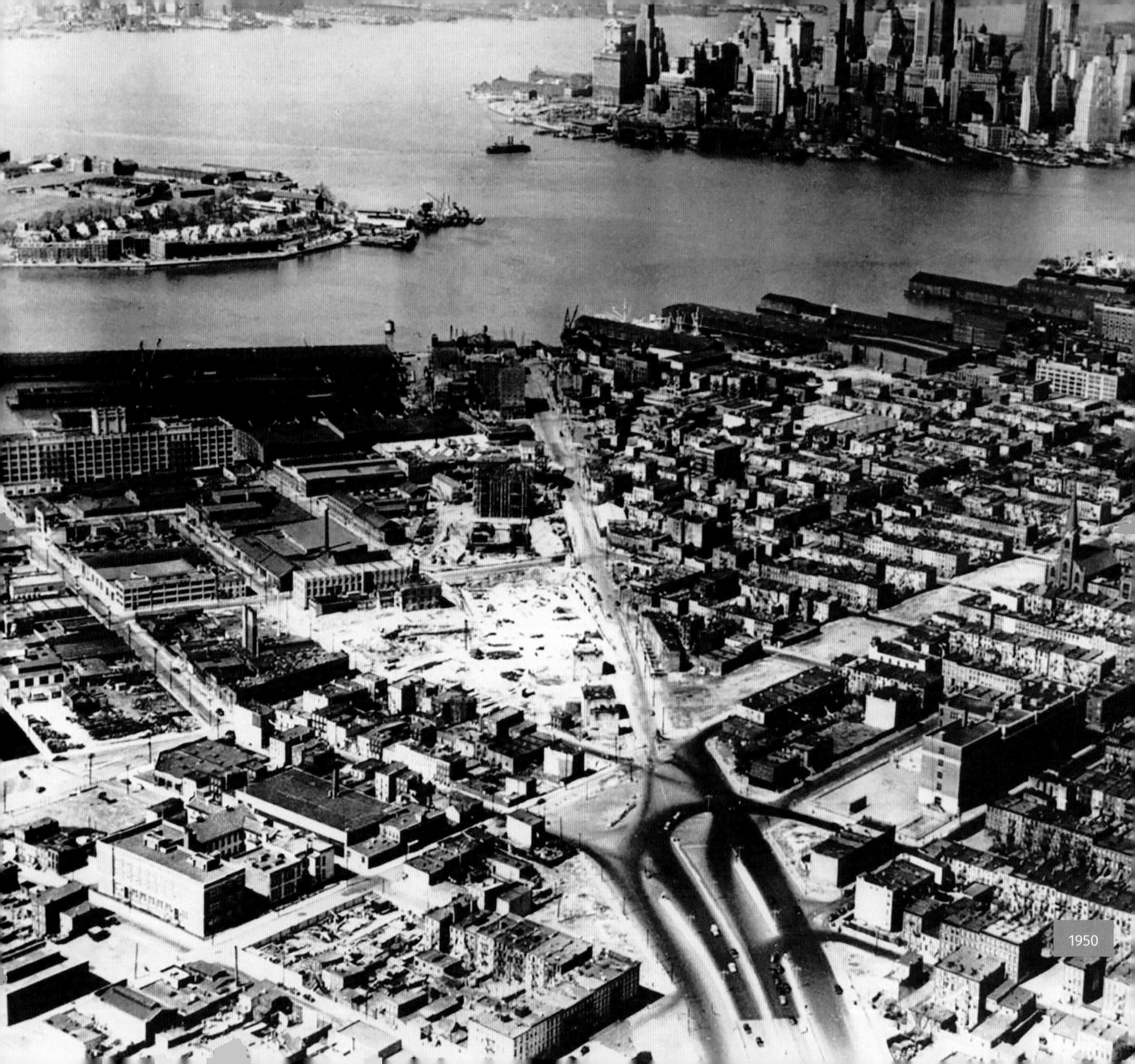
1950

RED HOOK

A gradual transformation from shipping hub to creative enclave

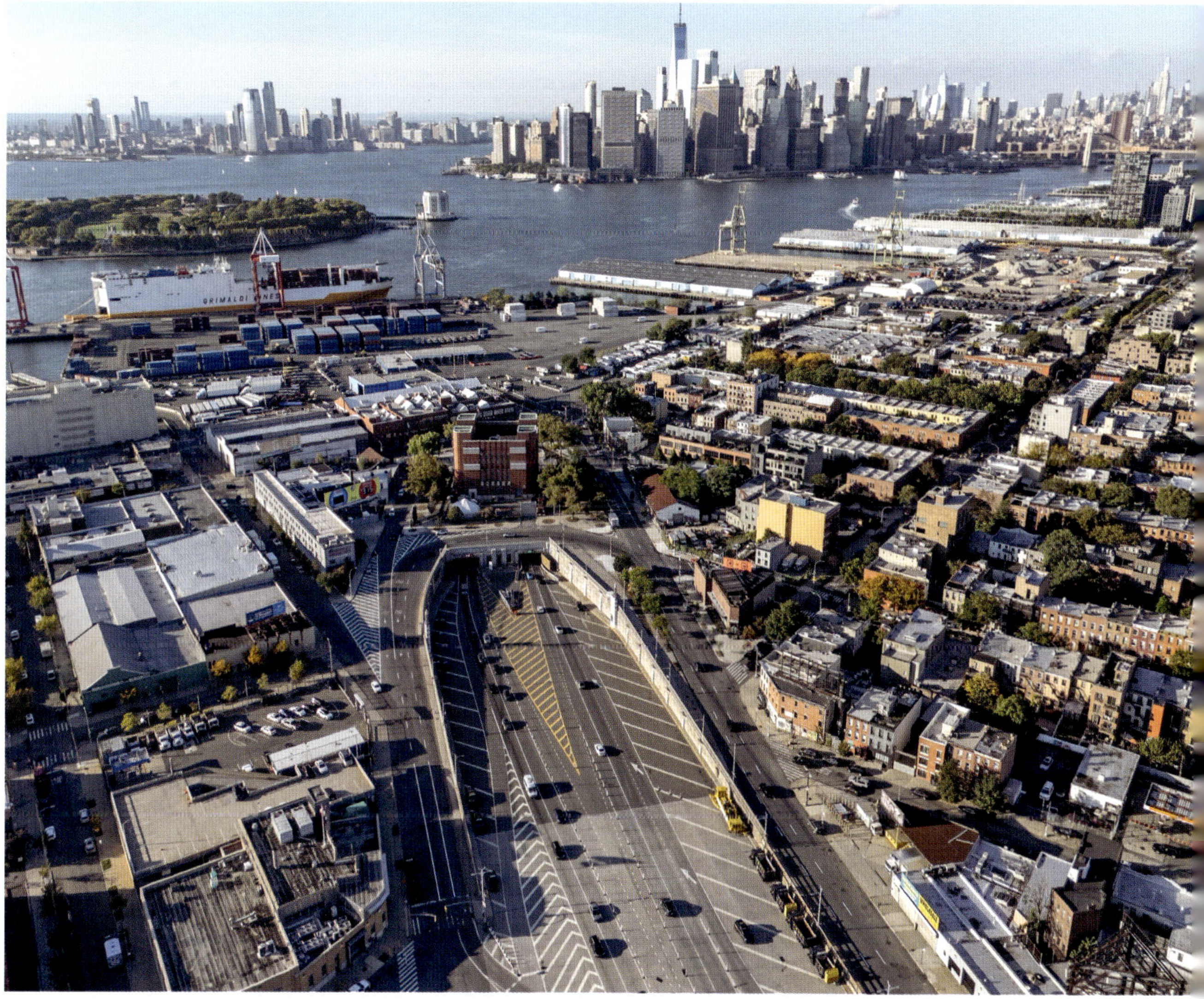

THEN: First settled by Dutch colonists in 1636, Red Hook is one of Brooklyn's earliest European enclaves. Named for its red soil and the pointed peninsula jutting into the upper New York Bay, the neighborhood had become an important maritime hub by the 1840s, reaching its industrial peak around 1950. That year marked the height of Red Hook's shipping activity. Thousands of longshoremen worked the bustling docks, handling massive amounts of cargo daily. The neighborhood was crowded with workers and their families, many of whom lived in the Red Hook Houses. When it opened in 1939, Red Hook was the largest public housing complex of the time. It replaced many tents and temporary houses that had filled the area during the Great Depression. The waterfront's labor issues during that time provided the inspiration for the 1954 Marlon Brando film *On the Waterfront*, a reflection of the gritty riverfront identity and tough culture for those who tried to make a living and a life there. In 1950, the Brooklyn Battery Tunnel opened, connecting downtown Manhattan to Red Hook, changing the topography of the area and offering additional transportation to and for the rest of Brooklyn. However, Red Hook remained isolated from New York's vital lifeline: the subway system.

NOW: Red Hook was never connected by subway to the rest of Brooklyn because its geographic isolation and waterfront topography made it a challenge to dig the required underground tunnels, so residents relied mostly on bus services to get around. The transportation limits meant the area was slower than the rest of Brooklyn to shake the economic challenges stemming from the decline in shipping and industry. In 2008, IKEA opened on a former shipping yard and began providing a ferry service to and from the neighborhood to both Manhattan and other parts of Brooklyn. Slowly but surely, abandoned properties began converting to new businesses. The Red Hook renaissance now includes artisanal food producers like Widow Jane Distillery and Red Hook Winery, as well as many fine restaurants like Brooklyn Crab and Hometown BBQ. Waterfront parks, art galleries, and creative businesses now bring new life to the historic architecture.

The IKEA ferry route was incorporated into the main New York Ferry service in 2017, making Red Hook more accessible to community and visitors. The Red Hook renaissance has continued ever since, and it is now a diverse commercial hub that includes many new places to live, work, and eat, all built into the surviving and protected historic buildings from the last century. The Red Hook Houses are still central to the community, providing housing for approximately 6,000 people, who have been joined by residents in dozens of refurbished homes built into historic structures.

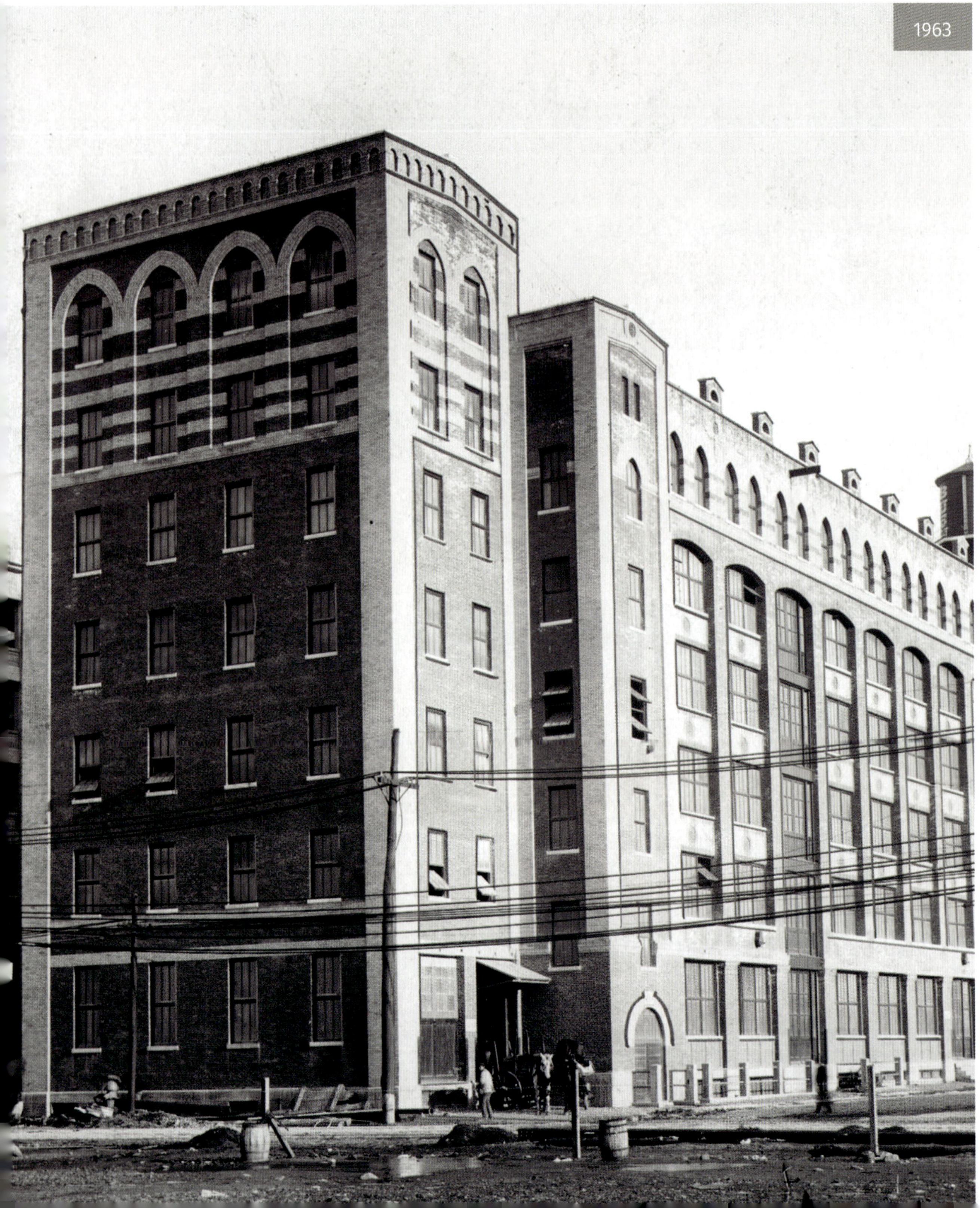

BUSH TERMINAL, INDUSTRY CITY

A waterfront industrial complex at the forefront of industrial integration

THEN: In 1895, Irving T. Bush began developing Bush Terminal in the Sunset Park neighborhood of Brooklyn. Bush was the son of Rufus T. Bush, owner of the Bush & Denslow oil refinery, which was sold to Standard Oil in the 1880s. When his father passed, 26-year-old Irving decided to use the inheritance to buy back that land to create the first freight terminal in New York City, combining shipping, manufacturing, and warehousing in one massive complex. He started with one building and turned it into six shipping piers, twenty-five industrial buildings, numerous warehouses, and integrated train tracks. At its peak, tens of thousands of workers were employed there. In spite of the initial opposition, Bush convinced railroads and oceangoing vessels to come directly to his Brooklyn terminal, pioneering the concept of integrated industrial complexes, which would be repeated worldwide. Bush extended his forward-thinking business practices into other areas, improving working conditions for employees and implementing strategic logistics systems, which anticipated and addressed supply-chain management challenges that wouldn't emerge for decades to come. In 1963, Bush Terminal was still operating at capacity, but manufacturing was shifting away from urban centers, a change that would impact Brooklyn's industrial waterfront development over the next half century.

NOW: The Bush Terminal Railroad was officially abandoned in 1971, the same year that the last remaining tugboat docked at the terminal. In 1974, the City of New York Department of Ports and Terminals hired a private company to fill the space between the piers to park shipping containers, but the operation was halted in 1978 after the city learned that toxic waste had been dumped at the site, creating a pollution issue. In 1986, Bush Terminal became Industry City, a rebranding intended to modernize the facility's image and attract lighter industrial and commercial tenants. The true reinvention began in 2013, when a new ownership group purchased a majority stake in the complex and invested $450,000,000 in redesigning the area. Today Industry City consists of sixteen buildings spanning thirty-five acres along the waterfront, with approximately 6,000,000 square feet of space. The interconnected buildings maintain the historic architecture outside and modern renovations inside. There are stores, restaurants, entertainment ventures, offices, furniture designers, food producers, and studio spaces. Major tenants include Amazon, media operations including Buck Productions and The Mill, and the New York City College of Technology. Today, Industry City represents a new kind of innovation hub, adapting Irving T. Bush's vision of integrated industrial complexes for the twenty-first century.

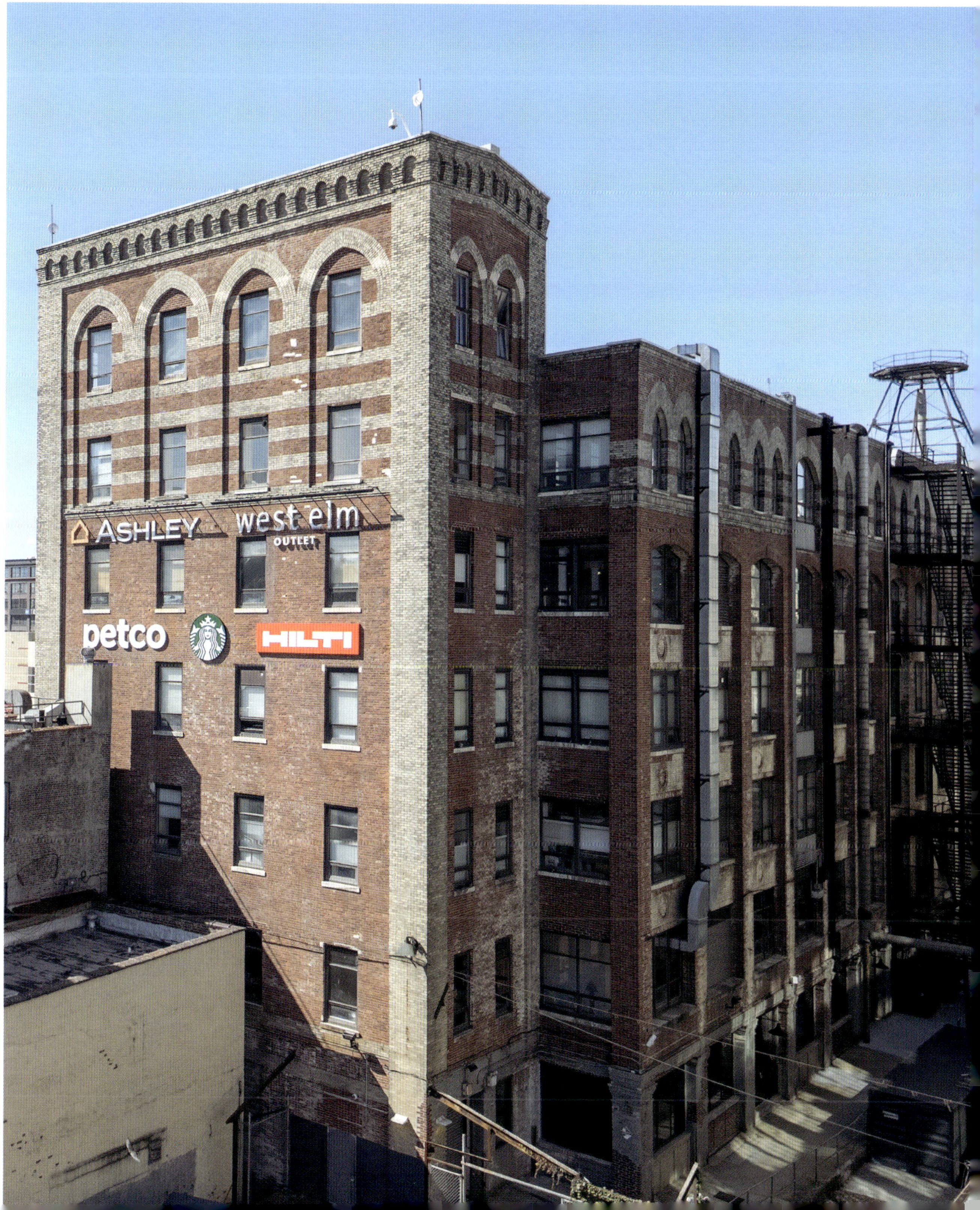

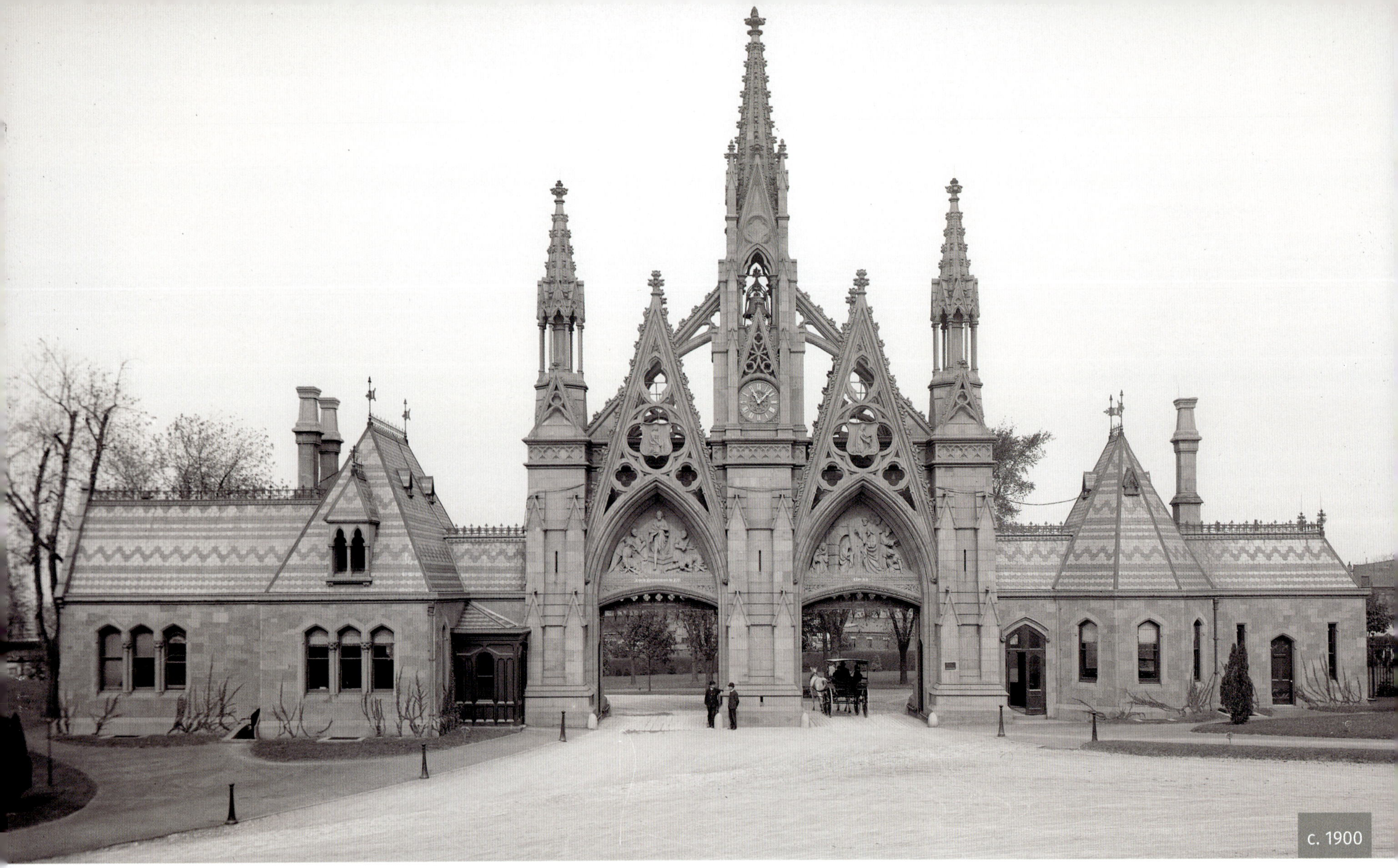

c. 1900

GREEN-WOOD CEMETERY

Victorian cemetery becomes a wildlife refuge and agroecology center

THEN: The Green-Wood Cemetery opened in 1838 and is considered one of the earliest rural cemeteries in America. It attracted the wealthiest and most elite families in Brooklyn for burials, and also included the Soldier's Lot, a section where Federal Soldiers who died in the Civil War were buried for free. Founder Henry Evelyn Pierrepont was a prominent land developer in Brooklyn, and a significant social influencer who believed that a cemetery should also attract the living. Green-Wood predates Prospect Park, and visitors came here to visit and bury their dead, as well as enjoy the bucolic surroundings. The original 178 acres were designed by David Bates Douglass, a military engineer and architect, who designed the topography with winding paths, hills, valleys, and a lake. By 1900, the urban landscape around Green-Wood Cemetery was expanding rapidly, becoming the developing residential neighborhoods of Sunset Park and Borough Park. The cemetery itself had grown to 478 acres and contained elaborate monuments, mausoleums, and landscaped grounds that reflected the Victorian-era attitudes towards death and remembrance among the most elite families in Brooklyn.

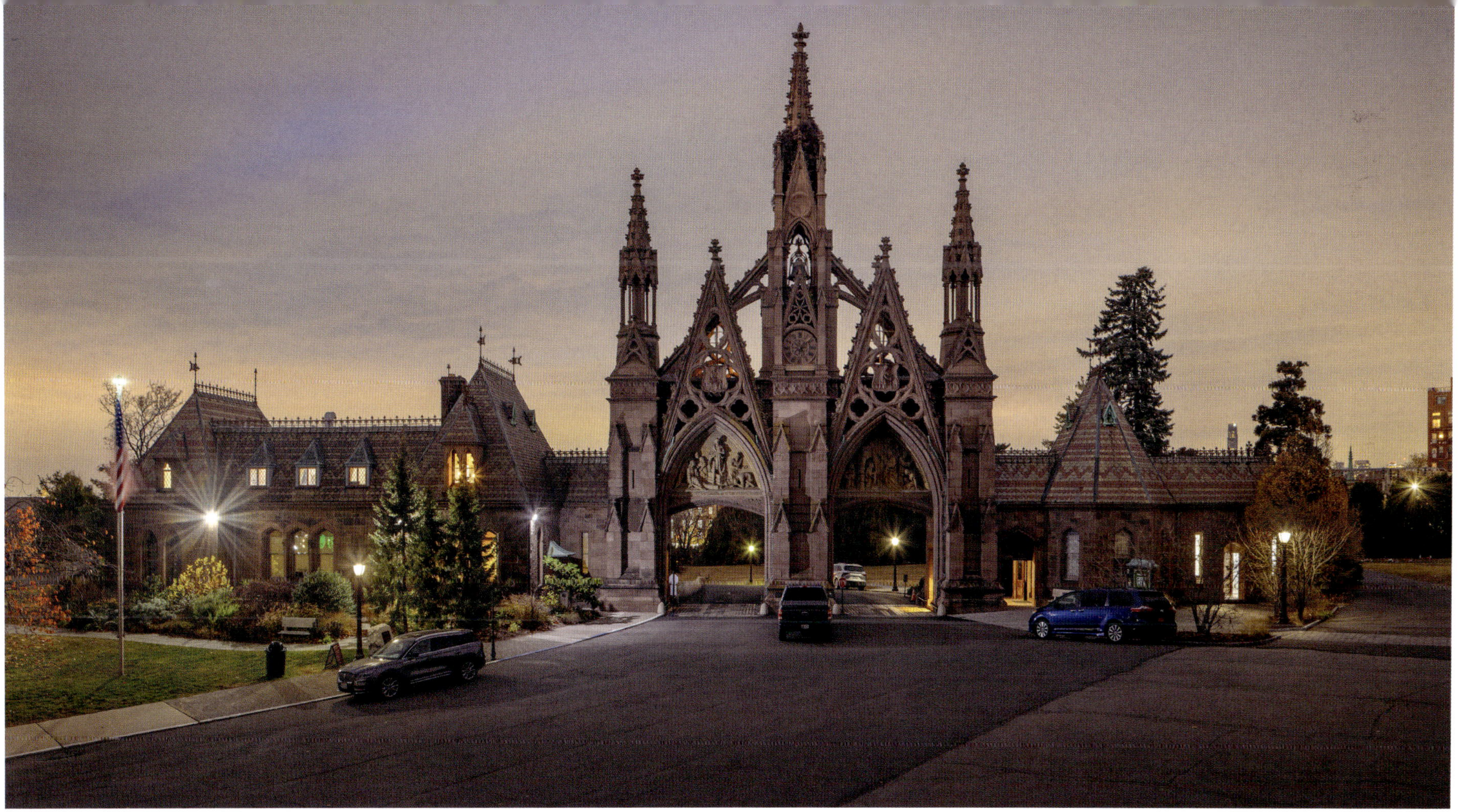

NOW: Visitors to the cemetery still enter from Fifth Avenue via the Gothic Revival gate, completed in 1865. It's the final resting place for 570,000 souls—and that number continues to grow today. The cemetery has become a cultural landmark, and hosts events like concerts, art exhibits, and educational programs throughout the year. The arboretum has over 700 species of trees, and the green space provides habitat for a number of wildlife species that would otherwise have been permanently displaced by the surrounding development. In addition to the Civil War soldiers, fifty victims from the September 11th attack at the World Trade Center are buried here.

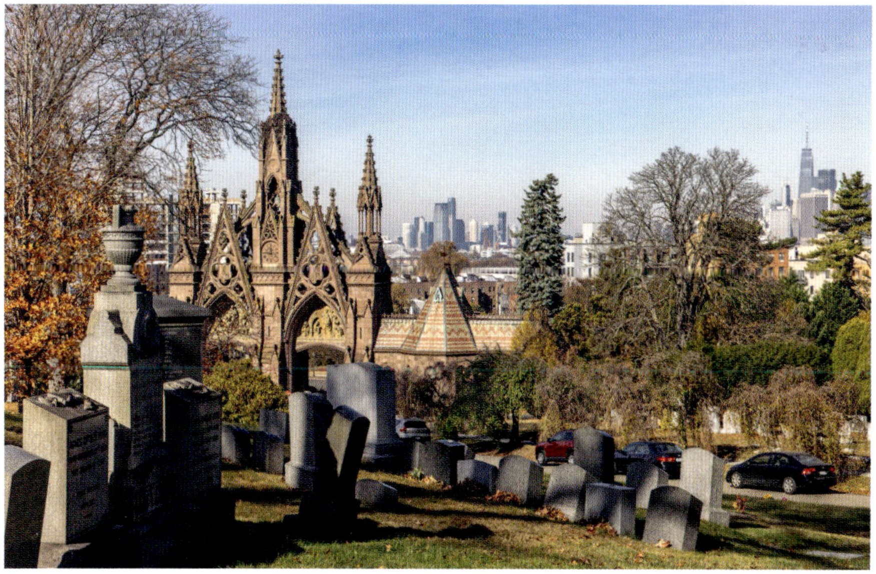

RIGHT: The Red Hook waterfront, One World Trade, and the Jersey City skyline are all visible from this old section of the cemetery, with gravestones from the 1800s that represent entire families.

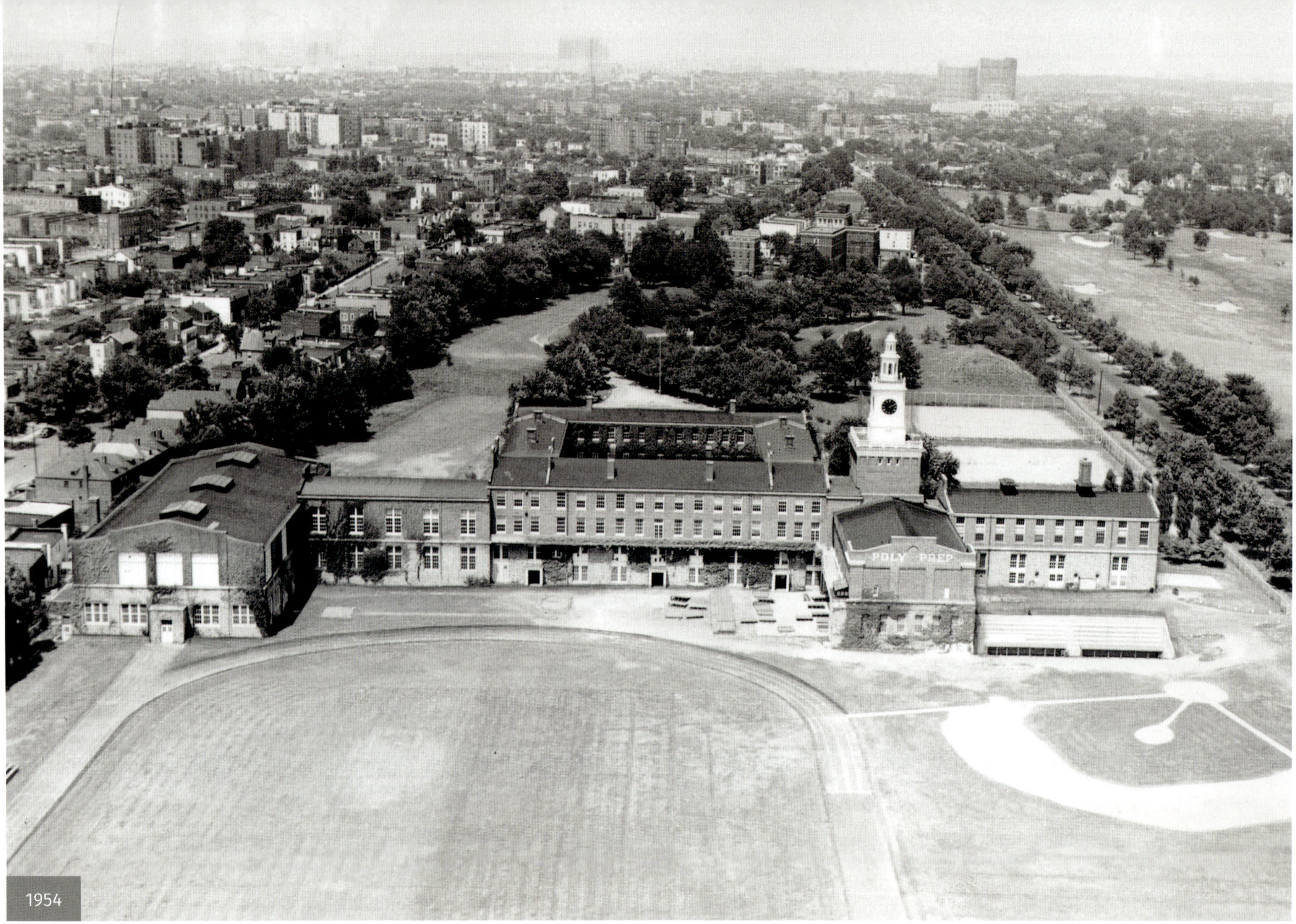

1954

POLY PREP, DYKER HEIGHTS

A prestigious private school provides peerless college prep programming

THEN: Poly Prep Country Day School was founded in Brooklyn Heights in 1854 to offer a rigorous academic institution in Brooklyn that could compete with boarding schools elsewhere in the state, with a focus on the technology and engineering that drove the Industrial Revolution. Initially located in downtown Brooklyn, the school quickly gained a reputation for academic excellence for the boys of Brooklyn's elite families, preparing students for college and even allowing them to study at the collegiate level. The curriculum was designed to prepare students for top universities and careers in the emerging fields of the time. In 1889, the school was reassessed, and the collegiate division was moved to a building next door. After decades and a series of name changes, this original building was acquired by New York University and

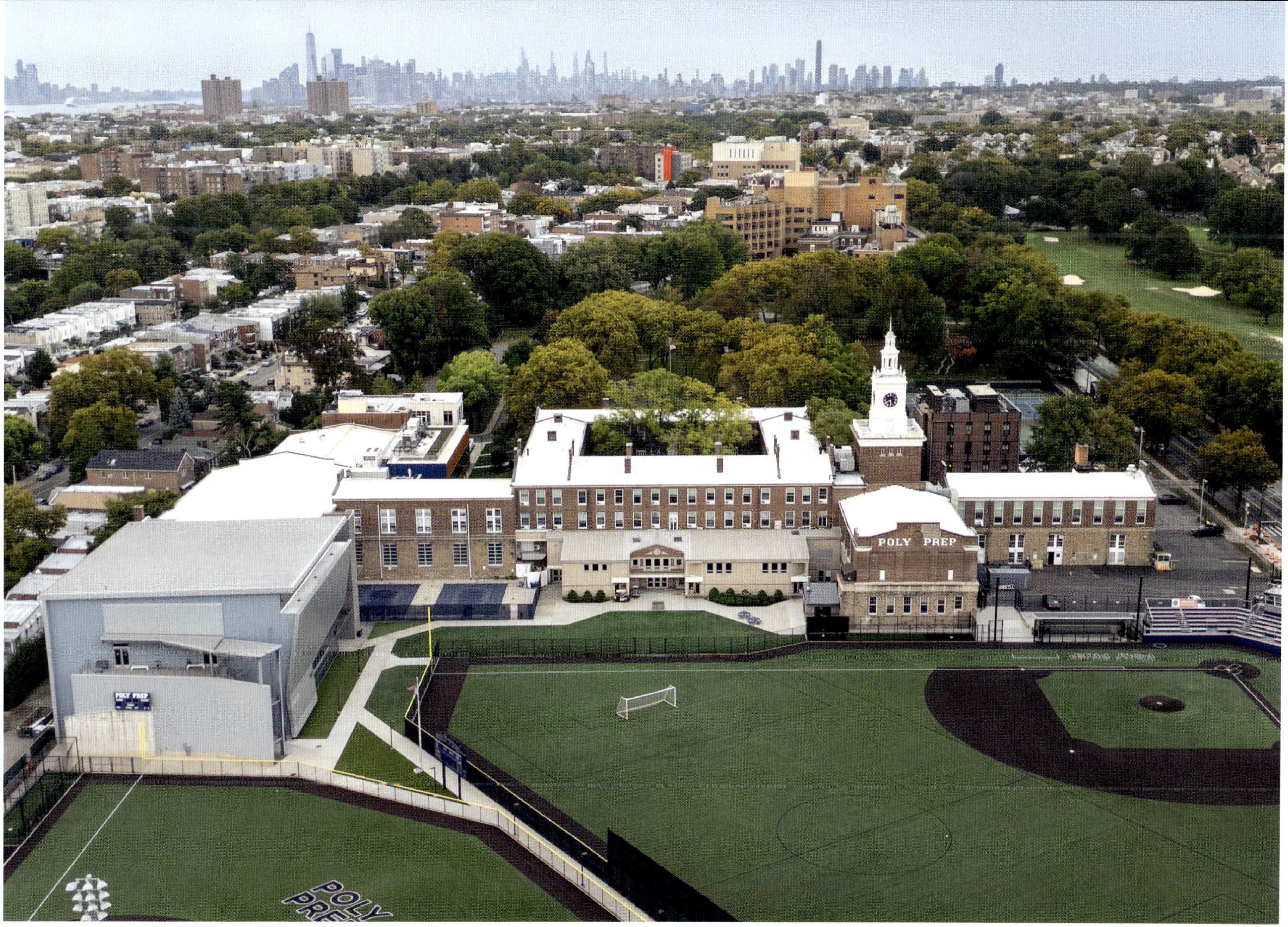

now houses their School of Engineering. As the school grew it focused on collegiate preparatory programming, expanding to include the humanities and athletics, while maintaining its strong emphasis on science and mathematics. Throughout the late nineteenth and early twentieth centuries, Poly Prep played a significant role in shaping Brooklyn's educational landscape, producing graduates who would go on to become leaders in various fields. In 1916, Poly Prep moved to a 25-acre campus, Dyker Heights. This picture opposite from 1954 is from that campus during Poly Prep's 100-year anniversary.

NOW: In the twenty-first century the school looks very different from when it was founded. The modern Poly Prep is known for its expansive campus, including state-of-the-art classrooms, laboratories, athletic fields, and theater. Female students have attended since 1977 and the school has worked to grow a student body that is more representative of the diverse range of backgrounds in the neighborhood. Its impact on the community is meaningful, serving as a major employer and cultural institution. Notable alumni of Poly Prep include a wide array of successful individuals in various fields, such as Jon Favreau (filmmaker and actor), John Rankin Rogers (third Governor of Washington State), and Rich Eisen (sportscaster).

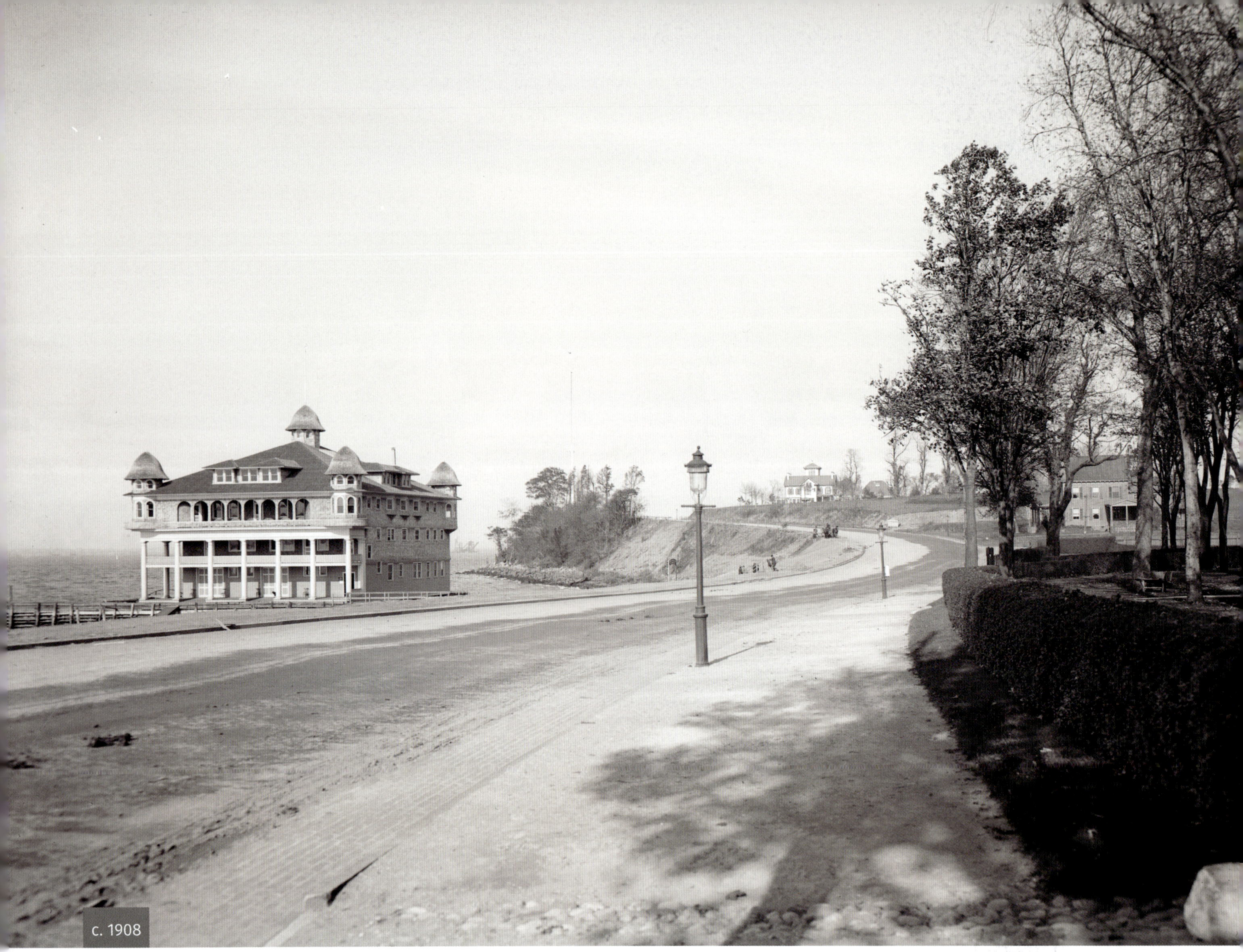
c. 1908

SHORE DRIVE, BAY RIDGE

The gold coast of Brooklyn

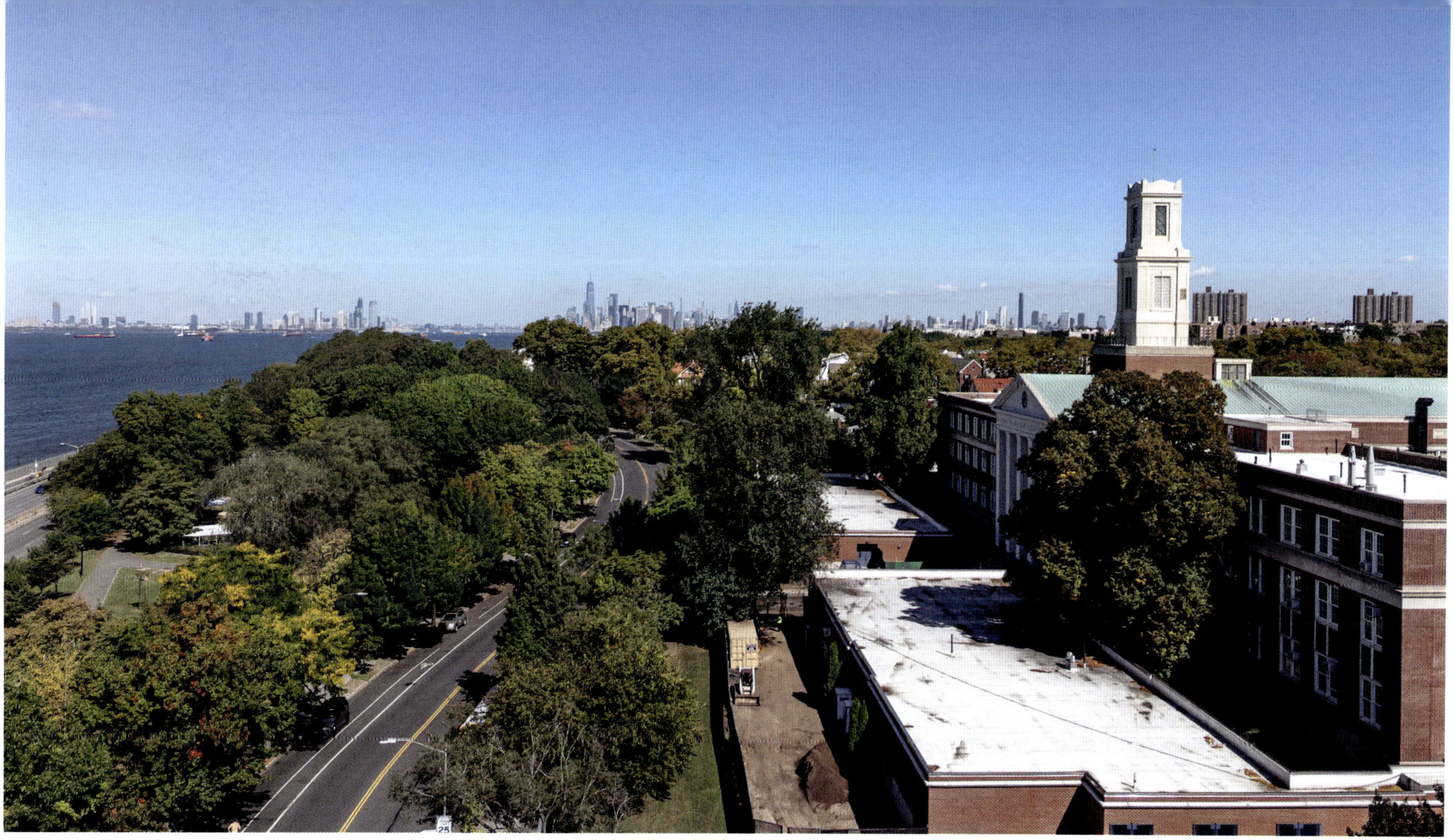

THEN: Brooklyn preacher Henry Ward Beecher penned a chapter in his book *Star Papers*, dedicated to the beauty and wonder of Shore Drive in 1855, describing the way the bay opened into 'shadows and light visible,' a welcome sight after the carriage drive from his home in Brooklyn Heights. By the late nineteenth and early twentieth centuries, Shore Drive—then called New Utrecht—had transformed from rural farmland into a gold-coast retreat for prosperous New Yorkers wanting scenic views and cool breezes off the harbor. Far from the urban centers of Manhattan and Brooklyn, it was still easily accessible by ferry and trolley for special day trips and summer homes. The waterside Crescent Boat House, visible in the photo, was part of an athletic club founded by Yale alumni in 1889. It offered exclusive social and sporting facilities for the area's affluent residents, with football, cricket, and rugby fields across the street. By 1908, a number of grand estates dotted the shore along the road, and the area had become a well-established luxury neighborhood. Several hotels also graced the drive, catering to summer visitors seeking respite from the city.

NOW: That period marked the height of Shore Drive's status as an exclusive enclave. At the end of the nineteenth century, Shore Drive was still private land that had graciously allowed visitors access. But it had been identified as a spot for a public park by Frederick Law Olmsted, whose office submitted a development plan in 1895. Just a year before, New Utrecht, including Bay Ridge and Fort Hamilton, became part of Brooklyn, and the city started a Parks Department, paving the way for the development finally to begin after Olmsted's death in 1903. Soon after, the elevated train, railroad, and subways would go deeper into Brooklyn and closer to Bay Ridge, contributing to the area's transition from a summer resort into a year-round residential neighborhood. Today, Shore Drive, now commonly known as Shore Road, has evolved into a diverse residential neighborhood that still maintains fragments of historic charm. While the area is still desirable for its waterfront access, the large estates and grand hotels are replaced by more modest homes and apartments. Fort Hamilton High School, built in 1941 on the site of the Crescent Club's athletic fields, is visible in the above picture. It provides an education and scenic water views to Bay Ridge students. The Shore Road Promenade offers waterfront access to all, and residents and visitors now enjoy the view that once attracted wealthy New Yorkers.

FORT LAFAYETTE

A vanished part of the country's coastal defense system

THEN: Fort Lafayette, a once formidable military installation in New York Harbor, was constructed between 1812 and 1822 as part of the city's coastal defense system, intended to work in conjunction with Fort Hamilton and Fort Wadsworth. It was an artificial island built on a reef in the Gravesend Bay, about 400 yards from what is now Sheepshead Bay, to protect New York City from naval attacks like one the British had launched from that location in the Revolutionary War. The fort was originally named Fort Diamond after its shape, but it was renamed in 1823 after the war to honor the Marquis de Lafayette, the French hero of the American Revolution. Though it was meant to defend New York City, it is most well known as a prison for Confederate soldiers, sympathizers, and political prisoners detained under Abraham Lincoln's selective suspension of the writ of Habeas Corpus during the Civil War, where it earned the nickname the "American Bastille." In 1868, the fort had a devastating fire that began in the artillery magazine, destroying most of its interior, and causing the outer walls to crack too. Several cannons exploded from the heat, and while it was renovated afterwards, it never went back to its original design. By 1900, the fort had evolved into an ammunitions depot supporting military operations along the East Coast, and it maintained an active military garrison where soldiers trained and stayed ready for potential conflicts.

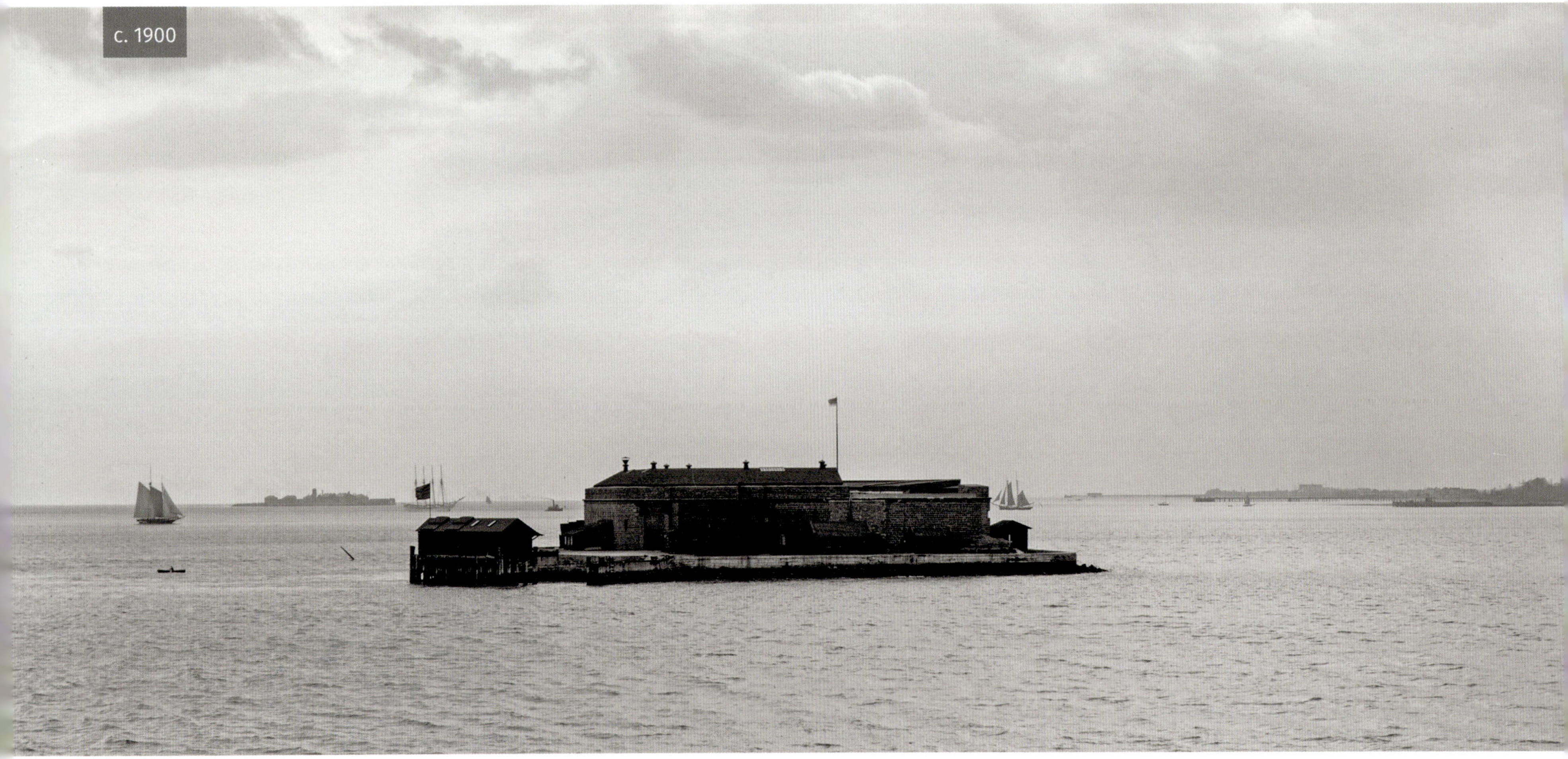

c. 1900

NOW: The buildings of Fort Lafayette were destroyed in the Sixties to make way for the Brooklyn tower of the Verrazzano-Narrows Bridge. The man-made island they stood on now holds a support shaft for the bridge, and bears no resemblance to the lost fort that once guarded the harbor. Despite its physical absence, Fort Lafayette remains a subject of historical interest and study, preserved in various museum exhibits and New York Harbor tours. Its memory serves to highlight the importance of New York's strategic position during conflict, and as a reminder that the needs of a growing metropolis are sometimes more important than preserving historical architecture.

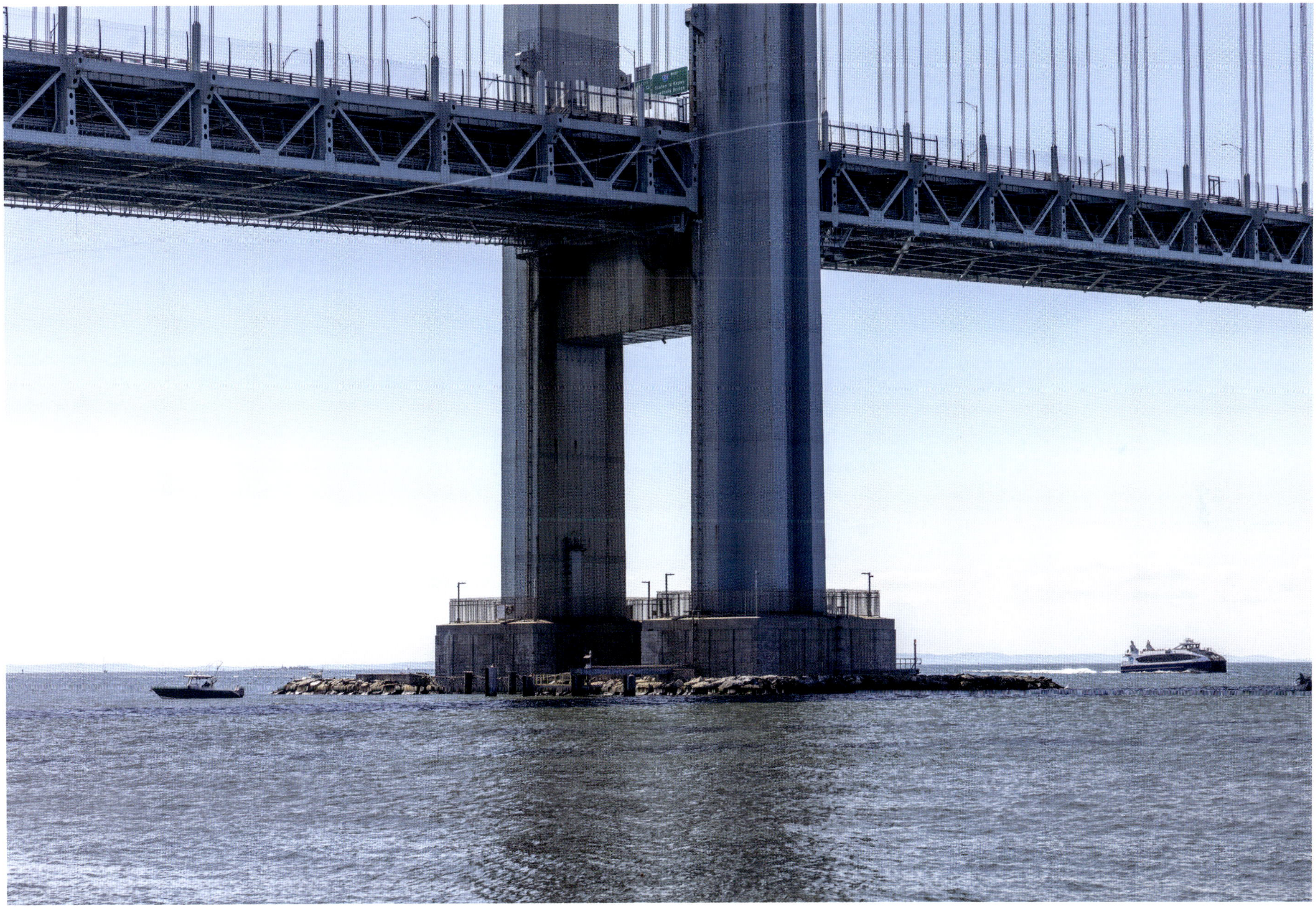

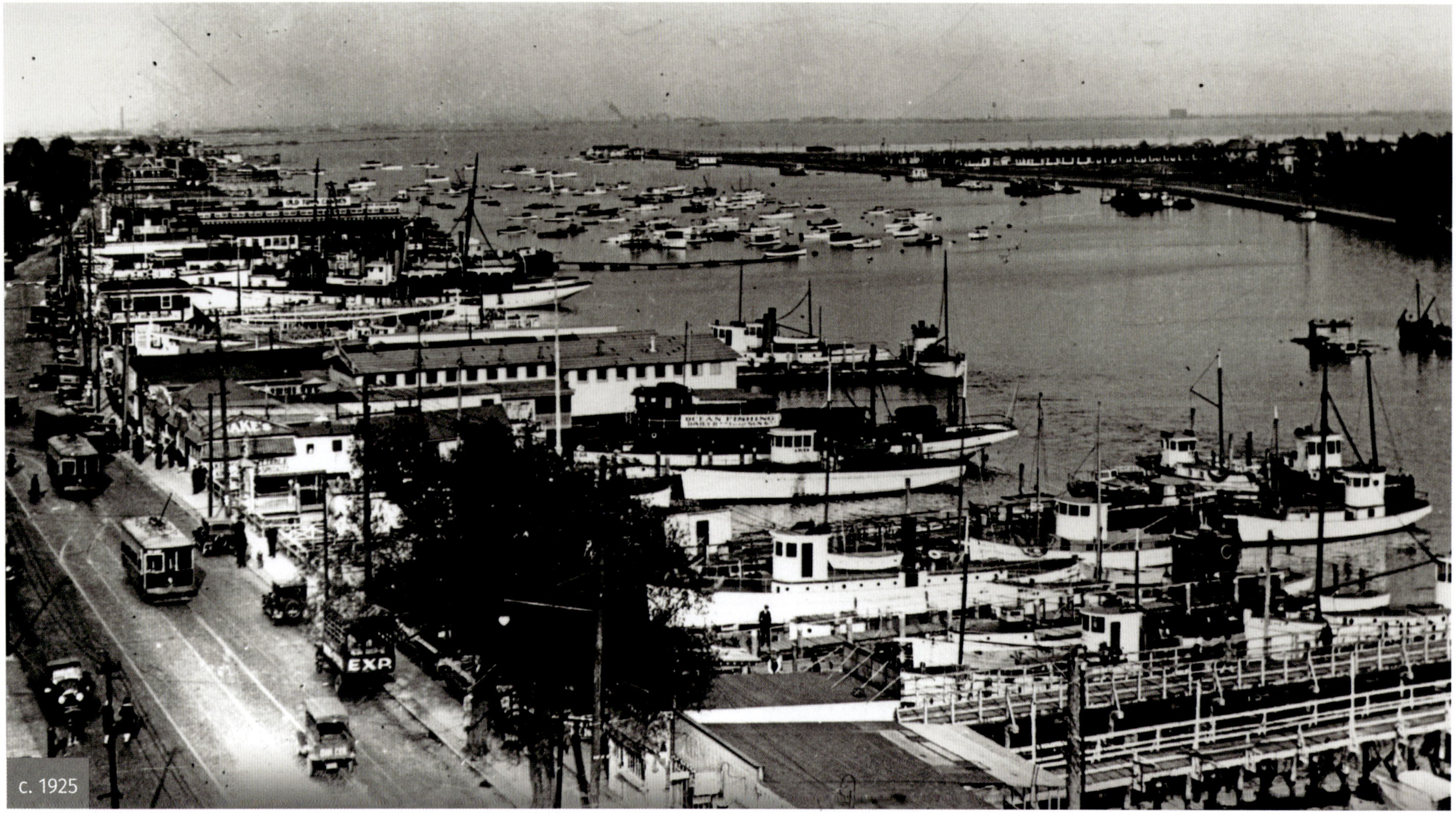

c. 1925

SHEEPSHEAD BAY PIERS

Brooklyn's original seaside resort

THEN: Sheepshead Bay Piers, originally constructed in the late nineteenth century, have served an important role in Brooklyn's maritime history. Sheepshead Bay was named for the sheepshead fish found in the waters, a popular and plentiful catch for fisherman since the Native Americans lived here. In the 1840s, city dwellers came to the community by trolley for fishing and hunting, and soon restaurants, hotels, and piers were built to serve the new inhabitants along Emmons Avenue, a once quiet street that ran parallel to the bay. By 1926, the piers were the nerve center of a thriving fishing industry and also a kind of seaside resort, and folks came by trolley car to enjoy the local fare. That same year, Irving Lundy opened Lundy Brothers Restaurant, which quickly became famous for shore dinners that included clams, lobster, and other local catches fresh out of the bay. Lundy had operated a clam shack on the piers since 1907, and by 1934 he owned most of the waterfront property in the village in addition to his restaurant, which had grown to become the largest in New York City.

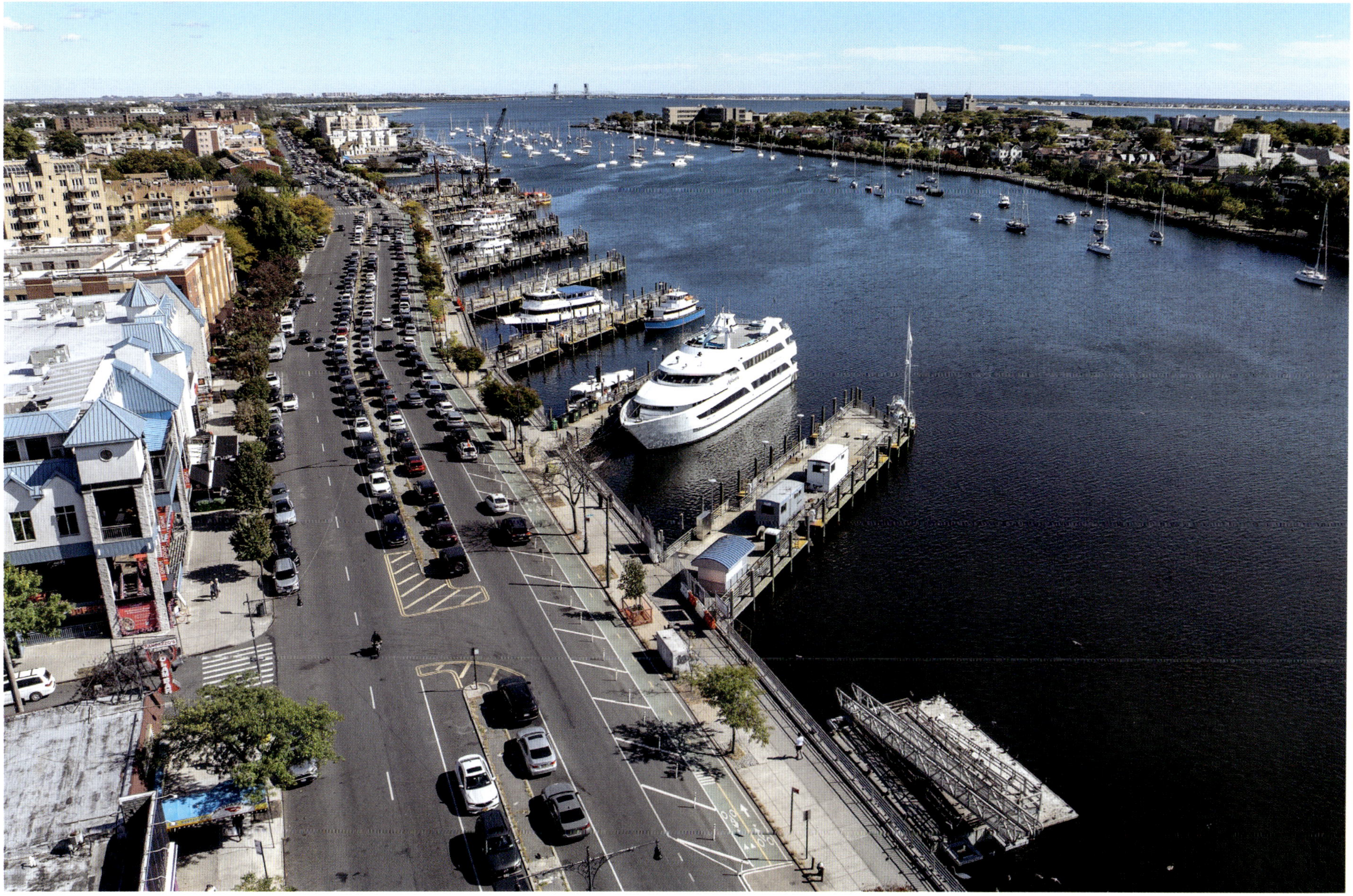

NOW: Since 1926, the piers have undergone significant changes. The decline of commercial fishing has meant a shift towards recreational use, and the professionals working the docks today operate fishing party boats and private charters. Many of the original wooden structures have been replaced by concrete docks for safety and durability. Lundy Brothers Restaurant closed in 2007 after decades of serving the day's catch, but its historic building still stands on Emmons. It sits among a collection of new restaurants that combine seafood with cuisines from the Caribbean and Mediterranean, reflecting the diversity of the current population of the waterfront community.

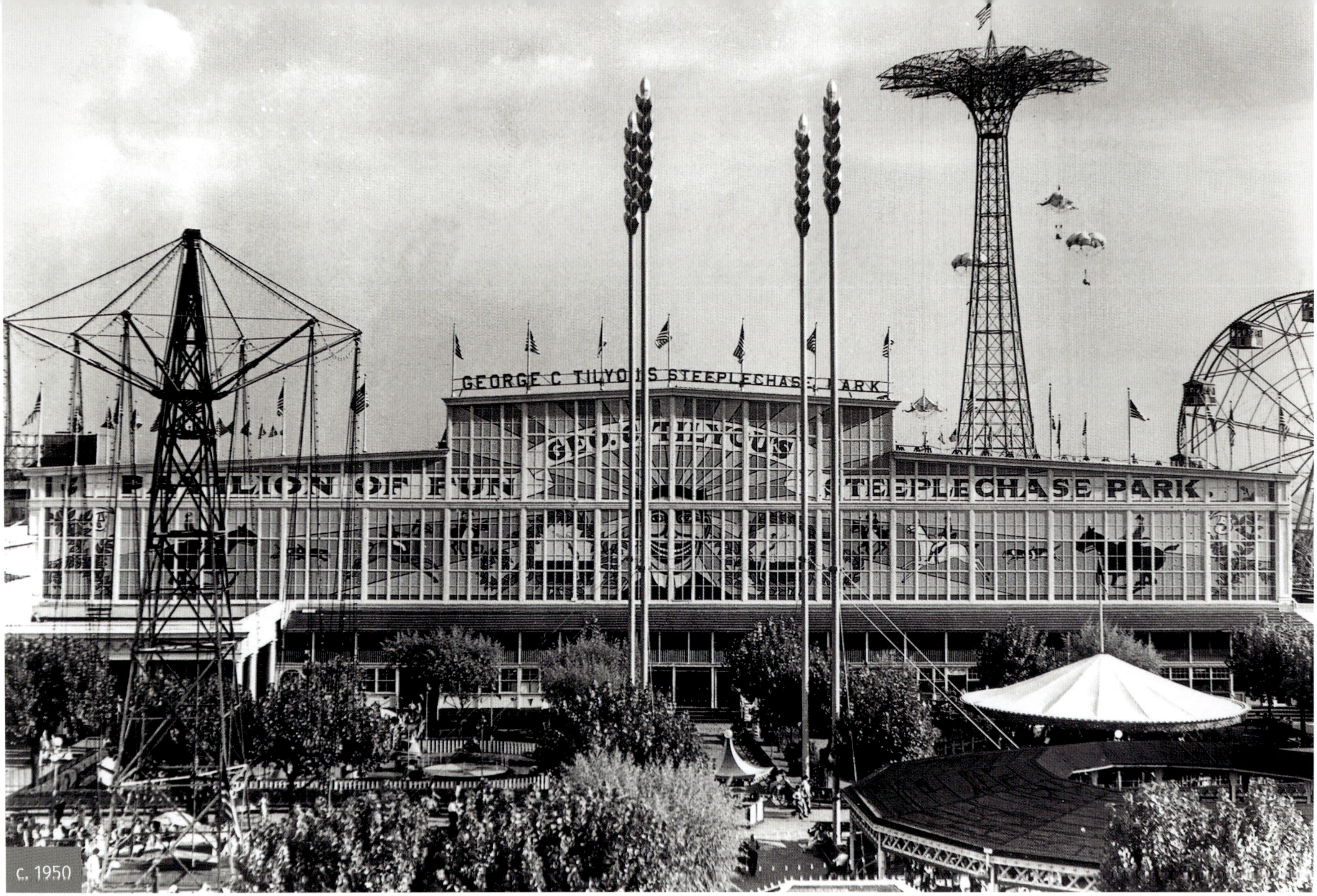

c. 1950

STEEPLECHASE PARK, CONEY ISLAND

Mechanical horse races gave the park its name

THEN: Coney Island was once an actual island separated from Brooklyn by Coney Island Creek. Between the 1900s and the twenty-first century, it went from a sleepy seaside resort to a bustling entertainment district. One of the area's three iconic amusement parks, Steeplechase Park, was created by Coney Island native George C. Tilyou, a pioneer of American amusement park development. He grew up working at various stands and small businesses around the boardwalk, and dreamed of opening an amusement center with a cohesive experience—he wanted it to be more than a collection of individual rides. He opened Steeplechase in 1897 and named it after the signature ride featuring a mechanical horse race. When a fire destroyed most of Steeplechase Park in 1907, Tilyou rebuilt it in only eighty-seven days. Steeplechase bounced back stronger than ever, becoming known for rides and attractions that were destined to bring strangers together in amusing—and occasionally embarrassing—ways, fostering a sense of shared adventure between visitors. In this image from the 1950s, the parachute tower, which had debuted at the 1939 World's Fair, is visible in

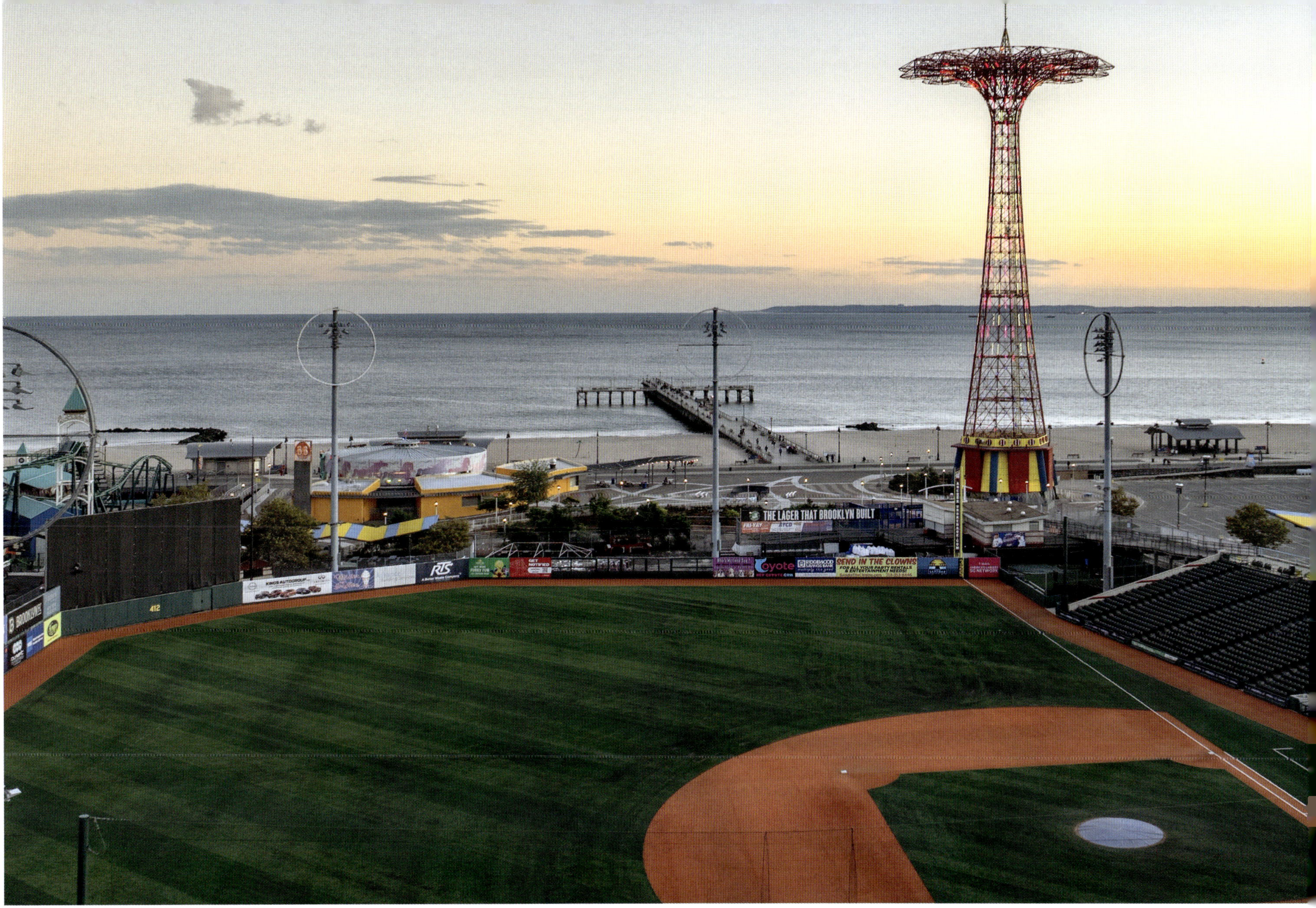

the background. The glass building is the Pavilion of Fun, a massive structure that housed a number of rides and attractions that connected to one another. The famous "funny face," viewable in the front, would become the iconic image for Coney Island. By the 1960s, Steeplechase was well past its heyday, and while the beach and other boardwalk attractions still attracted visitors, automobiles were common enough that folks started traveling further to go to less crowded beaches.

NOW: Tilyou passed away in 1914, but his family continued to run Steeplechase until it was demolished in the Sixties. The area remained empty for decades, a visual cue that Coney Island had fallen on hard times. In the 2000s, Coney Island was rezoned and redeveloped, and a new minor league baseball stadium opened on the Steeplechase Park site. The stadium became a home for the Brooklyn Cyclones, named after the boardwalk's iconic wooden roller coaster, located just a few blocks away. The Parachute Tower, a protected local landmark, still stands on the pier like a guardian of history.

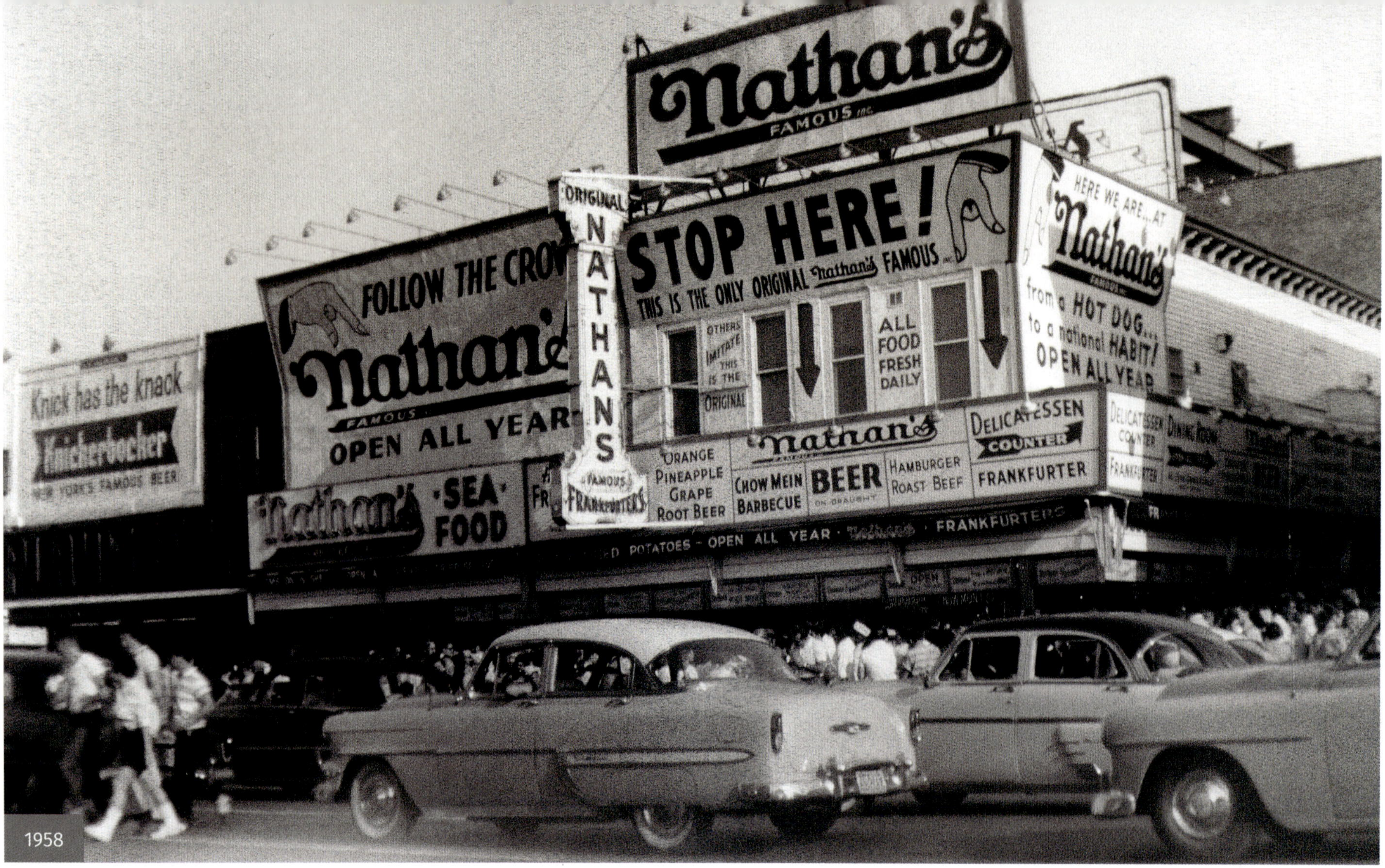

1958

NATHAN'S FAMOUS HOT DOG STAND, CONEY ISLAND

Hot dogs bring a century of visitors to the Brooklyn shore

THEN: Nathan's Famous, on the corner of Surf and Stillwell, was founded by Polish immigrant Nathan Handwerker in 1916 with a $300 loan from his friends and a recipe from his wife, Ida. Handwerker differentiated his hot dog stand from the rest of the competition on the crowded boardwalk by offering high-quality products at a lower price than competitors, as well as using creative marketing schemes to get attention. He hired undercover actors to wear lab coats while eating at the stand, giving the impression that doctors approved of his hot dogs, and he hosted the Fourth of July Hot Dog Eating Contest, which still today remains a beloved summer tradition. By the late Fifties, Nathan's had grown from a small operation to a beloved landmark, and no trip to Coney Island was complete without an "all the way" dog topped with sauerkraut, onions, and mustard. Nathan and Ida expanded the menu and regularly drew summer crowds like those in the picture, by offering seafood, hamburgers, and the unique chow mein barbecue sandwich. Part of the appeal was the culinary democracy, where everyone—regardless of class or status—stood in the same lines and received the same restaurant experience for the same cost. This appealed to locals who filled the space in the off season, using the restaurant as a neighborhood hangout and community space. This kept the business going strong during the second half of the twentieth century, when beach goers began to travel further and Coney Island suffered a steep economic downturn.

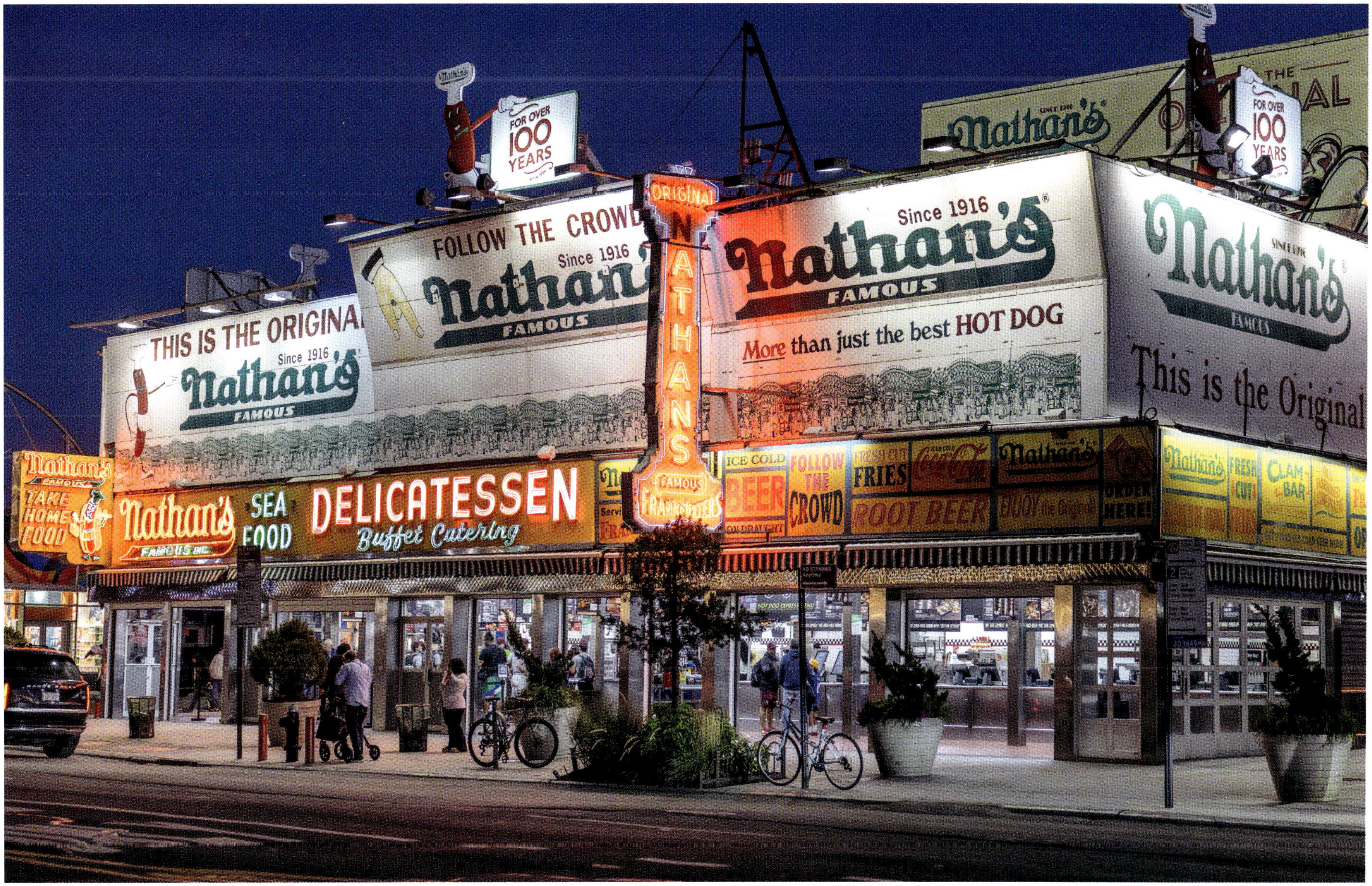

NOW: No matter what was or wasn't going on around it, Nathan's Famous remained a cornerstone of Coney Island, and the view from Surf and Stillwell remains much the same. The original location has been renovated and expanded over the years, and the business has grown far beyond the beach. Nathan's is now an international brand, with products in supermarkets and hundreds of hot dog stands around New York City and beyond. The Fourth of July Hot Dog Contest kept Nathan's in the public eye throughout Coney Island's decline and renewal, and is today a major televised event drawing competitors from all over the world. While Nathan's has become a large corporation, the original stand remains a vital part of Coney Island's identity and confirms that a low-cost, high-quality hot dog by the beach will have a place forever in our stomachs and our hearts.

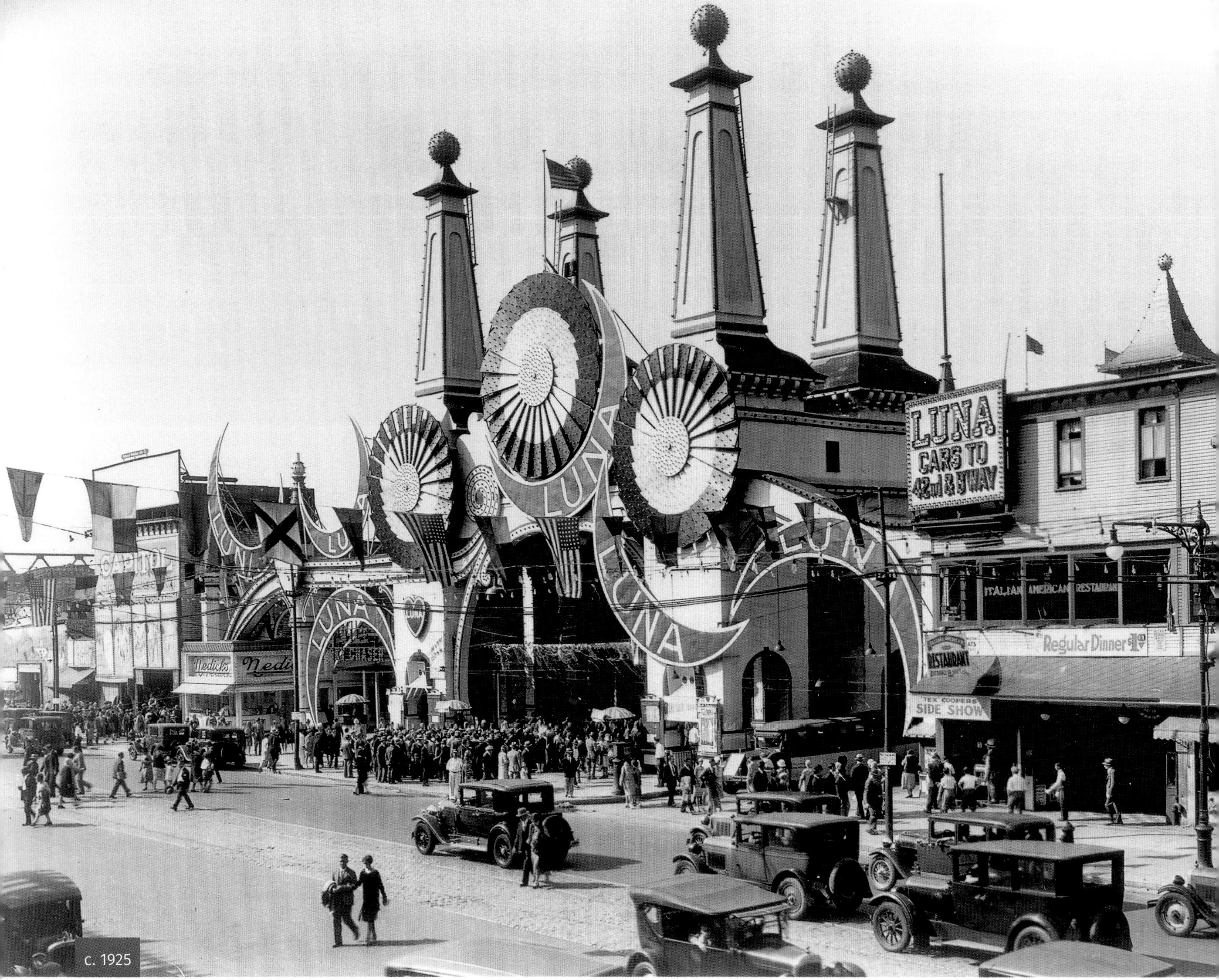
LUNA
CARS TO
42nd & B'WAY
LUNA
ITALIAN AMERICAN RESTAURANT
Regular Dinner
RESTAURANT
TEX COOPERS
SIDE SHOW
Nedicks
c. 1925

LUNA PARK, CONEY ISLAND

Coney Island's magic survives blaze

THEN: Luna Park opened in 1903, designed by Frederic Thompson and Elmer "Skip" Dundy. The name Luna Park was inspired by the sister of one of the founders, and the design was dedicated to Luna the Roman moon goddess. The entrance was marked by iconic towers, plaster minarets, Venetian archways, pagodas, and gargoyles. It dazzled at night, outlined by thousands of glittering lights that truly wowed crowds in the new age of electricity. By 1925, it had become a symbol of the escapist nature of Coney Island's amusements. A Trip to the Moon, simulating a lunar voyage, and Dragon's Gorge, an early scenic railway ride, were the most popular attractions. Luna Park also featured recreations of world landmarks, disaster spectacles, and ethnographic villages. Though some of these experiences would be unacceptable today, they were a huge draw at the time. Thompson and Dundy knew what customers wanted, and they were known for their continuous innovation. In 1925, crowds lining up outside were the norm, with millions of visitors coming through Luna Park each year.

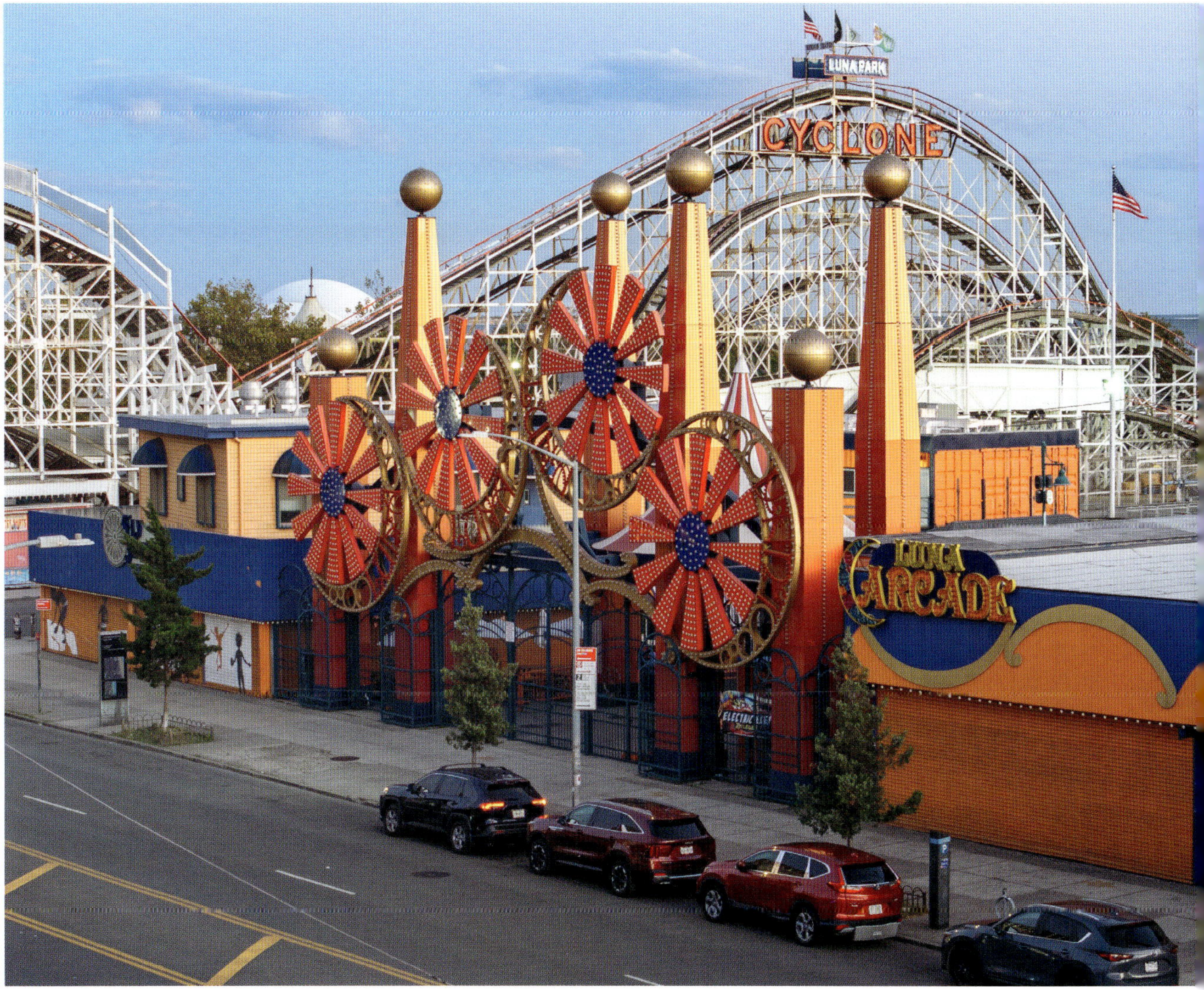

NOW: In 1944, a fire effectively destroyed almost all of Luna Park, though a small part limped along for a couple more years. Luna Park had provided a bird's-eye view of the 1907 Steeplechase fire and recovery, but its own rebuilding was impacted by World War II, and it never recovered. After the war, housing needs were prioritized and Luna Park was demolished to make room for the Luna Park Houses. The famous Coney Island boardwalk remained, lined with food stands, shops, and games, and the beach continued to attract sunbathers and swimmers during the summer months. However, the Coney Island boardwalk suffered through half a dozen more fires, destroying most of the original charm and physical details. In 2004, the Coney Island History Project started to preserve the area and teach visitors about the missing details and past. The organization made sure that redevelopment would protect any remaining history. In 2010, another Luna Park opened on Surf Avenue, offering a new amusement park behind a very familiar entrance, representing the iconic Luna Park entrance of the past. While the area has lost much of its mid-century grit and chaos, efforts have been made to maintain its unique character and history. The new Luna Park now entertains millions of visitors each year, just like its namesake.

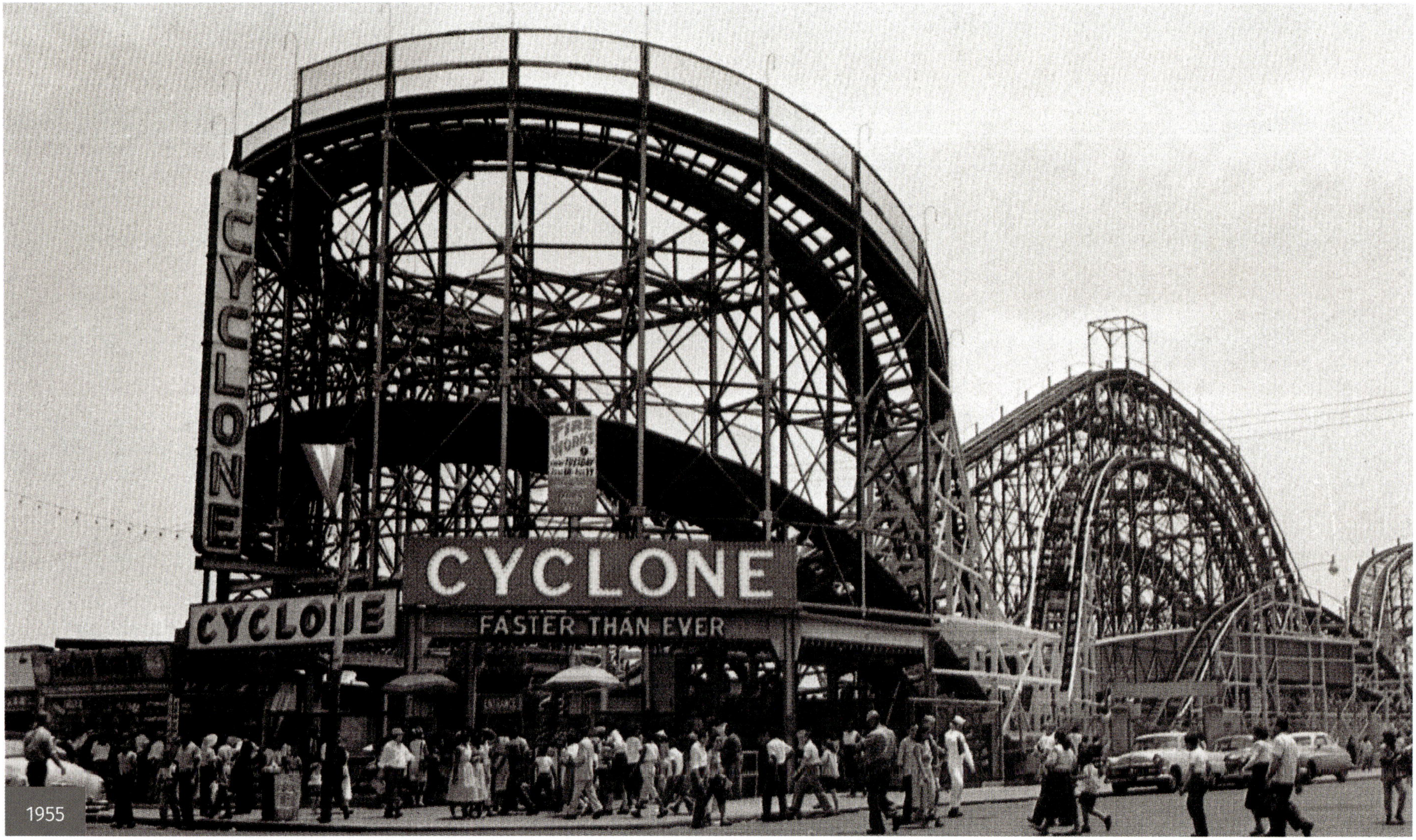

1955

CYCLONE ROLLER COASTER, CONEY ISLAND

America's most famous wooden coaster still thrills

THEN: The Coney Island Cyclone opened on June 26, 1927 on the site of what had been America's first roller coaster, the Switchback Railway. Designed by Vernon Keenan and built by Harry C. Baker, under the ownership of Jack and Irving Rosenthal, the Cyclone cost around $150,000 to build and only twenty-five cents to ride on weekdays—Sundays and holidays cost ten cents more. Standing eighty-five feet tall and featuring a first drop of sixty degrees, the Cyclone covered 2,600 feet of wood and steel tracks in under two minutes, with a top speed of sixty miles per hour. By 1965, Coney Island was suffering from the general urban decline that followed World War II, but the Cyclone remained a popular draw for thrill seekers from across New York, and it influenced the design of at least a dozen replica coasters around the world.

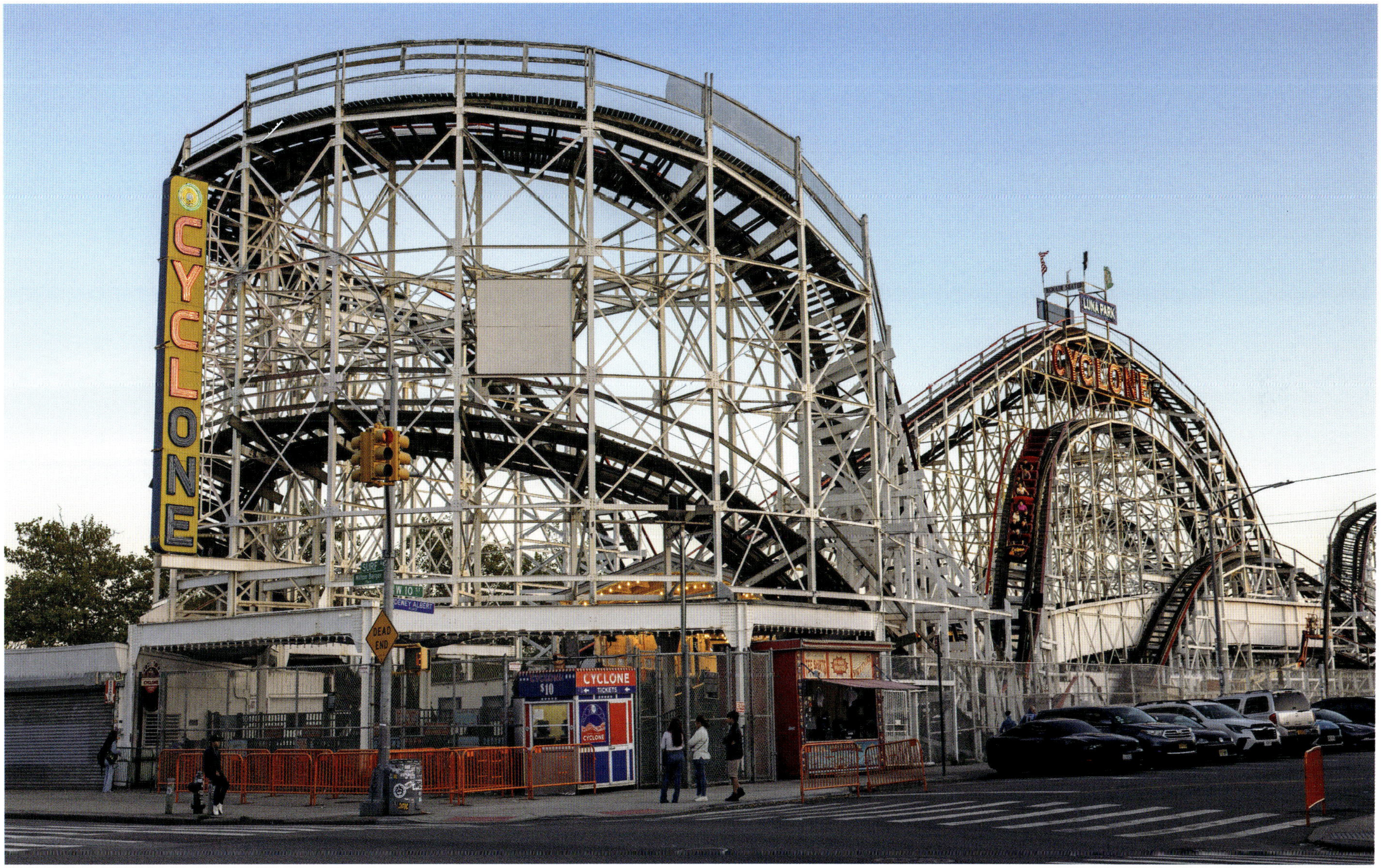

NOW: In spite of numerous threats to its existence over the decades, the Cyclone has stood as a distinctive part of the ever-changing Coney Island skyline, and continues to operate at the intersection of Surf Avenue and West Tenth Street. It was targeted for demolition in the Seventies, when Coney Island didn't have enough visitors to support the upkeep, but a "Save the Cyclone" campaign worked, and the coaster was declared a New York City Landmark in 1988. Over the years, the coaster has undergone several renovations and restorations to keep it operational. While the essential character is unchanged, modern safety features have been incorporated and regular maintenance ensures that it meets current standards. Today, it is owned by the City of New York, and operated and maintained by Luna Park. After almost 100 years, the Cyclone still stands as both a thrilling ride and a living piece of history, connecting modern riders to the spirit of excitement and innovation that has defined Coney Island for over a century.

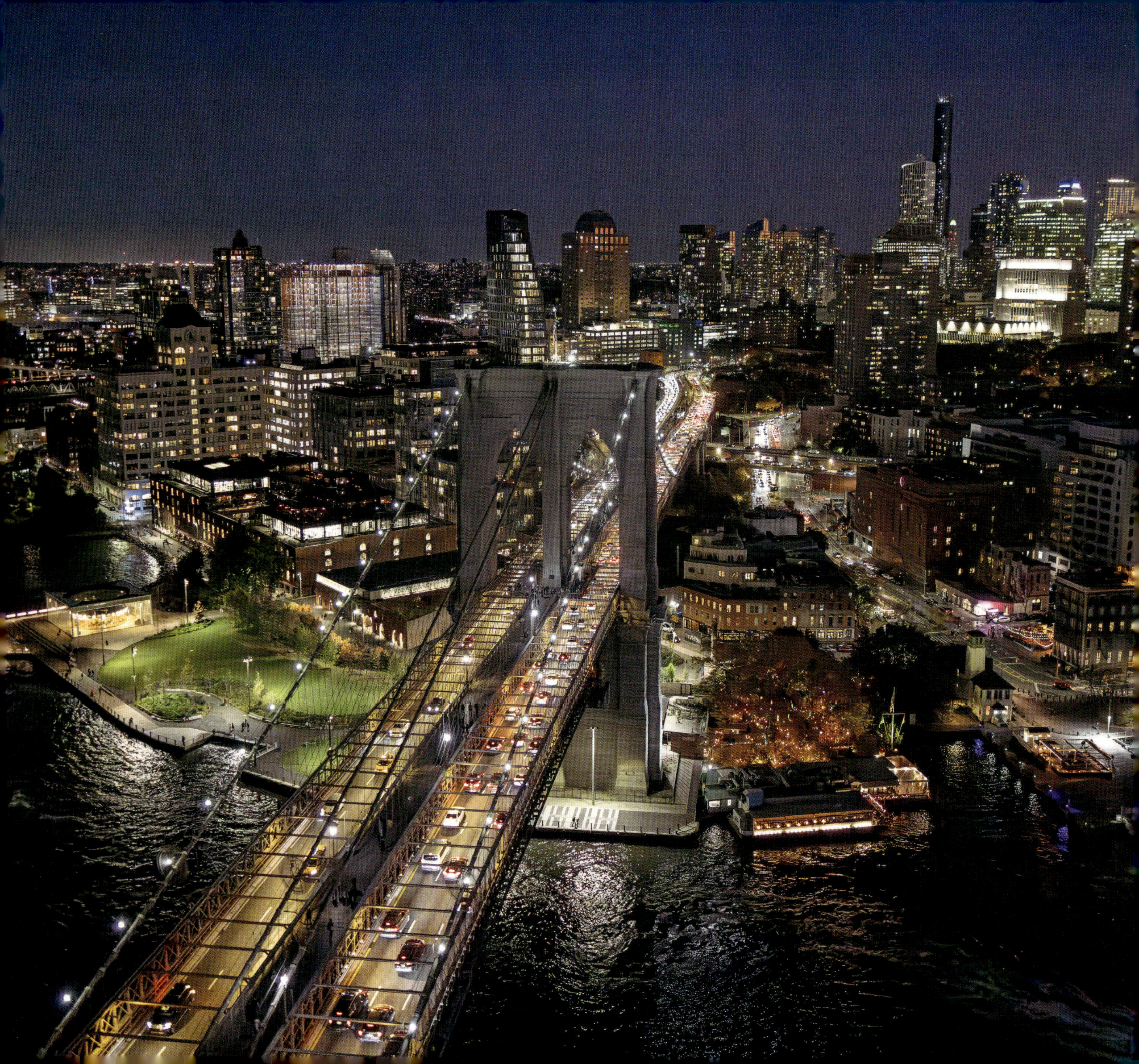

IMAGE CREDITS

All following images courtesy of Brooklyn Public Library, Center for Brooklyn History:

P8–9 *Back Cover and Brooklyn Waterfront*, [1910-1920?], V1976.2.268; Edward B. Watson photographs and prints
P14 *Fulton Ferry Landing*, 1891, V1986.18.1.9. Eugene L. Armbruster photographs and scrapbooks
P16 *Brooklyn Heights Promenade View*, 1961, HERZ_0312; Irving I. Herzberg photograph collection
P18 *Brooklyn Heights Promenade* [Brooklyn-Queens Expressway], [1948], V1973.5.1407; Brooklyn photograph and illustration collection
P20 *Plymouth Church*, [1954], CHUR_0123; Brooklyn Daily Eagle photographs
P24 *View from the Bossert Hotel, Brooklyn Heights*, 1929, NEIG_0486; Brooklyn Daily Eagle photographs
P26 *Montague and Clinton, Brooklyn Heights*, 1944, NEIG_0191; Brooklyn Daily Eagle photographs
P28 *The South Brooklyn Savings Bank, Cobble Hill*, [1941], BANK_0225; Brooklyn Daily Eagle photographs
P30 *Borough Hall*, [1896?], V1974.23.1.40; Art Work of Brooklyn, New York
P32 *Borough Hall Steps*, 1949, V1973.5.1804; Brooklyn photographs and illustration collection
P34 *Court Street*, 1941, V1987.10.13; Percy Varian Photograph collection
P36 *Cadman Plaza*, [1925-1935?], V1973.5.3602; Brooklyn photograph and illustration collection
P38 *Main Post Office and Brooklyn Eagle, Cadman Plaza*, [195-], NEIG_0562; Brooklyn Daily Eagle photographs
P40 *Fulton Street*, 1958, V1973.4.594; Postcard collection
P42 *Willoughby Street*, 1915, V1973.5.1869; Brooklyn photograph and illustration collection
P44 *The Brooklyn Paramount Theater*, 1962, HERZ_0331; Irving I. Herzberg photograph collection
P46 *Flatbush and Atlantic Avenues*, [1900-1925?], V1973.5.1862; Brooklyn photograph and illustration collection
P48 *Brooklyn Academy of Music*, [1900-1925], V1973.6.410; Brooklyn photograph and illustration collection
P50 *View from the Williamsburg Bank Tower*, [1936], NEIG_1980; Brooklyn Daily Eagle photographs
P52 *Fort Greene Park*, 1930, PARK_0113; Brooklyn Daily Eagle photographs
P54 *The Manhattan Bridge, DUMBO*, [1946–1954], BRID_0225; Brooklyn Daily Eagle photographs
P58 *Pratt Institute*, [c. 1930], SCHL_0237; Brooklyn Daily Eagle photographs
P60 *Williamsburg*, [1924?], V1972.1.605a; Early Brooklyn and Long Island photograph collection
P62 *Williamsburg Bridge*, 1900, V1974.8.144; Arthur Wilmott photograph collection
P64 *Williamsburg Bridge Plaza*, [1915-1925?], V1991.106.54; Eugene L. Armbruster photographs and scrapbooks
P66 *Williamsburg Bedford Avenue*, V1972.1.1109, 1895, V1972.1.1109; Early Brooklyn and Long Island photograph collection
P68 *Greenpoint*, [1915-1925?], V1973.5.1382; Brooklyn photograph and illustration collection
P70 *Bedford-Stuyvesant*, V1973.5.1871, [1890-1910?]; Brooklyn photograph and illustration collection
P72 *Weeksville Houses*, 1922, V1974.32.286a; Eugene L. Armbruster photographs and scrapbooks
P74 *Bedford Union Armory*, [1908?], ARM_0045; Brooklyn Daily Eagle photographs
P76 *Grant Square*, [1919-1929], V1973.5.1076a; Brooklyn photograph and illustration collection
P80 *Eastern Parkway*, 1897, V1974.8.154; Arthur Wilmott photograph collection
P82 *Brooklyn College, Midwood*, 1936, SCHL_0007; Brooklyn Daily Eagle photographs
P84 *Flatbush Reformed Dutch Church*, [189-?], V1972.1.617; Early Brooklyn and Long Island photograph collection
P92 *Brooklyn Public Library*, 1913, V1973.5.2468; Brooklyn photograph and illustration collection
P96 *Prospect Park Entrance*, [1900-1920?], V1988.54.54; Postcard collection
P98 *Prospect Park Long Meadow*, [1900-1925?], V1973.5.3422; Brooklyn photograph and illustration collection
P100 *Prospect Lake Boathouse*, [1897-1917?], V1973.4.1434; Postcard collection
P102 *Prospect Park Concert Grove*, [1870-1890?], V1986.250.1.41; William Schroeder, Sr. scrapbook collection
P104 *Litchfield Villa*, 1890?, V1973.5.1541; Brooklyn photograph and illustration collection
P106 *Park Slope Armory*, Old 14th Regt., 187th Field Artillery, 1951, ARM_0063; Brooklyn Daily Eagle photographs
P108 *Montauk Club*, [1905-1915?], V1974.022.9.260; Eugene L. Armbruster photographs and scrapbooks
P112 *South Park Slope, Fourth Avenue to Butler* [Fourth Avenue from Baltic Street], 1933, NEIG_1310; Brooklyn Daily Eagle photographs.
P114 *Carroll Street Bridge, Gowanus*, 1912, NEIG_2337; Brooklyn Daily Eagle photographs
P116 *Gowanus Canal*, 1952, NEIG_2343; Brooklyn Daily Eagle photographs
P118 *Smith Street at 1st Place* [Smith St. north at 1st Pl.], 1928, SMTH_0001; Smith and Jay Street collection.
P120 *Red Hook* [Aerial view of Red Hook], 1950, NEIG_1765; Brooklyn Daily Eagle photographs.
P122 *Bush Terminal, Industry City*, [193-?], WORK_0082; Brooklyn Daily Eagle photographs
P126 *Poly Prep, Dyker Heights*, 1954, SCHL_0552; Brooklyn Daily Eagle photographs
P132 *Sheepshead Bay Piers*, [1915-1925?], V1973.5.1497; Brooklyn photograph and illustration collection.
P136 *Nathan's Famous Hot Dog Stand, Coney Island*, 1958, V1974.4.1146; John D. Morrell photographs
P140 *Cyclone Rollercoaster, Coney Island*, V1973.4.1456.11; Postcard collection

With thanks to the Library of Congress for the images on pages:

Brooklyn Bridge Walkway: 12
Montague Street Ferry: 22
Brooklyn Navy Yard: 56
Union League Club: 78
Brooklyn Museum: 88
Grand Army Plaza. 90
Mount Prospect Reservoir: 94
Old Stone House: 110
Green-Wood Cemetery: 124
Shore Drive, Bay Ridge: 128
Fort Lafayette: 130

And to:

Alamy Images, *Brooklyn Bridge*: page 10

Louis Buhle, Courtesy of Brooklyn Botanic Garden: *Brooklyn Botanic Garden*: page 86

The Brian Merlis Collection for *Steeplechase Park*: 134
Luna Park: 138

All *Now* images taken by Evan Joseph.

OPPOSITE: Night falls and the lights of Brooklyn brighten the sky, as seen from a helicopter over the East River.

INDEX

A&S (Abraham & Strauss) 40, 41
Adams, John 56
Adams Street 40
Almirall, Raymond F. 93
Astral Oil Works 58
Atlantic Avenue 7, 24, 28, 46–7, 66, 71
Audubon Center at the Boathouse 101
Baker, Harry C. 140
Barclays Center Arena 45, 47
Bay Ridge 128–9
Bedford Avenue 74, 77, 79
Bedford Corners 71
Bedford-Stuyvesant 6, 66, 70–1
Bedford Union Armory, Crown Heights 74–5
Beecher, Henry Ward 6, 20, 129
Bergen Street 77
BFC Construction 75
Boerum Hill 24
Bond Street 51
Borough Hall 23, 30–3, 35
Borough Hall Transit Center 43
Bossert Hotel 24–5
Bossert, Louis 24
The Brooke 51
Brooklyn Academy of Music (BAM) 6, 48–9, 53
Brooklyn Battery Tunnel 121
Brooklyn Botanic Garden 81, 86–7
Brooklyn Bridge 6, 8–15, 24, 142
Brooklyn Bridge Park 7, 9, 15, 19, 23
Brooklyn City Railroad 66, 71
Brooklyn College, Midwood 82–3
Brooklyn Cyclones 135
Brooklyn Daily Eagle 30, 38–9, 93
Brooklyn Dodgers 21, 25, 33, 47, 107, 110–11
Brooklyn Heights 6, 17, 24–7, 126
Brooklyn Heights Promenade 16–19
Brooklyn Main Post Office 37, 38–9
Brooklyn Municipal Building 28
Brooklyn Museum 6, 81, 88–9
Brooklyn Navy Yard 6, 24, 52, 56–7, 67, 71
Brooklyn Nets 45, 47
Brooklyn Paramount Theater 44–5, 53
Brooklyn Point 51
Brooklyn Public Library (Main Branch) 81, 92–3, 95
Brooklyn-Queens Expressway 17, 19, 23, 24
Brooklyn Supreme Court 37
Brooklyn Tower 51
Brooklyn Waterworks 94
Bush & Denslow 122
Bush Terminal, Industry City 122–3
Bushwick 6
Butler Street 112–13
Cadman Plaza 24, 36–9
Campanella, Roy 33
Caputo's Fine Foods 119
Carnegie, Andrew 93
Carroll, Charles 118
Carroll Gardens/Park 7, 118
Carroll Street Bridge, Gowanus 114–15
Church Avenue 85
City Hall 30
City Point 31
Cleveland, Grover 109
Clinton Hill 59
Clinton Street 26–7
Cobble Hill 24, 28–9
Concert Grove, Prospect Park 102–3
Coney Island 6, 134–41
Continental Army Plaza 65
Court Street 28, 30, 31, 34–5, 118, 119
Crescent Boat House 129
Crown Heights 73, 74–5
Cyclone Roller Coaster, Coney Island 140–1
Davis, Alexander Jackson 105
de Blasio, Bill 107
Dean Street 77, 79
DeKalb Avenue 45, 50
DeKalb Market Hall 43
Dime Savings 51
Douglass, David Bates 124
Downtown 24, 31, 116–17
DUMBO 7, 15, 24, 54–5
Dundy, Elmer "Skip" 139
Dyker Heights 126–7
Eastern Parkway 80–1, 89
Eighth Avenue 109
Eisenhower, Dwight D. 109
Emmons Avenue 132
Extell 51
F. Monteleone Bakery 119
Fenner, Burt L. 39
Fifth Avenue 125
Flatbush Avenue 40, 45, 46–7, 50, 84–5
Flatbush Reformed Dutch Church 84–5
Fort Greene Park 52–3
Fort Hamilton High School 129
Fort Lafayette 130–1
Fourth Avenue 112–13
Fulton Ferry Landing 14–15, 22
Fulton Mall 41
Fulton, Robert 15
Fulton Street 30, 31, 40–1
Fulton Street Triangle 50, 51
Gowanus Canal 7, 112, 114–17
Graham, Augustus 89
Grand Army Plaza 90–1, 95, 97, 109
Grant Square 76–7
Green-Wood Cemetery 124–5
Greenpoint 58, 68–9
Greenpoint Savings Bank 68–9, 101
Handwerker, Nathan and Ida 136
Helmle, Huberty and Hudswell 101
Henry Street 20
Herts & Tallant 48
Hicks, John and Jacob 24
Hicks Street 20, 24, 25
Horn & Hardart Automat 40–1
Hunterfly Road Houses 73
IKEA 121
Imperial Apartments 77
Industry City 122–3
Invisible Dog Center 29
Jehovah's Witnesses 25
Jennewein, Carl Paul 39
Joralemon Street 28, 35, 36
Katz's Delicatessen 51
Keenan, Vernon 140
Kennedy, John F. 91
Kennedy, Robert F. 67, 71
Kimball, Francis H. 109
King, Gamaliel 30
Kings County Court 35, 42
Kirkwood, James P. 94
Korean War Veterans Plaza 37
Lafayette Avenue 48–9
Lauritzen, Peter 79
Lincoln, Abraham 20, 79, 91, 102, 130
Lincoln Place 109
Litchfield Villa 104–5
LIU Blackbirds Basketball 45
Live Nation Entertainment 45
Long Island Hospital 29
Long Island Railroad (LIRR) 46, 66, 71
Long Island University 45
Long Meadow, Prospect Park 98–9
Luna Park, Coney Island 138–9
Lundy Brothers Restaurant 132, 133
McKenzie, Voorhees & Gmelin 28
McKim, Mead & White 89
MacMonnies, Frederick 91
Macy's 41
Magnolia Plaza 87
Major R. Owens Health and Wellness Community Center 75
Manhattan Bridge 15, 54–5
MetroTech Center 31
Midwood 82–3
Moisseiff, Leon 62
Montague Street 24, 25, 26–7, 35, 48
Montague Street Ferry 22–3
Montauk Club 108–9
Morris, Montrose 77
Moses, Robert 19, 37, 47, 59
Mount Prospect Park 95
Mount Prospect Reservoir 94–5
Mundell, William A. 107
Nathan's Famous Hot Dog Stand, Coney Island 136–7
New York City College of Technology 123
New York University 126–7
Newcombe, Don 33
Nostrand Avenue 66–7, 71
NY Liberty 47
Old Fulton Street 15, 24
Old Stone House 110–11
Olmsted, Frederick Law 6, 52, 80, 87, 91, 97, 98, 102, 129
O'Malley, Walter 47
Orange Street 19, 20
Owens, Major R. 75
Pacific Street 77
Park Slope 7, 105, 106–9, 115
Park Slope Armory 106–7
Pearl Street 42–3
Pei, I.M. 67, 71
Peter Jay Sharp Building 49
Pierrepont, Henry Evelyn 22, 124
Pierrepont, Hezekiah Beers 24
Pierrepont Hotel 26
Pilcher and Tachau 74
Pilgrim Church 20–1
Pollard, Calvin 30
Poly Prep, Dyker Heights 126–7
Pratt Institute 6, 58–9
Pratt Library 58
President Street 74
Prison Ship Martyrs' Monument 52
Prospect Park 6, 80, 91, 96–103, 105, 124
Rapp and Rapp 45
Ratner, Bruce 47
Red Hook 6, 118, 120–1
Rich, Lorimer 39
River Park Development 29
Robinson, Jackie 33
Rockefeller, John D. 58
Roebling family 6, 12
Rogers Avenue 74
Roosevelt Federal Courthouse 37
Roosevelt, Theodore 57
Rosenthal, Jack and Irving 140
Royal Theater 42
Sahadi's Middle Eastern grocery 29
Sand Street 56
Schermerhorn Street 50, 51
Sharp, Peter Jay 49
Sheepshead Bay Piers 132–3
SHoP Architects 51
Shore Drive, Bay Ridge 128–9
Simon, Louis A. 39
Smith Street 118–19
Soldiers' and Sailors' Arch 91, 97
South Brooklyn Savings Bank, Cobble Hill 28–9
South Fourth Street 65
South Park Slope 112–13
South Sixth Street 61
Sovereign Bank 29
St. Mark's Avenue 79
St. Mary Star of the Sea Church 118
St. Vincent de Paul Church 119
Standard Oil 58, 122
Steeplechase Park, Coney Island 136–7
Steinhardt Conservatory 87
Stillwell Avenue 136–7
Stranahan, James 6
Sunset Park 122
Surf Avenue 136–7, 141
Tech Triangle 43
Thompson, Frederic 139
Tilyou, George C. 134, 135
Trader Joe's 29
Union League Club 77, 78–9
Union Street 74
Unity Club 79
U.S. District Court 37
Vaux, Calvert 6, 52, 80, 87, 91, 97, 98, 102
Verrazzano-Narrows Bridge 131
Walt Whitman Park 37
Washington, George 19, 65, 110
Weeksville Heritage Center 73
Weeksville Houses 72–3
Wells, Joseph, C. 20
West Tenth Street 141
Wetmore, James A. 39
Whitman, Walt 22, 30
Williamsburg 6, 7, 60–1
Williamsburg Bedford Avenue 66–7
Williamsburg Bridge 12, 60, 62–3
Williamsburg Bridge Plaza 64–5
Williamsburg Savings Bank 50–1, 60, 112–13
Willoughby Street 42–3
Willoughby Tower 43
Witkoff 51